Mappers of Society

Mappers of Society

The Lives, Times, and Legacies of Great Sociologists

RONALD FERNANDEZ

Westport, Connecticut
London

Library of Congress Cataloging-in-Publication Data

Fernandez, Ronald.
  Mappers of society : the lives, times, and legacies of great sociologists / Ronald
Fernandez.
     p. cm.
  Includes bibliographical references and index.
  ISBN 0–275–97434–0 (alk. paper)—ISBN 0–275–97435–9 (pbk. : alk. paper)
     1. Sociologists—Biography. 2. Sociology—Philosophy. I. Title.
HM478.F47 2003
301′.092′2—dc21   2003042056
[B]

British Library Cataloguing in Publication Data is available.

Library of Congress Catalog Card Number: 2003042056

ISBN: 0–275–97434–0
     0–275–97435–9 (pbk.)

First published in 2003

Praeger Publishers, 88 Post Road West, Westport, CT 06881
An imprint of Greenwood Publishing Group, Inc.
www.praeger.com

Printed in the United States of America

The paper used in this book complies with the
Permanent Paper Standard issued by the National
Information Standards Organization (Z39.48–1984).

10 9 8 7 6 5 4 3 2 1

To Rex Nettleford,
a role model for all seasons

Contents

Acknowledgments

At CCSU Pearl Bartlet and Antonio Garcia Lozada read portions of the manuscript and provided many useful ideas and criticisms.

Burt Baldwin read and reread the manuscript. He offered insights, suggestions, and a number of very helpful criticisms. I owe Burt a tremendous debt of gratitude; he is, of course, in no way responsible for the final product.

Praeger's Jim Sabin asked me to write this book. I want to say thank you. It was an absolute delight to research and write what Jim accurately titled, *Mappers of Society*.

The staff at Impressions Book and Journal Services, Inc. provided help and compassion to an impatient author. The copy edit of the manuscript was the best I have seen.

Brenda Harrison read every line of this book. It would not exist without her.

Introduction

MAPPING IT OUT

My wife loves maps. Not as much as the kids or the cats, but she loves maps with such a passion that on a trip, she never settles for the "junk" provided by the car rental companies. We go to a gas station, we buy the best map they have to offer, and after we study the road map, I drive and she provides the directions.

I used to be bothered by our reliance on maps. My arrogant attitude was, "Can't we just get going and forget the bleeping map? We'll find our way. I mean, we have educations and brains. How difficult is it to get from here to there?"

One answer is pretty hard. On a trip through Belgium, we not only got lost, but we somehow wound up in the middle of an international raceway. Luckily, no one was zooming around that day, but as we drove—wide eyed!—around the track, the need for assistance was startlingly obvious. My wife even reminded me that if we had taken a map and followed directions, we would not be driving around in circles.

Maps come in many forms, sizes, and shapes. But whether a map of Belgium, a seating plan for a theater, or an ocean chart indicating depth and hidden obstacles, all maps essentially perform the same service. They substitute for what the philosopher William James called "bloomin buzzing confusion" a sense of direction and order. With a good map in hand, we know where we are going, and we know how to get there.

Sociologists also work with maps. With a pinch of pretension, we like to call them paradigms, but whatever the label, sociologists are sometimes so audacious that they offer maps—conceptual maps—of how and why billions of people think and act as they do. Karl Marx believed he understood the order and direction of human history. Emile Durkheim offered two concepts—mechanical and organic solidarity—that allegedly explain the nature of social order in preliterate and modern societies. And Max Weber devised three types of authority—charismatic, traditional, and legal-rational—that supposedly offer significant insights into the functioning of, among others, Indian, Chinese, German, and American societies.

As scientists, these men never suffered from a lack of self-confidence. Each could have used *chutzpah* as his middle name. But in providing maps of how societies change, develop, implode, and explode, these theorists boldly underlined one of the essential prerequisites for sociology anywhere and anytime. Sociologists need conceptual maps to make sense of the world. Social, political, or economic reality is an amorphous mass— think of Silly Putty—until someone structures it with concepts, priorities, time frames, and (almost always) an expressed or veiled value judgment about the past, present, and future. Reading, for example, Georg Simmel you will find a deep sense of cynicism because he believed that money is the ultimate meaning of modern life; Karl Marx may have agreed, but his map nevertheless includes an optimistic end of the road—the coming of the communist state and the beginning of unprecedented measures of human equality.

Maps are so important that some scholars argue they are "a prerequisite to perception itself."[1] From this standpoint, only the very first human beings confronted social realities with no maps in their minds. But once theorists added order to the blooming confusion, maps functioned like a port of entry to social and physical reality. With a map in mind, we now perceive the world that is there *and* what we have been taught to see and not see.

Take, for example, Friedrich Engels's *The Condition of the Working Class in England*. Published in 1845, when Engels was barely twenty-five years old, the book focuses on the everyday living conditions of a new breed of humanity, factory workers. Engaging in what we would today call participant observation, Engels went into the streets, literally examined the homes of the workers, and then fabricated a portrait as vivid as anything from a novel by Charles Dickens. "In this part of the city [Manchester, England] there are neither sewers nor other drains. . . . All refuse, garbage and excrements of at least 50,000 people are thrown into the gutters every night, so that, in spite of all street sweeping, a mass of dried filth and foul vapors are created, which not only offend the sight and smell but endanger the health of the inhabitants in the highest degree."[2]

People lived with feces at their doorsteps. That was the undeniably odious reality experienced by Manchester's working class. But where Engels used his (and Karl Marx's) emerging paradigm of class conflict to see only the wretched exploitation of the workers by the owners, other analysts effectively told these same workers to eat nothing and die. Using the overpopulation map drawn by Thomas Malthus in 1820, these analysts argued that any help to the poor would only produce more poor. From Malthus's perspective, the problem was not too much profit but too many people. So, let them breathe in the harsh vapors, and when they failed to reproduce, they would at least lessen people's need for the world's scarce resources.[3]

As if air to a newborn, meaningful paradigms allow a science to breathe with the promise of progress. They theoretically make so much sense out of social realities that, whether it is religion or globalization, sociologists armed with a map all share the same assumption: they think they know how their part of the world works, and they agree to use the same, or similar, rules, methods, and standards to resolve the questions never answered by the original paradigm.[4]

In this book readers have the privilege of analyzing the maps drawn by eight great sociologists. Along the way you will meet some pretty irascible individuals. Thorstein Veblen, for example, always taught in a low monotone, his eyes fixed on his desk; he apparently hated to teach, so he made his first classes so boring that students withdrew in droves. And Karl Marx took criticism with all the grace of a lumbering hippopotamus. In response to one negative comment, he wrote a retort that exceeded 200 pages.[5]

Whatever their faults and eccentricities, these eight exceptional people provided maps that are a prerequisite for understanding the historical trajectory of the science of sociology. This book will examine their maps in some detail and, with the extraordinary advantage of a century of hindsight, will even risk criticizing the mapmakers. But before touching on specifics, first consider the contradictory consequences of adopting a particular map of the way the world works.

Say you have the wherewithal to read Georg Simmel's *The Philosophy of Money*. It is a spectacular book, but the prose is so painfully underwhelming that you constantly reach for a bottle of extra-strength aspirin. One of its original translators complained that the writing was so "heavy and opaque" that in the interests of intelligibility, he provided "an exposition rather than a translation." In this fashion the book might become intelligible to readers unaccustomed to paragraphs that, time after time, extend over two torturous pages.[6]

But remember, it's a great book—some would say it's as good as sociology gets. So although you are now exhausted, you are also impressed and overwhelmed. Simmel's map answered so many questions about the nature and realities of capitalism that the only job left for you is "mopping-up operations." That is, given the map's perceived brilliance and originality, your job is to actualize the map's promise by indefinitely extending its insights and possibilities. In addition, you also hope to increase the match between facts perceived and the predictions made by a particular mapmaker.[7]

This may sound boring, but it is actually quite fascinating for a problem solver—for a scientist. Any sociological map is always incomplete; it leaves a host of significant problems to solve and inconsistencies to reconcile. You could easily spend a lifetime working within the confines of a powerful paradigm. Thus, once a group of scientists begin to use a particular map, their research and publications can be called everyday science.[8] They work by trying to place, push, force, or twist the social world "into the preformed and relatively inflexible box that the paradigm provides."[9] In extreme cases adherents to a particular paradigm will publish in journals primarily read by one another.

Maps are therefore always double-edged swords. You need them to get a theoretically reliable fix on the nature of the social world that is there. But once you accept a map, your vision and research—the mopping-up operations—are limited by what the map asks you to see and not see. Remember Engels's and Malthus's diametrically different interpretations of the conditions of the English working class.

Maps are also personal. To become an expert in Marx or Weber requires a considerable time commitment. Eventually, you begin to call yourself a Marxist or a Weberian, and your speech patterns and publications reflect a singular fact: you have learned and internalized the esoteric vocabulary that mapmakers and their adherents always construct. Thus, as if Greek to a German, Marxists talk to an audience about absolute and relative surplus value while, for Veblen, you better learn the meaning of conspicuous consumption, the instinct of workmanship, and the unique way Veblen uses words like *imbecile, barbarity,* and *savagery.*

Accepting a map can make a scientist resistant to change. In essence, you think you know the way the world works, so why would you want to seek or accept new paradigms when you already have a reliable approach to social reality? It is a good question, so here is a good answer: the truth. All scientists seek solutions; our educations teach us to ask questions and demand empirical, hands-on proof of any assertion. So if somebody draws a new and better map of social reality, it will win over—however reluctantly—many adherents. If the new paradigm is as powerful as the work of Marx, Durkheim, or Weber, it can produce what amounts to a conceptual revolution.

The touchstone is the search for truth. Maps are simply the essential tools scientists use in their never-ending battle of ideas. Indeed, if we extend the battlefield metaphor, remember what happened at Waterloo in 1815. Because civilians were not yet targets of systematic and deliberate slaughter, they crammed into the bleachers (i.e., the Forest of Soignes), and with little threat of being harmed, peasants from the Waterloo district watched one of the great military confrontations of Western history.[10]

You have a similar opportunity in this book. From a point on high, you can safely watch, analyze, appreciate, and judge the peaceful (although sometimes quite personal) battle of ideas that helped produce the science of sociology. It is a spectacular story on at least two different levels.

First, like a stone thrown into a still pool of water, new maps always produce a variety of energizing intellectual reactions. Some of us applaud. Convinced by the arguments of the new mapmaker, we embrace his or her way of thinking and discard suddenly antiquated ways of perceiving social reality. More than thirty-five years later, I can still recall my first reading of George Herbert Mead's *Mind, Self, and Society*. I was dazzled and then hooked because Mead's work offered me an array of eye-opening concepts and insights.

However, not only can the same book produce different reactions, but it can produce a delayed reaction. Analysts sometimes forget that early responses to Marx's *Das Kapital* (*Capital*; published in 1867) included so much indifference that Engels tried to manufacture interest. He wrote a number of positive and negative reviews under a pseudonym and eventually managed to place seven of them, "each carefully tailored to the nature of the paper in which it appeared."[11]

It took four years to sell a thousand copies of *Das Kapital*.[12] Then, except in Marx's small circle of friends and followers, many of the responses that finally appeared were so negative that theorists only used Marx's work as a foil for their own efforts. Like a Microsoft watermark, Karl Marx appears on every page of Simmel's *The Philosophy of Money*, and much of Max Weber's best work is a long debate with the map produced by Karl Marx and Friedrich Engels.

For sociologists, the heated interest—the fascination—lies not only in the new ideas but also in the reactions, the ripple effects, those ideas produce in others. To use Marxian language, it is a dialectical process. One factor acts back upon the other, and the never-ending result is a variety of maps, all offering new insights about sociology's perpetual preoccupation: Why do people think and act as they do?

Remember that question. It a cornerstone of the discipline. The sociologists spotlighted in this book are so ambitious that they want to figure out everything. They are interested in suicide and self-conceptions, in religion and rumors of angels, in the nature of class conflict and the creation of a new moral order, in globalization and the social scripts that people use to deceive one another in ordinary and important forms of social interaction. For example, read Erving Goffman's *The Presentation of Self in Everyday Life*, and you learn that good liars can also be good people, especially when they are trying to save face for a person about to be humiliated by a lack of knowledge—say, someone's first time in a five-star restaurant or a person's first experiences in a new culture.

Our gift is the maps and, even more important, what is left when the battles are over. What is left is an intellectual inheritance that makes sociology the most liberating discipline in the modern world.[13] That is a giant claim. And you will, I hope, wait until the book's final chapter to agree or disagree with me. But in the meantime, read this book with the following firmly in mind. The second reason these maps are so fascinating is that they leave us with a marvelous legacy—that is, a science that has all the conceptual tools needed to produce peaceful yet revolutionary social change.

Idealistic? Full of value judgments? Of course! But even a supposedly conservative sociologist such as Emile Durkheim wrote these provocative lines nearly a century ago: "As long as there are States, so there will be national pride and nothing can be more warranted. But societies can have their pride, not in being the greatest or the wealthiest, but in being the most just, the best organized and in possessing the best moral constitution."[14]

Sociology's roots are in ideals. It is a proud tradition that can be easily nurtured if, as you read about the mapmakers, you remember a distinction between external and internal freedom. The former refers to public rights such as freedom of press, assembly, speech, and worship. In contrast, internal freedom refers to insight into self and world and the ability to act on those insights. Internal freedom underlines and endorses a human potential, the capacity to reflect on why we think and act as we do *and* the ability to change if we are unhappy with what we see.[15]

Thanks to the mapmakers, sociology's greatest promise is the gift of internal freedom. Using the concepts provided by these (and other) theorists, we can consciously and peacefully transform both the societies in which we live and ourselves.

Let me give a personal example. I was raised in the 1950s as a strict Roman Catholic. Nuns solemnly taught my fellow students and me about mortal (very serious) and venial (minor) sins; they even put lit matches under our fingers to simulate the devil's home. Thus my friends and I always worried about our behavior and its relationship to burning pain. Especially if we had committed a mortal sin, we supposedly roasted in hell forever—unless we first got to confession and had a priest provide us with absolution, with a clean slate.

My perplexing problem was that I had necked with a young woman. In my generation necking meant kissing and nothing more, not French, Turkish, or Mexican kissing, just kissing. Had I committed a mortal sin? Did I need to make a beeline to the confessional? Or was necking just a venial sin, which only sentenced me to indefinitely burn in purgatory until Saint Peter opened the gates of heaven?

Nuns told us that priests "were the representatives of God on earth." So I went to Father Sweeney for an answer to my conundrum. He told me—and this is the truth!—that if I kissed the girl for thirty seconds or less, that was a venial sin. Thirty-one seconds or more was a mortal sin. So as long as I necked with a stopwatch, I had a chance to kiss, tell, and walk through the pearly gates.

In telling you the story I am using the work of George Herbert Mead. I am looking at myself as an object in the world of experience, I am laughing at myself, and I am now consciously refusing to think as I was then taught to see myself—as a sinner with a one-way ticket to hell.

Fast-forwarding to chapter 8, my kissing story also underlines a crucial insight of Peter Berger. He writes that social reality—religion, politics, economics, education, family—is always a human construction. People, and only people, fabricate the values, beliefs, and practices that members of any society share. But sometimes people forget that they are in charge, that there is nothing inevitable or sacrosanct about any society on earth. For Berger one of life's great paradoxes is that people create a world of beliefs that denies their status as conscious agents of change.[16]

At the time I was born, the concepts of mortal and venial sin were easily more than a thousand years old. And Father Sweeney, a well-intentioned man, had used his stopwatch solution to sexual sin for many years, on many other worried young men. When we blindly accepted the ancient, conventional wisdom about sin, kissing, and hell, my friends and I forgot one of sociology's most powerful conclusions: we can reevaluate what people told us, and if we decide they were incorrect, we can walk into the future on the basis of a corrected past.

That is internal freedom. It is the mapmakers' everlasting legacy and the hallmark of a sociology that always aims to put people exactly where they belong—in charge and at the consciously creative center of every society on earth.

A FINAL WORD

I chose these eight sociologists for a variety of reasons. Four (Weber, Marx, Durkheim, and Simmel) are indisputably at the core of sociology's birth and growth. Like a rubber ball against a wall, we are still batting around the maps and concepts they devised. To exclude these four would be tantamount to heresy.

The next four came from a very long list that also included Robert Merton, C. Wright Mills, Talcott Parsons, Robert Nisbet, Harold Garfunkel, Karl Mannheim, Howard Becker, Vilfredo Pareto, and Alfred Schutz. These and other sociologists made significant theoretical additions to the science of sociology.

I chose Veblen, Mead, Goffman, and Berger because of their crucial conceptual contributions and also because they underline the length and breadth of sociology as a science. My overall aim is to show that the science of sociology offers important insights about virtually every aspect of human life. For example, where Marx and Weber focus on millions of people, George Herbert Mead spotlights the individual; like a dart to a bull's-eye, he wants to know why *you* think and act as you do. He offers insights as compelling and provocative as the work of Sigmund Freud.

Erving Goffman's work is utterly unique. In his world people have two selves: the one they show to others and the one they show to themselves. For Goffman the fascination is people using social scripts to manage themselves *and* the reactions of others. In the service of social order, people are magnificent manipulators in the sociology of Goffman.

Peter Berger took all the maps that existed and created a new one. His (and Thomas Luckmann's) focus on the social construction of reality helped change the research focus of countless sociologists. Suddenly, women and men were active agents in the never-ending creation and re-creation of their social worlds.

And Veblen? I focus on Veblen because I agree with the assessment of C. Wright Mills: "Thorstein Veblen is the best critic of America that America has produced. His language is part of the vocabulary of every literate American; his works are the most conspicuous contribution of any American to American studies."[17]

Veblen is the maverick, the social critic who often lies buried in the heart of many a sociologist. His work is value laden rather than value free. The captains of industry are barbarians on one page, imbeciles on the next. Yet his work still offers—with great passion and wit—an insightful map of American cultural beliefs, values, and practices.

For all their differences, each of the eight also shares this trait: they were interdisciplinary long before it became fashionable. Sociology is the hub of their thinking, but the spokes that radiate from each wheel include a wealth of nondisciplinary knowledge. Marx seems to have read every great work of literature; he moved from Cervantes to Shakespeare with ease, and he always underlined the importance of Balzac in his (and Engels's) understanding of the social comedy of capitalism. Weber and Simmel steeped themselves in history, philosophy, and religion; and Berger has a range that runs easily from philosophy to history to literature to economics. He also wrote a novel.

In a world that often asks students to specialize, this is the advice of a mapmaker such as Veblen. If you let "idle curiosity" be your guide, then, following Simmel or Durkheim, Mead, or Marx, someone may be avidly reading your books a hundred years after they first appeared.

NOTES

1. Thomas S. Kuhn, *The Structure of Scientific Revolutions*, 3rd ed. (Chicago: University of Chicago Press, 1996), 113. This entire section of the book is based on Kuhn's analysis of how all science proceeds and progresses.

2. Friedrich Engels, *The Condition of the Working Class in England* (New York: Oxford University Press, 1993), 48. For a superb overview of everyday life in the nineteenth century, see Otto L. Bettman, *The Good Old Days: They Were Terrible!* (New York: Random House, 1974).

3. See, for example, Robert Heilbroner, *The Worldly Philosophers* (New York: Touchstone Books, 1999), 83.

4. Ibid., 11.

5. On Veblen, see Joseph Dorfman, *Thorstein Veblen and His America* (New York: Augustus M. Kelley, 1966), 309; on Marx, see Francis Wheen, *Karl Marx* (New York: Norton, 2000), 168.

6. Georg Simmel, *The Philosophy of Money*, ed. David Frisby, 2nd enlarged ed. (London: Routledge and Kegan Paul, 1990), 521.

7. Kuhn, *The Structure of Scientific Revolutions*, 24–25.

8. Ibid., chapter 3.

9. Ibid., 24.

10. John Keegan, *The Face of War* (New York: Norton, 1968).

11. David McLellan, *Karl Marx: His Life and Thought* (New York: Harper and Row, 1973), 353.

12. Ibid.

13. Ronald Fernandez, *The Promise of Sociology* (New York: Praeger, 1975).

14. Emile Durkheim, *Professional Ethics and Civic Morals* (London: Routledge, 1992), 75.

15. Ronald Fernandez, *The I, the Me, and You* (New York: Praeger, 1977), 8–9.

16. Peter L. Berger and Thomas Luckmann, *The Social Construction of Reality* (New York: Doubleday, 1966), 82–83. It is important to remember that Thomas Luckmann also produced this important book. Because I am focusing on Berger's work I do not underline this fact in the principal text.

17. See Mills's introduction to Thorstein Veblen, *The Theory of the Leisure Class* (New York: New American Library, 1953), vi.

CHAPTER 1

Karl Marx

"Communism is the riddle of history solved, and it knows itself to be this solution."

Karl Marx, *The Economic and Philosophic Manuscripts of 1844*[1]

CARBUNCLES AND CAPTAIN SWING

It is a unique appendix. At the end of a long, intimate biography of Karl Marx, Saul Padover attaches a four-page list of "Marx's Illnesses during the writing of *Das Kapital*." Derived from personal correspondence, the seven-year inventory includes liver ailments—"it is swollen and I have piercing pains when I cough"—constant bile vomiting, and the ever-present carbuncles or boils that sprouted, like venomous weeds, over every part of Marx's body. In February 1866 Marx discovered "a virulent dog of a carbuncle on his left loin"; two years earlier the "perfidious Christian illness" appeared over his "whole cadaver," and in July 1864, he even had boils on his penis. He naturally shared that intimate information with his wife (and with Friedrich Engels), but despite the perpetual pain, Marx persisted. He finished the book, and when the public received it with "universal indifference," his wife lovingly wrote that "there can be few books written in more difficult circumstances. . . . If the workers had an inkling of the sacrifices that were necessary for this work, which was written only for them and for their sakes, to be completed they would perhaps show a little more interest."[2]

In accounting for the carbuncles that made Marx's everyday life a living hell, his biographer includes two modern-day medical comments from 1969 and 1970. One doctor assures that carbuncles were "not psychosomatic"; they were caused by an infection and could have been effectively treated with antibiotics. The other physician, Dr. Sigmund Gabe, indicates that it is "well established" that the skin responds to psychic stress; Marx might have endured "Job's disease," a common reaction in middle-aged men "to a reversal in their fortune or some other serious disaster." In Marx's case the physical afflictions were so numerous "that they might have overwhelmed even a Job."[3]

One thing is certain. Marx labored long, hard, and painfully to produce one of Western history's most influential books. Definitively deciding between a psychosomatic or biological explanation of the carbuncles is impossible; but the advice of Erik Erikson is nevertheless quite suggestive: "We have come to take it for granted that greatness also harbors massive conflict."[4]

Karl Marx had conflicts in spades. Reading his correspondence and a number of the biographies, you could even argue that Marx had as many everyday conflicts as there were conservative scholars in his beloved British Museum. Yet, as his wife justly cautioned, he wrote because he sought to end *social conflicts* that were every bit as virulent as the boils on his body. Massive social, political, economic, and technological change characterized Karl Marx's time. One great irony is that during Marx's most formative years, many of the greatest disturbances occurred against machines rather than capitalism, against farmers rather than factory owners. Marx somehow saw in capitalism's birth pangs the seeds of the class conflicts that would, as a matter of historical necessity, transform the world.

Marx was twelve when in 1830 the English protesters called their hero Captain Swing. Although historians argue about whether such a person actually existed, somebody signed the letters that bluntly told English farmers, "If your threshing machines are not destroyed by you directly, we shall commence our labours. Signed, on behalf of the whole, SWING."[5]

Swing lived in the countryside, with the vast majority of other English people and workers. Influenced by Marx, modern-day historians now call these men "rural proletarians." But a fairer contemporary judgment is "a hired man," a person who lived in a rural England that no longer provided, as a matter of tradition, the food and housing people needed to survive during hard times. As the English population grew, so did the need for food production and more cultivated land. Enclosure is the innocuous word to describe this process; farmers put rock walls around their land and enclosed it to meet the food needs of a burgeoning population. Unfortunately, small farmers, "cottagers," and squatters lost both security and a way of life when the land was enclosed. They became a workforce that a savvy farmer hired only when, for short periods, he needed the intensive efforts of a flock of dependent hired hands. "Instead of family, patronage or custom, there was now the straightforward nexus of wages, which bound the landless to the land."[6]

Enclosure was part of a problem that also included mechanization of agriculture and production for markets that, when boom turned to bust, left hired hands with no work and no food. Threshing machines therefore assumed great symbolic status because they helped eliminate what workers desperately needed: a job, a chance to earn a living.

On August 28, 1830, Swing and his coconspirators destroyed their first threshing machine. Well into October fires raged throughout England's center as workers burned farms, mills, and anything else that inflamed their passions. Over time the focus on machines turned to a question of wages. Swing's army wanted better pay and, for tenant farmers, lower rents on the land leased from the largest landowners and producers. The forces of law and order naturally tried to suppress the widespread rioting, but Swing was so successful that on November 22, 1830, a public placard appeared in Hungerford, England: "TO THE LABOURING CLASSES: The Gentlemen, Yeomanry, Farmers and others, having made known to you their intention of increasing your Wages to a satisfactory extent; and it having been resolved that 'Threshing Machines shall not be again used; it is referred to your good Sense . . .' to return to your work and accept that you won. The machines will not be used to destroy you and your families."[7]

And the farmers kept their word. The threshing machines never returned to their original levels. Thus, "of all the machine-breaking movements of the 19th century that of the helpless and unorganized farm-laborers proved to be by far the most effective."[8] Captain Swing was really a general, a leader who, however temporarily, silenced the winds of change that also brought in their wake what Frederick Engels called "some of the greatest marvels of modern times."[9]

Engels waxed eloquently about the industrial transformation that, as Captain Swing destroyed threshers, successfully placed even bigger machines in the cities and factories of Bolton, Rochdale, Oldham, and Preston. Engels writes that by the 1830s, the cotton industry had "thoroughly revolutionized" Lancashire county; cotton converted "an ill-cultivated swamp into a busy, lively region," containing great cities like Liverpool and Manchester. To Engels the remarkable growth in both productivity and population actually represented a series of "miracles" that deserved all the praise he could and did give them.[10]

Engels's attitude in *The Condition of the Working Class in England* suggests that for all their bitter criticism of capitalism, Marx and Engels also perceived its incredible ability to act as an engine of miraculous change. Yet they believed that capitalism's economic miracles would produce a heavenly life for the owners and a hellish existence for the workers. With equality as their moral guide, they keyed on the negatives; and the most remarkable thing of all is that in a Europe where agricultural interests still dominated, a man in his mid-twenties produced a theory about capitalism before capitalism and industrial production ruled the economies he meant to transform.[11] In the year that *The Communist Manifesto* finally appeared (1848), a Prussian census showed that only 4 percent of those employed worked in factories. And in 1848 France (along with Belgium, the most industrially advanced nation in Europe) possessed only 5,000 steam-powered machines.[12]

Karl Marx created a theory based as much on sheer brilliance as on the available evidence. He saw the future before it appeared, which is one reason his theory has more holes than a pasta colander. Yet, as Robert Heilbroner stresses, Marx is "unavoidable"; he is, in truth, "the great explorer whose footprints have been indelibly printed on the continent of social thought that [along with Engels] he discovered."[13]

JEWISH PROTESTANTS

Trier is the oldest city in Germany. Walk its streets today and you encounter a delightful sense of order and ease. In sharp contrast to the United States, shopping areas bar cars so pedestrians can meander in peace and see, prominently lounging around an ancient fountain, groups of skinheads, many with the latest tattoos and other signs of defiance. Under its soothing surface, Trier shares the world's conflicts, in the twenty-first century and in the nineteenth century.

On Brückengasse Street, near a small hotel, a modest brick structure posts a sign indicating that Karl Marx was born there on May 5, 1818. Today the house is a museum; then it sheltered Marx, his parents, and ultimately, seven brothers and sisters. Karl was special; his mother called him *Glückskind*, child of fortune; "his father thought he was possessed of a demon and feared for his future."[14]

Karl's father, Heinrich (originally Heschel) Marx, boasted rabbinical roots that stretched back for generations. With an immediate family that included fifteen other people, he was raised in a "dilapidated" synagogue house. But instead of following the family traditions, he broke with Judaism and tried to assimilate into the Prussian mainstream. After Waterloo, Prussia retained those portions of the Napoleonic codes that excluded Jews from a variety of professions. To save his position in the civil service, Heinrich wrote "abject petitions" seeking exemptions from prejudices that literally had millennial roots. In 1817, a year before Karl Marx's birth, his father became a Protestant in a Catholic city that blamed Jews for, among other things, the death of God. Heinrich Marx chose Protestantism because it represented to Prussia's rulers a religion that simultaneously separated them from Jews and from the Catholics who, living in the Rhineland, bore conspicuous evidence of Gallic or (how awful) French influence.[15]

Frank Manuel calls Marx the "alien of Trier"; along with other biographers, Manuel stresses Marx's status as a birthright outsider. He also focuses on Marx's alleged self-hatred because of his Jewish roots. When Marx fails, in his theories, to give due weight to ethnic and nationalistic factors, the blindness dates from his rejection of Judaism and himself. And when Marx venomously calls a political opponent a "Jewish nigger," that dreadful slur is also an assault on himself and his roots.[16]

Whether amateurs or the real thing, psychiatrists have always had a field day with the ethnic dilemmas of Marx's life. For the present purposes, this much is undeniable: he was always an outsider, and for all the pain he experienced and inflicted—as late as 1879 he wrote to Engels that a hotel was "full of Jews and fleas"[17]—Marx derived benefits from his alien status. Outsiders enjoy a distinct advantage when they try to analyze a problem; totally wedded to nobody's preconceived notions, outsiders are often open to fresh perspectives, to seeing the world from angles and attitudes never advanced by the in crowd.[18]

Karl Marx's home was as crowded as his father's. Besides a family of ten, it included two servants. Twelve people shared a small space, often dominated by the child of fortune. Using his brothers and sisters as horses, Marx rode them down the nearby streets and even "insisted" that they eat the "cakes" he molded with "dirty dough and even dirtier hands." When he angered his siblings with arrogance or other misbehavior, Marx soothed them with a skill he eventually used with his own children. Marx told "wonderful stories" rooted in a "fertile imagination" that never stopped his sisters from making this summary judgment of their brother. He was, as a youth, a "terrible tyrant."[19]

After his initial schooling at home, Marx entered the Gymnasium, a school of 300 to 500 students who came from a wide spectrum of the society. And for anyone who complains about the rigors of a U.S. education, consider Marx's curriculum. He took courses in religion, Greek, Latin, French, history, mathematics, and physics. The extensive and impressive references that, like stars, dot his writings trace their pedigree to this education. However, his teachers never saw a genius; instead, he seemed satisfactory rather than superb. It was only in an essay written as part of his final examinations that the seventeen-year-old Marx allowed his ambition and idealism to make an appearance: "When we have chosen the position in which we can do the most for humanity burdens cannot bow us down, because they are only sacrifices for all. Then we experience no meager, narrow egoistic joy, but our own happiness belongs to millions, our deeds live on quietly but ever actively, and our ashes will be moistened by the tears of noble men."[20]

Many biographers pay homage to these lines;[21] in a sense Marx wrote his own epitaph forty-eight years before he died.

From the Gymnasium Marx first went to the University of Bonn in 1835. After a year he transferred to the University of Berlin. At Bonn Marx majored in fun, alehouses—he was president of the university's Trier Tavern Club—and duels. He even got wounded in one of his eyes, and his father's letters accused him of everything from egoism to ingratitude, from neglecting his parents to neglecting his studies. His father demanded that he transfer to the "workhouse" atmosphere of Berlin, but before doing so, Marx returned to Trier to reaffirm his marital commitment to Jenny von Westphalen, the daughter of a German aristocrat and one of the most beautiful and eligible of Trier's young women.[22]

Why did the beautiful, aristocratic woman fall in love with the "swarthy" Jewish-Protestant, a man who was "exceptionally dark and conspicuously exotic among light skinned people?"[23] Biographers love to pose this question, but they sometimes forget about simple passion. Marx exuded intelligence and (when he wanted to) both charm and affection. Jenny von Westphalen was lovely, well educated, and dedicated to his well-being from the moment their attachment turned to love. Through almost forty years of the most torturous times (they married in 1843), she stayed by his side, and when his egoism allowed it, Marx expressed his love and gratitude. It was a marriage born of emotion and tested by Marx in every imaginable manner.[24]

Heinrich Marx died on May 10, 1838. This presumably touched Marx to the quick because he loved his father—Marx kept a picture with him all his life, and Engels put the picture in Karl Marx's coffin after his death[25]—and because his father's last letters included another long list of complaints about the son. As if a contemporary parent to his credit card hungry children, Heinrich Marx writes that "your pessimism disgusts me, and I least expected it of you. What reason can you have for it? Has not everything been smiling for you since your cradle? Has not nature endowed you richly? And had you not, in the most incomprehensible way, carried off the heart of a girl whom thousands envy you?" Yet all Marx wanted was more money, and his father, much too late in the game, blamed himself for overindulging a clearly gifted son.[26]

His father's death at sixty "was the termination of whatever dependence Karl Marx ever had on a parent." His relationship with his mother was tempestuous, and with his father's death, it centered on Marx getting whatever inheritance he could, as fast as he could. However, his mother held the financial reins tightly, and her understandable reluctance to shower more money on her irresponsible son only exacerbated what had always been a difficult bond. He hated "her propensity to take command," but he always needed (and despised) what she had become to him, "a possible source of money."[27]

At the University of Berlin, Marx became a "Young Hegelian," establishing ties to a philosopher whose influence Marx would never shake. Hegel, in sharp and deliberate contrast to French and English philosophers, argued for a "metaphysical historicism." In *The Philosophy of History*, this bulky phrase comes to include an Absolute Spirit or Idea that runs through all of human history. The spirit moves in a dialectical fashion of thesis-antithesis-synthesis, and as Bertrand Russell once noted with great sarcasm, "It [the Absolute Idea] seems to have been nearly, if not quite realized in the Prussian state" that employed Marx's father and educated his son.[28]

Hegel died in 1831, but his theories heavily influenced German philosophical thought during Marx's time at the university. Hegel provided an opus that explained all of human history, and to a man as ambitious as Marx, the Absolute Idea was initially as appealing as helping the masses to a better life. In 1841 Marx finally received his Ph.D. in philosophy, not from the University of Berlin but from Jena University, a small school "outside the jurisdiction of Prussia." In Berlin the government had appointed university officials determined to stamp out the influence of the Young Hegelians and anyone else with the audacity to criticize religion. Because politics would have prevented Marx from getting the degree he rightfully deserved, he transferred to Jena, filled out the appropriate forms, paid the legal fees, and submitted his already-written dissertation to a sympathetic audience. Within a week of its receipt, the Jena faculty made Karl Marx a doctor "in absentia." He was ready to begin his work life, as a journalist, as a revolutionary, as a pauper, and as an advocate for the world's proletarian masses.[29]

THE COMMUNIST MANIFESTO

Marx had a devilish sense of humor. When he served as editor of the *Rheinische Zeitung* (in 1842), Prussian censors cut portions of his stories as easily and frequently as a baker cut bread. Marx haggled with the censor each evening, but one night the official never received the proofs of the next day's paper. The officer, eager to attend a ball with his family, waited for hours. Finally, he sent his wife along first, waited a while longer, and eventually wound up using a carriage to reach Marx's "distant" lodgings. At eleven P.M., he urgently rang the bell again and again, finally receiving a response "when Marx stuck his head out of a third story window. The Proofs!" yelled the censor. "Aren't any," responded Marx. "We're not publishing tomorrow!" He then shut the window and left the official, so angry that "the words stuck in his throat," standing on the street."[30]

As writer, editor, and resident agitator, Marx worked for a variety of publications until he finally settled in London in late 1849. He traveled across Europe, living in cities like Cologne, Paris, and Brussels. Wherever he went he was often one step ahead of the law because Marx combined abilities and desires that are almost always separated. The scholar sat in libraries, reading the most obscure manuscripts and data; that Marx was as boring as a bureaucrat. Marx the journalist wrote prose that still sparkles with great wit, passion, and exuberance: for example, "the tradition of all the dead generations weighs like a nightmare on the living," and, discussing the rise to power of Napoleon's nephew, "Hegel remarks somewhere that all facts and personages of great importance in world history occur, as it were, twice. He forgot to add: the first time as tragedy, the second as farce."[31]

The third Marx was a dedicated revolutionary, a man who, despite his Ph.D., took to the streets and actually organized, supported, and financed violent struggles against the powers that be. When in 1848 he and his family desperately needed money to survive, he took the 6,000 francs he had just received from his father's estate and—instead of getting family possessions out of hock or buying a large stock of food—he gave the money to the workers, who used it to purchase "daggers and revolvers." When the Belgian authorities got wind of Marx's behest, Marx and his wife were arrested. She spent the night with "prostitutes and vagrants," sleeping on a "hard plank bed." In the morning she peered through the cell's window to see Karl "being led away under military escort."[32]

Somehow, Marx also found time to be profoundly influenced by two new acquaintances: Ludwig Feuerbach and Friedrich Engels. Among other books, Feuerbach published *The Essence of Christianity* in 1841. In it he argued "that the substance and object of religion is altogether human, . . . that divine wisdom is human wisdom." Instead of being the first cause, God took a back seat to man, who created God and sustained his life with a series of beliefs that represented "the nature of man objectively." Thus, "Man is the true God and Savior of Man." In a series of theses published in 1843, Feuerbach extended his attack on religion to philosophy; he said that one should forget aspirations like God and perfection and focus instead on "the finite, the particular, the real."[33]

If this sounds tame to modern ears, remember Hegel's assertion that something called the "Absolute Spirit" mindfully marched through history, guiding the affairs of man in a predirected fashion. But as Marx wrote in 1844, after reading Feuerbach, "philosophy is nothing else but religion rendered into thought and expounded by thought, hence equally to be condemned as another form and manner of existence of the estrangement of the essence of man." Feuerbach used a cannon of new ideas to shoot down the Absolute Spirit and bring his readers—and especially Karl Marx—back to earth. After Feuerbach, the "basic principle of the theory" needed to be "the social relationship of man to man." Suddenly, here on earth, in the social relationships that produced economic and political ties, Marx had discovered "true materialism" and, equally important, the need for a "real science" that would precisely explain the actual workings of the economic relationships that had nothing to do with God and even less to do with mysterious metaphysical absolutes wafting their way through human history.[34]

In analyzing the effect of Feuerbach, remember Marx's passion for change and justice. In the mountain of Marx biographies that exist, his negatives as a human being sometimes hide his positives as a sincere advocate for the poor, the exploited, and the oppressed. In his earliest newspaper work, Marx shows genuine outrage over both small and large injustices, such as when Prussian authorities erased an ancient right that allowed peasants to gather fallen branches for fuel. Under the new rules, collecting a twig could lead to jail; in addition, the peasant had to pay the forest owner the value of the twigs retrieved. Marx lambasted the authorities for this "legalized larceny." His anger represents a passion in search of a way to produce change.[35] Feuerbach helped Marx escape the dense forest of ideas represented by traditional philosophy; he was now ready to march with the peasants and with his new friend, Friedrich Engels.

Marx and Engels first met in Cologne in an 1843 encounter that impressed neither man in a deep way. But in Paris, in August 1844, they spent ten days together discussing every manner of economic, political, and philosophical question. Frank Manuel writes that it was "ideological identity at first sight"; the two rarely disagreed, and Engels, for all his brilliance, happily played second fiddle to Marx's lead. As he later noted, "Marx was a genius, the rest of us were talented at best."[36]

Engels was twenty-four when he and Marx formed a partnership that included an incredible irony: the champion of world communism lived off the money that Engels "borrowed" from his father's factory in Manchester, England. As one man researched the theory that would destroy capitalism, the other used its profits to support Marx, two homes in Manchester, and his affection for, among other hobbies, horses and fox hunting. In Manchester Engels maintained one home for appearances and the other for his real life with Mary Burns, a young Irish woman who epitomized England's exploitation of Ireland and its people. Like Mexicans in contemporary America, Irish immigrants crossed the seas and labored in the factories. There, Mary Burns and the factory owner's son formed a liaison that lasted for more than twenty years. Engels genuinely loved Mary Burns and, apparently, her sister as well. Lydia Burns also lived in the second home(s) that hid from Manchester's swells Friedrich Engels's life with the people.[37]

With Marx and Engels the facts are at times so unbelievably contradictory that they seem like the novels of Balzac, a writer who delighted both Marx and Engels. Balzac's kaleidoscope of the human comedy mirrored the lives they (especially Engels) led, and it adds a particular touch of the ridiculous to remember that when Engels brought Mary Burns to an entertainment sponsored by the League of the Just, the Marxes "held aloof from their friend. . . . Karl gave me to understand by a glance and significant smile that his wife declined in the most vigorous manner to make the acquaintance of that . . . lady."[38] Apparently, Feuerbach made Marx a materialist, but the revolutionary still had a real problem with the class conflicts that kept the Marxes and Mary Burns on very different sides of the railroad tracks. Engels rarely repeated his classless behavior, and the Marxes continued to ask for and receive the checks he sent from a city that hideously symbolized the conditions of the working class in England in 1845.

Engels wrote that when they first met, Marx had the basic elements of historical materialism already in place. *The Economic and Philosophic Manuscripts of 1844*—only published fifty years after Marx's death—underlines the accuracy of Engels's assessment. For example, the pages titled "Estranged Labor" contain the essential rudiments of Marx's theory of alienation. "Labor produces not only commodities; it produces itself and the workers as commodities." Under capitalism work is so foreign to the laborer that it "exists *outside him*, independently, as something alien to him, and it becomes a power on its own confronting him." And in a section, entitled "Private Property and Communism," Marx already suggests that "the entire movement of history" includes, as a substitution for "the vileness of private property," the sense of positive community that will be ushered in, as if a great liberator, by communism. In language that still sounds like the words of a German philosopher, he sees "communism as the positive transcendence of *private property*, as *human self-estrangement*, and therefore as the real *appropriation of the human essence* by and for man; communism [is] therefore the complete return of man to man as a *social* [i.e., human] being."[39]

The problem was the difference between the elements of a theory and its scientific proof. Marx sought nothing less than laws of history, so as he struggled, carbuncles and all, to discover those laws, he and Engels simultaneously fought with anyone who opposed their still-developing conception of the workingman's past, present, and future.

Through the years the two men—and especially Marx—argued with and alienated a host of opponents.[40] In Brussels in 1846 Marx encountered William Weitling, a tailor whose book *Guarantees of Harmony and Freedom* included lines like these: "We wish to be as free as birds in the sky; we wish to dart through life like them, carefree in joyful flight and sweet harmony." These wistful dreams nevertheless came from the pen of a real workingman, a fellow who had been imprisoned for openly criticizing the authorities. He was a hero on the streets, but in a presumably friendly gathering in Marx's home, the doctor abruptly questioned his student: "You [Weitling] who have made such a noise in Germany with your teaching; on what grounds do you. . . ." It was a pointed challenge to the unsuspecting tailor, who answered in a manner that produced a failing grade. "To rouse the workers without offering any scientific ideas or constructive doctrine, he [Marx] said, was equivalent to vain dishonest play at preaching which assumes an inspired prophet on the one side and on the other, only the gaping asses."[41]

When attacking an opponent, Marx aimed at and hit the jugular vein. He meant to bleed his opponents dry; they often attacked back, but until shortly after the Second Congress of the Communist League in London in late 1847, his opponents lacked a concise, written target. Marx and Engels provided it when the conference gave them an opportunity to offer, under the league's banner, their scientific view of the workers future.

To attend the conference, "Marx left his family in a wretched condition." His children were ill, and his wife, eight months pregnant, experienced both physical and emotional stress. In Marx's apt summary, "My economic condition at this moment is in such a crisis that my wife is literally harassed by creditors and finds herself in a thoroughly miserable embarrassment."[42]

Marx went to the conference. Engels had previously assured him that "this time we shall have it all our own way," and Engels (the Congress secretary) was right. After ten full days of debate, the league formally agreed to a new set of statues and a bold statement of goals. They included "the overthrow of the bourgeois, the domination of the proletariat, the abolition of the old bourgeois society based on class antagonisms, and the establishment of a new society without classes and without private property."[43]

To put meat on this revolutionary rhetoric, the Congress also charged Marx with the task of writing a "communist creed." In a draft, Engels took the creed charge so seriously that he produced a dry catechism of twenty-five questions and answers. Marx assumed the task of writing a manifesto that would arouse the masses. Unfortunately, he delayed his work for so long that the Central Committee of the Communist League sent him an ultimatum to finish the work by the end of January (1848) or the committee would take "further measures of an unspecified nature." Under great pressure Marx produced a document that is part "prophecy," part "history," part "morality"—and always revolutionary. The first line worried Western leaders for almost 150 years: "A specter is haunting Europe— the specter of Communism."[44]

Section 1 sets the stage. It is titled "Bourgeois and Proletarians" and begins with an incredibly audacious line: "The history of all hitherto existing society is the history of class struggles." *All* is a big word, and Marx was as serious as a recent religious convert. But because this was a political pamphlet—a clarion call to arms—the author provides no offer of proof, not even a definition of class. The reader is simply told that where past societies included "a manifold gradation of social rank," "our epoch . . . is more and more splitting up into two great hostile camps, into two great classes facing each other—bourgeois and proletariat."[45]

After "a series of revolutions in the modes of production and of exchange," the bourgeois took hold to such an extent that "the executive of the modern state is but a committee for managing the affairs of the whole bourgeoisie." If that line sounds like Ralph Nader in the year 2000 presidential elections, you get a hint of the influence that Marx, even after the collapse of the Berlin Wall, continues to exert. In what would later become "base" and "superstructure," Marx places economic relations at the foundation of any society. The floors that follow—the political, religious, educational, and military superstructure—rest on and are determined by the class interests of the dominant bourgeois, a group that uses the veils of religion and politics to hide "its naked, shameless, direct, brutal exploitation."[46]

Recall the novels of Charles Dickens, and you realize that Marx knew his world: a society that, for example, sent seven-year-old children to work ten-hour days in a factory deserved to be condemned. Marx did that and then put the exploitation into a perspective that included the entire world: "The cheap prices of its [the bourgeois] commodities are the heavy artillery with which it batters down all Chinese walls, with which it forces the barbarians' intensely obdurate hatred of foreigners to capitulate. It [capitalism] compels all nations, on pain of extinction to adopt the bourgeois mode of production. . . . In a word it creates a world after its own image."[47]

That image included some spectacular achievements. In lines that could have been written by the cheering members of London's Chamber of Commerce, Marx writes that "the bourgeoisie, during its rule of scarce one hundred years, has created more massive and more colossal productive forces than have all preceding generations together." Canals, railroads, the telegraph, agriculture, steam, navigation, "and the clearing of whole continents for cultivation—what earlier century had even a presentiment that such productive forces slumbered in the lap of social labor?"[48]

The prose is so evocative that the reader may forget that it is the father of communism praising the wonders of the capitalist system. Marx climbs out of this apparent hole by suggesting a theory of social change—once again, for all of human history. "We see then that the means of production and of exchange, which served as the foundation for the growth of the bourgeoisie, were generated in feudal society." Its antithesis—capitalism—grew in the womb of feudal society, and eventually "the feudal relations of property became no longer compatible with the already developed productive forces; they became so many fetters. They had to be burst asunder; they were burst asunder."[49]

Another explosion would shortly occur because modern bourgeois society "is like the sorcerer who is no longer able to control the powers of the nether world whom he has called up by his spells." Like the specter of communism, the specter of "overproduction" haunted the capitalist world. Machines produced more than people could consume, so the capitalists were forced to curtail production as they conquered new markets and more "thoroughly exploited" old ones. A new antithesis—communism—was about to be born in the womb of capitalism because "the weapons with which the bourgeoisie felled feudalism to the ground are now turned against the bourgeoisie itself."[50]

These lines were extraordinarily prophetic. On January 11, 2002, Ford jettisoned 35,000 workers and closed five plants. Yesterday and today overproduction is an endemic problem for all capitalist economies. Long before so many of his ideological opponents, Marx clearly understood the potentially fatal threat to capitalism posed by overproduction. And if he did not immediately see the capitalist's solution (e.g., cartels, price fixing, and production agreements between producers), Marx's argument nevertheless prophesized a possible future. Like Achilles' heel, overproduction could cripple capitalism and make way for the proletariat, the only "really revolutionary class."[51]

The bourgeoisie created the world-shattering proletariat when it stripped it of property (remember, for example, the enclosures of land that bothered Captain Swing). "They have nothing of their own to secure and fortify; their mission is to destroy all previous securities for, and insurances of, individual property." Marx perceived "a more or less veiled civil war, raging within existing society"; and the bourgeoisie were unfit to rule because "it is incompetent to assure an existence to its slave within its slavery, because it cannot help letting him sink into such a state that it has to feed him, instead of being fed by him."[52]

After surveying the communist movement's ties to fraternal organizations throughout the continent, Marx ends with these words: "Let the ruling classes tremble at a Communist revolution. The proletarians have nothing to lose but their chains. They have a world to win. Workers of the world, unite."[53]

In German, and with no mention of its authors' names, the Communist League printed 500 copies of the manifesto in February 1848. Two years later the first English translation appeared in *The Red Republican*, a weekly publication. The editor called the manifesto "the most revolutionary document ever given to the world." Fifty years later that claim made some slight sense, but in 1848 the manifesto had no influence on, of all things, the revolutions that suddenly broke out all over Europe. Like a match to a drought-ready forest, the fires erupted in Vienna, Brussels, Venice, and especially, Paris. In the city of lights, the proletariat acted on its own and with virtually no theoretical knowledge of the class struggles that determined history.[54]

CLASS STRUGGLES IN FRANCE

Engels declared that doubt was never a word in their vocabulary. When he and Marx saw Europe erupting "right up to the Russian frontier," when the Paris proletariat actually took charge of the one city that symbolized revolution, "for us, under the circumstances of the time, there could be no doubt that the great decisive struggle had broken out, that it would have to be fought out in a single, long and changeful period of revolution, but that it could only end with the final victory of the proletariat.[55]

Marx was in Brussels when the eruptions occurred. He immediately used that 6,000 francs from his father's inheritance to finance the fight, and after his arrest, the Belgian authorities quickly expelled him. He arrived in Paris on March 5, 1848, in a city that then made the heart of any revolutionary beat with a legitimate sense of great optimism.[56]

Over a series of six months, moderate Republicans pressed the monarchy for a series of electoral reforms. Rather than holding outright demonstrations, the moderates staged a series of banquets, and as they ate, they discussed the real main course: political change. By January 1848 King Louis Phillipe allowed worry to overtake common sense; the regime forbade a banquet scheduled for February 18; that aroused the opposition, and when a crowd of "well-dressed, respectable bourgeois" gathered for a protest on February 22, the king sent in the "Guard municipale, a sort of riot police that was heartily detested in the working-class quarters of the city for its arrogant and occasionally brutal enforcement of order." After a few casualties and shouts, the crowd began to disperse. But in the working-class districts, people quickly erected barricades, and the authorities ill-advisedly shut down the theaters and the Comédie française. Parisians believed that when the Comédie "shuts its doors in perilous times it is like the battening down of the hatches in dirty weather."[57]

From their barricades the people demanded the resignation of a hated minister. The king complied, but his troops in the streets produced a massacre when, confronting a crowd, they killed fifty-two people and wounded scores of others. An ingenious agitator found a huge wagon and a white horse; stacking the dead in the wagon, the driver and his comrades drove it around Paris until dawn. In many instances they actually knocked on doors, woke people up, and with a torch over the bodies, shed bright and bloody light on the king and his brutal messengers.[58]

Louis abdicated on February 24. In a nation where the regime's last chamber of deputies included "three times more landed proprietors than industrialists,"[59] Marx and Engels still believed the proletarian revolution was at hand. They had a point, especially if one checked the treeless streets of Paris's once-magnificent boulevards.

By one count the city contained no less than 1,512 barricades. Used since 1588 to defy authority, Parisians built the walls of resistance by "politely stopping omnibuses, unhitching the horses, assisting the passengers to alight, and then turning the vehicles over to be weighted down with stones." When they ran out of buses, they leveled more than 4,000 trees; the streets looked like a rain forest after a hurricane. They were stripped of beauty but full of the wooden shelters that now confronted anyone stupid enough to challenge the masses.[60]

The unemployed showed up on the Champs Elysées to sell anything imaginable. That may seem like a yawn today, but under Louis, common folk only appeared on Paris's main thoroughfare when, as a gift, the king let them walk there on holidays. When Marx arrived from Brussels, the masses were suddenly part of the mainstream, under a government that, to foster the arts, soon distributed free theater tickets to the poor. Meanwhile, it also became incredibly easy to read the news as Parisians, intoxicated by the prospect of a free press, established 479 new newspapers over a ten-month stretch of revolutionary time.[61] Marx walked the treeless streets, and whatever limitations he saw in the new government, the right-to-work law promised the proletariat a future in which their needs and desires stood center stage. The government presumably belonged to the people.

Marx left Paris on April 6. He and Engels went to Germany to assist and direct the struggle that was their primary responsibility as members of the Communist League. As they left, they must have passed some of the 100,000 Frenchmen who, lured by the prospect of work, rushed in from the countryside and overwhelmed a government that, at best, could provide 10,000 jobs a day. When the workshops created by the right-to-work law were dissolved in June of 1848, their rolls included 120,000 names "and 50,000 more unemployed hanging around Paris who had been refused admission."[62]

In *Class Struggles in France* (originally published in 1850), Marx clearly understood that despite his theories, the provisional government "could not be anything but a compromise between the different classes which together had overturned the July throne, but whose interests were mutually antagonistic."[63] For four months one side fought the other, but by June, they nevertheless united to erase the hopes and dreams of the Paris working class. "No one," wrote Marx, "fought more fanatically in the June days for the salvation of property . . . than the Parisian petty bourgeois. . . . The shopkeeper had pulled himself together and marched against the barricade, in order to restore the traffic which leads from the streets into the shop."[64] Shoulder to shoulder with the shopkeepers was an army of peasants who, when the government called for the closing of the workshops and the dismantling of the barricades, rushed in from the countryside. Fifteen hundred came from Brittany alone, traveling for 200 miles over terrain that lacked any railroads. The nation was once again in arms but this time against the proletariat. Only four months after the struggle began, "there was no doubt what the rest of France wanted, no doubt that the Paris workers suffered a complete ideological separation from the country."[65]

With full powers turned over to the minister of war, fighting broke out in July, lasting for three days. Government figures claimed only 2,000 dead, but the number certainly exceeded that; just as significant, the manner of death disgusted as many as it excited. When Minister Cavaignac received complaints about the shooting, he simply ordered his troops to fix bayonets and spear the workers to death.[66] Marx never forgot the July Massacre, but with the German, Italian, and Belgian revolutions of 1848 also fading as quickly as a shooting star, he and Engels needed to readjust their thinking. And they did. In Engels words, "Vulgar democracy expected a renewed outbreak from day to day; we declared as early as autumn 1850 that at least the first chapter of the revolutionary period was closed and that nothing was to be expected until the outbreak of a new world crisis."[67]

While the two men waited for the crisis, Engels moved permanently to Manchester, and the Marxes moved (in August 1849) to London. For more than fifteen years, the revolutionary put on the cloak of a scholar. Marx got lost in the British Museum, and when he reappeared, he finally had in hand a book that did in fact change the course of world history.

DAS KAPITAL

Think of what we take for granted. Most of us work from computers with word-processing systems that suggest grammatical improvements if we write a line in an inappropriate or clumsy fashion; the programs correct our spelling mistakes as we move across the page, and we can use a variety of fonts and type sizes to order instant copies from our laser printers. We can add borders, we can add a watermark as a trademark, and perhaps most important, we can easily save the documents in a variety of forms. After writing an article or book pages, a professor saves to disk (two times) to a portable computer and then attaches the chapters as documents to an e-mail. Arriving on campus, the professor now stores the chapters on the hard drive of another computer.

These are literal luxuries, especially if one considers what faced Marx, his wife, and Friedrich Engels. Marx wrote with a pen and put his thoughts on paper in a "careless style full of colloquialisms." He often wrote "coarse" jokes attached to this or that passage, and next to what was already written, he scribbled in, as notes, complete and incomplete ideas. To call his writing penmanship is to call night day. The mysterious ink marks drifted in an upward-moving angle, and even Engels was often unable to read the script. It was so indecipherable that after Marx's death, Engels actually gave translators a "course" in translating Marx. Thankfully, Jenny Marx often copied his work into legible pages, but storing those documents was a nightmare. Lose a piece of paper and you lost, forever, the work of years or even a lifetime.[68]

Marx worked when he rested. Even on casual walks he kept a notebook in his pocket and jotted ideas down as he strolled. The ideas often came from his research at the British Museum; on days he could actually work, he stayed there for nine hours, from ten A.M. to seven P.M. He read everything, including the ponderous but honest reports that came from investigators who worked for the government. Like the U.S. General Accounting Office today, one arm of the British government published, free of charge, scathing criticisms of what other government agencies happily supported. Marx footnotes these reports through *Das Kapital* (*Capital*), and they provided grist for a mind that milled them into passionate prose. When Marx writes about the working day and "the werewolf-like hunger for surplus labor," he is using the reports produced by a British government that also provided him with a library, workspace, and a chair.[69]

David McLellan's biography provides a picture of the corner of the British Museum frequented by Marx. It was a pleasant space, and the cubicle offered the comforts of fine wood. The photo even shows the chair that Marx preferred. Unfortunately, he could not sit in the chair for long periods because, along with his carbuncles, Marx also suffered from hemorrhoids. In January 1852 he had an attack and told Engels that they "have affected me this time more than the French Revolution. . . . To go to the Library, the rear conditions do not permit this yet." Even when the hemorrhoids subsided, Marx often stayed home "because he was unable to get his suit and overcoat out of hock." As always, the family was destitute, but in the early 1850s, the madness of Marx's everyday life reached new heights.[70]

In November 1850 the Marxes lost a child. Their son Heinrich Guido succumbed to illness after a year of terrible grief for all concerned. Despite great pain in her back and breast, Jenny Marx had fed a son who nursed so hard that "he created an open sore on her breast, from which blood would spurt into his trembling little mouth." Meanwhile, the rent collectors arrived and in the middle of this horror evicted the family. Jenny Marx sold the beds to raise the rent, but the bailiffs put their possessions on the street. While the landlord complained that they had stolen something, a crowd of 200 or 300—the "riff-raff" of Chelsea—appeared, and the family's private degradation became a public humiliation. Eventually, Marx found new rooms and the family moved into those, servant and all.[71]

Helene "Lenchen" Demuth was the family's savior. Sent by Jenny Marx's mother when the family lived in Brussels, she stayed with the Marxes for a lifetime. When Jenny Marx was away, Helene Demuth and Marx produced a child of their own. Freddy was born on June 23, 1851, and despite a striking resemblance to Marx, all concerned agreed to blame Engels for the new addition to the world. He willingly assumed responsibility, and biographers suggest that Jenny Marx believed the lie. Only she, however, had the solution to that particular puzzle.[72]

To earn a living, Marx wrote for the *New York Herald Tribune*. Over the years he submitted roughly 500 articles (the *Tribune* did not have to accept the submissions). Engels wrote at least half of them because Marx was either too busy with serious research, too overwhelmed by family problems, or too sick to work. On March 10, 1853, he told Engels that "I came near to croaking this week" from a "grave liver inflammation." In addition to writing the newspaper pieces, Engels provided the lion's share of the family's actual income by beginning in these years to steal from the factory's coffers the money that kept Marx and family off the streets and, however crowded, under one roof. This was difficult indeed because, in any one month, Engels paid more to keep his horse stabled than Marx earned. Thus, over a twenty-year period, Engels religiously sent about 200 pounds a year. He paid for the writing of *Das Kapital* in every imaginable way and fashion.[73]

This short summary only takes us to the mid-1850s. One could go on endlessly repeating stories that help explain why, under these living and working conditions, it took Marx almost seventeen years to complete his most important book. Along the way he did publish *A Critique of Political Economy* (1859); however, for the present purposes the focus of attention remains *Das Kapital*. The first volume appeared on September 14, 1867. Volumes 2 and 3 are posthumous publications. Together, the volumes add up to an analysis of more than 2,700 pages. The books are enormous, and the prose, occasionally studded with mathematical formulas, is much heavier than Marx's journalistic work. A German professor wrote *Das Kapital*, but a world-class revolutionary and a great journalist also made significant contributions. The books are therefore an adventure; the reader never knows when the journalist or revolutionary will push the professor aside and produce prose that is, all at once, both angry and magisterial.

GOLDEN EGGS

Marx begins *Das Kapital* with a warning. Although he does not "by any means depict the capitalist and the landowner in rosy colors," he analyzes their efforts "only in so far as they are the personifications of economic categories, the bearers of particular class-relations and interests." In *Das Kapital* he perceives the development of economic relationships "as a process of natural history"; individuals can valiantly try to rise above the process, but ultimately, it is a futile effort. One cannot, after all, "make the individual responsible for relations whose creature he remains."[74]

These lines represent a significant hardening of Marx's views. In the 1844 manuscripts, "just as society itself produces man as man, so is society produced by him."[75] The relationship was dialectical, and people always played an active part in shaping the society that shaped them. By 1867 people are like a flatbed on a long freight train. The economic engine moves everything, and people are the passengers who come along for a ride that ends with the inevitable coming of communism.

The first chapter of *Das Kapital*, titled "The Commodity," seems both harmless and boring. Marx states that wherever capitalism prevails, the wealth of the society appears as "an immense collection of commodities." What are commodities? They are *things* that "satisfy human needs of whatever kind."[76] You could have a side of beef, ten acres of land, or a thousand human beings. If you think of them as things, they are commodities that can be used, like a magic wand, to satisfy the hunger pangs of your stomach or the status-seeking needs of your imagination. A meal and a Rolex watch are both commodities from this perspective.

To put commodities in perspective, Marx makes a crucial distinction between use and exchange value. The former revolves around the efficacy or utility of, for example, land or tools. You realize a use value when, after harvesting the crop, you consume the bounty. Exchange value refers to the process of trading one thing, one commodity, for another; I swap a quantity of corn for a piece of land. But "when commodities are in the relation of exchange, their exchange-value manifests itself as something totally independent of their use-value." Focus on the words "totally independent" because Marx is rightfully fascinated by a system that exchanges a particular quantity of money for a particular number of machines. Even more to the point, he is fascinated by a system that exchanges substantial amounts of property for pieces of paper, that is, stock in a company.

Marx makes a beeline to the question of what determines value when people exchange the most diverse commodities. Already in this first chapter, he is absolutely unequivocal in arguing that "what exclusively determines the value of any article is the amount of labor socially necessary, or the labor-time socially necessary for its production." Thus, whatever it is that people exchange—goods, time, sex—"as exchange values, all commodities are merely definite quantities of *congealed labor-time*."[77] This is such a hard and fast rule that even when, in volume 2, Marx discusses a company's buyer of goods and services, he stresses that a buyer "adds nothing" to the value of the commodities exchanged. Even the savviest of salespeople cannot add value because value exists only as a result of the labor time involved in the commodity's production.[78]

This is the labor theory of value. As many commentators stress, Marx "offers no adequate proof of his labor-value theory."[79] In fact, he offers no proof at all. It is, however, an assertion that is at the core of his overall theory, particularly his argument that capitalism is nothing more than an "epoch making mode of exploitation."[80]

As an internal necessity, capitalism endlessly exploits the workers because, as part of an historical process, it revolutionized two aspects of economic life: the *continual* mechanization of production and the *unique* organization of the labor process. Each adds its own dimension to capitalism's effects, but it is the new organization of labor that first catches Marx's attention. Under capitalism labor power is a commodity, a thing with no more inherent value than a quantity of coal or a pile of horse manure. The notion of people as things is both morally offensive to and economically catastrophic for the worker because, under capitalism, "labor power is a commodity only in the hands of its seller." The worker exchanges his labor power for money and, after a ten- or twelve-hour day, goes home. Meanwhile, the buyer—the employer—uses that labor power as a way to make money. The buyer *transforms* labor power into capital, but "human labor-power is by nature no more capital than are the means of production." It acquires this specific *social character* only under capitalism and, at the core of capitalism, is the "circulation of commodities."[81]

Here Marx is at his best. He perfectly catches a process that is as contemporary as a trip through any mall or a visit to a trade fair hawking the latest versions of a computer's hardware and software. Think, says Marx, of the circulation of commodities as a series of three letters: M-C-M. The letters stand for money-commodity-money. Marx explains that when, for example, I use money to buy labor power, I turn it into *productive capital* when the laborers produce something that I can eventually sell (i.e., the commodity) for money, preferably for far more money than it cost me to produce the clothing, pottery, or flatware.

The M-C-M process is both a ceaseless and an endemic part of capitalism because "capital has one sole driving force, the drive to valorize itself."[82] By definition capitalists need to take their money, convert it into a commodity, and complete the process by accepting money (or an equivalent, such as stock) for whatever they produced. If your money just sits there, it is, like a wad of cash under your bed, sleeping on the job. Value is added only when you turn money into a saleable commodity; you can produce medicine to cure cancer or a pill that produces the erections required for sex. You can produce movies that artfully depict the horrors of the Holocaust, or you can produce horror flicks with Santa Claus as the killer. Commodities are value neutral; they are "born levelers and cynics" because they are part of a circulatory process that only has one, soulless goal: to add value the capitalist can then use in another variation of the M-C-M process.

In capitalism, the workingman is an integral—if reluctant—part of an endless circulatory (M-C-M) process; "and the characteristic thing is not that the commodity labor power is purchasable but that labor power appears as a commodity." Of course, in the factory it interacts with the means of production used by the capitalist who, to his great satisfaction, discovers that the circulatory process "brings forth living offspring, or at least lays golden eggs." The eggs appear when, at the back end of the M-C-M process, the capitalist suddenly has more money than before, even after deducting for the costs of labor power and the means of production.[83]

What creates this value? No matter what goods and services are exchanged, the value of all commodities is solidly rooted in labor power—in the amount of time it took workers to produce a particular commodity. The beauty for capitalists is that they pay the worker enough for the worker's survival, and when that survival is assured, the laborer still works additional hours, punching a time clock marked profit for the owners of the means of production. Capital creates "vampires" posing as the beacons of civilization; capital lives "by sucking living labor, and lives the more, the more labor it sucks."[84]

Another term for this sucking process is *surplus value*. When the worker labors for his sustenance, that is "necessary labor time"; it is what he gets from the capitalist as a living (never a just) wage. But, say it takes the worker six hours of labor to earn his daily keep. When he works for the additional four or six hours, "he creates no value for himself." On the contrary, as a commodity used in the M-C-M process, the laborer creates "surplus value, which, for the capitalist, has all the charms of something created out of nothing." In essence, the system allows the vampire to endlessly suck the blood from his prey because, in control of the means of production, the capitalist can buy—often at a great discount—the only thing the worker has to sell: his labor power. Meanwhile, that labor power is the only thing that creates economic value in any process of exchange.[85]

Marx subdivides surplus value into two types. When the owners lengthened the working day, they got much more for the same basic pay. This robbed labor power "of its normal moral and physical conditions of development and activity." Capitalists heartlessly extended "the worker's production time within a given period by shortening his life"; while this was a worker's tragedy, the longer he labored (and lived), the more the worker's production spelled *absolute surplus value* for the capitalist. When the owners mechanized or otherwise changed the productive process in an effective manner, that was *relative surplus value*. And if particular owners managed to force the proletariat to work longer hours with better machine tools, they won the prize for profit. They literally made money coming and going.[86]

With his concept of surplus value, Marx believes he has explained the origins of profit and the historical reality of the exploitation that must produce class conflict. Capitalists got something for nothing; they laughed all the way to the bank, and there were no exceptions to this rule. "You may be a model citizen, perhaps a member of the R.S.P.C.A. [Royal Society for the Prevention of Cruelty to Animals], and you may be in the odor of sanctity as well; but the thing you represent when you come face to face with me [the worker] has no heart in its breast." You are a capitalist, and as a representative of that system, your role is to create value from the

M-C-M process. The worker is nothing but a commodity and, simultaneously, the source of the golden eggs collected by all capitalists, in any country, at any time.[87]

Those golden eggs produce competition. Because all capitalists want to collect them, the search for the profitable goose means that all capitalists, as a matter of systemic necessity, try to undercut or destroy their marketplace opponents. Quoting from a book about the advantages of the Indian colonial trade to England, Marx notes that "if my neighbor by doing much with little labor, can sell cheap, I must contrive to sell as cheap as he."[88] Think of modern-day competing ads for desktop computers. Marx correctly underlines an elemental part of the capitalist system. All players are perpetually and inescapably vulnerable to the competitive efforts of others.[89] Imaginative competitors can undercut you and even force you to sell short in the interest of maintaining market share. Ultimately, that is ruinous; the smart capitalist always looks for an edge and correctly grasps that even fourteen-hour days are no response to a competitor who gains a marketplace advantage by adroitly mechanizing the productive process.

Here we find the Trojan horse of the capitalist system.[90] To compete with one another, all capitalists must mechanize the production process. This, too, is an element of the system that Marx grasped with great force and intelligence. Recent books about globalization stress the same dynamic perceived by Marx.[91] You bring those robots into the automobile factory, or you watch market share disappear as quickly as snow under a heat lamp.

But for Marx, "machinery, like every other component of constant capital, creates no new value." Only labor power did that. Therefore, as competition produced greater and greater mechanization, the capitalist would be squeezed because machinery "never adds more value than it loses, on the average, by depreciation."[92] Today's advantage is tomorrow's weakness; because the "sole driving force" of the entire system is the need to increase value, each capitalist initiates and continues the mechanization process that inexorably squeezes profits from his business *and* from the entire capitalist system. Ultimately, a crisis occurs, and capitalism collapses under the weight of the machines that "create no new value."[93]

As the machines displace labor, one sure consequence is an "industrial reserve army." Marx calls this the "general law of capitalist accumulation." In its absolute form, the machines that erase the need for people leave in their wake "the mass of a consolidated surplus population, whose misery is in inverse ratio to the amount of torture it has to undergo in the form of labor." On the job the worker is pushed till he drops; when a machine replaces him, he is swiftly discarded along with the other waste products of the capitalist system. Modern analysts use words like underclass or homeless, but Marx simply discusses paupers. "The more extensive the pauperized sections of the working class and the industrial reserve army, the greater is official pauperism."[94]

Once again Marx caught an elemental and persisting aspect of the capitalist system. When present-day analysts discuss the acceptable rate of unemployment (is it 5 percent, 8 percent, 12 percent?), they are referring to surplus workers. Marx broke them down into three types—the floating, the latent, and the stagnant—and he correctly grasped that the capitalist system let them float or, in today's world, migrate. There are now 100 million men and women (from countries like the Philippines, India, El Salvador, and Mexico) "floating" through the global marketplace in search of jobs, and when they find employment, they send most of their money home to support the family members who cannot find work in their country of origin. Whether it is villages in Algeria or Guatemala, floating armies of migrants provide the revenue that allow people to purchase goods and services on the home front. Meanwhile, capitalists happily hire illegal workers (in 2002 the U.S. estimate exceeds 6 million) and pay them as little as is competitively possible.[95]

Although labor migration has many causes besides capitalism, Marx's vision proved remarkably accurate in a variety of ways. All over the globe, reserve armies of surplus (or disposable) people are a historical constant, and their existence is intimately related to the exigencies of the capitalist system outlined by Marx. However, where an analyst today sees a systemic weakness, Marx saw those armies as the ultimate weapon of the proletariat. In a chapter in *Das Kapital* titled "The Historical Tendency of Capitalist Accumulation," he writes that "one capitalist always strikes down many others." Forever thirsty, the biggest capitalists gulp down the profits of their competitors so that "along with the constant decrease in the number of capitalist magnates, who usurp and monopolize all the advantages of this process of transformation, the mass of misery, oppression, slavery, degradation and exploitation grows." Ultimately, at some totally undefined time, "the centralization of the means of production and the socialization of labor reach a point at which they become incompatible with their capitalist integument. This integument is burst asunder. The knell of capitalist private property sounds. The expropriators are expropriated."[96]

This is an "inexorable" process. Like a caterpillar that transforms into a butterfly, communism grows within the womb of capitalism, and when the proletariat takes charge, that is "negation of the negation." The miseries produced by private property and the capitalist mode of production become positives when the world's workingmen and women use their justifiable rage to drive a stake through the heart of the vampire whose real name is capitalism.[97]

This prophecy changed the world. From Lenin to Mao to Castro, communists produced revolutions rooted in Marx's dream. But was the dream realized through the efforts of people or the simple working out of the laws of historical materialism? In the lines previously quoted, people can seemingly wait for the inevitable explosion. But one could also argue that however important the role of crises and economic depressions, activists needed to create the sense of class consciousness that moved the masses to action. Marx himself spent almost a decade organizing the International Working Men's Association. However, if people produced change, that meant they created society as much as society created them. In action, the class-conscious workingman was the negation of Marx's theory. After all, if the laws were inexorable why did the worker need to produce the explosion that supposedly occurred in an inevitable fashion?[98]

A fatal flaw in Marx's map is the labor theory of value. Once you add other variables to the process of production (e.g., machines, scarcity, colonialism), explaining exchange value only in terms of congealed labor power is difficult indeed. When the English opened Indian markets for British textiles, they did so by eliminating the competition in a brutal manner. On at least two occasions, they cut off the thumbs of whole communities of Indian weavers to open the way for the products of Lancashire. The exchange value of those textiles must be seen, at a minimum, in terms of labor power *and*, as a hideous addition to value, the thumbs lost to British colonialism.[99]

Surplus value collapses as an explanation of profit once we turn to realities such as cartels, monopolies, and simple corruption. Marx certainly knew these practices existed, but in search of a theory that focused on exploitation of the worker, he neglected the other variables that can dramatically increase profit without the worker's assistance or labor. Americans, for example, pay approximately three times the world-market price for sugar. The United States maintains higher profit margins for the growers by refusing to allow cheaper sugar to enter the U.S. marketplace. It would be hard to explain these profits as resulting from a longer working day or mechanization. On the contrary, they are a result of the political power that, as Marx well knew, allows producers to receive government subsidies as they simultaneously close the market to "unfair" competition.[100]

Almost 140 years after its publication, shooting holes in *Das Kapital* remains an international pastime. But for all its faults, Marx's map is the blueprint still consulted by anyone trying to understand everything from exploitation to the circulation of commodities, from reserve armies of labor to the class conflicts that shake nations. Equally important for sociological theory, Marx's map was the catalyst that initiated some of the greatest books and insights the discipline has. Neither Simmel nor Weber can be understood without first grasping that they read Marx and in reaction produced maps that built on the extraordinary stimulus titled *Das Kapital*.

THE PARIS COMMUNE AND THE FUTURE

Marx and Engels rarely fought. But in January 1863 Engels turned ice cold when Marx responded to news about the death of Mary Burns. For Engels her death was a catastrophe; he truly loved his companion and explained to Marx that "I simply can't convey what I feel." Marx answered with a letter that included a one-line expression of sorrow and a long litany of complaints about his own problems in London: the family needed money, the children's clothes were in hock, and as always, Marx felt terrible. "Engels read this with anger and amazement." He was so disgusted by Marx's egotism and selfishness that he remained silent for days; when he did respond, he told Marx that "my own misfortune and the frosty view you took of it should have made it positively impossible for me to reply to you any sooner." Even "philistine acquaintances" expressed far more sympathy for Engels than his best friend and comrade who, by the way, lived on the money sent by Engels.[101]

Marx apologized by blaming his callousness on Jenny Marx and her "exacerbated nervousness." His wife caused him to forget the most obvious decencies, and he regretted any incident that threatened a "rift in their friendship." Engels accepted the apology, sent some money as a gesture of reconciliation, and Marx went back to work and to complaining about the horrors of his life.[102] As if glued to a mirror, he continually focused only on himself and his work. That could be horrible for family and friends, yet it did allow him to devote his best energies to *Das Kapital* and, after 1864, to the International Working Men's Association.

For eight years Marx tried to create the revolution by organizing—in the streets—the workers of the world. England offered the best opportunities because, in sharp contrast to the Continent, activists here experienced "neither police brutality nor intellectual persecution." One could organize at will and feel secure that, with its relative freedom of the press, English and other workers would get the message. So when Marx received an invitation to attend a public meeting of workers in September 1864, he agreed to become involved because "the international was a once-in-a-lifetime chance for action and expression through an organized channel that had the possibility of reaching the world proletariat." In addition, the movement offered Marx a chance to escape his life in the library. The chance to meet and shape the masses allowed a solitary scholar the chance to once again be a man of action.[103]

Marx wrote the International Working Men's Association's "inaugural address." It is a surprisingly tame document. As he explained to Engels, "It will take time before the reawakening of the movement allows the plain speaking of the past." Thus Marx even deleted the word "profit-mongers" from the association's preamble to satisfy his concerned comrades.[104]

Addressed to "Workingmen," Marx's address explains that despite "unrivaled" growth of industry and commerce, "the misery of the working man has not diminished from 1848 to 1864." Using official reports of the English government, Marx cites a series of studies that condemned everything from working to health conditions, whether in the factories or on the farms. Meanwhile, "in all countries of Europe, it has now become a truth demonstrable to every unprejudiced mind . . . that no improvement of machinery, no appliance of science to production, no contrivances of communication, no new colonies, no emigration, no opening of markets, no free trade, not all of these things put together, will do away with the miseries of the industrious masses."[105]

Only one thing could help the masses. They needed to cooperate. But instead of immediately storming the Bastille, Marx proposed that "the great duty of the working classes" is "to conquer political power." Because "the lords of the land and the lords of capital" used their authority to demoralize and depress the masses, workers needed to struggle within the system to gain political power in all the world's nations. Eventually, "the bonds of brotherhood" could create a situation in which, at long last, workers followed Marx's advice: "Proletarians of all countries, unite!"[106]

This was admittedly mild stuff compared with the fire and brimstone of the *Communist Manifesto*. Engels was so unimpressed that despite Marx's enthusiasm, he remained for many years "distinctly reticent" about the International Working Men's Association's achievements and possibilities. He even failed to form a commission for the workers of Manchester.[107] Marx nevertheless labored with such passion that at one point, he pretended to be away from London so that he could actually continue writing *Das Kapital*.

By the time of the International Working Men's Association's first Congress in 1866, seventeen unions had joined the movement and another thirteen considered affiliating with the workers of the world. It was a considerable achievement, at considerable expense. So many unions meant compromises to satisfy the diverse viewpoints of workers who sometimes started in the middle of the political road. And as always, Marx battled with anyone who sought to move the organization in a direction he opposed. His fights with the Russian revolutionary Mikháil Bakúnin caused both men endless problems and a legacy of rancor that divided as much as it united the proletariat.[108]

The press grossly exaggerated the influence of the International Working Men's Association. Some commentators even suggested the association caused the great Chicago fire of 1871. As Marx answered these and other charges, he became a "notorious" celebrity. Yet in England the total number of the association's individual members was 254. Germany had 58 branches, which may sound like great progress until one examines the number of members: 385 workers in the 58 branches. France, Italy, Spain, and even the United States also had chapters; but in truth, the International Working Men's Association was a worldwide movement with the depth of a puddle.[109] Engels seemed to be right. Then suddenly, the workers of the world did unite—behind the heroic efforts of the Paris proletariat. As in 1848, France again offered hope of a real revolution, and Marx entered the fray with a small book, *The Civil War in France*.

France and Prussia fought a war in 1870. As much as anything else, it revolved around the territorial ambitions of Prussia's Chancellor Otto von Bismarck. Wanting to create and unify a nation, he helped engineer a war that quickly ended with France's total defeat.[110] However, with Prussian troops still surrounding the city, the people of Paris refused to surrender even when their government did so. In fact, when General Claude-Martin Lecomte tried (on March 18, 1871) to suppress the revolt of the masses, troops sided with the people; three times General Lecomte told his troops to fix bayonets but instead, Lecomte was arrested, placed in prison, and soon executed by the leaders of the Paris Commune of 1871.

In Paris more than 600 barricades kept the French army at bay; and while French authorities—with Bismarck looking over their shoulders—decided what to do, the people of Paris created a government composed, to a great degree, of workingmen. As far away as Australia, the bourgeoisie worried because, as the *Sydney Morning Herald* told its readers, "the object of the Red republicans is to remodel society, to appropriate the accumulated fruits of labor and to ensure the establishment of a government which shall revive the (1848) policy of the national workshops."[111]

Marx was delighted by the revolution and by the aims of workers who wanted far more than national workshops. In an address to the International Working Men's Association in May 1871, Marx explained that the workers were elected by universal suffrage "in the various wards of the town, responsible and revocable at short terms." *Everything* was now in the Paris Commune's hands, so they quickly destroyed "parson power"; clergy "were sent back to the recesses of private life, there to feed upon the alms of the faithful in imitation of their predecessors, the apostles." Education was instantly open to all, and with the church and state on the sidelines, "science freed itself from the fetters which class prejudice and governmental force had imposed on it." Most important, "nothing could be more foreign to the spirit of the Commune than to supercede universal suffrage by hierarchic investiture."[112]

Some scholars suggest that the emphasis on decentralization offers us the first, hazy glimpse of Marx's vision of a communist future.[113] That seems just if one also remembers that "the working class did not expect miracles from the Commune." Nobody had "ready made utopias" to offer the proletariat; instead what the commune did was to "set free the elements of the new society with which old collapsing bourgeois society is pregnant." The baby was being born in the streets of Paris, and like any parents, Marx and the other members of the International Working Men's Association would need to wait many years as their child developed into maturity. Meanwhile, the Paris Commune "was the first revolution in which the working class was openly acknowledged as the only class capable of social initiative."[114]

That initiative was brutally destroyed on May 27–28, 1871, as French troops entered the city. The government estimated the dead at 17,000; other estimates go as high as 30,000 Parisians killed. One contemporary account reports that close to one of the boundary points, a natural hollow was now filled with the dead: "There they lay, tier above tier, each successive tier powered over with a coating of chloride of lime—two hundred of them patent to the eye, besides those underneath hidden by the earth covering layer after layer."[115]

Although Marx condemned the slaughter in the strongest terms, he was powerless to stop the collapse of the Paris Commune and in 1872 the disintegration of the International Working Men's Association. Bitter feuds fractured the movement to such an extent that some talked of moving the headquarters to New York. In the new world the workers could get a new start. Instead, the association died a slow death as its demise became to Marx and Engels another symbol of the need for patience. Capitalism was pregnant, but nobody knew when the communist baby would actually announce with a catastrophic economic crisis its first signs of real life.

THE FINAL YEARS

Engels "was flourishing his walking stick in the air and singing, and laughing all over his face." The observer was Marx's daughter Eleanor, and the occasion was Engels retirement from business in 1869. He had used a large inheritance from his father to become a partner in the Manchester firm in 1864; five years later he sold his half of the business. Until his death in 1895, Engels lived very well indeed because, for all his criticisms and reservations, he was a first-class capitalist, a splendid success in a world he tried to destroy.[116]

Engels's generosity exceeded all expectations. Before closing the books on his business, he put aside enough money for the Marxes to live comfortably for the rest of their lives. Even then Marx spent more than they had "and frequently asked for more handouts." Today we might call it a sense of entitlement or even welfare. Marx called it a way of life and moved the family into comfortable quarters in a well-heeled section of London. While his garden was still covered with the "black snow" called coal, after 1869 the pollution caused by capitalist growth was, thanks to

Engels, nothing more than a nasty footnote to a now-ensured life of leisure.[117]

If the snow got too deep, there were vacations at the seashore and a series of "cures" in Europe's most-renowned spas. In London, where Engels also had a home, the two men saw each every day. Through the 1870s they customarily met in the early afternoon and discussed, in Marx's study, everything from the most esoteric to the most commonplace aspects of capitalist development. At one point Marx focused on the role of Jewish and Christian bankers in the early Middle Ages. Each man studied the issues, and when they later compared thoughts and opinions, they used Marx's study as an exercise area. "One man walked diagonally in one way, the other in the other." For hours the fathers of communism discussed the direction of human history and the crisis that, as it ushered in communism, would presumably destroy the annuities that secured their existences.[118]

Marx loved children in general and his own grandchildren in particular. One friend relates that on an extended visit, Marx's grandson Johnny used Marx as an omnibus (i.e., he rode on his grandfather's shoulders); with Engels and the friend as horses, Johnny drove them all over London. The boy issued marching orders in English, German, and French, and the delighted men played "until Marx was dropping and then we had to parley with Johnny and a truce was concluded."[119]

Marx continued to update volume 1 of *Das Kapital*, which would prove to be the only section published during his life. Reading through a detailed chronology of his last years, the pages cite one trip after another to spas designed to cure his and Mrs. Marx's many health problems. In August 1876 he arrived in Karlsbad for his "third" cure. Two years later he traveled to the Isle of Jersey for medical assistance, and a month later, he took his wife to Waterloo for her needed care. When Jenny Marx died in December 1881, Marx was too ill to attend the funeral. He labored on for two more years. Not quite 65 years of age, Karl Marx died on March 14, 1883.

Marx is buried in Highgate Cemetery in London. The eulogy given by Engels offers a wonderfully biased summary of Marx's life, achievements, and predictions. "Nobody can fight for a cause without making enemies. . . . Throughout the greatest part of his political life he was the most hated and calumniated man in Europe, . . . but at the end of his life, he could proudly glimpse millions of followers. . . . He saw his economic theories becoming the indisputable basis of socialism throughout the whole world."[120]

Engels was right. Yesterday and today, Marx's work remains the indisputable starting point for anyone seeking, as in contemporary Colombia or Peru, the overthrow of capitalism and the coming of the communist state.

NOTES

1. Karl Marx, *The Economic and Philosophic Manuscripts of 1844*, ed. Dirk J. Struik (New York: International Publishers, 1964), 135.

2. The list of illnesses appears in Saul K. Padover, *Karl Marx: An Intimate Biography* (New York: McGraw Hill, 1978), 639–43; the quote appears in Francis Wheen, *Karl Marx: A Life* (New York: Norton, 1999), 313.

3. Padover, *Karl Marx*, 643.

4. Erik Erikson, *Young Man Luther* (New York: Norton, 1958), 245.

5. E. J. Hobsbawn and George Rudé, *Captain Swing* (New York: Pantheon, 1968), 204.

6. Ibid., 29–35.

7. Ibid., 97, 137.

8. Ibid., 298.

9. Friedrich Engels, *The Condition of the Working Class in England* (New York: Oxford University Press, 1993), 21.

10. Ibid., 21; see also the entire introduction.

11. Reference is to Marx's *Economic and Philosophic Manuscripts*.

12. George Fasel, *Europe in Upheaval: The Revolutions of 1848* (Chicago: Rand McNally, 1970), 2.

13. Robert Heilbroner, *The Worldly Philosophers: The Lives, Times, and Ideas of the Great Economic Thinkers*, 7th ed. (New York: Touchstone, 1999), 168.

14. Padover, *Karl Marx*, 1.

15. Frank E. Manuel, *A Requiem for Karl Marx* (Cambridge, Mass.: Harvard University Press, 1995), 5–6; also see Wheen, *Karl Marx*, 11.

16. Manuel, *Requiem for Karl Marx*, 15–16.

17. Ibid., 16.

18. See Thorstein Veblen, "The Intellectual Preeminence of the Jew in Modern Europe," in *Thorstein Veblen*, ed. Bernard Rosenberg (New York: Crowell, 1963), 91–100.

19. Padover, *Karl Marx*, 27; also see David McLellan, *Karl Marx: His Life and Thought* (New York: Harper and Row, 1973), 9.

20. Padover, *Karl Marx*, 45.

21. Besides Padover, *Karl Marx*, see McLellan, *Karl Marx*, 15; also see Franz Mehring, *Karl Marx* (Ann Arbor: University of Michigan Press, 1962), 5.

22. See, for example, Edmund Wilson, *To the Finland Station* (Garden City, N.J.: Doubleday, 1940), 116; also Wheen, *Karl Marx*, 16.

23. Padover, *Karl Marx*, 45–47.

24. See, for example, Padover, *Karl Marx*, 46–56; see also Manuel, *Requiem for Karl Marx*, chapter 2.

25. Wilson, *To the Finland Station*, 117.

26. Padover, *Karl Marx*, 105.

27. Ibid., p.110; and Manuel, *Requiem for Karl Marx*, 29.

28. Georg W. F. Hegel, *The Philosophy of History* (New York: Dover, 1956); Bertrand Russell, *A History of Western Philosophy* (New York Simon and Schuster,

1945), 735; Isaiah Berlin, *Karl Marx: His Life and Work* (London: Oxford University Press, 1978), 34–40.

29. Padover, *Karl Marx*, 124–25.

30. Wheen, *Karl Marx*, 45–46.

31. Karl Marx, *The Eighteenth Brumaire of Louis Bonaparte* (New York: International Publishers, 1963), 15.

32. Padover, *Karl Marx*, 252–53.

33. Ludwig Feuerbach, *The Essence of Christianity* (New York: Harper and Row, 1957), 270 and 277; also see McLellan, *Karl Marx*, 68.

34. Marx, *Economic and Philosophic Manuscripts*, 172; for this discussion, I also relied on Wilson, *To the Finland Station*, 125–27.

35. See Wheen, *Karl Marx*, 45.

36. Manuel, *Requiem for Karl Marx*, 58; Wilson, *To the Finland Station*, 147.

37. See J. D. Hunley, *The Life and Thought of Frederick Engels: A Reinterpretation* (New Haven, Conn.: Yale University Press, 1991), esp. chapters 1 and 2.

38. See Wilson, *To the Finland Station*, 177.

39. Marx, *Economic and Philosophic Manuscripts*, 106–9, 135; on alienation see Dirk Struik's excellent introduction, esp. 46–47.

40. See, for example, the posthumously published Karl Marx and Friedrich Engels, *The German Ideology* (New York: International Publishers, 1947).

41. Wheen, *Karl Marx*, 104; for the same story, also see Manuel, *Requiem for Karl Marx*, 76–77.

42. Padover, *Karl Marx*, 244.

43. McLellan, *Karl Marx*, 117. Engels statement about having it their own way is quoted in Padover, *Karl Marx*, 242. For a third, similar version of this congress, see Wheen, *Karl Marx*, chapter 5.

44. Karl Marx and Friedrich Engels, *The Communist Manifesto* (New York: International Publishers, 1948), 8; on the ultimatum from the conference and the manifesto's four elements, see Padover, *Karl Marx*, 248–49.

45. Marx and Engels, *Communist Manifesto*, 9.

46. Ibid., 11.

47. Ibid., 13.

48. Ibid., 14.

49. Ibid.

50. Ibid., 15.

51. Ibid., 15–19.

52. Ibid., 20–21.

53. Ibid., 44.

54. Padover, *Karl Marx*, 249–50.

55. See Engels's introduction to Karl Marx, *Class Struggles in France, 1848–1850* (New York: International Publishers, 1964), 13.

56. For specific dates, I have used the chronology provided by Padover, *Karl Marx*, 593–613.

57. Fasel, *Europe in Upheaval*, 46–47; see also Priscilla Robertson, *Revolutions of 1848: A Social History* (Princeton, N.J.: Princeton University Press, 1952), 30.

58. Robertson, *Revolutions of 1848*, 33.

59. See Jean Sigmann, *1848: The Romantic and Democratic Revolutions in Europe* (New York: Harper and Row, 1970).

60. Robertson, *Revolutions of 1848*, 35.

61. Ibid.; on the newspapers, see p. 55; on the Champs Elysées, see p. 65.

62. Ibid., 69.

63. Marx, *Class Struggles in France*, 39.

64. Ibid., 63.

65. Robertson, *Revolutions of 1848*, 90; also see Fasel, *Europe in Upheaval*, esp. chapter 5, "The Triumph of the Counterrevolution."

66. Fasel, *Europe in Upheaval*, 146–47; Robertson, *Revolutions of 1848*, 94.

67. See Marx, *Class Struggles in France*, 13.

68. See Engels's introduction to volume 2 of Karl Marx, *Capital*, 3 vols. (London: Penguin Classics, 1991), 2:1–2.

69. On the notebook see *Marx and Engels through the Eyes of Their Contemporaries* (Moscow: Progress Publishers, 1972), 63; for the quote about werewolves, see Karl Marx, *Capital*, 3 vols. (London: Penguin Classics, 1991), 1:353.

70. David McLellan's fine biography also provides a number of interesting portraits and glimpses of Marx's life; see McLellan, *Karl Marx*; concerning the hemorrhoids, see Padover, *Karl Marx*, 313.

71. Manuel, *Requiem for Karl Marx*, 37–38.

72. Wheen, *Karl Marx*, 171–76.

73. Padover, *Karl Marx*, 295.

74. Marx, *Capital*, 1:92.

75. Marx, *Economic and Philosophic Manuscripts*, 137.

76. Marx, *Capital*, 1:125.

77. Ibid., 1:130.

78. Ibid., 2:135.

79. Thorstein Veblen, "The Socialist Economics of Karl Marx and His Followers," in *Thorstein Veblen*, ed. Bernard Rosenberg (New York: Crowell, 1963), 66. See also Joseph Schumpeter, *Capitalism, Socialism, and Democracy* (New York: Harper and Row, 1947), esp. part 1.

80. Marx, *Capital*, 2:37.

81. Ibid.

82. Ibid., 1:342.

83. Ibid., 1:255.

84. Ibid., 1:342.

85. Ibid., 1:325.

86. Ibid., 1:432; on the effects of the working day see 1:376–77.

87. Ibid., 1:343.

88. Ibid., 1:436.

89. See Robert Heilbroner's discussion of vulnerability and the M-C-M process in his *The Nature and Logic of Capitalism* (New York: Norton, 1985), 56–57.

90. I got this notion from Robert Heilbroner, *Worldly Philosophers*, 159–60.

91. See, for example, Rosabeth Moss Kantor, *World Class: Thriving Locally in the Global Economy* (New York: Simon and Schuster, 1995); also see William Greider, *One World, Ready or Not* (New York: Simon and Schuster, 1997).

92. Marx, *Capital*, 1:509.

93. Heilbroner, *Worldly Philosophers*, 160–61.

94. Marx, *Capital*, 1:798.

95. See, for example, Ronald Fernandez, *America's Banquet of Cultures: Harness-*

ing Ethnicity, Race, and Immigration in the Twenty-first Century (Westport, Conn.: Praeger, 2000), chapter 2.

96. Marx, *Capital*, 1:929.

97. Ibid., 1:929.

98. Veblen, *Thorstein Veblen*, 71.

99. See Shashi Thadoor, *India: From Midnight to the Millennium* (New York: Harper, 1997), 14; also see Joseph A. Schumpeter, *Capitalism, Socialism, and Democracy* (New York: Harper Torchbooks, 1962), 24.

100. See, for example, the chapter titled "Cultural Constants" in Ronald Fernandez, *Cruising the Caribbean U.S. Intervention and Influence in the Twentieth Century* (Monroe, Maine: Common Courage, 1994).

101. Wheen, *Karl Marx*, 263; Manuel, *Requiem for Karl Marx*, 67–69.

102. Manuel, *Requiem for Karl Marx*, 69.

103. Padover, *Karl Marx*, 381, 394–95; also see Mehring, *Karl Marx*, chapter 11.

104. McLellan, *Karl Marx*, 365.

105. Karl Marx, "Inaugural Address of the International Working Men's Association, October 21–27, 1864," [www.ex.ac.uk/Projects/meia/Archive/1864-IWMA/1864-b.htm]. (Accessed October 12, 2001.)

106. Ibid., 5.

107. McLellan, *Karl Marx*, 369.

108. Ibid., 368; see also Wilson, *To the Finland Station*, esp. chapter 14.

109. McLellan, *Karl Marx*, 386, 401.

110. For example, D. G. Williamson, *Bismarck and Germany 1862–1890*, 2nd ed. (London: Longman, 1998).

111. See the *Sydney Morning Herald*, May 12, 1871 [www.arts.unsw.edu.au/pariscommune/news/sh/she_0002.html]. (Accessed October 14, 2001.)

112. Karl Marx, *The Civil War in France* (New York: International Publishers, 1962), 59.

113. See, for example, McLellan, *Karl Marx*, 400.

114. Marx, *Civil War in France*, 61–62.

115. See Norman Barth, "The Paris Commune of 1871," *Paris Kiosque* [www.paris.org/Kiosque/may01/commune.html]. (Accessed October 20, 2001.)

116. Padover, *Karl Marx*, 340.

117. On the "black coal" see *Marx and Engels through the Eyes of Their Contemporaries*, 72; also see Padover, *Karl Marx*, 341.

118. *Marx and Engels through the Eyes of Their Contemporaries*, 43.

119. Ibid., 72.

120. Padover, *Karl Marx*, 591.

CHAPTER 2

Emile Durkheim

"We may say that what is moral is everything that is a source of solidarity, everything that forces man to take account of other people, to regulate his actions by something other than the promptings of his own egoism, and the more numerous and strong these ties are, the more solid is the morality."

Emile Durkheim, *The Division of Labor in Society*[1]

A TIME OF ULTIMATE TURMOIL

God is dead. Like a knife in the heart of Jesus, Buddha, or Allah, Friedrich Nietzsche in 1883 eagerly announced God's demise. In France Emile Durkheim was only twenty-five years old, but if he heard Nietzsche's news, the young teacher could easily fit God's obituary into an accepted intellectual framework.

Recall that with a pronounced sense of superiority, a principal aim of the eighteenth-century European Enlightenment was to forever weaken the hold of all religious superstitions.[2] In France debunking religion became such an obligation that when Thomas Paine lived in Paris during the French Revolution, he published the *Age of Reason*, a book that harshly criticized all brands of Christianity. "My own mind is my own church," said Paine, because divine revelation lost all credibility—the bible was "hearsay"—when reasonable men and women subjected it to the penetrating light of scientific standards.[3]

Emile Durkheim's philosophical inheritance always included a long line of thinkers who undermined the ultimate moral values spiritually linking the members of Western societies. Nietzsche's chilling, contemporary con-

tribution was to take the rule of reason to its ultimate conclusion. Where
men like Paine still believed in a God who was omnipresent yet unin-
volved, Nietzsche erased all divinities, all devils, and all hopes of another
world. Human beings lived on earth and all alone. This might be nihilistic
to some, but Nietzsche expressed relief: "Your soul will be dead even
before your body; therefore fear nothing any more."[4]

Philosophers feared nothing; sociologists expressed great concern. How
could any society achieve a sense of solidarity if people followed the advice of a world wrecker like Nietzsche? He called man the great evaluator;
good and evil not only shaped people's thoughts, but they were the greatest powers on earth. Unfortunately, "much that seemed good to one people seemed shame and disgrace to another; . . . I found much that was
called evil in one place was in another decked with purple honors."[5] God's
death led to the conclusion that one set of moral beliefs merited no more
ultimate value than another. Like a house of cards, everything was relative, nothing certain or secure.

Nietzsche preached the coming of a superman. Particularly in the
United States, the word *superman* suggests extraordinary extremes. It con-
jures up images of Nazi Germany or, for those wedded to television, Clark
Kent, phone booths, and peculiar caped costumes. Nietzsche, however,
used the word to suggest a need for disregarding, for overcoming the
barriers created by *any* inherited set of moral beliefs. "Free from what?"
Nietzsche did not care about that question. The case was closed the moment he killed God and the ten, twenty, or fifty commandments that always accompanied, as "slave ethics," any system of religious beliefs.

From the perspective of social solidarity, Nietzsche committed two mortal sins. He cavalierly erased the moral beliefs that provided one basis for
social order, and as a replacement, he offered what amounted to eternal
anarchy. "Can you furnish yourself with your own good and evil and
hang up your own will above yourself as a law? Can you be judge of
yourself and avenger of your law?"[6] If so, you were the superman that
Nietzsche desired. *You* created your version of morality, *you* judged yourself, and *you* followed no leaders. Nietzsche repeatedly told his students
to "lose me and find yourselves; and only when you have all denied me
will I return to you."[7]

Nietzsche's challenge symbolizes a theme that dominated Emile Durkheim's many books. Durkheim achieved his maturity when European philosophers were asking the most monumental questions about the meaning
of human life. Agree with Nietzsche, and nothing—neither religion, the
family, nor politics—is solid or sacred. Even the natural law so important
to the French and American revolutions got thrown out the window when
philosophers emphasized the provisional nature of all social norms.

Durkheim also certainly perceived the profoundly unsettling consequences of capitalism, industrialization, and democratization. In his time

French governments had as much stability as loose Jell-O. But in an intellectual atmosphere that belittled the legitimacy of religious beliefs, Durkheim also stressed—with great sociological clarity—the import of the loss of God. What would hold societies together once they lost the ultimate arbiter of all crucial social questions? Would men and women argue, like Raskolnikov in Dostoyevsky's novel *Crime and Punishment* (published in 1866) that everything is permitted, nothing forbidden? Would people, without the threat of hell, do as they pleased, oblivious to the needs and desires of their fellow citizens?

Emile Durkheim was a decent man. And his decency informs all his work. He knew that the genie of individualism was forever out of the bottle,[8] but he also wanted a world in which people willingly recognized and accepted the need to sacrifice their individuality for the sake of society, for the sake of other human beings. As the young teacher told his students in the same year Nietzsche announced God's death, "Maintain a very vivid sense of your own dignity, . . . but also do not believe that you will become much greater by never permitting anyone to raise himself above you. *Do not glory in being self sufficient, in owing nothing to anyone; for then, in order to humor a false pride, you would condemn yourself to sterility*" (emphasis added).[9]

Like Nietzsche, Durkheim always focused on the big questions. In a nation and continent dominated by monumental social change, what creates a sense of social solidarity? And in a Europe where "the unleashing of economic interests has been accompanied by a debasing of public morality,"[10] how does one achieve a sense of justice that recognizes—with no gods in sight—the inherent dignity of all people, all the time?

These are great questions. And Durkheim has answers that are as provocative today as they were in 1900.

BEGINNINGS

It was summer in Paris. Two of Durkheim's students took a break from their work in the Sorbonne. They strolled over to a sidewalk café, sat in the sun, and sipped a beer (or two), theoretically free of any concerns or obligations. Suddenly, one of the men—Durkheim's nephew—spotted the professor coming out of a university courtyard. "Quick hide me! Here comes my uncle!" pleaded Marcel Mauss. Luckily, the café used orange trees as decoration so, as his uncle marched by, the nephew weaved himself into a citrus tree, and his uncle was never the wiser.[11]

Emile Durkheim walked through life in a very deliberate manner. Friends noted that his parents instilled such a strong sense of duty and obligation that he always manifested a "serious, indeed austere view of life." One friend reported that Durkheim "could never experience pleasure without a sense of remorse."[12]

What a way to live! And what a dedication to work! A dedication that has its deepest roots in the rabbinical training that was supposed to be Durkheim's future. He was born on April 15, 1858, in Épinal, a part of the Lorraine region of France. Like Marx, his family had provided rabbis for the community for more than a century. But unlike Marx, Durkheim grew up "within the confines of a close-knit, orthodox and traditional Jewish family."[13] His father ruled the roost and wanted Emile to be the next rabbi in the family. Initially, the son agreed. He practiced his Hebrew, read and reread the Talmud, and all the while also followed a regular course of instruction in the region's secular schools.[14]

Durkheim's intelligence so impressed his teachers that he quickly skipped two grades. He was an excellent student but a lackluster rabbi. Even before his adolescence, he wanted a different career. His father finally agreed, under one condition: he had to be serious, hard working, and dedicated.[15]

Durkheim grew up in a France that remained virulently anti-Semitic. Although the Catholic Church no longer taught that Jewish people were born with tails and a funny odor, Jews nevertheless experienced personal and institutional prejudices in virtually every corner of French life.[16] In Durkheim's case the Germans occupied Alsace Lorraine during the Franco-Prussian War (1870–71), and the twelve-year-old boy tried to make sense of French neighbors blaming Jewish people for France's defeat.[17]

It was an ugly experience with institutionalized hate, yet in sharp contrast to Marx, Durkheim seems comfortable with his Jewish roots. In fact, although he resolutely rejected the religious side of his inheritance, Durkheim never turned away from either of his ethnic legacies. He was French and Jewish and apparently quite satisfied with his dual identity. Admittedly, sociologists turned into amateur psychiatrists argue that Durkheim's passionate commitment to France derived from his need to prove himself to real Frenchmen.[18] Of course, there is no way to know his actual motivations. The one certainty is that Durkheim was an outsider, never within the religious traditions that dominated his home and never within a society full of anti-Semitism.

However difficult on an everyday level, outsider status also offers its own great advantages. Like an acrobat on a high wire, the outsider stands above the fray, with a view that sees into every corner. As Thorstein Veblen suggested, because many Jewish scientists and scholars were never completely wedded to either side of their dual inheritances, they thankfully achieved insights denied to contemporaries who, with all the hard work in the world, remained the prisoners of their solidly endorsed traditional beliefs, values, and practices.[19]

Durkheim had a dream. After getting his first degrees (in 1874–75), he wanted to enter the École Normale Supérieure, France's version of Harvard, Yale, and Princeton all rolled into one. Unfortunately, his father fell ill, and along with the pressures of preparing for the rigorous exams, the seventeen-year-old student also tried to help his family. One biographer writes that "his days were passed in daily anguish."[20] Durkheim worried about his parents, his future, and his living arrangements. In Paris he scraped by in a *pension* reserved for students. Conditions were less than delightful, and all the while he prepared for the exams that would decide his future.

Durkheim failed—not once, but twice. On the third try he finally passed the now-hated exams, and he entered the École Normale in 1879. For a contemporary student—think of life without your cell phone, computer, and food card!—the École Normale resembles a prison in need of repair. The university—eager to prevent distractions—happily offered its students sparse furnishings, bad lighting, lousy ventilation, and the hygienic practices of life in the wilds of Montana. Somehow France's best and brightest survived, but fun was never a part of the curriculum. Faculty literally locked students in the buildings; indeed, except for attending classes, students only received a prison pass on Sunday and Thursday afternoons. Once a month the young men could stay out until midnight.[21]

Students fought to enter the École. Like the yellow brick road that led to Oz, the École provided the best education available, it opened the doors to faculty appointments at the finest universities, and as a final bonus, students networked with one another. Friendships formed at the École could help a person throughout his life.

Durkheim eagerly joined in the discussions, arguments, and debates that characterized life at the École. In his first year, for instance, France's political left and right locked horns over the role of the Church in French education. Anticlerical forces wanted a clean sweep of priests and nuns, whereas more traditional forces saw no reason to remove Jesus and religious authority from their central place in the public school system. Ultimately, a moderate reform plan won the day—for example, new secular schools, especially for women were built, and over time clergy lost their opportunity to teach in the public school system—but friends indicated that Durkheim could talk for hours, mesmerizing his listeners with arguments full of high principles and great logic. He always stayed above the fray; personalities and political intrigue were not to his liking. Instead he optimistically saw politics as a way to create the sense of unity so obviously lacking in French society.

The issues never failed to appear. Democracy or monarchy? Sacred or secular? Communist or capitalist? Divorce or no divorce? France experienced every imaginable argument in Durkheim's youth, and one friend suggested that it was the debates at the École that helped lay the groundwork for Durkheim's later argument that only sociology provided the insights needed by a perpetually and deeply divided France.[22]

After graduation Durkheim faced another battery of exams, the so-called *agrégation*, the passport necessary for admission to the teaching staff of France's secondary schools. This time Durkheim passed at once, and for five years he taught philosophy in the *lycées*, or secondary school system. In fact, when Durkheim told students to "maintain a very vivid sense of your own dignity," he was offering the "prize day" address to the students of the Lycée of Sens in August 1883.[23]

By 1887 Durkheim settled at University of Bordeaux, which had created a lectureship in social science especially for the young scholar. Then (as today) sociologists aroused a good degree of distrust in academia. They tried to generalize about everything on earth, and to achieve their insights they crossed disciplines and created a new one to boot. Durkheim's passion and intelligence sometimes overwhelmed his critics, but he always had to prove the worth of his new science. Arguably, that is the lot of any pioneer; however we read about his problems, he lived through them. And as anyone familiar with university life would stress, professors can be as brutal as any politician, soldier, or businessperson.[24]

Also in 1887 Durkheim married Louise Dreyfus, beginning a marriage that was by all accounts happy, loving, satisfying, austere, and entirely centered on the work of Emile. His wife "never left his side"; she copied manuscripts, corrected proofs, and allowed her husband to create a home life centered on a rigid time table and great discipline. For example, even after the appearance of two children, Durkheim would "talk at mealtimes but not afterwards."[25]

In his early years at Bordeaux, Durkheim focused on his Ph.D., a mountain of work under the prevailing system. Candidates then wrote not one but two dissertations; the first was in French, the other (this was a mandate) in Latin. Durkheim wrote his Latin thesis on Montesquieu, a forerunner of sociology because of books like *The Persian Letters* (1721) and *The Spirit of the Laws* (1748).[26] Durkheim argued that these books established two prerequisites for the science of sociology, the ideas of type and law. Type is another word for concept; Montesquieu looked at different civilizations, established classifications, and thus allowed scholars "to compare societies in their whole structure and existence." Law is a word that, especially in his early years, was very dear to Durkheim's heart. He sought the laws that governed societies and paid due homage to Montesquieu as one of the first to persuasively argue that "social phenomena have a fixed and necessary order."[27]

Durkheim's second theses became (in 1893) *The Division of Labor in Society*. From his first lectures at the University of Bordeaux, Durkheim wanted to know only one thing: "What are the bonds that unite men with one another?"[28] For reasons that sometimes defy understanding, both Durkheim's advocates and critics continually call this a conservative passion.[29] Apparently, if you are seriously interested in order and morality, you drive through life using the rearview mirror; if not always opposed to social change, you are at least leery of it. In what follows I avoid political classifications. One of the most delightfully provocative things about the entire body of Durkheim's work is that he utterly defies one political label. Moral issues are certainly at the center of his thought, but dubbing that focus as conservative says more about the labeler—and his or her motives—than it does about the sociology of Emile Durkheim.

THE DIVISION OF LABOR IN SOCIETY

Durkheim was a positivist. It is an awkward word, and sometimes it seems to mean only one thing: Durkheim is positive he is right! Especially in *The Division of Labor in Society*, he seeks to discover the "laws" of human solidarity, and in his eagerness to uncover the truth, he moves from assumption stated to assumption proved with breathtaking speed. His confidence is both admirable and worrisome. You ask yourself: Why not wait a while? Give us a few more facts before you claim to have uncovered one law after another.

Durkheim's impatience derived from a laudable ambition. Following in the footsteps of Henri de Saint Simon and Auguste Comte, Durkheim saw a place for a new science of man. He told his students that positivism grew out of a disenchantment with the increasing specialization of scientific inquiry. An apparent fragmentation of knowledge produced such a sense of frustration that "one might wonder whether humanity's early aspiration for unity of knowledge could henceforth be considered an illusion."[30] Positivism stepped into this paralyzing intellectual void, producing one of the most important movements "in the entire history of French philosophy." In the future, "philosophy, instead of seeking to go beyond the sciences, must assume the task of organizing them, and must organize them in accordance with their own method—by making itself positive."[31]

A rough synonym for positive is *scientific*, and a sure synonym for the organizing science par excellence is *sociology*. Durkheim explicitly indicates that "in full justice" Saint Simon was the true father of sociology; he was the first to see that between the narrow specialization of the particular sciences and the metaphysical flights of the philosophers, there was "a place for a new enterprise," for a science that integrated all knowledge in an innovative and intellectually satisfying manner. Durkheim stresses that creating a new science is a "very laborious operation," but because this new science would be "more productive than the annexation of a new continent to the old continents,"[32] Durkheim happily took the helm and steered sociology in a positive direction.

In the first line of the first preface to *The Division of Labor in Society*, Durkheim announces that "this book is above all an attempt to treat the facts of moral life according to the methods of the positive sciences." He labored to create the new science of morality, yet he constantly uses the word *moral* without explicitly defining the word until the very end of the text. It is enormously frustrating, so, as my own personal contribution to this book, I will begin with Durkheim's belated definition of morality: "Moral is everything that is a source of solidarity, everything that forces man to take account of other people, to regulate his actions by something other than the promptings of his own egoism."[33]

Durkheim is neither a cleric nor a self-help therapist. Moral simply means being forced to put yourself in the other person's shoes. It is synonymous with a sense of empathy *and* the perceived necessity to curb personal desires in the interests of, for example, social order, cohesion, and predictability.[34]

Durkheim starts with an apparent contradiction. As he methodically examined the evolution of societies such as France or England, he perceived that people achieved increased degrees of individuality. From the budding women's movement to the constitutionally based rights of man, people became more and more "autonomous," more and more in charge of their own destinies. Yet people also depended more than ever on society. In economic and political affairs, the interdependencies of all people were as obvious as the need for sociology. How, Durkheim asked, can we square this circle? His answer is that "what resolved this apparent antimony was the transformation of social solidarity which arises from the ever-increasing division of labor."[35] Somehow modern societies simultaneously championed the individual and the group; Durkheim wanted to know how and why this happened.

Durkheim uses the word *function* as a beacon light. It means the need theoretically served by a particular form of social organization. Durkheim's contention is that following the lead of Auguste Comte, he has discovered the "true function" of the division of labor. That function is to create a feeling of solidarity between people who, in the extreme, may have absolutely nothing in common. Durkheim repeatedly stresses that he is not referring to the division of labor in a factory; business enterprises create effective and efficient coordination of a diverse labor force for the purposes of profit. Durkheim sees the division of labor acting as the moral axis for social cohesion. It will somehow positively bind atheists and true believers, Catholics and Protestants, conservatives and socialists, feminists and traditional men.[36]

Durkheim's problem—especially urgent for a positivist—was that "social solidarity is not amenable to exact observation and especially not to measurement." Like a shadow, social solidarity was impossible to catch, much less quantify. So, in search of something tangible, Durkheim focused on the law. This was arguably quite arbitrary; he himself noted that "it may certainly be objected that social relationships can be forged without necessarily taking on a legal form."[37] But by keying on the law, Durkheim grabbed a tool that he effectively used to delineate the forms of social solidarity that, in his mind, characterized all past, present, and (presumably) future societies.

One pole for Durkheim is *mechanical solidarity*, or solidarity by similarities. It is ironic that Durkheim chose a modern symbol—the well-oiled machine—to characterize early societies, but "mechanical" does catch the sense of lock-step cohesion that he wanted to emphasize. Law under mechanical solidarity is always repressive; yet instead of singling out the threat of force or the actual use of violence to maintain social solidarity, Durkheim employs a concept called "the collective or common consciousness."[38] In societies characterized by mechanical solidarity, people share a cultural (a cognitive) consensus that borders on unanimity. Values, beliefs, and practices are so successfully transmitted and endorsed that they become the external "embodiment of the collectivity." Like a strong tent that covers people during a wedding reception, the collective consciousness ultimately achieves a power all its own. It stands over the society because "its real function is to maintain inviolate the cohesion of society by sustaining the common consciousness in all its vigor."[39]

From this perspective murder and theft are crimes not in and of themselves but only because they offend the collective consciousness. Durkheim never condemns specific acts because they are crimes; on the contrary, they are only crimes because they are condemned by the collective consciousness successfully embodied, via socialization, in the minds and actions of men and women living their daily lives.[40]

For an American example of the common consciousness, consider "the Middletown spirit." This is the label attached to the beliefs and values that characterized the city of Muncie, Indiana, in the 1930s. Sociologists Robert and Helen Merrel Lynd wanted readers to understand what heartland folks believed, so they coined the phrase "Middletown spirit" to catch what was in Muncie yet external to it. Components of the spirit included these ideas and values:

- Americans are the freest people in the world.
- Washington and Lincoln are the greatest Americans.
- Jesus is the Son of God, and what he said is true for all time.
- Schoolteachers are usually people who couldn't make good in business.
- Competition is what makes progress and has made the United States great.
- Most foreigners are inferior.[41]

To the extent that you have learned these beliefs—or endorsed them— you proved the present-day validity of Durkheim's concept. In short, you internalized parts of a common consciousness that retains its influence seventy years after it was first "discovered" by the Lynds.

Durkheim was among the first to perceive the coercive power of the collective consciousness, but in sharp contrast to societies as wildly diverse as our own, the concept of mechanical solidarity rests on a consensus best characterized by small, self-contained civilizations. Especially in a preliterate society, the collective consciousness is passed on orally, and even if it changes from one generation to another—think of the child's game of telephone—the lack of a written record makes it very difficult to compare one set of beliefs with another. You are padlocked by your collective inheritance because it is the only spirit available. Moreover, when the laws are enforced with harsh sanctions (e.g., losing a hand for theft in contemporary Kuwait), that is to maintain the collective consciousness in full force. Homogeneity is the rule that will prevail.

Durkheim always emphasizes the importance of religion in creating and sustaining the collective consciousness. Originally, "religion extended to everything; everything social was religious—the two words were synonymous."[42] He is also, not for the first time, sarcastic about religious explanations; they are a "figment" of people's imaginations. Yet despite his own beliefs, he nevertheless comprehends the importance of religion in offering God's imprimatur to everyday beliefs, values, and practices. Durkheim stresses that "it is invariably the fact that when a somewhat strong conviction is shared by a single community of people it inevitably assumes a religious character."[43]

In Durkheim's work, religion was, once upon a time, the most powerful social force imaginable. However, as societies moved from a lower to a higher level, the significance of religious superstitions considerably diminished. Remember that Durkheim wrote under the shadow of Charles Darwin. Published in 1859, *The Origin of the Species* instantly moved scientists to argue that, like animals, societies also evolved.[44] And given the assumption—in Europe's common consciousness—of a so-called primitive mind, it is no surprise that in Durkheim's mind, societies evolved by climbing the ladder of cultural superiority. At times the ardent positivist let values and emotions so color his prose that he championed the "absolute grandeur" of the division of labor and the *organic solidarity* that characterized the advanced societies.[45]

Organic solidarity is rooted not in similarities but in the differences that typify modern life and modern societies. Standing on a corner in Durkheim's Paris, you would see people from all classes, all walks of life, all parts of France, and even all parts of the world. Differences produced the contrasts that allowed people to question, challenge, and even reject the collective consciousness. The trouble was that for all their obvious differences, people still needed to effectively cooperate with one another in economic, political, and personal relationships. The legal invention that produced social cohesion was the contract, an agreement by the most different types of people to precisely specify the rights and obligations that one party had to another. Individuals voluntarily entered into contracts and if violations occurred, justice restored rather than oppressed. Durkheim used the cumbersome phrase "restitutory sanctions" to refer to the financial and other penalties imposed on those who violated a contract.[46]

In an America where the common consciousness teaches that lawyers are great white sharks, Durkheim's strong support of contracts as a form of social glue may be hard to understand. But contracts were simply a means to an end; that end was a society guaranteeing both freedom of thought and social cohesion. The division of labor rested on the functional interdependence[47] of people from different religions, ethnicities, nations, and social classes; so, if contracts provided the ground rules for uniting a diverse labor force in the service of a *particular* task, work proceeded efficiently, but it never interfered with a person's most important beliefs and values. As an ideal, citizens of any society grasped their inevitably increasing interdependence. In the service of social harmony, they performed their allotted tasks, they received just compensation, and society's needs were effectively achieved without the stultifying sense of social similarity demanded by the earliest societies.

This ideal was Durkheim's way of putting Humpty Dumpty back together again. Organic solidarity would provide social harmony if people used sociology's insights about the course and direction of human history.

In his analysis of the causes of the increasing division of labor, Durkheim focused on what he called moral density. Recalling that morality refers to whatever forces an individual to take account of other people, Durkheim stressed factors such as migration, population, technology, and the phenomenal growth of cities. On the farms tractors displaced people, who migrated to cities, which suddenly needed to provide ever-increasing amounts of every imaginable service—housing, transportation, sanitation, education, and the storing and distribution of food for millions of people.

Paris, for example, boasted 580,000 people in 1807; the number for 1861 was 1.7 million people, and the number for 1891 was 2.4 million. London had close to a million inhabitants in 1801; the figure for 1851 was 2.4 million, and in 1891 London contained over 4.2 million people. Finally, New York contained 76,000 people in 1800; the number for 1860 was 1.1 million inhabitants, and the number for 1890 was 2.5 million New Yorkers.[48]

Given this degree of growth, the need for functional interdependence was obvious, and the division of labor a prerequisite. But as Otto Bettman reminds us in *The Good Old Days: They Were Terrible!* the actual realities of life in late nineteenth-century cities produced optimism only if you closed your eyes and held your nose. In 1882 New York only 2 percent of homes had water connections, and pigs accompanied people as they walked the streets. And the manure endlessly emanating from real horsepower never smelled sweet. Windows stayed closed in the summer as a way to lock out foul odors and the dust that came from unpaved streets. Outside open barrels with cinders from parlor and kitchen stoves sent up the dust clouds that moved people to tears, and crossing the street required a shield to survive. One recent estimate is that horse-drawn vehicles produced ten times as many deaths as cars do today. Finally, employers boasted that "we take them [children] as soon as they can stand up." In European and American cities, children labored in glass factories from five P.M. to three A.M.: "As molder boys they replaced men, who found the work too hot."[49]

Durkheim fully understood that modern societies languished between past and future. He also repeatedly underlined the "debasement of human nature" that characterized work in most factories. As if a livid line by Marx, he writes that a worker is "no more than a lifeless cog, which an external force sets in motion and impels always in the same direction and in the same fashion."[50] This line illustrates one reason Durkheim's work remains so provocative and relevant: globalization today produces the same horrible living and working conditions from Bangkok to Los Angeles, from Manila to Mexico City, a metropolis where well-heeled people and their dogs *both* wear masks when they take a walk.[51]

In accounting for the chasm that separates the ideal from the real, Durkheim discusses "the anomic division of labor." *Anomie* refers to the admitted sense of normlessness—of moral chaos—that characterized the condition of the cities seen by Durkheim. Durkheim's pressing theoretical problem was to explain the causes of the pollution that sullied his ideal; until he positively explained the actual origin of the problems, "the division of labor might be suspected of logically implying them."[52]

Durkheim now reached for a word—*abnormal*—that many of his greatest advocates wish he had never used. Having established what organic solidarity could produce, he now married his ideal to the about-to-happen;[53] he called that nonexistent yet inevitably evolving condition normal, and he explained social problems as a wretched way station on the road to a world united by the benefits of organic solidarity.

Calling problems abnormal rightly satisfied none of Durkheim's critics. In truth, it was an intellectual escape that hindered or prevented any systematic investigation of the very problems perceived. Why, after all, scrutinize the possibly systematic causes of ruthless competition, class conflict, and dehumanization if they were temporary and not permanent, abnormal rather than endemic?[54] This was arguably Durkheim's biggest failure, a mistake than can be accepted if one remembers that in the closing pages of *The Division of Labor in Society*, Durkheim the positive sociologist makes way for Durkheim the ardent idealist.

Dreams ordered problems to stand aside. The normal would prevail.

This was Durkheim's conundrum. The "perfect spontaneity" he envisioned "was nowhere encountered as a fact realized in practice." Yet "the task of the most advanced societies" was to produce justice.[55] He grasped with great clarity that (among other things) the French, industrial, and philosophic revolutions of his time liberated the individual from the shackles of religious and political authority. However, he saw no chance of justice unless people relinquished portions of the freedom they had or were about to receive. "The only power that can serve to moderate individual egoism is that of the group; the only one that can serve to moderate the egoism of groups is that of another group that embraces them all."[56]

These lines underline Durkheim's principal fear. The common consciousness of his time "was increasingly reduced to the cult of the individual." Durkheim was offended by the selfishness and egoism of the first me generation, yet he still perceived in modernity a source of solidarity that was "more human, more rational" than anything else in history. Simply put, society needed people to cooperate effectively in order to fulfill all the functions of increasingly complex and interdependent cities, regions, and nations. Get people focused on the whole, and you would once again achieve a sense of social solidarity that made anomie a bad dream. "It requires us only to be charitable and just towards our fellow men, to fulfill our task well, and to work towards a state where everyone is called to fulfill the function he performs best and will receive a just reward for his efforts."[57]

If this sounds terribly idealistic, it was nevertheless rooted in reality because it mirrored the way Durkheim actually lived his life. Over the years he would fill in the blanks with a series of intelligent, detailed, and even rabble-rousing proposals for everything from the role of the state to the crucial importance of professional groups. The one constant was a problem as evident then as it is today: How do you create a sense of social solidarity when people are increasingly different *and* increasingly devoted to the individual rather than the group?

The Division of Labor in Society is a work of a science and a call to action. As Durkheim put it in the final lines of the book, "Our first duty at the present time is to fashion a morality for ourselves."[58]

METHOD RULES

In creating a science of sociology, Durkheim worked in the shadow of Auguste Comte, a predecessor who left a bushel of bad memories. For example, especially as he aged, Comte spoke to audiences that often contained only old men and Parisian workers. He relished these listeners because, quite frankly, no one else wanted to read what he wrote or hear what he said. Criticized on all sides, by 1849 this father of sociology even announced that he no longer read the works of other scientists; this helped maintain a sense of "cerebral hygiene" while his small band of cult followers provided the funds that allowed Comte to spread the word. As secular pope of Europe, the former prophet of positivism now headed the new religion of humanity. Headquartered in his home, Comte preached— to people who were arguably hard of hearing—a gospel that sometimes sounded like the words of leftist revolutionaries. Workers had a "natural aptitude to become the auxiliaries of spiritual power"; they would fan out, one on one, introducing the gospel of Comte as he sent "epistles and missives" to converts in other lands and even to the heads of national governments. In Paris many people were positive of only one thing: the father of sociology was a lunatic, acting in the service of a science that had somehow become a religion.[59]

Comte's shadow put Durkheim on the defensive; Durkheim had to legitimate the science he was simultaneously trying to create. This war of words is most evident in *The Rules of the Sociological Method*, a small volume published in 1895 that moved critics to protest "so loudly that for a time it was almost impossible for us to make ourselves heard."[60]

Thankfully, Durkheim never answered his critics with the vehemence of Marx. Two hundred-page bursts of anger were not his style. Instead, he added a twenty-page preface to the second edition of the book, in which he explained why his critics were wrong and he was right.

The concept of social facts bothered every critic in Paris. Durkheim refused to understand their problem. His definition was clear: "A social fact consists of ways of acting, thinking and feeling, external to the individual and endowed with a power of coercion, by reason of which they control him."[61]

Take this example. In 1962 anthropologists filmed an actual preliterate war between members of the Dugum Dani in New Guinea. In one scene about 500 warriors are on the field; they scream obscenities at one another while proudly strutting their spears and feathers. This war is relatively tame, often with more talking than fighting. Suddenly, it begins to rain, and all fighters leave the field. It seems a mystery until the anthropologists explain that no one fights with wet feathers. When wet, feathers lose their magical ability to protect; fighters need the sun—or at least dry conditions—to try and kill one another.

The belief in the need for dry feathers is a Dugum Dani tradition. Because it existed prior to that battle, it is *external* to any particular group of warriors. As the mass departure from the battlefield shows, a social fact (in this case a tradition) is capable of exerting a *coercive* effect on members of the society. When the rain starts to fall, hundreds of men quickly leave the field.

I used a fairly recent example because Durkheim's concept of social fact remains an impressive tool for sociologists of all persuasions. He clearly caught the power of widely accepted beliefs and practices to control the way people think and act, and he explained to his critics not only what they were missing but also what made sociology so utterly unique and important.

Believing that society only contains individuals, "the common-sense view still holds that sociology is a *superstructure built on the substratum of the individual consciousness* and that otherwise it would be suspended in a social vacuum" (emphasis added).[62] Nonsense, said Durkheim. Although individuals are the obvious core of any society, when individuals coexist over time, they create "states of collective consciousness" that have a totally different substratum. To capture the essence of these states of collective thinking and acting, Durkheim used the term *social fact* and always offered a variety of examples to his critics. Religious beliefs, the language we speak, the laws we submissively follow, the rights and obligations of professors—"here are ways of thinking and acting that present the noteworthy property of existing outside the individual consciousness."[63]

With social facts Durkheim believed (quite correctly) he had an object of study that was uniquely sociological.[64] In the future the principal task of progressive sociologists would be to examine social facts of every type and variety and do so with a particular disposition: treat social facts as things. This admonition, "the proposition at the very basis of our method,"[65] moved critics to use the strongest words. They labeled Durkheim's request "ridiculous," and he told them what to do with their assessment of his work. He stressed that his method focused on "a certain mental attitude" toward social facts. Because any serious scientist always aimed at truth, all Durkheim wanted was a method that studied social facts "objectively as external things, for it is this character that they present to us."[66]

To be fair to his critics, Durkheim's demands pushed a variety of hot buttons. In his zeal to lay out a precise agenda for sociology, he offhandedly relegated psychology to an almost nonexistent role. Even more important, Durkheim's insights forced readers to ponder questions and answers that threatened to undermine the notion of free will and personal control. For example, if social facts actually exercised the coercive power highlighted by Durkheim, what chance did men and women have to create new futures? Didn't social facts significantly impede both free will and social change? And, even more ominously for those who read Nietzsche, were human beings as controlled by social facts as they once were by the notion of God? Or was humankind a paradox, free and socially determined at one and the same time?

Durkheim's small book poses gargantuan questions. And with a touch of arrogance, he knew it. Unfortunately, Durkheim gave critics real ammunition in a section of the book titled "Rules for Distinguishing between the Normal and the Pathological."[67] Durkheim wanted to help both France and Europe. "Why strive for knowledge of reality if this knowledge cannot serve us in life?"[68] The goal is laudable and, like his dual ethnic heritage, an integral part of Durkheim's life and work. But in searching for an objective criterion to judge societies, he chose the words *normal* and *pathological*, and then in a giant leap of faith, he argued that "we shall call 'normal' these social conditions that are the most generally distributed, and the others 'morbid or pathological.' "[69]

To Durkheim (but not to his critics) "it would be incomprehensible" if the most widespread forms of social organization were not also—"at least in their aggregate"—the most advantageous.[70] Critics asked, advantageous to whom? Was an aristocracy advantageous to the peasantry? Was Christianity advantageous to Jews? Was a patriarchal system advantageous for women?

Durkheim responds with less-than-satisfying qualifications. He writes that the conditions of normal and pathological can never be defined "in the abstract and absolutely"; they are always relative to particular societies and *to particular stages of social development*. In the middle of *The Rules of the Sociological Method*, Darwin suddenly makes an appearance because Durkheim now discusses lower, higher, and most recent societies. Each manifests a law of evolution, although "for the most recent societies this law is by definition unknown since they have not yet accomplished their entire course."[71]

The critics' questions never receive a compelling answer. Durkheim simply argues that the discipline needed a precise focus, so "in order that sociology may be a true science of things, the generality of phenomena must be taken as the criterion of their normality."[72] In this manner sociologists could use their knowledge to serve society. They would foster the normal, erase the abnormal, and all the while, explain social facts by keying on causes *and* functions. In a chapter titled "Rules for the Explanation of Social Facts," Durkheim writes that by first seeking the causes of social facts, it will be much easier to discover "their function in the establishment of social order."[73]

This assumption (that social facts function to create social order) added another element to Durkheim's analysis. Not satisfied with sharply underlining the power of social facts, he demands that sociologists also ascertain the role of any social fact "in putting society in harmony with itself and with the environment external to it."[74] Here Durkheim asks sociology to be not simply a science but the scientific proponent of moral order. In short, these are the social facts; and this is how order does or does not occur.

Durkheim's focus on function produced diverse reactions. In the United States an entire school of sociology—structure functionalism—owes an enormous debt to Durkheim's methodological analysis.[75] Durkheim's influence is also evident on sociologists as different as Peter Berger and Erving Goffman.

Although social order is undoubtedly a profound need of all human beings,[76] critics stressed that in focusing on cohesion, Durkheim grossly neglected the causes of and the need for social change. Indeed, he and his analysis supported society's most reactionary forces because in super gluing the normal to the most general, Durkheim's arguments sanctified the status quo.

Durkheim's desires (for social cohesion) did in fact determine his functional method; reading his work, it is easy to argue that the normal, the general, and the status quo are one and the same thing. However, critics were dead wrong about Durkheim's politics or his attitude toward social change. This is nowhere more evident than in his discussion of "social superiority." As if a Marxist, Durkheim states that anyone exercising superiority over another "because he is stronger or wealthier, especially if this wealth does not express his social value, is *abnormal* and can only be maintained by violence" (emphasis added).[77]

The obvious question is, "Abnormal in relation to what?" Durkheim seemed to be contradicting himself because in 1895 many European aristocracies still generally exercised significant authority on the basis of inherited wealth; and force was quite normal in the gaining and maintenance of political power: remember Napoleon's coup d'état in France (1848) or Germany's forceful acquisition of Durkheim's birthplace during the Franco-Prussian War of 1871.

Durkheim squares this circle by again imposing an evolutionary order on history. Once sociologists explained the significance of social facts, people would grasp "how much the social being is richer, more complex and more permanent than the individual being"; eventually, "reflection can only reveal the intelligible reasons for the subordination demanded of him and for the sentiments of attachment and respect which habit has fixed in his heart."[78]

In the future only one form of constraint would dominate, that of social superiority rooted in "intellectual or moral" achievements. That would be tomorrow's norm because "the principle [of social facts] we have just expounded would create a sociology which sees *in the spirit of discipline* the essential condition of all human life, while at the same time founding it on reason and on truth" (emphasis added).[79]

Scrap Durkheim's faith in evolution, and *The Rules of the Sociological Method* still asks the big questions. Were people spitting in the wind when they resisted the power of social facts? Could anyone successfully avoid the coercive power of external beliefs and practices? Or to reverse the equation, why not willingly submit to the new social facts that people could create if they reasoned together?

Ultimately, Durkheim's book moved sociology in a new direction. He successfully created a specific focus of analysis and (with evolutionary lapses) a rigorously scientific approach to the data. Meanwhile, on a personal level, his faith in the power of reason was severely tested when he intimately involved himself in one of France's ugliest political controversies. The Dreyfus affair made history, and so did Emile Durkheim.

"INDIVIDUALISM AND THE INTELLECTUALS"

Devil's Island. The words suggest danger; you imagine an isolated inlet full of pirates or prisoners. In this case, you would be right. Located in the Atlantic Ocean, off the northeastern coast of South America, Devil's Island belonged to the French. In the nineteenth century, they used it to house their worst prisoners, who, even with a limited sentence, rarely returned to Europe. Once the scorching heat slowed their metabolism, many inhabitants failed to digest whatever food guards gave their keep. At one point the French even removed a leper colony from the island to save the sick from a certain fate.[80]

Captain Alfred Dreyfus arrived in 1895. Already in a colonial Alcatraz, his guards nevertheless built a special hut for his incarceration. It measured roughly ten feet by five feet; outside guards maintained a twenty-four-hour watch, and over time they added details to the French fortress. Five feet from the hut they built a high wall that prevented any view of the ocean; they then built a second wall to protect the first wall, and they locked down their prisoner with a double *boucle* at night. Imagine the stocks from Puritan times, and you get a feel for this iron *boucle*. At night Dreyfus put his ankles though the bands, a guard slipped on the iron bar that extended across the foot of the bed, and the prisoner tried to sleep. Perhaps he would die.[81]

Details like these made the Dreyfus case an international controversy throughout the late 1890s. Defenders such as Durkheim came to the captain's defense for a very simple reason. Dreyfus was guilty of nothing. With walls and iron, generals tried to block off the truth, but by 1898 the following facts began to emerge.

In 1894 Captain Dreyfus served on the French general staff in Paris. His appointment caused consternation because, despite his brilliance and dedication to France, Dreyfus was Jewish and had a somewhat arrogant personality. Colleagues often resented or hated his presence. So when a case of espionage occurred, and the supposed traitor's name began with a D, Dreyfus took the blame for another's work.

The actual traitor was Major Marie Charles Esterhazy. He traitorously exchanged documents with German officials and mentioned the "scoundrel D" in correspondence obtained by French intelligence. Investigators realized that the D could be code for someone else, but when they read down the list of officers on the general staff and saw the name Dreyfus, each came to the same conclusion: "It was the Jew."[82]

In a rigged trial handwriting experts under pressure from the general staff testified that the writing on the schedule was Dreyfus's. Jurists obediently disregarded exonerating evidence, and as a final touch of malice, the French minister of war sent the judges a secret (from Dreyfus's lawyer) message as they deliberated the captain's fate. Pleading national security and secret evidence of guilt, "the court-martial judges were being told that if they found Captain Dreyfus innocent, they would be flouting the Minister of War."[83]

Because Dreyfus's brother Mathieu was loyal, dedicated, and wealthy, he used a variety of resources to keep the case in the public eye. Over time the Dreyfus controversy seemed to symbolize every underlying battle in French society. Religious and political forces weakened by social change rallied to the army's battlefield banners; even if Dreyfus was innocent—and certainly he was not!—what did the life of one man matter beside the honor of the army? Could France survive if yet another bastion of traditional authority was fatally weakened?

A. A. Milne once said that a patriot is someone who thinks someone else is not a patriot.[84] In France in 1898, the nation boasted a small army of patriots, many convinced that they saw in the Dreyfus case the unseen hand of Jewish conspirators. In a nation of 39 million people, France contained only 70,000 Jews. Because most lived in Paris, few French citizens ever saw or met a Jewish person. That never stopped the ignorant from teaching that "there was something monstrous about these descendents of the crucifiers of the Son of God."[85]

Dreyfus made manifest a latent anti-Semitism. Like mosquitoes carrying disease, conspiracy theories filled the air. Jews, for example, worked with France's other enemies to humiliate the nation as badly as the Germans did in the 1871 Franco-Prussian War. Everyday life became so intolerable that it became the fodder of cartoonists. In one drawing (from February 1898) a group of well-to-do citizens are about to enjoy a fine dinner. The host stresses that there will be "absolutely no talk of the Affair." In the next drawing, one man is strangling a woman, another woman is pummeling a man, and the entire group is at war with itself. The caption reads: "They talked about it."[86]

In January 1898 Emile Zola published "I accuse," a frontal assault on the army and every one of its traditional defenders. By this time the actual traitor had been publicly exonerated in a formal trial. Zola magnificently laid out the case with such force that his public condemnation sold 300,000 copies on its first day at the newsstands. Zola rightfully feared for his life, and so would anyone else brave enough to defend the alleged traitor.[87]

On Devil's Island the army increased Dreyfus's guard to thirteen men and a warden. Soldiers built a tower to watch over the sea and installed a cannon to fire at any suspicious vessels. Dreyfus, chained to his bed, never knew what was happening. The army cut off all communication with his family, so the captain had no idea he was both a world celebrity and the possible cause of either a civil war or a coup d'état.[88]

Emile Durkheim publicly entered this minefield with an essay published in the middle of 1898, "Individualism and the Intellectuals." Although it contains none of the purple prose produced by the novelist Zola, the essay is arguably much more important. Durkheim takes the Dreyfus case and explains its significance in terms of the moral forces dividing the modern from the ancient regime—organic solidarity from its anachronistic predecessors.

Durkheim proudly admits to be guilty as charged; he and his colleagues absolutely refused "to bend their logic before the word of an Army general." They defended the "inalienable" rights of any falsely accused individual, and they did it in the name of reason and "the religion of humanity."[89]

Generals and other defenders of a dead past argued that individualism represented "the great sickness of the present age." If they spotlighted only economic issues, Durkheim agrees; it was easy to denounce "this crass commercialism which reduces society to nothing more than a vast apparatus of production and exchange." But when generals condemned the rights of man that derived from the French Revolution, they committed heresy. Those rights protected the individual valiantly championed by Rousseau; those rights were in fact "the basis of our moral catechism."[90]

Durkheim repeatedly uses religious symbolism. He seeks to hoist the generals on the petard of social solidarity by stressing the moral beliefs of the ever-evolving new age. "The cult of which he [the individual] is at once both object and agent, does *not* address itself to the particular being which he is and bears his name, but to the *human person* wherever it is to be found and in whatever form it is embodied." For Emile Durkheim "the individualism thus extended is the glorification not of the self but of the *individual in general*. It springs not from egoism but from sympathy for all that is human, a broader pity for all sufferings, for human miseries, a more ardent need to combat them and mitigate them, a greater thirst for social justice" (emphasis added).[91]

These lines are as relevant today as they were more than a century ago. In Rwanda or Colombia, in the Balkans or the Middle East, Durkheim preaches that *all* human beings have rights—inalienable rights—that transcend specific cultures, ethnicities, or political conflicts. Opponents of justice will always build high barriers around the world's Devil's Islands, but Durkheim hopes that those brick walls can eventually collapse—think of Berlin—if people ceaselessly demand recognition of the human rights of any woman, man, or child.

Durkheim explains why walls fall when he discusses details of the moral catechism. Its "primary dogma" was the "autonomy of reason," and "its primary rite the doctrine of free inquiry." When the generals demanded blind obedience to traditional authority—"it's a question of national honor"—they contemptuously spit on the core moral beliefs of modern men. "My reason requires reasons before it bows to someone else's. Respect for authority is in no way incompatible with rationalism as long as the authority is rationally grounded." Opponents needed to realize that if a number of artists and scholars now openly challenged the army and the government, the challenge derived not from a sense of superiority but from a firm commitment to the rule of reason. "Since they are accustomed by the practice of the scientific method to reserve their judgment as long as they do not feel themselves enlightened, it is natural that they should yield less easily to the sway of the masses and the prestige of authority."[92]

Remember that Durkheim was a Jew in a nation full of anti-Semitism. He risked his career with these lines, but instead of wavering, his essay concludes with a grand design for social cohesion.

Individualism, instead of being anarchical, "was the only system of beliefs which could ensure the moral unity of the country." Religion normally implied symbols and rites, priests and golden temples. In reality these represented a superficial facade; religions expressed their actual essence in a system of "beliefs and practices endowed with a certain authority." Using arguments from *The Division of Labor in Society*, Durkheim writes that as societies evolved, traditions voluntarily or involuntarily surrendered to cultural and thus moral diversity; everyone tended to go their own way, with this eventual result: "The members of a social group will have nothing in common among themselves except their humanity. . . . Nothing remains which men can love and honor in common if not man himself. That is how man has become a god for man and why he can no longer create other gods without lying to himself."[93]

Durkheim later noted that in 1895, he first began to fully comprehend the importance of religion as a force for order and harmony.[94] That new insight influenced "Individualism and the Intellectuals." A critic could certainly argue that the religious imagery produced confusion because it pointed to the supposedly dead past, but for Durkheim the inalienable rights of the individual actually possessed a sacred quality. Only respect for the individual in general maintained France's precarious moral solidarity. Thus, although he certainly sought justice for Dreyfus, the deepest cause of Durkheim's efforts was this: "A religion which tolerates sacrilege abdicates all dominion over the minds of men." Dreyfus represented a terrible test; believers supported his cause because in denying Dreyfus you undermined the religion beliefs that offered the only chance for man's dignity and society's moral cohesion.[95]

Durkheim's essay ends with an emphasis on France's past. In the nation that devised the "Rights of Man," "today, the urgent task which must come before all others is to save our moral patrimony; once it is secure, we will see that it prospers."[96] Ultimately, the generals were no match for opponents with a faith as profound as Durkheim's own. Because individualism was the sacred key to social solidarity, "it would therefore seem impossible that these dilettantes' games could so long succeed in holding back the masses if we knew how to act. But also, what a humiliation it would be if reason, dealing with so weak an opponent, should end by being worsted, even if only for a time."[97]

Reason lost, for quite a while. Dreyfus received a second trial in 1899, the generals ordered the judges around like privates in the army, and this kangaroo court again issued a guilty verdict. To end the nation's agony, officials offered Dreyfus a pardon. To the dismay of some of his supporters (who never lived on Devil's Island), Dreyfus reluctantly accepted. In 1906 the High Court of France finally set aside the military rulings; it broadcast the truth—Dreyfus was guilty of nothing—and restored the former captain to his rightful place in the army and in French society.[98]

Although the case was closed, Durkheim's "Individualism and the Intellectuals" remains a vital document. In it Durkheim deliberately underlined a new use of the word *intellectual*. When Dreyfus's supporters first issued their "Manifesto of the Intellectuals" (in January 1898), Durkheim called it "pretentious";[99] "intellectual" raised artists and scholars to the rank of supermen. Eventually, this sociologist as intellectual produced an essay that admirably combines scholarship and criticism, knowledge, and the advocacy of moral principles that did in fact evolve into international standards. Is there any way to read a document like the United Nations' 1948 *Declaration of Human Rights* and not see in its support for the individual in general, the legacy of bitter struggles to free prisoners as innocent as Captain Alfred Dreyfus?

SUICIDE

It seemed like a strange topic. After an effort as ambitious as *The Division of Labor in Society*, why would Durkheim opt to write a book on suicide, one of life's most solitary acts? If sociology focused on collective representations and social facts, what moved Durkheim to take aim on the individual rather than the group, one person rather than France's 39 million?

One explanation is personal. During his years at the École, Durkheim found a friend forever. With Victor Hommay, he "lived the same life. We worked in the same room, we pursued the same studies, we even spent together almost all our days of freedom."[100] After graduation, Hommay taught in the provinces; he desperately missed Paris, and he only endured rural exile by burying himself in books. One day he entered his rooms, sat on the edge of a window that had no ledge, and "a few moments later he was picked up in the courtyard, his book of notes beside him."[101]

With *Suicide* (published in 1897) Durkheim certainly settled some personal scores. He wanted to comprehend his friend's pain, but he also wanted to once again respond to sociology's critics. They never ceased their assaults on Durkheim's work, so he settled on suicide as a way of piercing the armor of his severest critics. Even the introduction to the book is full of the quantitative data that government agencies throughout Europe carefully compiled. Because, then and now, numbers carried intellectual weight, Durkheim uses them to underline the scientific character of sociological investigations. The real beauty of suicide, however, was this: if Durkheim could show that the most private act had collective roots and causes, it would be a "triumph" for sociology. His critics would fall as fast as a line of dominoes, and as a final blow to his detractors, Durkheim would also show that suicide rates were intimately linked to a lack of social solidarity. Like his friend Hommay, people needed group supports to feel connected to society and to one another.[102]

Durkheim begins by eagerly eliminating traditional explanations of suicide. In a chapter titled "Suicide and Cosmic Factors," he meticulously—and I mean meticulously!—examines "the monthly variations of suicide with the average length of the day in France," "the proportional share of each season in the annual total of suicides of each Country," and "the seasonal variations of suicide in several large cities compared with those of the whole country." It may seem like battles with an army of straw men, but Durkheim needed to get rid of traditional explanations. He agrees with the irrefutable numbers: throughout Europe voluntary deaths increased from January to July. But instead of looking for causes in the cosmos, he came down to earth. Citing everything from railroad statistics to the number of fashion shows, Durkheim concludes that it was the intensity of social life—and not the weather—that moved people to take their own lives.[103]

The intensity of social life is hardly a viable explanation of suicide, and Durkheim knew it. He needed to show exactly how collective life caused suicides, so he devotes the principal portion of the book to establishing three sociological types: egoistic, altruistic, and anomic. Connecting the different dots are the collective factors that cause all three forms of suicide.

Egoistic suicide is "special"; its roots lay in the "excessive individualism" that characterized so many modern societies. Durkheim persuasively argues that suicide varies inversely with an individual's integration into a variety of social groups, the most important being the family, political organizations, and religious institutions. Weave a set of ties to important, vibrant collectivities, and you offered "a constant interchange of ideas and feelings from all to each and each to all, something like a mutual moral support."[104] But create a nation of religious doubters, or people without positive family ties, and the result is a desperation as awful as that experienced by a suicidal person. Egoists are mysteries to their own minds; their pain is intense because they are perpetually unable to "escape the exasperating and agonizing question: To what purpose?"[105]

Although egoistic suicide was especially prominent in modern societies, it could occur in any period where people lost their social moorings. Think of the Protestant Reformation or the ripple effects of the work of scientists like Galileo or Newton.[106] Society came before the individual; the former produced the latter. People therefore expressed and served societies' needs. If you weakened ties to the groups that nurtured society, you abandoned the individual as cruelly as a parent abandoning a child.

In a rare burst of sarcasm, Durkheim writes that "the essence of civilized man" is to be at sea in a world of illusions. The individual is "the masterpiece of existence"; he looks in the mirror, only sees himself, and always misses the most obvious truth: lose society and you lose your reasons for living.[107]

Altruistic suicide revolves around a sense of duty. In sharp contrast to the egotistical, altruists lose themselves in the group. People surrender their individuality to exterior beliefs, values, and goals, and acting on behalf of others, men and women commit suicide because it is an obligation impossible to avoid. Although the word *altruism* can connote only positive acts, Durkheim makes no value judgments. He simply seeks to delineate a form of suicide that keys on selflessness; he refers to "feeble individuation," which accurately captures his focus on the individual's willing submission to the group and its goals.[108]

Suicide contains a long section on soldiers; they epitomize the sense of sacrifice that characterizes altruistic suicide. But in the final paragraphs of his analysis, Durkheim raises an issue that is as modern as the hideous bombing of New York's Twin Towers on September 11, 2001. Ever the scientist, Durkheim wants to remain objective. Thus, "if the inhabitant of the Canary Islands who throws himself into an abyss to do honor to a god is not a suicide, how give this name to a Jain sectary who kills himself to gain entry into oblivion." Each selflessly dies for the group's shared values, so "according to what standard will the division be made? When does a motive cease to be sufficiently praiseworthy for the act it determines to be called suicide?"[109]

These questions are also our own. Were the nineteen men actively involved in the Twin Towers' slaughter martyrs or beasts, mad or simply selfless exponents of a form of altruistic suicide? Durkheim's work still animates a twenty-first-century mind because he fully realizes a predicament that is as contemporary as today. Because sociology teaches that everything is relative to the group and its values, Durkheim deliberately avoids a definition that judges values, beliefs, and practices. It is an altruistic suicide if the person is obligated to selflessly die for the religious beliefs that clearly make him a hero at some of the mosques in Afghanistan, Pakistan, or the Palestinian West Bank.

In *Suicide* Durkheim never offers the key to this conceptual maze. As a sociologist he only seeks to create definitions that are as objective as the accompanying statistics. But, remembering his essay on the Dreyfus case, Durkheim offers a touchstone that can conceivably transcend the theoretical relativity of all values and beliefs. Our standard is the individual in general; our never-wavering banner is the inherent dignity of any human being, any time, anywhere. Thus, the nineteen men on the planes each committed an altruistic suicide, but they were also barbarians because they utterly disregarded the individual in general—that is, the at least three thousand innocent women, men, and children who were burned alive or reduced to human rubble.

In 2003 we still lack a world consensus about moral values. Muslims (or others) who support the suicide bombers would ridicule my analysis. But that, of course, is Durkheim's point. If we are increasingly diverse, how do we achieve a sense of moral solidarity? And if we cannot agree about mass slaughter, is there anything more important than Durkheim's search for social cohesion?

Durkheim begins his discussion of *anomic* suicide by underlining the aggravating effect of economic crises. He travels from one European nation to another, cites the rise in suicide associated with depressions or (what we would call) recessions, and blames the rise in suicides on "disturbances of the collective order." Once again this is an intangible phenomenon, so he tries to clarify the concept by distinguishing it from egoistic suicide. The latter revolves around the lack of attachment to meaningful social groups; anomic suicide revolves around society's inability to regulate the individual's moral beliefs and practices.[110] At the north and south poles of a circle, the egoist exists without group ties; the anomic person exists without norms. They know what they reject; they know what they are supposed to affirm.[111]

Anomic suicide is especially characteristic of modern society—and its best-educated inhabitants. Those with intellectual careers are the most prone to anomic suicide because, by definition, their job is to challenge and reassess inherited beliefs and practices.[112] Anthropologists or sociologists would be especially good suicide candidates because one conclusion drawn from cross-cultural studies is that norms are culturally and historically relative. Nothing is certain except the new beliefs that challenge and undermine the former cornerstones of a person's worldview.

Durkheim is particularly critical of the economic changes that characterized his time. Like people who eat until they burst—think of the football-long buffets in Las Vegas—appetites for profit lacked "any limiting authority." Formerly a means to an end, money had become "the supreme end of individuals and societies alike." Meanwhile, religion had lost its power to provide moral guidance, "and government, instead of regulating economic life, has become its tool and servant." The result was a world where "from top to bottom of the ladder, greed is aroused without knowing where to find ultimate foothold."[113]

Anomie thus refers to a sense of normlessness that existed in the family and the economy, the church, and the government. Some people eventually got so dizzy that, like a ride on a never-ending Ferris wheel, the nauseous only had one solution: suicide.

The book draws to a close with a section on the "Social Element of Suicide." Durkheim repeats his arguments about the power of social facts and maintains, with a good degree of legitimacy, that he has scientifically shown many social roots of what was formerly perceived to be a solitary act. Sociology's power to explain why we think and act as we do is therefore undeniable. Durkheim's critics could go whistle in a windstorm.

Suicide's final chapter is called "Practical Consequences." Recalling his dictum that knowledge needs "to serve us in life,"[114] Durkheim is at first relentlessly honest. Given the social forces (e.g., science, philosophical, religious, economic, and political change) that promote individualism, why be surprised that people have a high opinion of their own abilities and prospects? "Where man is God to mankind,"[115] people make their own rules and disregard society's anachronistic, superstitious, or invalid beliefs and values. *"The entire morality of progress and perfection is inseparable from a certain amount of anomy"* (emphasis added).[116]

Then and now, Durkheim was perfectly correct. He splendidly caught modernity's power to undermine our sense of personal and cultural order. But ever the optimist, Durkheim now argues that the suicide rates are in fact abnormal. "We may begin by affirming that they result not from a regular evolution but from a morbid disturbance which, while able to uproot the institutions of the past has put nothing in their place; for the work of centuries cannot be remade in a few years."[117]

In a footnote Durkheim makes this important point: "When a state is said to be normal or abnormal, one must add, with reference to this or that, or else one is misunderstood."[118] In this case "this or that" referred to the dead world of the past; Durkheim faithfully believed—he did not know[119]—that modern societies would achieve a new, harmonious synthesis over time. This faith in moral solidarity weakens the book because it is an order imposed on the future. As critics never tired of noting, if an essential component of modernity was to forever ask questions, how would people ever achieve the harmony that was their supposed inheritance?

Some suggested the imposition of severe penalties; force people to behave properly by threatening them with the most horrible punishment. This never appealed to Durkheim, so he ends the book with a plea for interstitial groups like the family and professional associations. The state was a distant bureaucracy, the corporation an entity that divided labor in the pursuit of profit and efficiency. But in-between groups related to life as it was actually lived; Durkheim felt that these groups offered such hope that he taught a course about them at the Sorbonne. After his death those lectures were published in book form.[120] They reveal a man who has something provocative to say about every important issue in French and European societies.

PROFESSIONAL ETHICS AND CIVIC MORALS

One stereotype of university life suggests that it is an ivory tower. Absent-minded, bleary-eyed professors pursue their disciplines with disinterest and dedication. Knowledge is the watchword in a rarefied atmosphere where real life never intervenes.

In truth universities are closer to political pits. Many professors have Ph.D.s in mud wrestling, and the turf battles over issues as different as course offerings and office space require strategic thinking and the tactical precision of a stiletto. Get twelve Ph.D.s in an enclosed space for a departmental meeting, and the room is filled with enough pomposity to fill the Goodyear blimp. Meanwhile, promotion and tenure committees are cleverly stocked with friends or supporters of the petitioners; a quick wink of the eye indicates that I will support your candidate if you do not mess with mine.

Emile Durkheim experienced France's brand of university warfare when in 1902 he reluctantly allowed his name to be put forward for a professorship at the Sorbonne. In a letter to a close colleague—they do exist!—he wanted to avoid any suggestion that he sought "to insinuate himself into Paris. I find the idea of giving such an impression repulsive." In addition, Durkheim noted that he was a "poor politician" and, given his somber personality, "far from an expert in selling himself."[121]

Others did the job. Unable to bring a socialist to the Sorbonne, they settled for a sociologist. He would "furnish them with a doctrine to propound," so behind the scenes, Durkheim's advocates easily won the day. A large majority agreed to appoint him professor of education, and Durkheim agreed to focus his educational lectures on issues of morality. "There I feel at home."[122] (In 1913 the chair changed its name to Science of Education and Sociology.)

On a university stage Durkheim's manner repeated his other presentations of self in everyday life. He had the "face and body of an ascetic"; his manner was stern, somber, and professional. He quickly began new lectures with a summary of the previous week's discussion and then immediately got down to business.

Emile Durkheim never sold himself; his ideas did that. At the Sorbonne he soon had a legion of disciples masquerading as students because the small, gaunt man with odd spectacles offered courses full of the most challenging ideas and possibilities.[123]

In his courses on moral education, Durkheim consistently took a number of stinging swings at economists from Adam Smith to Karl Marx. The idea that the self-guiding hand of free markets or the "blind mechanisms" of historical forces would somehow produce social harmony seemed absurd to the Sorbonne's new professor. Only anarchy would prevail if class conflicts made economic life a stage for the pursuit of selfishness. "We find that the manufacturer, the merchant, the workman, the employee, in carrying on his occupation, is aware of no moral influence set above him to check his egoism; he is subject to no moral discipline whatever."[124]

To today's ears Durkheim sounds like a television preacher; with stern prose, he wants to bring back some of that old-fashioned discipline. In truth, he was simply a superb sociologist trying to juggle a variety of conflicting moral beliefs and economic priorities. If mechanization and standardization only produce "warfare," are they worth the price? And in a France where overproduction turned workers into spare parts in the economic machine, "a high rate of output is not everything. Value attaches to regularity as well." It provides regular work, regular wages, and a regular life. "There should not be alternating periods of over and under production. *No regulated planning means no regularity*" (emphasis added).[125]

In his essay on professional ethics, the political state is the "social brain" of a modern society.[126] Durkheim has no problem assigning the state significant regulatory functions, but he seeks to supplement the state by creating groups that are rooted in the everyday lives of everyday people.

Representing millions of people, the state exists at a level of abstraction that, by definition, cannot easily speak to the particular cultural, ethnic, religious, and class concerns of its increasingly diverse population. So, between the state and the average person Durkheim sought to institutionalize a new sense of moral solidarity by establishing professional organizations that would create, nurture, and judge the moral beliefs and practices of its members. Durkheim did not care if membership was voluntary or involuntary. Once they were up and functioning, the group's importance would be so obvious that only fools would refuse to join. But when it came to "the respective place and part of employer and employed, . . . it seems to me obvious that both should be represented in the governing body responsible for supervising the general affairs and well-being of the association. Such a body could only carry out its function provided that it included both these elements."[127]

This suggestion never satisfied many owners and workers. At the extreme ends of the economic continuum, communists and free marketers both wanted the same thing: total control of the productive process. Durkheim spoke to those seeking a middle ground. He saw the professional organizations providing "a special form of common morality." They would also be linked to the common consciousness of the state, but as interstitial groups, they would provide ideals able to closely bond lawyers and sociologists, engineers and machinists, doctors and government workers.[128] At their best professional groups would serve as the economic "heirs of the family," watching out for individual interests with all the diligence of a parent or a sibling.[129]

Today these professional associations often act only in their own self-interest. In Connecticut, the professor's association (we are not supposed to call it a union!) diligently lobbies for my interests, yet students always get an empty chair. Durkheim demanded that professional associations consider the larger society as well as their own narrow interests. A direct descendant of his thinking is the contemporary German practice of including labor representatives—by law—on any corporation's board of directors. Equally suggestive, a German firm cannot summarily fire workers. German corporations must have a *Sozialplan* (a social plan) in place if they plan to lay off workers. By definition the corporation has an obligation not only to its stockholders but also to its employees, their families, and the larger society.[130]

Durkheim also tried to create the "civic morals" that would weave a new common consciousness for modern societies. Two of his central ideas revolve around the role of the political state and the legitimacy of inherited wealth. Where American and French philosophers believed in the existence of natural rights—think of Jefferson's captivating prose in the Declaration of Independence—Durkheim stressed the revolutionary consequences of a sociological perspective. The only thing natural in human life was the ability to create new beliefs and values; political or otherwise, natural rights existed not in nature but in the eye of the beholder. Their legitimacy "depended entirely on the state of public opinion."[131]

In a world where rights depended on the shape of public opinion (i.e., of the common consciousness), the state's primary responsibility was to institute and protect the ever-evolving rights of man. "What yesterday seemed but a kind of luxury becomes overnight a right precisely defined. The task incumbent on the state, then, has no limits."[132] This line can be construed to authorize a state with as many arms as an octopus. Durkheim is admittedly sketchy here, but his political conception only authorizes a state whose principles derive from a "higher degree of consciousness and reflection." The root conception is the right of the individual to develop in a manner that allows for free expression and free thought. So the state protects the lone individual from arbitrary abuses of (political, economic, or religious) authority, *and* it also protects the individual from "secondary groups" such as the family or the church. These groups need to know that they have no right to "curb and monopolize" a modern citizen; all people deserve to exercise their right to evolve, so the state acts as a powerful barrier to all forms of potentially suffocating authority.[133]

These ideas suggest one of sociology's most liberating consequences. If beliefs, values, and practices are relative, people have the opportunity to compare, contrast, deliberate, and decide. No one ever works from a clean slate (think of Durkheim's passionate commitment to the rights of man), but the power to consciously create a different world nevertheless exists. Durkheim remains provocative because he offers the skeleton of a sense of moral solidarity that protects the individual and the group, the *rights* of the individual and the *obligations* of a citizen to the state and to all the other members of his or her society.

One final example concerns Durkheim's assessment of inherited wealth. Ever the advocate of reason and logic, he argues that "if equality were the rule," inherited wealth is "is contrary to the spirit of individualism." Anyone born with a silver spoon in his or her mouth has a decided advantage over the other members of a society. Therefore, if merit and individual achievement are the actual goals of modern man, Durkheim suggests the abolition of inherited wealth. "We might for instance imagine that every head of a family would have the right to leave to his children specified portion of the heritage. The inequalities that would then continue would be so slight as to not affect" the competition for political and economic power.[134]

Think, for example, of Al Gore and George W. Bush. Would either have achieved political prominence without the inherited wealth of their well-to-do families? In Durkheim's brave new world, each citizen would compete only on the basis of his or her intelligence, tenacity, and ambition. It is a conception as radical today as it was when the gaunt man with the odd spectacles offered it to his students at France's version of Yale, Harvard, and Princeton.

THE ELEMENTARY FORMS OF RELIGIOUS LIFE

Do you remember Wonder Bread? It is the "staff of life" with as much physical substance as a piece of onionskin paper. Wonder Bread builds strong bodies in eight ways because if you roll up a piece of the white bread, you can use it as a ball and get exercise in a variety of team sports. Wonder bread is arguably one of the most *profane* things on earth. Especially if you spread peanut butter and jelly on the bread, the sandwich is a dripping testimony to irreverence.

But take that *same* piece of Wonder Bread, use it during a Roman Catholic mass, and the bread becomes the body of Jesus Christ. The priest's blessing transforms the bread into a *sacred* object. You now approach the bread with a sense of awe and respect. God is on your tongue because of one of the most miraculous transformations in human life. "In all the history of human thought there exists no other example of two categories of things so profoundly differentiated or so radically opposed to one another." The difference between the sacred and the profane is "absolute."[135]

Take another example. On a recent university-sponsored trip to Cuba, one of our Israeli students wanted to locate synagogues. The one in Havana is quite large and easy to find. Religious symbols are all over the building. But the synagogue in Camagüey (Cuba's third-largest city) was located in a remote part of the city. It looked just like any other home, so while we waited for the rabbi to come, we walked in and sat down. He arrived, instantly dipped into a waiting box to get a yarmulke and put it on because he—and we!—had entered a sacred enclosure. The difference, of course, is that he knew the absolute difference that we absolutely failed to perceive.[136]

The distinction between the sacred and profane is a key to any understanding of Durkheim's *The Elementary Forms of Religious Life*.[137] Whether it was a city as large as Jerusalem, a building as magnificent as the cathedral in York, England, or the shrines in many traditional Vietnamese homes, any and all religions dichotomize social reality into sacred and profane aspects. Theoretically, all aspects of human life could acquire a sacred quality; but whether diffuse or contained, the existence of the sacred demands a disposition that always includes attitudes such as awe, reverence, and respect. Almost always special figures like rabbis and mullahs maintain the sacred objects and places because they can so easily be contaminated by the presence of the profane, for example, my students and me in Camagüey, Cuba.

Religious *beliefs*—about the soul, about the origin of fire (think of Prometheus), about the origin of life—represent a collective expression of the nature of sacred things. Religious *rites and ceremonies* "were the rules of conduct which prescribed how a man should comport himself in the presence of these sacred objects."[138] In Brooklyn nuns solemnly taught us to genuflect in front of the altar as we simultaneously made the sign of the cross. And if we passed a Catholic church on an object as profane as a New York bus, we were to bow our heads and once again make the sign of the cross.

The sacred correctly assumes a tremendous significance in Durkheim's thought. He seeks to do nothing less than provide "an understanding of the religious nature of man, that is to say, to show us an essential and permanent aspect of humanity."[139] He argues that if you could get beyond a particular symbol—go "underneath" the sacred—you could conceivably find the thread that linked all religions, all the time. His entire study rests on the postulate "that the unanimous sentiments of the believers of all times cannot be purely illusory."[140]

Durkheim got in trouble when he sought the *one* origin of religion. He declared that it existed in the totemic beliefs of the Australian aborigines. Anthropologists quickly pilloried him for this error, while other social scientists seriously doubted his principal conclusion: after burrowing under all the mythologies on earth, Durkheim claims that "the universal and eternal objective cause" of all sacred sensations was society.[141] People worshiped not gods or demons but the collective representations that men and women created when, as a group, worshipers joined hands.

The soul of religion was the idea of society.[142] Ever the positivist, Durkheim never minced words. Neither did his critics. One sarcastically stressed that "in the beginning was the end." Like God the Father, Son, and Holy Ghost all turned into one, Durkheim always explained everything in a monotheistic fashion. Society produced social facts, those social facts were external to the individual, and especially with religious beliefs and practices, those social facts led people to worship the gods who were actually nothing but human manifestations of the religious common consciousness.[143]

This gross oversimplification ignores at least one obvious fact. Religions try to answer the most important questions about human life: What is the ultimate origin of the solar system? Why do innocent children experience the most agonizing pain? Who painted a sea as blue as the Caribbean in Puerto Rico or Tobago? Why are we here? What happens when we die? The actual soul of religion is as complex as the *ultimate* answers to these questions; thus few if any sociologists today accept Durkheim's explanation of what lies beneath all manifestations of the sacred.

But, and this is a big but, *The Elementary Forms of Religious Life* nevertheless laid the groundwork for the scientific study of religious beliefs, values, and practices. The distinction between the sacred and profane is as important and influential today as it was when Durkheim first published his book in 1912. Contemporary sociologists of religion start with the assumption that human beings create religious beliefs and practices. Few doubt the importance of rituals, rites, and ceremonies in creating a sense of social order, and as the religious resurgence in South America or the Middle East underlines, religions can certainly offer the profoundest sense of social and moral solidarity.

One final explanation of this book's importance rests on Durkheim's attempt to offer an understanding of the categories of human thought. What were the ultimate origins of ideas like the sacred? He sought to provide a middle ground between those who argued that categories of thought existed prior to the individual (i.e., they were innate or a priori) and those who argued that our beliefs lacked any solidity at all. The a priori thinkers left no room for human creation, whereas the empiricists contended that categories of thought only arose from the minds of individuals. For the empiricists, "the categories of human thought are never fixed in any one definite form."[144]

Durkheim built two straw men, and he knocked them down. His opponents' arguments were far more subtle than that. But in citing the utter uniqueness of social facts and collective representations, Durkheim penned a line that had a profound influence on sociology. Categories of thought were neither innate nor artificial; they were "*in a sense a work of art, but of an art which imitates nature with a perfection that is capable of increasing unlimitedly*" (emphasis added).[145]

At the very end of *The Elementary Forms of Religious Life*, we read about "the consciousness of the consciousness."[146] When sociologists understand the origin and development of particular social facts, they become acutely conscious of the beliefs that shape their categories of thought. Like a curtain that hides a treasure, sociologists suddenly see how and why they—and the other members of society—think and act as they do. Society is therefore a work of art because only people painted the beautiful or ugly picture. Admittedly, everyone on earth inherits a "finished" portrait; yet that work of art is capable of unlimited perfection because, with our consciousness of the categories of human thought, we can knowingly alter, modify, or even discard our inherited beliefs, values, and practices.

In the introduction to this book, I discussed internal freedom, the notion that people can gain insight into how and why we think and act as we do. That notion is firmly rooted in Durkheim's thought. Part of his immense legacy is a body of work that shows both the power of social facts and our potential ability to overcome the coercive influence of facts we did not accept or respect. Thus he concludes *The Elementary Forms of Religious Life* by focusing on "historic souvenirs"; like Nietzsche, he stresses that "the old gods are growing old or are already dead, and others are not yet born."[147] Durkheim believed he had scientifically proven that reasonable people had the power to consciously create new forms of moral solidarity. Thus he hoped that his analysis of religion offered the hints and insights that would allow people to begin to use sociology to take charge of their own destinies. "There are no gospels which are immortal but neither is there any reason for believing that humanity is incapable of creating new ones. As to the question of what symbols this new faith will express itself with, whether they will resemble those of the past or not, . . . that is something which surpasses the human faculty of foresight."[148]

SLAUGHTER ON THE WESTERN FRONT

The Literary Digest was the *Time* or *Newsweek* of its day. For Americans it offered a weekly summary of news from throughout the nation and the world. On August 12, 1916, the *Digest* published a small chart summarizing the results of two years of war. The chart's three columns matter-of-factly listed "killed," "wounded or missing," and "total casualties." Russia had 1 million dead and 4 million wounded or missing. Germany's total included over 900,000 killed and 2.25 million wounded or missing. Finally, France's total indicated that 800,000 men had died and more than 1.2 million were wounded or missing.[149]

The chart borders on the obscene. Millions of deaths are calculated like so many gallons of gasoline or Model T cars off Henry Ford's assembly line. As if a social fact, World War I trained people to think of mass slaughter as a fixed part of modern war and modern life.[150] It was an impersonal catastrophe that affected Emile Durkheim in the most personal fashion imaginable.

Durkheim and his wife loved their son Andre with a tremendous passion. He was a fine student who, after the war broke out, eventually found himself on the Bulgarian front. In January 1916 the Durkheim family learned that Andre "had been declared missing in the retreat from Siberia." For three months the odious reality of the statistics was a living nightmare for the family. In a letter Durkheim writes, "I do not have to tell you of the anguish in which I am living. It is an obsession that fills every moment and is even worse than I supposed."[151]

After three months of agony, the family finally learned of Andre's death. It was a blow that soon killed the father. He returned to work because "it prevented the suffering from overwhelming me completely, driving it back and localizing it. From there it cannot be driven out. But it is perhaps possible to render it less acute."[152]

Durkheim failed. In late 1916 he suffered a stroke, and on November 15, 1917, he died at the age of fifty-nine. His and his wife's terrible grief remind us that statistics can be a sedative. They numb the mind and close our eyes to the families who lost both a son and their peace of mind.

World War I also challenged Durkheim's hopes for a new moral solidarity. His sociological insights were as valid as ever, yet instead of embracing reason, Europe embraced rage. The new symbols of solidarity were rooted in hate and the death of more than 10 million Andres over four horrible years. It was hard to be optimistic standing over the graveyards that, like a perpetual pall, covered countries from Russia to England, from Austria to the Paris of Emile Durkheim.

NOTES

1. Emile Durkheim, *The Division of Labor in Society* (New York: Free Press, 1984), 331.

2. See Peter Gay, *The Enlightenment: An Interpretation* (New York: Macmillan, 1996); also see Durkheim's comments in Emile Durkheim, *Socialism* (New York: Collier, 1962), 223–24.

3. Thomas Paine, *The Selected Work of Tom Paine* (New York: Modern Library, 1945), 285, 287.

4. Friedrich Nietzsche, *Thus Spoke Zarathustra* (London: Penguin, 1969), 48; see also Friedrich Nietzsche, *The Will to Power* (New York: Random House, 1967); and Friedrich Nietzsche, *On the Genealogy of Morals* (New York: Random House, 1967). For an overview of Nietzsche's work, see Walter Kaufmann, *Nietzsche* (Cleveland, Ohio: Meridian Books, 1956).

5. Nietzsche, *Thus Spoke Zarathustra*, 84.

6. Ibid., 89.

7. Ibid., 103.

8. See, for example, the essay titled "Civic Morals" in Emile Durkheim, *Professional Ethics and Civic Morals* (London: Routledge, 1992), 56–57.

9. *Emile Durkheim on Morality and Society*, ed. Robert Bellah (Chicago: University of Chicago Press, 1973), 33. The quote is from a speech Durkheim made to the graduating class of his secondary school, "Address to the Lyceens of Sens."

10. Durkheim, *Professional Ethics*, 12.

11. *Emile Durkheim on Morality and Society*, vii.

12. Steven Lukes, *Emile Durkheim: His Life and Work, a Historical and Critical Study* (London: Penguin, 1973)., 40. Especially for personal details, I have relied heavily on Lukes's superb summary of Durkheim's life and work.

13. Ibid., 39.

14. Lewis Coser, *Masters of Sociological Thought* (New York: Harcourt Brace, 1971), 143.

15. Lukes, *Emile Durkheim*, 41.

16. For a short but solid overview, see J. Milton Yinger, *Anti-Semitism: A Case Study in Prejudice and Discrimination* (New York: Freedom Books, 1964).

17. Ibid., 41.

18. Coser, *Masters of Sociological Thought*, 163.

19. See Thorstein Veblen, "The Intellectual Preeminence of the Jew in Modern Europe," in *Thorstein Veblen*, ed. Bernard Rosenberg (New York: Crowell, 1963), 91–100.

20. Lukes, *Emile Durkheim*, 42.

21. Ibid., 45–46.

22. Coser, *Masters of Sociological Thought*, 156–57; Lukes, *Emile Durkheim*, 46–47.

23. Bellah, *Emile Durkheim on Morality and Society*, 33.

24. See Henri Peyre, introduction to *Montesquieu and Rousseau: Forerunners of Sociology*, by Emile Durkheim (Ann Arbor: University of Michigan Press, 1965), viii–ix.

25. Lukes, *Emile Durkheim*, 99; see also Robert Alun Jones, *Emile Durkheim: An Introduction to Four Major Works* (Beverly Hills, Calif.: Sage, 1986).

26. See Montesquieu, *Persian Letters* (London: Penguin, 1977) and Montesquieu, *The Spirit of the Laws* (New York: Hafner, 1966).

27. See Durkheim, *Montesquieu and Rousseau*, 62–64.

28. Lukes, *Emile Durkheim*, 139.

29. See, for example, the otherwise excellent study by Robert Nisbet, *Emile Durkheim* (Englewood Cliffs, N.J.: Prentice Hall, 1965); see also Nisbet's *The Sociological Tradition* (New York: Basic Books, 1966). For another perspective see Anthony Giddens, *Capitalism and Modern Social Theory: An Analysis of the Writings of Marx, Durkheim, and Max Weber* (Cambridge, England: Cambridge University Press, 1971), 65–118.

30. Durkheim, *Socialism*, 142.

31. Ibid., 142.

32. Ibid., 142–43; also see 165–66. For a short overview of Saint Simon's work, see Henri De Saint Simon, *Social Organization, the Science of Man, and Other Writings* (New York: Harper Torchbooks, 1964).

33. Durkheim, *Division of Labor*, 331.

34. For what could arguably be called the epistemology of Durkheim's thinking, see his 1914 essay "The Dualism of Human Nature and Its Social Conditions," in *Emile Durkheim on Morality and Society*, ed. Robert N. Bellah (Chicago: University of Chicago Press, 1973), 149–63.

35. Ibid., xxx, the preface to the first edition of the book.

36. Ibid., 16–17, 23–24.

37. Durkheim, *Division of Labor*, 24–25.

38. As many analysts indicate, Durkheim owes a debt of gratitude to Rousseau. He openly indicated this in *Montesquieu and Rousseau;* see especially 102–4.

39. Durkheim, *Division of Labor*, 63.

40. Ibid., 40.

41. Robert Lynd and Helen Merrell Lynd, *Middletown in Transition* (New York: Harcourt Brace, 1937), 402–86.

42. Durkheim, *Division of Labor*, 119.

43. Ibid., 119.

44. For the influence of Darwin's *The Origin of the Species* in the United States, consider Richard Hofstadter, *Social Darwinism in American Thought* (Boston: Beacon Press, 1955); also see the superb chapter on race in Michael Hunt, *Ideology and U.S. Foreign Policy* (New Haven, Conn.: Yale University Press, 1987), 46–91.

45. Durkheim, *Division of Labor*, 122.

46. Ibid., 81–2.

47. I am relying here on Giddens, *Capitalism and Modern Social Theory*, 77.

48. See, for each city, The Wendell Cox Consultancy, *Demographia* [www.demographia.com]. (September 13, 2001.)

49. Otto Bettman, *The Good Old Days: They Were Terrible!* (New York: Random House, 1974), 2, 8, 79; for an overview of the development of cities, see Lewis Mumford, *The City In History* (New York: Harcourt Brace, 1961).

50. Durkheim, *Division of Labor*, 307.

51. See, for example, William Greider, *One World, Ready or Not* (New York: Simon and Schuster, 1997); also see Kevin Bales, *Disposable People* (Berkeley: University of California Press, 1999).

52. Durkheim, *Division of Labor*, 291.

53. Lukes, *Emile Durkheim*, 177.

54. Ibid., 174–75.

55. Durkheim, *Division of Labor*, 313, 321.

56. Ibid., 337.

57. Ibid., 338–39.

58. Ibid., 340.

59. Coser, *Masters of Sociological Thought*, 38–39.

60. Emile Durkheim, *The Rules of the Sociological Method* (New York: Free Press, 1964), xli.

61. Ibid., 3.

62. Ibid., xlvii.

63. Ibid., 1–2.

64. Ibid., 27.

65. Ibid., xliii.

66. Ibid., 28.

67. Ibid., chapter 3, 47–75.

68. Ibid., 48.

69. Ibid., 55.

70. Ibid., 58.

71. Ibid., esp. 60–61.

72. Ibid., 75.

73. Ibid., 58.

74. Ibid., 97.

75. See, for example, Talcott Parsons, *The Social System* (New York: Free Press, 1964).

76. See, for example, Peter Berger and Richard John Neuhaus, *Movement and Revolution* (New York: Doubleday, 1970), especially 25–26.

77. Durkheim, *Rules of the Sociological Method*, 123.

78. Ibid., 123.

79. Ibid., 124.

80. Nicholas Halasz, *Captain Dreyfus: The Story of a Mass Hysteria* (New York: Simon and Schuster, 1955), 62–63.

81. Ibid., 63.

82. Ibid., 18; see also David L. Lewis, *Prisoners of Honor: The Dreyfus Affair* (New York: William Morrow, 1973).

83. Lewis, *Prisoners of Honor*, 52.

84. A. A. Milne, *Peace with Honor* (New York: Dutton, 1934).

85. Halasz, *Captain Dreyfus*, 93.

86. Lewis, *Prisoners of Honor*. The cartoon appears, with other illustrations, in the center of this book.

87. Halasz, *Captain Dreyfus*, 129.

88. Ibid., 119.

89. See Emile Durkheim, "Individualism and the Intellectuals," in *Emile Durkheim on Morality and Society*, ed. Robert N. Bellah (Chicago: University of Chicago Press, 1973), 43–57.

90. Ibid., 43–45.

91. Ibid., 48–49.

92. Ibid., 50.

93. Ibid., 51–52; for a similar argument from an American, see John Dewey, *A Common Faith* (New Haven, Conn.: Yale University Press, 1934).

94. See Giddens, *Capitalism and Modern Social Theory*, 105.

95. Durkheim, "Individualism and the Intellectuals," 53.

96. Ibid., 56.

97. Ibid., 56–57.

98. See Halasz, *Captain Dreyfus*, part 5; Lewis, *Prisoners of Honor*, chapter 14.

99. Lewis, *Prisoners of Honor*, 218.

100. This section on *Suicide* rests on the insights of Lukes, *Emile Durkheim*, 49–51 and chapter 9.

101. Ibid., 51.

102. Ibid., 192–95.

103. Emile Durkheim, *Suicide* (New York: Free Press, 1966), 122–23, chapter 3.

104. Ibid., 210.

105. Ibid., 212.

106. See, for example, Alexandre Koyre, *From the Closed World to the Infinite Universe* (New York: Harper Torchbooks, 1958).

107. Ibid., 213.

108. Ibid., 220, 236.

109. Ibid., 239–40.

110. Ibid., 258.

111. See, for example, José Ortega y Gasset, *Man and Crisis* (New York: Norton, 1962).

112. Durkheim, *Suicide*, 258.

113. Ibid., 257.

114. Ibid., 49.

115. Ibid., 363.

116. Ibid., 365.

117. Ibid., 369.

118. Ibid., 365.

119. For the distinction between believing and knowing, see Peter Berger, "Protestantism and the Quest for Certainty," *The Christian Century*, August 26–September 2, 1998, 782–96.

120. Emile Durkheim, *Professional Ethics and Civic Morals* (London: Routledge, 1992).

121. Quoted in Lukes, *Emile Durkheim*, 365–66.

122. Ibid., 365–66.

123. Ibid., 369–71.

124. See Durkheim, *Professional Ethics*, 12.

125. Ibid., 16.

126. Ibid., 30.

127. Ibid., 38.

128. Ibid., 39.

129. Ibid., 218.

130. On Germany, see Hedrick Smith, *Rethinking America* (New York: Random House, 1995), 211, 240.

131. Durkheim, *Professional Ethics*, 67.

132. Ibid., 68.

133. Ibid., 62.

134. Ibid., 217.

135. Emile Durkheim, *The Elementary Forms of Religious Life* (New York: Free Press, 1965), 52.

136. This trip occurred in June 2001.

137. Durkheim owed a great deal here to one of his teachers, Fustel de Coulanges, *The Ancient City* (Washington, D.C.: Johns Hopkins University Press, 1980).

138. Durkheim, *Elementary Forms*, 56.

139. Ibid., 13.

140. Ibid., 14; See Lukes, *Emile Durkheim*, 459, for an especially good analysis of this point.

141. Durkheim, *Elementary Forms*, 465.

142. Ibid., 466.

143. Lukes, *Emile Durkheim*, 482.

144. Durkheim, *Elementary Forms*, 28.

145. Ibid., 32.

146. Ibid., 492.

147. Ibid., 475.

148. Ibid., 476.

149. *The Literary Digest*, August 12, 1916, 342.
150. See, for example, General J. F. C. Fuller, *The Conduct of War, 1789–1961* (New Brunswick, N.J.: Rutgers University Press, 1961).
151. Lukes, *Emile Durkheim*, 555.
152. Ibid., 556.

CHAPTER 3

Max Weber

"For the last stage of this cultural development, it might well be truly said: Specialists without spirit, sensualists without heart; this nullity imagines that it has attained a level of civilization never before achieved."

Max Weber, *The Protestant Ethic and the Spirit of Capitalism*[1]

CHARGE OF THE LIGHT BRIGADE

Henry VIII married so many women that, from books to movies, his endless escapades and beheadings still attract great attention. Less well known are Henry's exploits as commander-in-chief of Britain's Army Royal. He headed a force so overloaded with aristocratic privileges, it is amazing anyone had time to fight.

In 1513 more than 2,000 "soldiers" (out of an army of 16,000) did nothing but care for the king; if he stayed home, so did they. In this instance Henry took the field but in a unique way. Even as a young man, Henry ate well; "the king's household"—the soldiers who provided and prepared his food—included 276 men. Long before Versace or Ralph Lauren, Henry also liked to dress properly; the king's "wardrobe of robes" contained 49 soldiers. When he wanted to pray, 115 men maintained a chapel fit for a king. The gentlemen ushers, grooms, and pages totaled another 579 men. And when Henry wanted to laugh, his 10 minstrels and players told the latest jokes and sang whatever songs pleased the king's discriminating ears.[2]

On the battlefield Henry VIII used tents for his enormous entourage; he even had a gold one that occupied a full wagon. Meanwhile, Henry resided "in a prefabricated timber house, complete with fireplace and chimneys, the component parts of which occupied twelve carts." The house's main room was twenty-seven feet by fourteen feet, with walls eight feet high to the eaves. The second, smaller room only had seven-foot ceilings, but Henry was, after all, on the battlefield. War required royal sacrifices. Historical records fail to show if Henry had the house assembled for an overnight stay; but as one historian notes, "few of Henry's actions on the 1513 campaign were governed by common sense and it may well be that the pavilioners' first task when the Army halted was to assemble the King's house of timber."[3]

History fascinated Max Weber. Among the eight magnificent minds profiled here, he is arguably the best historian. Besides a lifelong interest in fascinating facts, however, Weber used history to win a variety of intellectual battles with Karl Marx. If economic factors determined social class, how does one explain the privileges of Henry VIII? For Weber social class was determined, for much of human history, by esoteric questions of social honor. *Who* you were was more important than *what* you did. At times, according privilege based on royal ancestry produced the most absurd results. Fully 250 years after Henry did battle, French officers in the Seven Years' War (1756–63) could serve their aristocratic colleagues—in the field—as many as thirteen separate dishes in a two-course meal.[4] This greatly impeded military efficiency, but as Weber well knew, when aristocrats ruled the world, efficiency meant nothing. Traditions—not reason—dictated your behavior. You became an officer because of your blood, and if, as at the Charge of the Light Brigade (1854), the officer was a royal idiot, men died, all in the name of social honor and traditional authority.

Five years after Marx and Engels published the *Communist Manifesto*, the English fought in the Crimean War (1853–56). The two communists argued that economic factors determined questions of power and privilege. Unfortunately, no one told the English. Three-and-a-half centuries after Henry VIII, aristocrats still made the best officers, and when Lord Cardigan (who led the charge) was born in 1797, the royal right to rule even included the following military tradition. As a matter of honor, officers were mortified if they knew the words of command. When officers drilled troops, "an intelligent sergeant whispered from time to time the word of command which his captain would have been ashamed to have known without prompting."[5]

Was this crazy? Of course it was—but only from the point of view of rationality. Another principal theme of Weber's work is the profound significance of tradition in human history. Weber came to his maturity when the new and old worlds were still very much in competition. Thus he brilliantly caught the power of tradition to make intelligent people *celebrate* and *legitimate* norms of conduct that had nothing to do with common sense, intelligence, or facts. Traditions looked backwards, and they dominated because people accepted this rule: we behave this way because our ancestors behaved this way.

The seventh earl of Cardigan came from an "ancient" family. He traced his blue blood back to the fourteenth century, when his forebears first established close ties to the crown. "His enormous faith in himself was based on the principle of hereditary aristocracy. . . . The question was one of divine right; his rank gave him a divine right to command and to be obeyed."[6] Granted, Cardigan's displays of arrogance demanded a special gold medal from the queen, but he was not *that* different from his peers. The duke of Wellington ruled the army in Cardigan's day, and he would recommend, for example, "only staff officers, who usually had aristocratic connections, for decorations and distinctions." In the nineteenth century, one purchased his commission and promotions in the British army. This tradition dated back to the seventeenth century when, after Cromwell's revolution, the aristocracy maintained power by assuring itself that only those with a landed stake in the country officered the army. Occasionally, a person with only money broke through the ranks, so habits like Wellington's assured aristocrats of their divine right to embarrass themselves if they knew the words of command.[7]

Cardigan bought a lieutenant-colonelcy of the fifteenth Hussars (in 1831) for almost 40,000 pounds. This was a princely sum, but given Cardigan's landed wealth, the peasants would pay the piper. For twenty years Cardigan made an absolute fool of himself. He created so many disturbances in the army that his appearance at the theater moved audiences to boo and riot. At one point he lost his command, and at another he drove through London with the curtains tightly shut. Thus he was already hugely unpopular when, during the Irish famine, he evicted no less than 40,000 men, women, and children. Even his peers thought this excessive, but Cardigan (a friend of the queen) nevertheless became a brigadier-general when the Crimean War began.[8]

One of Cardigan's senior officers actually had combat experience. It dated back twenty-six years, but the fellow could still mount a horse. None of the other cavalry officers, including Cardigan, "had any experience of active service." So they substituted aristocratic arrogance for military expertise and sent Cardigan and his Hussars into the valley of death. The Russians had guns everywhere, but Cardigan chose a uniform of "brilliant cherry color and blue," fitted with "fur, plume and lace." He looked every bit as dashing as Henry VIII when he rode off to certain defeat. Seven hundred soldiers charged into the valley; 195 returned. Over 500 horses died. Lord Cardigan—he survived!—retreated to his yacht, "had a bath and a bottle of champagne with his dinner and went to bed." When he finally returned to England, his contemporaries feted him as a military hero; his gallantry remains alive in Tennyson's poem, a traditional way to celebrate England's aristocracy and its military heroes.[9]

These events occurred a decade before Max Weber's birth in 1864. Weber grew up in a Europe transforming itself through industrialization but ruled, in many instances, by aristocrats.[10] Weber lived with tradition and science, the old world and the new; through great intelligence and exceedingly hard work, he used that "confusion" to create a theoretical overview of history that is both grand and solidly rooted in the facts. As a consequence he achieved new and enduring insights into, for example, the nature of social class, the importance of tradition, the legitimacy of political authority, the role of religion (especially in "creating" capitalism), and the significance of "ideal types" as conceptual guides to understanding human behavior.

Weber was a sociological giant who spent good parts of his adult life in sanitariums and asylums. He was often incapable of work. Amazingly, for the relatively short time he could focus, few have matched his achievements or insights.

AT THE SEASHORE

Max Weber's wife wrote a huge biography of her husband (first published in 1926). It offers a degree of intimacy and detail that exists for none of the other sociologists discussed in this book. One story seems especially important. As a child Weber contracted meningitis; for a while the four-year-old boy slept in a bed with padded sides. "The danger of dying or becoming an imbecile cast a shadow over the weak child and over Helene's [his mother's] happiness." She rarely left his side and never left the house without making it quite clear where she was if an emergency arose. In later years, it was so hard for her to leave her offspring that she considered "trips taken by parents without their children as frivolous temptations of god."[11]

Weber recovered, but his body still refused to cooperate. His head "grew conspicuously while his limbs remained girlishly small." Childhood was less than a pleasure, so his mother took him to the shore. "At Borkum she used to carry the five-year-old boy into the ocean, thinking that this would make him stronger. But every day there was so much screaming that the bathers demanded a stop to the treatment. Even as a young man Weber did not forget the terrors of this procedure."[12]

Weber remembered many scary things from his childhood in Berlin. Born on April 21, 1864, he grew up in the home of parents joined in matrimony yet separated by personalities as harmonious as lemon and milk. Max Weber Sr. was a jurist, a member of the municipal diet of Berlin, and ultimately a member of the new Reichstag. If his political label seemed confusing—he was a right-wing liberal—his overbearing personality erased any chance for clarification. "He claimed intellectual authority and did not really like the young people to hold different opinions." When conflicts arose with any member of the family, he solved the problem by stressing that "he was in the right." There was no conflict, just his way of doing things his way.[13]

Helene Weber genuinely loved her children, but carrying a heavy cargo of trauma, she passed on her anxieties and inhibitions in a forceful and frightening way. "When she was sixteen, a chaste, closed bud of a girl," a teacher and close friend of the family sexually assaulted her. She avoided a nervous breakdown, but "from that moment on she regarded physical passion as guilt laden and subhuman." Sex was difficult at best; this made a poor match even harder to sustain, but given the depths of her contempt for sex, she taught her son to fear his own body. "Without using words— for in those days the dark substrata of life and their menacing problems were left under thick wraps, . . . she implanted in him indestructible inhibitions against a surrender to his drives." Freud would call it sublimation, but for Max Weber the quantities of food that sometimes led to a "robust corporeality" offered one way to cope with a mother who, as with trips to the seashore, turned the most natural aspects of life into a cause for guilt, fear, anxiety, repression, and ultimately, a complete inability to think, work, or teach.[14]

Throughout his life, but especially as a young man, books offered the shy adolescent a way to travel to other worlds. History proved to be such a favorite that as a thirteen-year-old, Weber gave a family member historical essays as belated Christmas gifts. His first paper was titled "About the Course of German History with Special Regard to the Positions of the Emperor and the Pope." His second essay focused on the Roman imperial period beginning under Constantine. The young author even dedicated his first scholarly efforts. The formal opening begins: "Dedicated by the Author to His Own Insignificant Self as well as to his parents and siblings."[15]

Weber lost some of his insecurity when he attended Heidelberg University in 1881. Although reading still absorbed him, joining his father's fraternity offered alternatives he genuinely relished. Instead of class he went out drinking with his classmates, and the "manliness" demanded at the time sent Weber to the dueling hall. The macho ideal in Heidelberg included the notion that "the brothers did not associate with friendly warmth but were as cold as ice to one another." So, instead of friendship, the men fought like fools. Weber later said "that were no *problems* for us; we were convinced that we could somehow solve everything by means of a duel." Sword in hand, Weber fought with his fraternity brothers and even acquired a dueling scar that he wore with pride. When he returned home for a visit, his mother was so startled by his appearance that her only response was a swift slap in the face.[16]

Weber also served his mandatory year in the army. But he was now so "stout" that none of the uniforms in the army depot fit around his frame. Eventually, his commanders squeezed him into "a mess sergeant's uniform." That made him look like a soldier, but the young man who never exercised suddenly faced serious problems when his commanders demanded that he drill, run, and jump with his comrades. According to his wife, "His delicate feet and ankle joints had trouble supporting his heavy body and broke down during the hours of military drill." Weber also despised "the monstrous stupidity" of the drills and the mandatory badgering by junior officers. He hated the army and drank so much that he went through "military routines in the daze of a moderate hangover." In later years, these experiences assumed a halo effect. He wrote "that the training for haughty aggression in the dueling fraternity and as an officer had a strong influence on me. It removed the shyness and insecurity of my adolescence."[17]

Outside his home Weber lost some of his insecurities. Unfortunately, after he completed his studies to be a "junior barrister" in 1886, he saw no alternative but to return to his parents' home. His problem was money. He had none, and the salary of a young attorney offered no means to self-sufficiency. He "voluntarily" returned to the nest but confessed that "it is a peculiar feeling when one outgrows one's student shoes and yet has to wait for years before one can stand on one's own feet; at least this is how I feel, and I simply have to swallow the idea almost every day."[18]

Weber sought such a quick escape that he complemented his legal studies with the acquisition of a doctorate. He relished the knowledge he acquired and, equally important, the knowledge that he could use a Ph.D. to leave home in a shorter period of time. It still took seven long years. And because Weber "never relieved himself by a frank discussion of the problems"—his wife noted that "he repressed everything"—Weber painfully swallowed the resentments that rarely reached the surface. "For years I have realized with *infinite bitterness* that I was unable to obtain a position that would give me an independent income. . . . The only thing that attracted me was my own bread and the fact that it was denied me made my family home a *torment*" (emphasis added).[19]

Weber's first serious love affair was with a young woman who spent considerable periods of time in a mental hospital. The affair lasted for six years and ended when Weber met Marianne Schnitger, a grandniece of his father. Marianne fell in love with Max and accepted his profound sexual inhibitions, as well as his other sources of guilt, repression, and anxiety. For example, when Weber told his previous fiancé about his new fiancé, the young woman was in a period of recovery. The news naturally unsettled her, and "Weber never forgot that he had caused suffering to this tender girl." Guilt clouded his life with such a dark cover that he also felt terrible about winning the heart of Marianne. She had been courted by one of his friends, and here too the break was less than pleasant. As if caught in a Greek tragedy, Weber seemed unable to experience joy without the fates adding a heavy dose of guilt and remorse.[20]

The Webers married in the fall of 1893. By this time Weber had his Ph.D. and a full professorship at Freiburg University. Two years later he received an offer from Heidelberg, replacing one of the nation's most eminent historians. His wife wrote that "the new life quickly brought forth rich blossoms." A measure of independence from his parents had been achieved when, "in the early summer of 1897, a great crisis arose" and "it left an indelible mark on all involved."[21]

His mother wanted to spend time with the young couple. Although they happily agreed, Weber's father demanded the rights of any traditional patriarch. Helene Weber belonged to him, and his needs demanded so much attention that he alone would determine when and for how long she could vacation. Max and Marianne disagreed with the father, and when the inevitable confrontation occurred, the years of "infinite bitterness" produced a startling reaction. "The son was no longer able to contain his pent-up anger. The lava erupted and the monstrous thing happened: A son sat in judgment on his father."[22]

In contemporary America such judgments are an everyday affair. Some of us even instruct our children to stand up to their parents and have a mind and say of their own. For Weber the confrontation occurred in a society where sons dutifully obeyed their father; under the best of cases, this was a burden for men with a mind, but for Max Weber the decisive battle occurred after thirty-one years of repression. He suddenly had a target for all his justifiable rage. When he told his father that they would have no relationship unless his mother was permitted to visit, he did what he thought was right. Tragically, he simultaneously sowed the seeds of a lifelong sense of guilt. His father died soon after the horrendous argument occurred, and Weber never made peace with what soon became an unbearable burden.[23]

Within months he was unable to teach. Just beginning "his descent into hell," he had a particular problem talking; it produced an especially "disagreeable effect." He was also unable to concentrate—"intellectual activity was poison"—and eventually wound up in "a small mental institution" and stayed there for weeks. Even after he left the asylum, he would sit, "just picking at his fingernails. . . . He claims that this does him a lot of good."[24]

Weber was now thirty-four years old. Until his death he would suffer from bouts of depression or a sense of anxiety that produced what his wife called paralysis. As a man of honor he tried to resign from his position at Heidelberg, but the university generously chose a form of perpetual leave and his salary to boot. He could return when he was well; in the meantime he tried to recover by visiting, among other places, Venice and Corsica. He also made periodic visits to a variety of Europe's best rest homes.

The Webers inherited money, and their ability to live well created a situation whereby, despite his illness, Max Weber sometimes managed "manic spurts of extraordinary intellectual activity." At any moment the paralysis might reappear, but when he was mobile, he worked with passion, intensity, and brilliance. As he later told an audience in 1918, "In the field of science only he who is devoted *solely* to the work at hand has personality. And this holds true not only for the field of science; we know of no great artist who has ever done anything but serve his work and only his work."[25]

Max Weber was a great artist with great conflicts. He worked through those conflicts when he could, and the result is a body of work that includes a wonderful essay: "Science as a Vocation."

SOCIOLOGY AND CLARITY

In 1918 Weber spoke to a group of students at Munich University. By this time he was a professor of international distinction, so the students (it is hoped) listened with both respect and interest. The professor began by spotlighting a passion. Anyone who wanted to be a scientist needed to know that "nothing is worthy of man as man unless he can pursue it with passionate devotion." You must be lovingly wedded to your work, but never assume that passion alone gives birth to great and new ideas. Granted, ideas often occurred at the strangest times, when a person walked or, sat with friends, smoking a Cuban cigar. An amateur might assume that the idea came from nowhere; a scientist knew that, as much as two plus two equals four, no idea would ever "come to mind had we not brooded at our desks and searched for answers with passionate devotion."[26]

Scientists also embraced a peculiar sense of satisfaction, the knowledge that successors inevitably improved or surpassed even the best work of the best scientists. This was the "very meaning of scientific work," the certainty that "every scientific fulfillment raises new questions; it asks to be surpassed and outdated." In principle, this progress lasted forever, so "why does one engage in doing something that in reality never comes, and never can come, to an end?"[27]

What a great question. Were scientists just a bunch of masochists? Why work with passion, devotion, and tenacity, knowing all the while that in ten, twenty, or (if you were very lucky) fifty years, you would be thrown on the scrap heap, replaced by the latest formulations and theories?

This is Weber's answer: "Scientific progress is a fraction, the most important fraction of the process of intellectualization which we have been undergoing for thousands of years." Think of a Native American. He knows "incomparably more about his tools" than we know about many vital aspects of our civilization. How does a plane fly or a computer process its information with such incredible speed? Most of us are ignorant of the workings of the tools we use everyday yet the beauty of science— its significance for everyone—is "the knowledge or belief that if one wished one *could* learn it at any time. Hence it [science] means that in principle there are no mysterious, incalculable forces that come into play, but rather that one can, in principle, master all things by calculation."[28]

Weber now introduces one of the principal themes of his work: the world is disenchanted. The gods are gone and we are here, with no need to resort to mysterious forces or prayers to the spirits that supposedly inhabit the universe. Science replaces faith with reason; the sociologists' job is to use "technical means and calculations" to achieve greater knowledge of how the world actually works, knowing all the while that this knowledge is so hard to get, their work will inevitably be surpassed by those who pick up a calculator after their death.

But what about someone like Tolstoy, the masterful Russian novelist? Tolstoy writes that "science is meaningless because it gives no answer to our question, the only question important for us: 'What shall we do and how shall we live?' "[29] Weber confronts this conundrum with a blunt instrument: the truth. Science can never answer Tolstoy's question. Go to a church, synagogue, or mosque if you seek those answers. But if you accept that science provides knowledge that is "worth knowing," then it—and especially sociology—can provide a good measure of assistance, even with the questions posed by Tolstoy.

Weber emphatically underlines that science must be pursued objectively. Teachers never have the right to impose their political, religious, or economic beliefs on students. For example, Weber passionately discussed politics when friends and colleagues came to his home. He called Germany's Kaiser Wilhelm II "the crowned dilettante" and also announced that "a nation which has never chopped off the head of its monarch is not cultured." Weber had beliefs and a decided willingness to proclaim them openly. But in one heated gathering, the conversation instantly stopped because "there are students here now, and, naturally, I don't have the right to talk about politics in front of them; it might influence them."[30]

Weber had no problem with influencing students; however, he meant do it in a scientific fashion. "The primary task of a useful teacher is to teach his students to recognize *inconvenient* facts—I mean facts that are inconvenient for their party opinions." From this perspective the scientist—the sociologist—introduces the knowledge acquired through passion and hard work and then lets students use it as a means to a clearer, truthful articulation of their particular set of beliefs, values, and practices. Never come to lecture hall or read a piece of (scientific) sociology imagining that you will receive answers to political questions and dilemmas. The soci-

ologist is a teacher, not a leader. Go to a party meeting for political propaganda; come to a lecture hall because you want the one gift that the
science of sociology can provide: clarity.[31]

Clarity has a special meaning for Weber, a meaning that is arguably as
relevant today as it was in 1918. Clarity signifies that if we are "competent" in our work, "we can force the individual, or at least we can help
him, to give himself an *account of the ultimate meaning of his own conduct"*
(emphasis added). By offering a series of inconvenient facts—for example,
about the crucial, continuing role of tradition in shaping military beliefs
and practices—teachers demand that students rethink their inherited and
learned assumptions. In deliberately challenging the traditional wisdom
about the way the world works, the sociologist "stands in the service of
'moral' forces; he fulfills the duty of bringing about self-clarification and
a sense of responsibility." Equally important, any sociologist will produce
the greatest successes "the more conscientiously he avoids the desire personally to impose upon or suggest to his audience his own stand."[32]

Stay in the background. Guard the combination to the value judgments
locked away in your mind. But never forget to be ruthlessly honest. "The
fate of our times is characterized by rationalization and intellectualization,
and, above all, by the disenchantment of the world." If not dead, God was
dying, yet Weber had more respect for someone who retreated to the
churches than for an "academic prophet" who forgot "that in the lecture-
rooms of the university no other virtue holds but plain intellectual integrity."[33] Facts worth knowing were the sociologist's only stock in trade.
And yes, it was very difficult to live at a time when science undermined
the legitimacy of the religious truths that provided the answers sought by
a writer like Tolstoy. But that was the "fate of the times," and the sociologist still performed an invaluable role by offering the inconvenient facts
that "forced" people to ask the ultimate questions that no sociologist—as
a sociologist—could ever answer.

How did sociology do its job? Weber answered that question with a
precise definition of the discipline: "Sociology is a science which attempts
the interpretive understanding of social action in order thereby to arrive
at a causal explanation of its course and effects."[34] Focus on the words
action and *interpretive*. Weber is interested in action in the broadest sense;
it includes "all human behavior," yet action is social only when "one actor
takes account of the behavior of others and is thereby oriented in its
course." Walking is human behavior; I am in action when I power walk
each and every day. But that solitary action becomes social when, after
years of experience, I jump onto the sidewalk every time I see an SUV. I
am especially afraid—in Weber's terms I take particular "account"—of
SUVs driven by people holding a cup of coffee in one hand and their cell
phone in the other.

Interpretation is what sociologists do when they try to understand so-

cial action. Like the great ideas that supposedly come from nowhere, Weber understood that sociologists actually worked for their knowledge and
only achieved their aims through a process of interpretation. Social actions
"did not speak for themselves."[35] No one would or could offer instant and
precise explanations of complex human behaviors. But what sociologists
could do—and it was a great deal—was to try and grasp the subjective
meaning that individuals attached to their actions. When Lord Cardigan
rode into the valley of death wearing a cherry uniform full of fur, plumes,
and lace, what did the uniform mean to him at a subjective level? And
what did his colleagues and subordinates think of his costume? If we can
establish that they approved of his behavior, why did they do so? Was it
spontaneous or a matter of learning to like fur, lace, and plumes?

In interpreting the social actions of others, sociologists shelve (as much
as possible) their own beliefs and values. *Weber wanted to understand the
world as it is, not as it ought to be.*[36] In Weber's view, sociologists tried to
grasp the subjective meanings that people attached to their actions; by
definition, this was an approximation because the sociologist's interpretations always stood, like a great portal, between the actions of others and
the explanations ultimately offered by sociology. Mental distance always
impeded perfect understanding, but by deliberately shelving their own
values, sociologists could nevertheless achieve exceptional explanations
and understandings of the world that was, is, and will be.

Weber was highly ambitious. He focused on the biggest questions possible. Thus in laying his groundwork for concepts that could cut through
any society on earth, he describes four types of social action. First is "rational orientation to a system of discrete individual ends." When I see
SUVs during my early morning walks, I jump on the sidewalk (the means)
with a particular end in mind—survival. Especially if the SUV drivers are
drinking coffee *and* talking on the telephone, the street is the last place a
sane person wants to be. Second is "rational orientation to an absolute
value"; the value could be communism or nirvana, but all my rational
actions are directed only to achieving this absolute end. Here the means
can shift, but the end always remains the same. Third is "affectual orientation, especially emotion, determined by the specific effects and states
of feeling of the actor." Think of falling in love and the anxieties and
tensions that arise when you wonder if the other person also loves you.
Fourth is social action that is "traditionally oriented, through the habituation of long practice." Many families, for example, celebrate holidays by
going to the house of a particular relative. The house may be way out of
the way, and Aunt Sadie or Uncle Bill may not be the most beloved member of the family. Yet Thanksgiving would not be Thanksgiving unless we
all ate together at Sadie's or Bill's.[37]

With this typology of social action in place, Weber now moves to the
creation of "ideal types." Over the years these constructs have produced

great controversy, so I will try here to interpret what Weber (and not his critics) actually said. Remember his ambition. While he sought types that were always firmly rooted in historical fact, he also wanted to delineate concepts that cut across civilizations as wildly diverse as ancient China and eighteenth-century Europe. He understood—perfectly—that he sacrificed varying degrees of specificity by creating typologies of such enormous breath, but he also argued that the ideal, the "pure," typologies would meaningfully sensitize us to the types of social action *shared* by many millions of people, in different societies, even at distant points in human history.

This is a classic case of the proof being in the pudding, in the value of the concepts that Weber offered. So we need to precisely grasp his intent: "In *all* cases, rational or irrational, sociological analysis both abstracts from reality and at the same time helps us to understand it, in that it shows with what degree of approximation a concrete historical phenomenon can be subsumed under one or more of these concepts."[38]

One of Weber's justly famous essays, "Bureaucracy," focuses on the ideal typical bureaucracy. He specifies its characteristics wherever the phenomenon exists—for example, "there is the principle of fixed and official jurisdictional areas that are generally ordered by rules"—and with these details in mind he argues that we can understand the subjective meaning of social actions wherever bureaucracies exist or dominate.[39] For example, if the Department of Motor Vehicles represents "the concrete historical phenomenon," how different is your experience as you move through the fifty states? Each clerk stands below a sign that indicates their jurisdictional area, and as they push you from window to window—"that's not my area"—they remind you to read the documents that spell out the rules and regulations required to register a car or get a driver's license. Typically, the clerk is deliberately taught to see only a client or customer, and affective social action (a smile, too much emotion) is inhibited in the service of rationally and objectively (no preferences here) performing the job "by the book."

If those examples reflect your experiences, then Weber's "pure types" do sensitize us to forms of social action that are both widely shared and subjectively understandable. In fact, whether in Texas or New York, Montana or Florida, clerks who want to help—"I really do"—but nevertheless push you to another window are, typically, neither mean spirited nor malicious. They are simply behaving like bureaucrats, like people trained to indifferently perform a task "ordered by rules, that is, by laws or administrative regulations."[40]

Ideal types are both "abstract and general." They never describe a "concrete course of action, but a normatively ideal course, assuming certain ends and modes of normative orientation as binding on the actors."[41] The purity of Weber's concepts will always be sullied by the real world, by societies full of atypical cultural beliefs, unique personalities, and specific historical events and circumstances. Nonetheless, Weber still chose to use these types as his principal sociological tools because he wanted to do nothing less than conceptualize the monumental changes of his time. While that effort obviously required a significant degree of abstractness, Weber's principal goal was to provide more accurate maps of the way societies actually functioned and changed.

Recall Weber's intellectual opponents. In sharp contrast to Marx and Durkheim, Weber saw nothing as inevitable as the coming of communism or the eventual dominance of organic solidarity. Living in a disenchanted universe, Weber imposed no ultimate order on history. He tried to interpret the world as it was, not as it ought to be. Thus, despite their "purity," his types are firmly rooted in the facts of everyday life and the changes he perceived. Even a century later, his concepts arguably offer a degree of concreteness that neither Marx nor Durkheim ever achieved. They are the interpretive schemes of a scientist who, for years, focused on history and then decided to be a sociologist.

THE TYPES OF AUTHORITY AND IMPERATIVE COORDINATION

In approximately 1580 the French philosopher Michel de Montaigne wrote an essay titled "On Cannibals." Explorers returning from the "New World" told stories of strange people who ate one another. His contemporaries thought the natives behaved like barbarians, but Montaigne had serious doubts. Discussing the tortures and burnings at the stake of his time, he argued that there is "more barbarity in roasting a man bit by bit" than in eating him once he is dead. Montaigne was so open minded that he even discussed his conversations with a captive brought to Europe by the Portuguese. The fellow was startled by this fact: Why did "so many grown men, bearded, strong, and armed" obey the will of a child? What made adults accept the authority of a boy they called the king?[42]

Those questions go to the root of Weber's three types of authority. He is interested in what legitimates the domination of a child over men. He wants to grasp—in their pure form—the beliefs, values, and practices that allow people to accept and obey particular forms of political, religious, military, educational, familial, and economic authority. And for those of us who are as haughty as Montaigne's contemporaries, why did Americans, especially during the Vietnam War, legitimate beliefs as questionable as "my country right or wrong but my country," "my president right or wrong but my president"? The logic of these statements is that if you jump off the bridge, I will follow; yet young men used these beliefs to legitimate the political and military authority of the officials who sent them to fight and die in Vietnam.

In *The Theory of Social and Economic Organization*, Weber analyzes three types of authority: charismatic, traditional, and legal-rational. As if the axis of a planet in its orbit, societies revolve around these types of authority. In principle, a particular type can spread through all the institutions and practices of the United States in 2002 or Germany in 1902.

Charisma refers "to a certain quality of an individual by virtue of which he [or she] is set apart from ordinary men and treated as those endowed with supernatural, superhuman, or at least specifically exceptional powers or qualities."[43] The pure type of charismatic authority is always a religious leader, and the exact quality is impossible to discern because charisma refers to a *relationship* between the person claiming to be special and those who accept that claim. For example, the African-American leader Malcolm X was handsome, intelligent, articulate, and a workaholic. Elijah Muhammad, the spiritual leader of the Black Muslim religion, was small and not especially good looking, and he spoke with a squeaky voice. Yet it is Malcolm X who tells us that this "little, gentle, sweet man" was the messenger of Allah. He saved Malcolm X, and thus "I have pledged on my knees to Allah to tell the white man about his crimes and the black man the true teachings of our Honorable Elijah Muhammad. I don't care if it costs my life."[44]

"It is the recognition on the part of those subject to authority which is decisive for the validity of charisma."[45] When I was a boy living in New York, my friends and I would often go to Times Square to listen to individuals who claimed they were God. Many of the speakers gave eloquent presentations, but so far as I know, none of us became converts. Our disbelief meant that these gods never came to life. In essence the individuals lacked charisma because we refused to recognize their claims to it.

In charisma's religious form, the charismatic leader comes with a mission. Elijah Muhammad taught that the world was soon coming to an end and that he was the "messenger" issuing the clarion call of God: follow me and you will be saved. If you believed what he said, recognition signaled that it was your *duty* to accept, above all else, the authority of the charismatic figure. Remember, for example, the boxer Muhammad Ali's refusal to accept military service during the Vietnam War. The law said he must go, but for this devout Muslim, the authority of the charismatic figure superceded the authority of the law. *Nothing* is more important than the word of the charismatic figure if we recognize his or her claim and the teachings that always accompany that claim.[46]

"Charismatic authority is thus specifically outside the realm of everyday routine and the profane sphere."[47] In its pure religious form, it is the only type of authority recognized; and whatever rules and norms exist are determined by the charismatic authority in the course of fulfilling his or her message. In Montana the many followers of Prophet Claire moved from California because "Mother" predicted that earthquakes would soon drag California into the sea. And soon after they built their new home in Montana, followers once hid in mountainous bunkers for a full week. She had predicted the end of the world, and they obediently waited for an end that never arrived. Her charismatic authority initially reigned supreme, but when the predictions failed, many followers left the fold. Charisma is a relationship, and if the charismatic leader fails to deliver, followers can disperse as quickly as a flock of frightened sheep.[48]

By definition charismatic authority is short-lived. Rooted in the individual whose charisma is recognized, the authority presumably dies when the messenger or prophet passes on. However, Weber is especially insightful when he discusses the routinization of charisma. This seems like a contradiction in terms; how can you routinize authority that is individual and at times whimsical? Weber's answer is that the movement must do so if the group is to survive the death of its charismatic leader. So, like Jesus with Saint Peter, "the original charismatic leader" can designate "his own successor and his recognition on the part of his followers." In Roman Catholicism the now-traditional authority of the pope still rests on the passing of the charismatic mantle by Jesus. Compare this with the death of Muhammad. Because no recognized successor existed, the Muslim religion spilt into parts—Sunni and Shiite Muslims—that are still battling one another almost 1,400 years after the death of Muhammad in 632. The Shiites believe that Muhammad's son-in-law should have succeeded him, while the Sunnites believe the first four caliphs after Muhammad were "rightly guided" by the word of the now-dead charismatic leader.[49]

Weber knew that charismatic authority was an exceptional phenomenon. Yet, when the relationship exists, it is as powerful and all-pervasive a form of domination as traditional or legal-rational authority. Equally important, with examples as diverse as David Koresh in Texas and Shōkō Asahara (with the Aum) in Japan, it is quite clear that Weber delineated an ideal type that is as real today as it was a century or a millennium ago.

The following illustrates the second authority type, *traditional* authority. During the Opium War (1840–42), the English battled a Chinese army even more bound by tradition than its own. In front of the soldiers that approached the English, the Chinese sent warriors "brandishing swords in both hands and uttering strange cries varied by terms of opprobrium." Some soldiers took a break by performing Olympic quality somersaults on their way to the attack, and the best warriors defended themselves against modern weapons by using "rattan shields painted with the head of devils or ferocious animals." Soldiers also wore "tiger-head caps when they could get them"; meanwhile, their commanders, who "prided themselves on their calligraphy," prepared a strategy that included writing victory announcements in verse before the battle began.[50]

Weber writes that "a system of imperative co-ordination will be called *traditional* if legitimacy is claimed for it and believed in on the basis of the sanctity of order and the attendant powers of control as they have been handed down from the past, *have always existed*" (emphasis added).[51] The Chinese who faced the English always fought with swords, fiercely painted shields, and a strategy laced with beautiful calligraphy. The English—for all the ridiculousness of their system—fought with many modern weapons and a level of rationality that far exceeded the strategy and tactics used by the Chinese. As if a dinosaur footprint in stone, the Chinese army froze its level of development. It somersaulted forward by looking in the rearview mirror of tradition. Like many of the armies encountered by European colonialists in South America and Africa, one crucial reason the Chinese fell so easily was that they revered the past—the norms and practices that had always existed.

In discussing traditional authority, Weber makes a bold assertion: "In prerationalistic periods, tradition and charisma between them have almost exhausted the whole of the orientation of action."[52] Weber offers no specific year or century indicating the beginning of the end for traditions. Although one could easily come up with a number of arbitrary dates (e.g., Galileo's proof that the sun, not the earth, was the center of the universe)[53] Weber's contention underlines his desire to delineate precisely yesterday and today, rational from nonrational societies. Because the legitimacy of traditions is the *root orientation of thought* for the vast majority of societies that have ever existed, traditions help us to understand obedience to authority in entities as different as the family in ancient Persia and the divine right of kings in seventeenth- and eighteenth-century Europe.

Under traditional authority, "obedience is not owed to enacted rules but to the person who occupies a position of authority by tradition or who has been chosen for such a position on a traditional basis." Weber is very careful to leave room for "personal decision," for the force of a powerful personality. However, once traditions are in the saddle, they dominate the exercise of authority and constrain even the most forceful and beloved of kings. When he came to the throne, Louis XIV harbored great ambitions, yet he also understood "that the King's power to command and to exact obedience was strictly limited in a society in which there were many stubborn wills to be reconciled and many traditions to be recognized." For example, if Louis seriously threatened the ancient prerogatives of the aristocracy, he would simultaneously undermine his own authority. Both the king and his court dominated because traditions legitimated their power and privileges; challenge the counts and marquises of the land and you challenged yourself.[54]

From the perspective of science and reason, the social organization of a traditional society always includes many irrational or nonrational elements. Incumbents, for example, receive positions of political, military, or family authority not because of technical training or personal competence but because traditions dictate that authority figures must be members of, for example, particular families, religions, tribes, ethnicities, or genders. Intelligence or ability is beside the point because thought is oriented to what was and must be. In Rwanda, being a Hutu or a Tutsi explains a great deal about who does what and who gets what.[55] Moreover, from a rational point of view, it is utterly irrational to exclude systematically more than half of the human race (i.e., women) from positions of political, military, economic, educational, religious, and familial authority. However, until very recently, women never broke free of the traditions that limited what they can and cannot do—according to tradition, according to what people have always done.

Although traditions are, by definition, barriers to social change, Weber made no value judgment about the worthiness of traditions versus laws and rules and regulations. His aim was to compare and contrast and, in the process, force readers to raise a series of possibly inconvenient facts about the way the world works. Thus, if traditions stop change, that could be a very good thing. Instead of fancy uniforms, modern soldiers wear camouflage gear; they blend into the background because bright uniforms make anyone an easy target. While clothing that hides the soldier makes great sense, when a society uses reason and science to foster the arts of war, one result is a world of nuclear weapons. In the world's war colleges, we have actually institutionalized the search for scientifically better ways to kill one another. The ultimate *irrationality* is that, as a result of using science, we can now drop the nuclear weapons that, as they destroy the enemy, simultaneously destroy us with fallout, genetic mutations, and nuclear winter.[56]

With his three types of authority, Weber offers us the conceptual tools required for comparing one society or one period with another. He wants to flesh out the root differences, especially in his analysis of the third type, *legal-rational authority.* "The effectiveness of legal [rational] authority rests on the acceptance of the validity of the following mutually interdependent ideas."[57]

• Officials establish legal norms "by agreement or by imposition, on grounds of expediency or rational values or both."

• Every body of law or regulations contains "essentially a consistent system of abstract rules which have normally been intentionally established," for example, by a legislature or a university office of student affairs. Administration of justice consists "in the application of these rules to particular cases."

• The typical person in a position of authority "occupies an office." That person issues commands to others and is also subject to the *impersonal* order of the laws he or she enforces and obeys. For example, if a university administrator violates the contract while disciplining a faculty member, he or she is guilty (or not guilty) in relation to the impersonal rules—one size fits all—established by said contract.

• The person "who obeys authority does so, as is usually stated, only in his capacity as a member of the corporate group and what he obeys is only the law or the rules and regulations." At home or at play, work rules hold no sway; for example, once discharged from the army or navy, I am no longer subject to its laws and codes.

• Finally, and arguably most important, people who obey a police officer, a judge, or a dean do not owe obedience to the person as an individual but to the *impersonal order* that the authority figure represents. I obey the law, not the person; and when I, as a town official, enforce zoning regulations that forbid this or that type of structure, I enforce and you obey the impersonal body of rules that we both find in the town's body of approved procedures for residential construction.[58]

In presenting the preceding list of interdependent characteristics as an ordered list, I have tried to give a feel for what Weber means by legal-rational authority. With just cause, critics note that many modern office buildings look like filing cabinets. There is a place for everything and everything in its place. The rules are objective; they theoretically apply in the same way (one size fits all); and officials interpret, enforce, and continually improve those rules based on the competence they acquired when, in sharp contrast to traditional societies, they received specific training—often for as much as six or eight years.

Despite their impersonality, laws (and rules and regulations) offer societies a much greater degree of flexibility than other forms of overarching authority. Where followers look to the charismatic leader and traditions look backwards, laws allow a society to create norms that more accurately reflect the world that is there. If, as with the great scandal surrounding the Texas-based Enron Corporation, legislators believe that business auditors need much tighter regulation, they can easily create new laws that (theoretically) eliminate the dangers suddenly obvious to all. If our beliefs about sexual orientation change, lawmakers can pass (as in Vermont) a bill that legitimates marriage and adoptions for gay Americans. Finally, after the hideous attacks of September 11, 2001, observers perceived canyonlike holes in U.S. airport security. They then quickly passed national legislation that specifically mandates, among other things, much greater training for airport security personnel.

This is sensible, reasonable, and intelligent. In fact, rules and regulations offer such a flexible tool for order and change that Weber makes the following argument: "The decisive reason for the advance of bureaucratic organization has always been its technical superiority over any form of organization." Think of Lord Cardigan or the somersaulting Chinese soldiers when you read this line: "The fully developed bureaucratic mechanism compares with other organizations exactly as does the machine with the non-mechanical modes of production."[59]

In accounting for the juggernaut march of legal-rational authority, Weber focuses on the principle of rationalization. With Durkheim, he grasps the importance of the division of labor in creating (for government as well as business) organizations that use reason and logic as the building blocks of social organization. Moreover, with Marx, he perceives the effects of capitalism in, for example, impersonally separating the worker from the means of production. However, while always arguing that *many* factors account for social change, Weber nevertheless concludes that behind the centuries-long transformation of religious, military, political, familial, educational, and economic institutions lies the dominating force of rationalization. Once people start to ask, "Does it make sense? Is it logical to behave that way?" both thought processes and social institutions fall to the power of reason as harshly as pins to the bowler of a perfect strike.[60]

Under legal-rational authority, root thought processes celebrate values like logic, efficiency, competence, calculation, precision, exactness, punctuality, impersonality, and a deliberate dehumanization of everyday life. Weber himself witnessed a ghastly example of dehumanization when he visited the United States in 1904. He saw how Chicago trolleys killed or maimed 400 passengers a year, yet he perfectly grasped the inhuman rationale offered by the owners who refused to buy new cars. Each death cost the company $5,000; an injury cost $10,000. Multiply the costs of the deaths and injuries, compare that cost to the cost of safe machinery, and the passengers must continue to die. It was simply cheaper that way.[61]

On rare occasions Weber let his beliefs appear. In a line written in 1904, he notes that "for the last stage of this cultural development, it might well be truly said: Specialists without spirit, sensualists without heart; this nullity imagines that it has attained a level of civilization never before achieved."[62] Weber never liked everything he saw; but the force of rationalization was so powerful that he correctly predicted its increasing dominance throughout the twentieth century.

Critics argue that Weber's pure concepts neglect the complex realities of real life. In any actual corporation or government office, people often receive positions based on who they are, or whom they know, rather than what they know. As in any society on earth, the United States continues to prefer less-qualified people for a variety of positions. Veterans, for example, can score lower on a wide assortment of civil service exams and still get the job. In many of the United States' finest universities, "legacies" (the sons and daughters of alumni) receive a lovely letter of admission even though their scores are substantially lower than their competitors' are. In addition, in many universities and businesses, seniority—rather than competence—is a major criterion in awarding everything from office space to office hours.

Recite these criticisms, and you fight with a straw man. Weber understood the complexities of actual life, but his focus was always on the *orientation* of thought—on what legitimates a person's right to a position of authority. Thus, in the continuing and controversial battle about affirmative action, opponents argue that giving preference to women or minorities violates the accepted legitimacy of legal-rational authority. Merit—what you know and can do—is the only acceptable basis for offering people a position in any modern organization. Quite paradoxically, this critique ignores the accepted preferences cited previously (e.g., veterans, seniority, and legacies), but from Weber's perspective, the key factor remains the orientation of thought. Oppose affirmative action because the most competent person failed to get the job, and you affirm the legitimacy of legal-rational authority and the values it celebrates.

The pure types sensitize us to the real world and allow us to perceive not only our own contradictions but also the dilemmas between competing values and orientations. Since at least 1890, for example, the United States gives preferences to immigrants based on the value of family reunification. Even today far more close relatives of U.S. immigrants enter the United States than those who possess the skills needed for the U.S. economy. In purely rational terms, we should welcome only those who have the needed competencies.[63] In real life the values compete, but the differences are so obvious only because we have the luxury of using Weber's conceptual tools.

For all their problems and impersonality, laws (and rules and regulations) do help eliminate many of the biases and prejudices that exist anywhere on earth. Indeed, to the extent that laws and rules treat everyone in the same fashion, they offer an ideal that is as rational as a meritocracy. The problem, however, is to wear a blindfold and not see the religious, tribal, ethnic, gender, age, class, and other variables that, like glue, often stick to our thought processes.

Except for a rare slip of the tongue, Weber made no judgments about the best world or the most equitable society. His only aim as a sociologist was to offer us the possibility of greater clarity about the ultimate meaning of our existences and our world. In Weber's opinion only we, as struggling human beings, can resolve the conflicting legitimacies and values.

THE PROTESTANT ETHIC AND THE SPIRIT OF CAPITALISM

Weber's *The Sociology of Religion* was first published in 1922.[64] In sharp contrast to Karl Marx, Weber stresses the crucial significance of religious beliefs, values, and practices in explaining human behavior. Thus, Weber analyzes everything from the rise of religions to the idea of God to the different roads to salvation. His *Sociology of Religion* stands on its own as a significant contribution to our understanding of the relationship between "this world," the one inhabited by people, and the "other worlds" (Heaven, Hades, Hell, Nirvana), the ones inhabited by the gods.

In *The Protestant Ethic and the Spirit of Capitalism* (1904) Weber links his interest in religion to his belief in the multiple causes of social change. He then asks a series of truly provocative questions. Suppose that religion influenced the economy as much as the economy influenced religion. And suppose a scholar could prove that capitalism itself had deep roots in religious beliefs and practices. Would that not be a wonderful irony of Western intellectual history, that the development of the capitalism depicted by Marx was significantly influenced by the religious forces that Marx disregarded as much as the factory owner ignored the well-being of his workers?

These are great questions, so Weber begins by sounding just like Karl Marx. "Capitalism is identical with the pursuit of profit, and forever *renewed* profit, by means of continuous, rational, capitalistic enterprise. For it must be so: in a wholly capitalistic order of society, an individual capitalistic enterprise which did not take advantage of its opportunities for profit-making would be doomed to extinction" (emphasis in original).[65]

Competition drives each capitalist to search out any and all sources of profit. Although that is a fundamental aspect of the system, Weber focuses on the *spirit* of capitalism. Citing figures like Benjamin Franklin—with his dictum that "time is money"—Weber argues that the spiritual "essence of the matter" is the pursuit of money as an end in itself. In precapitalist periods, economic acquisition was "subordinated to the satisfaction of material needs"; under capitalism the "natural" situation totally reverses itself. People now seek to make as much money as possible, oblivious to anything but acquiring mountains of wealth. The *duty* to accumulate riches is "thought of so purely as an end in itself, that from the point of view of the happiness of, or utility to the individual, it appears entirely transcendental and absolutely irrational."[66]

So far, Weber sounds like Marx's echo. The difference arises in accounting for a capitalist spirit that pursues profit with irrational exuberance. To understand why capitalists work with the zealousness of a true believer, Weber begins with Martin Luther's notion of the "calling." As a matter of faith, the Catholic Church sent its best and brightest to monasteries and nunneries, where, incidentally, they took a vow of *poverty*. It was obviously quite hard to be a successful capitalist if religious ideals preached penury rather than profit. However, once Luther tacked his protests to the cathedral door, he told other protestants "that the fulfillment of duty in worldly affairs was the highest form which the moral activity of the individual could assume." Luther puts God's imprimatur on the activities of everyday life when he teaches that "the only way of living acceptably to God was not to surpass worldly morality in monastic asceticism, but solely through the fulfillment of the obligations imposed upon the individual by his position in the world. That was his calling."[67]

Luther took his followers out of the monasteries and nunneries. Calvin turned them into capitalists. Calvin agrees that this worldly activity is God's desire, but with Calvinism, believers approach a God "who does not exist for men but men for the sake of god." Only a select few can possibly discern the little that God has decided to reveal. The vast majority exist with precious little divine knowledge, and they should never assume that their actions have anything to with their ultimate destination in the next world. Calvinists learned that "to apply earthly standards of justice to His sovereign decrees is meaningless and an insult to His Majesty, since He and He alone is free, i.e., is subject to no law."[68]

The God of Calvinism leaves people utterly alone and utterly vulnerable. Only the select know history's cosmological trajectory, and their news is bad news: God decided everyone's ultimate home in heaven or hell before they were born. Everyone's eternal fate was settled from eternity because God *predestined* the few who would be saved and the endless multitude whom God indifferently condemned to damnation. In the most important question to any person living through the Reformation—what happens when I die?—Catholics received everyday assurances from priests, penance, sacraments, and the community of the Church. Calvinists not only got no help at all, they even had to do without God: "For even Christ had died only for the elect, for whose benefit God had decreed his martyrdom from eternity."[69]

Calvinists also rejected any "magical means" of eliciting God's favor or discerning his will. Serious Calvinists actually buried their dead "without song or ritual in order that no superstition, no trust in the effects of magical and sacramental forces should creep in." The result was a religion that expressed a decided antipathy toward sensuous forces of all sorts. Ultimately, Weber coined the lovely term "inner worldly ascetic"; like a monk who wore a hair shirt, the Calvinist lived a life of abstinence, a life free of everyday comforts and extravagances. However, unlike a monk, Calvinists lived in this world, totally dedicating their time to ascetically serving a God who had, given their slim odds of election to heaven, condemned them to hell long before they appeared on earth.[70]

In Europe Calvinists (and Methodists and Baptists) competed with other religions; in the New World, they established their sects free of the weight of the past. In fact, as the cornerstone of Puritan America, Calvinism was also a cornerstone in creating colonial culture, the world that eventually turned into the United States. Because Weber is tracking the root beliefs of the most successful capitalist society on earth, he focuses his attention on the Calvinist's sociopsychological reaction to the doctrine of predestination and the necessity of living without any help from sacraments, magic, penance, or even religious hymns.

In theory, Calvinists were obligated to assume their membership in the tiny group of God's elect. In reality, they experienced never-ending anxiety because they lived their entire lives with no certain answer to the only question that really mattered: Was I (forget my spouse or children) going to heaven or hell? One response was to find sinners. Think of Nathaniel Hawthorne's *The Scarlet Letter.* By sewing the "A" (for adulterer) on her dress, Hester becomes a living source of solace to the rest of the community. You feel better when you can pin God's hellish judgment on someone else's frame; instead of "there but for the grace of God go I," the Calvinist looks at the scarlet A and says, "What a relief; she is going to hell."

Sinners helped. They made Calvinists feel more secure. Nevertheless, Weber sees the real—religious—roots of the spirit of capitalism in the need to find, beside sinners, everyday signs of election to heaven. Weber's argument is that the only way Calvinists could feel secure about their destiny was by material success in this world. If you did well in Massachusetts, that was God's way of telling you that heaven was your final resting place. Weber stresses that this was a sociopsychological reaction to the Calvinist's predestined predicament. "The Calvinist . . . himself creates his own salvation, or, as would be more correct, *the conviction of it*" (emphasis added).[71]

The problem is that the anxiety is never ending. You will never know your actual destination until the day you die. So, as if a perpetually self-sustaining mine of energy and effort, the Calvinist's anxiety moves him or her to work harder and harder to achieve the enormous wealth that can never completely allay the fear propelling the furious effort in the first place. Remember, too, that the condemnation of sensuous and spiritual means of salvation leaves the Calvinist with work and this worldly success as the only source of spiritual solace. For Weber many all-American traits (e.g., being a workaholic) trace their ancestry to the Calvinists' need to work like the devil in order to know they were destined to live with the angels.

At one point Weber uses the phrase "acquisitive machines."[72] It catches the essence of his argument, especially if we recall that Calvinists were self-made. Because God predestined all human beings, no one could help you, and you could not help anyone else, even the closest members of your own family. Arguably, the American focus on individualism and making it on your own also have at least partial roots in the religious beliefs and practices of the earliest English settlers. In Weber's apt summary, the Puritan outlook "favored the development of a rational bourgeois economic life; it was the most important, and above all the only consistent influence in the development of that life. It stood at the cradle of the modern economic man."[73]

But what happened when the economic man grew up? Weber argues that the forces of rationalization—the disenchantment of the universe—eventually undermined the validity of religious beliefs. As with Benjamin Franklin, the Enlightenment turned true believers into skeptics. Americans soon placed religion in the background, but they still methodically embraced a culture that fostered the values, beliefs, and practices so essential to capitalist success. "The Puritan wanted to work in a calling; we are forced to do so. For when asceticism was carried out of monastic cells into everyday life, and began to dominate worldly morality, it did its part in building the tremendous cosmos of the modern economic order."[74]

Note Weber's language. The Puritan ethic did "its part" in building the modern economic order. Also crucial were the process of rationalization and "the technical and economic conditions of machine production which today determine the lives of all the individuals who are born into this mechanism . . . with irresistible force." Weber never saw one factor that moved history or one factor that, all alone, created the spirit of capitalism. What he does argue is that as religion lost its legitimacy, "the spirit of religious asceticism escaped from the cage." Calvin frowned on material goods; in Weber's time America celebrated the Gilded Age, a period in which industrialists like Gould, Fisk, and Vanderbilt flaunted their wealth and possessions with all the power at their disposal.[75] It is as if, when the industrial revolution occurred, the Calvinists gave Americans a gigantic head start; their religious ethic laid the foundation for a set of (eventually) secular beliefs that preached a methodical devotion to success in this world, achieved through a ceaseless devotion to hard and never-ending work.

Weber never liked what he saw. He even noted that new economic order might determine people "until the last ton of fossilized coal is burnt." That was prophetic indeed, but from a sociological perspective, Weber's book brilliantly served two purposes. First, it showed that religion could influence the economy as much as the economy influenced religion. Marx was wrong, and that was that. Equally important were the unintended consequences of human behavior. Calvinists certainly never meant to help produce an economic system that endorsed everything from luxury to hedonism. Yet that was their legacy. So, as Weber suggests, beware of precise prophecies. No one knows exactly what will happen "at the end of this tremendous development." Sociology can sensitize us and provide crucial clues; but as with the Calvinist legacy, human beings are so cantankerous that they can even turn a religious ethic into the spirit of capitalism.[76]

SOCIAL CLASS AND SOCIAL HONOR

When Max and Marianne Weber visited the United States in 1904, they stopped in Tuskegee, Alabama, to see the college made famous by the work of Booker T. Washington. "What they found probably moved them more than anything else on their trip. The great national problem of all American life, the showdown between the white race and the former slaves, could here be grasped at its roots." So-called mixed-race Americans rapidly increased as a part of the total population, yet the "master race" of whites treated them so abominably "that they were excluded from the [Tuskegee] community as though they bore a stigma." In law slavery no longer existed; in reality the mixed children did every nasty job imaginable, but "anyone who played host to a mulatto thereby permanently removed himself from association with his own race."[77]

Thirty years after the Webers visited Tuskegee, the college's board of trustees met for one of its scheduled meetings. Local officials returned home after the day's events while outsiders stayed overnight. The white trustees roomed at the prestigious "campus guest house, Dorothy Hall." The black trustees "stayed in student dormitories." And although the trustees met together to conduct business, "the whites were served in the Dorothy Hall dining room and the blacks ate in the faculty dining room." There they at least ate on time; however, when the black trustees used the trains to come to Tuskegee, they arrived for dinner "only after the third call and then only behind a curtain drawn around a few tables at the end of the car, separating black from white."[78]

Weber understood the prejudice that still poisons American life. He grasped as well the complex nature of social stratification in any society on earth. The essence of social ordering is power and privilege.[79] Those with the power get the privileges; those without it ignominiously eat leftovers behind curtains. In an essay titled "Class, Status, and Party," Weber shows that the basis of social power included, besides economic variables, something called social honor. He writes that "we wish to designate as 'status situation' every typical component of the life fate of men that is determined by a positive or negative social estimation of honor."[80]

Human beings typically inherited cultures mandating that certain groups of people possessed—at birth—social honor and that others (as members of a group) did not. When Marianne Weber writes about the "stigma" attached to mulattos, she underlines the lack of honor that attached to those youngsters long before they got a job or engaged in any form of economic enterprise. Instead of the bottom rung of the ladder of success, they never even got a chance to climb because, as "half breeds," mulattos often encountered as much rejection from blacks as they did from whites.[81]

Weber argues that questions of social honor played a powerful role in building and sustaining the social stratification system of virtually every precapitalist society. While European aristocrats offered an obvious example, in *The Religion of India* Weber analyzes a stratification system of castes that had its roots in questions of honor determined by *religious* beliefs and values. For example, the casteless untouchables represented a substantial minority of the Indian people, but they were born with such an absolute lack of social honor that they needed to maintain, at all times, ninety-nine feet of distance between themselves and the highest caste, the

Brahmins. "By some rules an Untouchable had to shout a warning before entering a street so that all the holier folk could get out of the way of his contaminating shadow." In other instances the untouchable needed to maintain a low voice because even the sound of his could thoroughly "pollute" the ears of a Brahmin.[82]

Whether rooted in the prejudices of religion or biology, groups of people, as groups, initially gain wealth, power, and privilege from other than economic sources. Weber once again tries to correct Marx, especially when he argues that for most of human history, any status situation also included "a specific style of life that can be expected from all those who wish to belong to the circle."[83] The lower groups often imitate the trends, styles, fashions, and practices set by their betters; the stratification system maintains and nurtures itself by this imitation and by the prior acceptance of the society's inherited basis for according social honor to particular groups of people.

When he turns to social class, Weber sounds very much like Karl Marx. Market situation determines class situation; that is, in a society dominated by capitalism, you climbed the ladder of social classes because of your "power to dispose of goods and services for the sake of income." If you owned property (e.g., a factory or a farm), you had power; if you did not, you worked for the wages paid by property owners and under the conditions set by property owners. Equally important, your power to dispose of your goods and services also determined your chance for "a supply of goods, external living conditions and personal life experiences."[84]

Given sufficient income, you could live in the best suburbs and have the opportunity to buy the freshest, juiciest fruits and vegetables. Trees lined the streets and the lawns offered a manicured precision because the lower classes properly cut the grass. As the hired hands worked, parents used Range Rovers to drive their children to gymnastics classes in the early morning and fine arts classes in the late afternoon. Income determined your access to this lifestyle; indeed, when the working classes returned to their crowded communities in the congested cities, that only reemphasized that "property and lack of property" determined where you lived, whom you met, and what you did with your time.[85]

Whether discussing status groups or social classes, Weber uses the word "fate." Each of these forms of social stratification produced such an arbitrary and powerful impact on people's lives that, despite all the persistence and tenacity a person could manage, class situation or social honor could alone determine the ultimate outcome of any person's existence.[86]

What makes Weber's analysis especially important is that in sharp contrast to Marx, he stresses that "class distinctions are linked in the most varied way with status distinctions."[87] For the purposes of analysis, a sociologist can discuss one factor separated from the other. In real life the two basic sources of power and privilege are as intermingled as the knots in a fine rug. For example, an individual who owns a series of successful adult video shops certainly has the power to dispose of his or her goods in return for large amounts of income. Such a person may live in the best neighborhoods, but the minute that individual indicates the source of his or her income, questions of status honor appear. The person—and the person's family—suddenly lacks honor because of the source of their undeniable wealth.

Another example appears in the work of the sociologist William Julius Wilson. He initially argued that in the United States, race was of declining significance in explaining the economic success or failure of African Americans. However, in *When Work Disappears* (published in 1996), Wilson forcefully explains that "employers make assumptions about the inner-city black workers *in general* and reach decisions based on those assumptions before they have had a chance to review systematically the qualifications of an individual applicant." Lacking social honor, the "net effect" for African Americans is that they often fail to get even an entry-level position because prejudice acts to "screen them out" before any interview or examination occurs.[88]

In Tuskegee in 1904 or Chicago in 1996, the African American's lack of social honor acts as an institutionalized impediment to power and privilege. Combine this with the relative absence of any jobs in many of America's central cities, and you see the continuing significance of prejudice and Weber's correction of Marx. In the real world class and status group distinctions *together* produce the most varied outcomes. In the case of the rich owner of adult video stores, the two variables work against one another. In the case of the African American living in inner-city Chicago, the two factors work together in a terribly negative fashion. And in the case of the successful child of old-money Protestants, the class and honor factors produce Americans at the very top of our social stratification system.

Fate can be determined from birth. Weber's continuing significance rests on an explanation of social stratification that always includes economic *and* social honor variables.

"POLITICS AS A VOCATION"

After their nation's disastrous defeat in World War I, Germans asked every imaginable political question. A colleague of Weber's noted that "we have turned from being Monarchists at heart to being Republicans by reason." Weber entered the political fray with a speech titled "Politics as a Vocation."[89] He now taught at the University of Munich (he accepted the position in 1918), and he tried to offer his students a perspective that eclipsed the ideological battles that then—and now—attracted the greatest attention. Weber focused on the hard truths of political life in any society, at any time; his essay seems a perfect way to end the present discussion because Weber's arguments and insights are especially poignant in the twenty-first century. After only three years of the new millennium, our world already boasts as much political turmoil and violence as the Germany of 1918.

Weber starts slowly. "A state is a human community that (successfully) claims the *monopoly of the legitimate use of physical force* within a given territory." Territory is important because, while other officials (e.g., police or the National Guard) often get the right to use force, that right exists only to the extent that the state permits it. "The state is considered the sole source of the right to use violence. Hence, politics for us means striving to share power or striving to influence the distribution of power, either among states or among groups within a state."[90]

How do you make the striving for power—politics—a vocation? Weber states that while the contrast is by no means exclusive, a person can live "for" politics or "off" politics. Many people love power and its trappings, the offices, the adulation, the hand shaking (think of former President Clinton), the chance to decide the fate of nations. It is a psychological high, but the person lives "for" politics only if he or she can afford to do so. Weber stresses that any politician who "lives under the dominance of private property" needs wealth to enjoy the luxury of focusing only on the fate of nations and their citizenry. Thus, U.S. political administrations throughout the twentieth century included any number of "dollar-a-year" politicians. They never needed a real job, and neither do many current members of the U.S. Senate. John Kerry (D., Mass.) is our richest senator with a bottom-line net worth of $550 million dollars, but Jay Rockefeller (D., W.Va.) has $200 million of his family's fortune, and Barbara Feinstein (D., Calif.) needs to get along on a mere $50 million of wealth derived from, among other sources, a series of trust funds.[91]

Most politicians live "off" politics. They actually need to work for a living, so they receive their paycheck from public funds. Individuals (e.g., governors or mayors) earn income, but "all party struggles are struggles for the patronage of office, as well as struggles for objective goals."[92] In Weber's essay, these lines appear with all the surprise of the sun in August. Weber is not a cynic; he is a sociological realist. People need to eat, and if you want them to spend all their time engaged in politics, expect them to want money, and expect political parties to use the lure of a job to influence everything from votes to the shaping of local and national policies. Political payrolls are normal because only the wealthy live "for" politics. The rest of us live off it, and if that is dirty or unsavory, open your eyes and savor the pork that is as essential to politics as the love of power and the need to use force.

Weber's arguments spotlight one of our contemporary political debates: the need for campaign finance reform. To advertise on television, today's politicians need money; the politicians who live "off" politics are especially needy. No money equals no serious campaign equals no job in Congress or the state legislature. Pressed by their constituents—and a series of scandals—some politicians my actually press for reform; meanwhile, the large majority resist it because, living "off" politics, they need to finance the campaigns that become more and more expensive with each passing year. New York's Mayor Michael Bloomberg recently spent (in 2001) more than $60 million of his own money to achieve victory; how can the average politician match that without the contributions that corrupt or a system of public financing of all elections? That is our dilemma, but as Weber suggests, the great irony is that politicians who live "off" politics will significantly shape the legislation that theoretically curtails or erases the source of their political and economic well-being.

Weber criticizes political "infants." Money is one problem, but he returns to the issue of violence when he distinguishes between an "ethic of ultimate ends" and an "ethic of responsibility." An ethic of ultimate ends is not necessarily identical with an ethic of irresponsibility. A believer in communism or (later) Nazism carries "the flame of pure intentions"; their ardor fuels their politics and a type of reasoning that easily argues that the end justifies the means. Discussing socialists during World War I, Weber explained to his Munich students that the socialists accepted "some more years of war" because the avalanche of deaths promised the social crisis needed to usher in the rule of socialism and equality.[93]

Weber challenges any ethic of ultimate ends by citing the incredible dilemma posed by Dostoyevsky in *The Brothers Karamazov:* Would you kill one innocent child if that death promised a world without violence? Answer with a "yes," and Weber argues that you refuse to face "the ethical irrationality of the world." True believers conjure up wonderful rationalizations, but "from no ethics in the world can it be concluded when and to what extent the ethically good purpose justifies the ethically dangerous means and ramifications."[94] An "ethic of responsibility" understands that "he who lets himself in for politics, that is, for power and force as means, contracts with diabolical powers and for his action it is *not* true that good can follow only from good and evil only from evil, but that often the opposite is true. Anyone who fails to see this is, indeed, a political infant."[95]

Some might argue that those are the words of a political conservative. Others would contend that Weber rooted his conclusions in an accurate reading of history. For example, in the civil war now raging in Colombia, both revolutionary and counterrevolutionary forces subscribe to an ethic of ultimate ends. In the name of communism and "the old order," each slaughters civilians with ease, but the counterrevolutionary forces win the prize for cruelty—they are now beheading people with chain saws. Meanwhile the United States provides the Colombian government with military assistance, but even the best intentions produced dreadfully unexpected results. Our military allies assist the counterrevolutionaries, and they use our gasoline to do it. A recent study by the Government Accounting Office indicates that U.S. officials cannot account for 20 percent of the gasoline (469,000 gallons) given to the Colombians between 1995 and 1999. The good news is that the counterrevolutionaries only got part of the gas; some of it went to the forces growing the cocaine our assistance supposedly stopped. Between 1995 and 1999 Colombia doubled its production of cocaine, and *all* parties to the civil war now actively and profitably participate in its growing.[96]

Weber offers insights that are hard to take. His world of "ethical irrationality" is arguably still very much our own. "However, it is immensely moving when a *mature* man—no matter whether old or young in years— is aware of a responsibility for the consequences of his conduct and really feels such responsibility heart and soul. He then acts by following an ethic of responsibility and somewhere he reaches the point where he says, 'Here I stand; I can do no other.' "[97]

Weber took a stand on the facts he saw. He never offered panaceas, only the hope that we might live in a world full of mature men and women. His ideal politician is a person who feels an overwhelming sense of responsibility for any use of violence. Weber always argued that, as in Colombia, even the best intentions can produce the most unexpected and ghastly results.

Max Weber died from pneumonia in June 1920. He never lived to see a future that included, instead of an ethic of responsibility, an ethic of ultimate ends that, as in Germany, Russia, or China, slaughtered many of the most innocent people on earth.

NOTES

1. Max Weber, *The Protestant Ethic and the Spirit of Capitalism* (New York: Charles Scribner's, 1958), 182.

2. C. G. Cruickshank, *Army Royal: Henry VIII's Invasion of France* (Oxford: Clarendon Press, 1969), 29.

3. Ibid., 44–45.

4. Lee Kennett, *The French Army in the Seven Years' War* (Durham, N.C.: Duke University Press, 1967), 67.

5. Richard Glover, *Peninsular Preparation: The Reform of the British Army, 1795– 1809* (Cambridge: Cambridge University Press, 1963), 117.

6. Cecil Woodham-Smith, *The Reason Why* (New York: McGraw Hill, 1954), 33, 2–3.

7. Ibid., 136.

8. Ibid., 69–73, 113–15.

9. Ibid. For the experience see page 132; for the uniform see page 236; for the number of dead see page 249. The battle itself is recounted in chapter 12, 229–49.

10. See, for example, Richard A. Preston, Sydney F. Wise, and Herman O. Wer-

ner, *Men in Arms: A History of Warfare and Its Interrelationships with Western History* (New York: Praeger, 1965).

11. Marianne Weber, *Max Weber: A Biography,* ed. Harry Zohn (New Brunswick, N.J.: Transaction Books, 1988), 32–33.

12. Ibid., 33.

13. Ibid., 61; also see Hans Gerth and C. Wright Mills, eds., *From Max Weber* (New York: Oxford University Press, 1946), 3.

14. Ibid., 91–92, 69; also see Arthur Mitzman, *The Iron Cage: An Historical Interpretation of Max Weber* (New York: Grosset and Dunlap, 1969).

15. Marianne Weber, *Max Weber,* 46; see also Reinhard Bendix, *Max Weber: An Intellectual Portrait* (Garden City, N.J.: Anchor, 1962).

16. Marianne Weber, *Max Weber,* 69–70.

17. Gerth and Mills, *From Max Weber,* 7; Marianne Weber, *Max Weber,* 71.

18. Marianne Weber, *Max Weber,* 162.

19. Ibid., 185, 148.

20. Gerth and Mills, *From Max Weber,* 10.

21. Marianne Weber, *Max Weber,* 230.

22. Ibid., 230.

23. Ibid., 231; also see Gerth and Mills, *From Max Weber,* 10.

24. Marianne Weber, *Max Weber,* 238.

25. Max Weber, "Science as a Vocation," in *From Max Weber,* ed. Hans Gerth and C. Wright Mills (New York: Oxford University Press, 1958), 137.

26. Ibid., 135–36.

27. Ibid., 138.

28. Ibid., 139.

29. Ibid., 143.

30. Paul Honigsheim, *On Max Weber* (New York: Free Press, 1968), 3, 6, 13.

31. Max Weber, "Science as a Vocation," 145–51.

32. Ibid., 152.

33. Ibid., 145–47.

34. Max Weber, *The Theory of Social and Economic Organization* (New York: Free Press, 1964), 88.

35. See Peter Berger and Hansfried Kellner, *Sociology Reinterpreted* (London: Penguin, 1981), 17.

36. Ibid., 18.

37. Max Weber, *Theory of Social and Economic Organization,* 115.

38. Ibid., 110.

39. Girth and Mills, *From Max Weber,* 196.

40. Ibid.

41. Ibid., 11–14.

42. Michel de Montaigne, *The Complete Essays of Montaigne* (Stanford, Calif.: Stanford University Press, 1948), 159.

43. Max Weber, *Theory of Social and Economic Organization,* 358.

44. Malcom X, with the assistance of Alex Haley, *The Autobiography of Malcolm X* (New York: Grove Press, 1964), 210; see especially the two chapters titled "Saved" and "Savior," 169–210.

45. Max Weber, *Theory of Social and Economic Organization,* 359.

46. See, for example, E. Essien Udom, *Black Nationalism* (New York: Dell, 1964).

47. Max Weber, *Theory of Social and Economic Organization*, 361.

48. Ibid. The material on Prophet Claire is based on conversations with a member of my family who was, for almost twenty years, a devout follower of Prophet Claire.

49. See, for example, Don Belt, ed., *The World of Islam* (Washington, D.C.: National Geographic, 2001).

50. Peter Ward Fay, *The Opium War, 1840–42* (New York: Norton, 1975), 344–45.

51. Max Weber, *Theory of Social and Economic Authority*, 341.

52. Ibid., 363.

53. See Ludovico Geymonat, *Galileo Galilei* (New York: McGraw Hill, 1957).

54. John B. Wolf, *Louis XIV* (New York: Norton, 1968), 73–74.

55. Philip Gourevitch, *We Wish to Inform You That Tomorrow We Will Be Killed with Our Families* (New York: Farrar, Straus and Giroux, 1998).

56. See, for example, Herman Kahn, *On Thermonuclear War* (New York: Free Press, 1960); Spencer Weart, *Nuclear Fear: A History of Images* (Cambridge, Mass.: Harvard University Press, 1988).

57. Max Weber, *Theory of Social and Economic Authority*, 329.

58. Ibid., 329–30.

59. Max Weber, "Bureaucracy," in *From Max Weber*, ed. Hans Gerth and C. Wright Mills (New York: Oxford University Press, 1958), 214.

60. See Gerth and Mills, *From Max Weber*, 50–51, 54.

61. Marianne Weber, *Max Weber*, 287.

62. See Max Weber, *Protestant Ethic*, n1.

63. See Ronald Fernandez, *America's Banquet of Cultures Harnessing Ethnicity, Race, and Immigration in the Twenty-first Century* (Westport, Conn.: Praeger, 2000), chapter 1.

64. Max Weber, *The Sociology of Religion* (Boston: Beacon Press, 1964).

65. Max Weber, *Protestant Ethic*, 17.

66. Ibid., 53.

67. Ibid., 80.

68. Ibid., 103.

69. Ibid., 104.

70. Ibid., 105.

71. Ibid., 115.

72. Ibid., 170.

73. Ibid., 174.

74. Ibid., 181.

75. See, for example, Ray Ginger, *The Age of Excess: The United States from 1877 to 1914* (New York: Macmillan, 1965).

76. Max Weber, *Protestant Ethic*, 182.

77. Mariannee Weber, *Max Weber*, 295.

78. Frederick D. Patterson, *Chronicles of Faith*, ed. Martia Graham Goodson (Tuscaloosa: University of Alabama Press, 1991), 49, 108.

79. See, for example, Gehard Lenski, *Power and Privilege* (Chapel Hill: University of North Carolina Press, 1984).

80. Max Weber, "Class, Status, and Party," in *From Max Weber*, ed. Hans Gerth and C. Wright Mills (New York: Oxford University Press, 1958), 186–87.

　81. See, for example, Gregory Howard Williams, *Life on the Color Line* (New York: Dutton, 1995).

82. Max Weber, *The Religion of India* (New York: Free Press, 1958), especially chapters 2 and 3; Harold Issacs, *India's Ex-Untouchables* (New York: John Day, 1965), 27–28.

83. Max Weber, "Class, Status, and Party," 187.

84. Ibid., 181.

85. Ibid., 182.

86. Ibid., 183.

87. Ibid., 187.

88. William Julius Wilson, *When Work Disappears: The World of the New Urban Poor* (New York: Random House, 1996), 137; his earlier book was *The Declining Significance of Race* (Chicago: University of Chicago Press, 1978).

89. Gerth and Mills, *From Max Weber*, 23; Max Weber, "Politics as a Vocation," in *From Max Weber*, ed. Hans Gerth and C. Wright Mills (New York: Oxford University Press, 1958), 77–128.

90. Max Weber, "Politics as a Vocation," 78.

91. "The Fifty Richest Members of the U.S. Congress," *Roll Call Online* [www.rollcall.com]. (Accessed November 4, 2001.)

92. Max Weber, "Politics as a Vocation," 121.

93. Ibid., 120–21.

94. Ibid., 121–22.

95. Ibid., 123.

96. See, for example, Gabriel Marcella and Donald Schulz, *Colombia's Three Wars: U.S. Strategy at the Crossroads, U.S. Army War College* (Carlise, Penn.: Army War College, March 5, 1999); Government Accounting Office, *Drug Control: Challenges in Implementing Plan Colombia*, GAO-01-76T (Washington, D.C.: Government Accounting Office, October 12, 2000), 8; finally, Ronald Fernandez, "Colombia RX Will Work in Theory, but Not in Reality," *The Hartford Courant*, February 2, 2001, A13.

97. Max Weber, "Politics as a Vocation," 127.

CHAPTER 4

Georg Simmel

"Money is the secular God of the World. . . . It is the absolute means which is elevated to the psychological significance of an absolute purpose."

Georg Simmel, *The Philosophy of Money*[1]

THE FOURTH LATERAN COUNCIL

In 1215 Catholic bishops arrived at the Lateran Church in Rome. Pope Innocent III, "a particularly energetic church politician," convened the conclave because he was engaged in a fierce battle with the Holy Roman Empire. Nobody amassed troops, yet the struggle for pontifical power contained all the elements of a real war. In Europe Church and State had already clashed for more than a millennium, and Innocent was a strange name indeed for a pope who played politics with all the skill of a city hall shark.[2]

As one symbol of who ruled the Roman day, Innocent and his colleagues solemnly reenacted previous imperial legislation—or canons—about the rights and place of Jews. The pope's intent was to assert his authority over that of Emperor Frederick. Neither man won the battle. It was a draw, except for the Jews. The Canons of 1215 posted the pope's imprimatur on commandments that institutionalized a prominent form of hate throughout the Holy Roman Empire.[3]

One especially odious canon—the second—focused on "distinctive dress." In 1215 Jews and Christians still managed to, if not intermarry, at least engage in sexual congress. So Innocent instituted this rule: Jews must wear a distinctive badge so that as if a gruesome germ, Christians would instantly think of Jews as a danger to their spiritual health. Because bishops never mandated the exact design of the sign of shame, specific countries fabricated their own. In England, bishops chose a badge depicting two stone tablets indicating the Ten Commandments. In France St. Louis directed two badges, made of red or saffron yellow cloth, cut in the shape of a wheel and worn in front and rear. Other localities only used a yellow circle, the color symbolizing the Jews' alleged love of gold.[4]

Georg Simmel was Jewish. And if popes never forced him to wear the mark of Cain, he paid dearly for his inheritance of holy hate. Despite one important book after another, Simmel never received the jobs or honors he deserved. One principal explanation for a lifetime of academic dead ends rests on his Jewish ancestry.

Jews wore the badges for more than six centuries. "They were the personal ghettos in which every Jew had to live."[5] But, especially after the French revolution, enlightened thinkers whittled away at the great wall of prejudice built by popes who were never innocent. In a precedent that influenced other nations, Napoleon decreed that Jews could be equal citizens in France *if* they ceased being traditional Jews and embraced instead the identity "Frenchmen of the Mosaic persuasion." In practice this meant that Jews needed to abandon their claim to being a distinct people as well as disband the rabbinic courts that then adjudicated the everyday lives of countless European Jews.[6]

Given a starting point of yellow badges, Mosaic Frenchmen signaled some progress. However, in 1808 Napoleon promulgated what was soon called "the infamous degree." It mandated restrictions that created badges of a different kind. Jews now faced restrictions on the loans they could provide; they needed special permits to trade, their entitlement to migration was restricted, and they were even refused the right—granted to other French citizens—of providing a substitute for military service. In essence Napoleon said that Jews could and would die for France but never as equal citizens, Mosaic or otherwise.[7]

After Napoleon's defeat at Waterloo, the 1814 Congress of Vienna established a constitution for the thirty-six states of the new German Federation. While progressive delegates tried to remove many of Napoleon's legal "innovations," German states received great flexibility in dealing with Jewish residents. Thus, as with Marx's father, a Jew could become a Protestant and succeed or stay Jewish and live in a ghetto. In Simmel's birthplace, Berlin, no less than four of Moses Mendelssohn's children chose to be baptized. A grandson became the famous composer Felix Mendelssohn, yet even holy waters never cleaned up the past. In nineteenth-century Germany a Jew always wore the Lateran mark whether he was religious or secular, baptized or bar mitzvahed.[8]

Georg Simmel grew up in a society that invented the word *anti-Semitism*. In 1879—Simmel's twenty-first year—the journalist Wilhelm

Marr used the word to describe the many existing forms of political opposition to Jews. Originally, anti-Semitism never denoted an antipathy toward Jewish culture; activists "only" focused on keeping Jews out of mainstream political and economic institutions. They meant to establish a respectable, scientific form of prejudice against Jews. Yet by the end of the year, a famous professor of history at the University of Berlin expanded the bounds of anti-Semitism. Heinrich von Treitschke wrote a series of newspaper articles that included a horribly memorable line: "The Jews are our misfortune." It was a phrase that "rings with the self-pity of the oppressor," a phrase that would be used by the ugliest of Germany's anti-Semites.[9]

When economic slumps occurred, Jews received the blame for the decline and little if any praise for the good times. On street corners rabble-rousers openly expressed their views, and political groups discovered previously uncovered revelations in everything from the Talmud to the work of Darwin. Racial theories began to sprout, providing the "real reason" for Jewish malevolence and a scientific rationale for the exclusion of Jews from Germany. The chaplain to the imperial court, Adolf Stöcker, never went that far, but he did openly suggest that Jews do two things: stop criticizing Christians and stop amassing great fortunes.[10]

Like the gold badge from 1215, business success haunted German Jews in the late nineteenth century. Christians threw stones because the Jews killed Christ; racists proved their inferiority; and Communists in search of a new world argued that Jews epitomized the robbery that, however ironically, a Jew name Karl Marx discovered at the heart of capitalism. In 1890 five anti-Semites won seats in the Reichstag; by 1893 the figure climbed to sixteen, as anti-Semitic leagues and parties fed on one or all forms of anti-Semitism.[11]

In his history of Zionism, Walter Laquer explains the desire and need for a Jewish state. He argues with great force that for German Jews, the 1880s marked a decisive turning point. "The new anti-Semitism meant the end of assimilation, the total rejection of the Jew."[12] Zionists looked to Palestine or Argentina as a possible shelter from the storm of hate, while Georg Simmel, fortune in hand, never wanted to leave Berlin. He loved the city and was literally born at its version of Times Square on March 1, 1858.[13]

LEIPZIGERSTRASSE AND FRIEDRICHSTRASSE

At the very end of his *Philosophy of Money*, Simmel discusses a new invention: the slot or vending machine. He calls it "the ultimate example of the mechanical character of the modern economy" because vending machines perfectly symbolized the increasingly impersonal spirit of everyday life in Berlin, Paris, London, or New York. Through all of human history, people actively participated in the art of exchanging goods and services; haggling was often such an integral and anticipated part of the purchasing process that families sent their best negotiator to the bargaining table. The vending machine instantly erased the need for people. Anyone on earth could put money into a slot, receive their merchandise in another of the machine's cavities, and never have a human contact of any kind. Indeed, especially if the machine failed to function, what did you do? Scream at a piece of metal or kick it?[14]

Like a hunter after a meal, Simmel always caught, with great precision, the nature of social change. He used supposedly inane examples to underline a transformation that he witnessed, firsthand, from the day he was born. In the second half of the nineteenth century, the streets Leipzigstrasse and Friedrichstrasse "emerged as two of the most important commercial corridors in Berlin." The new city was built right beside the heart of the old city—the Stadmitte—so Simmel walked out of the family apartment and literally saw the transforming power of capitalism, industrialization, urbanization, and raw power politics. As a thirteen-year-old, Simmel watched the victory parades celebrating Germany's unification and victory in the 1870 Franco-Prussian War. He grew up as Berlin surpassed Paris as the cultural, political, and economic center of Europe. It was an exciting time to be young, and the Simmel family experienced all the highs and lows of life in a city on the move.[15]

Simmel's father, Eduard, started his Berlin business life importing and distributing fine French jams for Germany's elite. He soon had such a prosperous line of culinary goods that he and his associates created a chocolate business that was the Godiva of its day. The Prussian royal family put its stamp of approval on the chocolate produced by Simmel's father, but for unclear reasons, Eduard broke with his partners and subsequently experienced hard times until his death in 1874. That left Simmel, his mother, Flora, and six brothers and sisters with no visible means of support. They struggled until Jules Friedländer—"Uncle Dol"—became a member of the family. He was much older than Flora Simmel, but, besides being kind, he was enormously wealthy. Perceiving the desires of a middle class that aimed to imitate its betters, Friedländer sold cheap, classical sheet music for the piano and other stringed instruments. He made one fortune, sold the music business for 1 million marks, and then made another fortune by investing the profits in "property management and the acquisition of real estate in and around Berlin."[16]

At one point Georg Simmel collected rents for his uncle. A Herr Guggenbuchler never paid the bills, so, acting on behalf of his uncle, Simmel moved to evict the tenant. In response Guggenbuchler took a first-class carriage to Simmel's apartments, argued with him, and then took a pistol out of his pocket. The first shot missed its target, but as Simmel ran down the hallway, his assailant fired one shot that grazed Simmel's head and another that pierced his shoulder blade. One biographer writes that the experience acted as the catalyst for Simmel's later focus on avarice and greed. That may be true, but this is a fact: Simmel always lived quite well off an economy he often despised with all the vigor and force of Karl Marx.[17]

Simmel's uncle bequeathed him a huge fortune, enough money to never work for the rest of his life. That gave Simmel time to increase his extensive collection of Asian porcelains, take full advantage of Berlin's cultural richness, and write books that would and did offend the academic sensibilities of traditional professors. Thanks to his uncle's generosity and business acumen, Simmel could always do as he pleased.

At the University of Berlin, professors sarcastically rejected Simmel's first dissertation. His "Psychological and Ethnographic Studies on Music" included, in the last section on *yodeling*, one of the first questionnaires used by social scientists. Simmel published the questionnaire in the *Journal of the Swiss Alpine Club*, but this only added insult to his readers' injury. They complained about misspellings, and in a criticism that would last for a lifetime, they grumbled about "stylistic errors." Simmel never included enough footnotes, which, along with the other mistakes, so offended his readers that one offered this assessment: "We would be doing him a great service if we do not encourage him further in this direction."[18]

With a prize-winning study of Immanuel Kant, Simmel eventually completed all the work for his doctorate in 1885. He gave the obligatory public lecture and then assumed the status of Privatdozent at the University of Berlin. Although the title may sound prestigious, it symbolized such a low rung on the academic ladder that Simmel needed binoculars to see the summit. The American rank of adjunct professor catches the position's essence, except that Simmel never even received a salary. He relied on student fees for the money he never needed, and he further antagonized his colleagues by being one of the most popular lecturers in the entire university.[19]

While still a Privatdozent, Simmel soon taught in the largest lecture theater in the entire university. He told a friend, "I am rather proud of the fact that I have over seventy students in a private seminar on social psychology. This is a lot for such a remote and unpractical area." Simmel was right, but in a course actually titled "On Pessimism," he somehow managed to enroll 269 students. He mesmerized his listeners with a spirited speaking style, and his students included a number of women, surprising for the time. Women never entered the University of Berlin as full participants until 1908. Simmel paved their way fifteen years earlier, so, as if being Jewish, wealthy, and footnote free was not enough of a challenge to the establishment, Simmel added women's rights and, in the early 1890s, a public association with socialism and its advocates.[20]

Simmel led the charge of the avant-garde. As if a kaleidoscope, he swirled in all the colors of social change, losing no opportunity to voluntarily or involuntarily offend those wedded to the past. In 1890 he married Gertrud Enckendorff. She was twenty-six, a writer, a philosopher, "and a sworn enemy of Victorian marriage." In their salon the Simmels set such a tone that the leading figures in art and literature frequented their home. And if a famous artist failed to appear, Simmel could easily drop in on them. Fascinated by the work of Rodin, Simmel visited Paris on many occasions to talk with and learn from one of the West's greatest sculptors.[21]

As with couples today, this two-career marriage produced its inevitable challenges. After the birth of their son Hans in 1891, Gertrud reluctantly agreed to stay home. This produced so many problems that "until she found her voice as a writer, marriage was a living hell." She experienced everything from chronic back pain to "deep bouts of depression." Both partners soon realized that an avant-garde lifestyle produced problems not only in the university but also in the home.[22]

Simmel nevertheless chose to be the willing harbinger of change. If he wanted, he could have written in the approved style or, even more to the point, stopped jumping from one topic to another. In theory academics praise what we today call an interdisciplinary approach to the pursuit of knowledge; in practice professors need a disciplinary pigeonhole, and Georg Simmel fit into no available boxes. The same man who wrote about Dante, Goethe, Rodin, and Rembrandt also produced a biblical size book about money and the challenging outlines of a new discipline called sociology. Simmel truly deserved the term "an original," yet it was 1914 before he finally received a full professorship; even then he served in Strasbourg, at the margins of the academic universe, rather than at its sun in Berlin.[23]

Perhaps with his uncle in mind, Simmel wrote his own epitaph shortly before his death in 1918: "My legacy will be like cash, which is distributed to many heirs, each transforming his portion into a profit that conforms to his nature; this profit will no longer reveal its derivation from my legacy."[24]

Simmel was wrong. As sociologists we know exactly whom to thank for a view of sociology that focused, with a sure touch of genius, on "the pure forms of sociation."

"HOW IS SOCIETY POSSIBLE?"

Like Peter Berger today or Max Weber in his own time, Georg Simmel was a superb historian. Instead of statistics, his work used the facts of history to help establish the science of sociology. Sometimes, in one paragraph, the reader starts in Palestine, travels to Greece, Italy, and Czechoslovakia, and ends the tour in the United States.[25] It is a breathtaking display of knowledge that Simmel used in an inventive manner. From the perspective of society—of how people interacted—"history was an un-differentiated whole" of fascinating and horrible, unbelievable, and mun-dane facts. To create something that was specifically sociological, the scientist needed to induce from the heterogeneity that was history, the pure forms of social interaction. Simmel said to think of grammar, which first isolates and then analyzes verbs, nouns, adverbs, and adjectives. Us-ing history as its database, sociology could and should focus its attention on the "identical forms of behavior" that, like clouds, soar over the history of humankind.[26]

One of Simmel's most provocative books is titled *Conflict and the Web of Group Affiliations*. It exemplifies his approach to sociology because he for-gets specific manifestations of conflict or competition (e.g., the Crimean War or games of sport) and only focuses on what he, via a process of induction, has isolated from the raw facts of history. Discussing compe-tition, he underlines its "poisonous, divisive and destructive effects," but he also calls our attention to its "immense" ability to connect the com-petitors. To beat an opponent, I need to "come close to him, establish ties with him, find his strengths and weaknesses and adjust to them, find all bridges or cast new ones" that might link us instead of divide us. Simmel loved to see all the consequences of a social form, and as with business mergers, cartels, or political federations (e.g., the European Economic Community), he suggested how conflict could also lead to cooperation.[27]

By focusing on forms, Simmel fenced in what was uniquely sociological. He wanted to create the subject matter of a new science, and he did it in such an original manner that few have followed his lead. He always seems to see what the rest of us miss. Consider, for example, his answer to a crucial question for any sociologist: "How Is Society Possible?" Can we abstract from history the essential elements—the pure forms—that allow thousands or even many millions of people to successfully interact over and through the manifold experiences of everyday life? How do people who have never met one another, and may never again see one another (e.g., on a line in a store or in a theater audience), manage to interact in a cooperative or even pleasing manner?

Simmel thrived on these questions. Like a drill in search of water, he always drove his mind to the core of a social form. In the case of society, he argues in "How Is Society Possible" that it was possible because of three factors, each common to any society on earth.

He starts with distortions. None of us can ever perceive the individu-ality of another. Don't waste your time. It is impossible because "all re-lations among men are determined by varying degree of incompleteness." I never see the core of your individuality because I also see you—in all social interactions—generalized in some measure or form.[28] If I introduce Brenda, my wife, I demand that you see the unique person *and* the social type *wife*. If I introduce Paul, "he is a cop," I have attached to Paul, as an inseparable piece of the interaction, an identity that instantly puts the unique person into a general category.

As a test try this exercise. Think of anyone you know—Sally, Burt, Ernestina—and try to talk about them without using a social type, such as sister, colleague, mother. In my experience it is impossible to discuss anyone without soon using the general categories that "lift or lower" the person in my and other people's eyes. This is "the president"; this is a "homeless person." You are raised or degraded by the categories we all employ as the conceptual tools of everyday life.

Using a lovely metaphor, Simmel argues that social types act as a veil, a veil that hides my uniqueness as it simultaneously gives it a new form. Call me a teacher, and you place the veil over my individuality; lift the veil, and you have the set of assumptions that allow otherwise anonymous interactions to proceed. Teachers do this, students do that, and successful interaction in the classroom occurs because the veils disregard what is irrelevant in specific social situations.[29]

Social categories distort the picture of another person, and the more highly differentiated the society, the greater the frequency and degree of distortion that occurs. Go buy a pair of sneakers at the mall, tell the clerk you are an eight wide, and you become a shoe size. The generalization momentarily turns you into a numerical category, but if the clerk has what you want, you get the shoes and you go home. After all, you did not want a new friend, just a pair of serviceable or stylish sneakers.

The veils make society possible because they allow us to act on the basis of the assumptions we have learned to attach to a particular generalization. Conversely, if we disagree about the meaning of a particular category—for example, what is a good husband or wife in twenty-first century America—society is impossible because the veils hide not shared assumptions but different definitions of the marital situation.

Remember that Simmel only seeks to isolate the forms that prevail in all societies, anytime, anywhere. Social categories are crucial, but so too are what Simmel calls the "extrasocial nature" of any human being. It is an awkward phrase, suggesting that all people are simultaneously inside and outside of any society on earth. Indeed, "the fact that in certain respects the individual is not an element of society constitutes the positive condition for the possibility that in other respects he is."[30]

If it seems like a paradox, that is exactly Simmel's point. An a priori of social life is that life is not entirely social. Individuality, not to mention social change, sneaks in at least two ways: via a person's temperament, fate, interests, and worth as a personality and via the impossibility, even in the simplest of societies, of perfectly socializing any human being. Discrepancies between what people are supposed to do and what they actually do inevitably produce a universal fact of life: people are contained in society and, at the same time, confronted by it.[31] For example, when you or I disregard a social category—say, as a man, I wear a pleated dress instead of pleated pants—you have the social space required for questions about the person *and* the category. Maybe Fernandez is a pacesetter? Perhaps all men should wear polka-dot day dresses?

Ask the question, and you are outside of society. This can include, as with Simmel, a process of deliberate reflection or simply a knee-jerk rejection of what others say you must do. Either way the individual enters social interaction in an original manner, and this allows for social change, *even if no one recognizes that change has occurred.* Analyzing preliterate societies, different generations of anthropologists have recorded the same myths. But the written record indicates that the oral record changed because, like the children's game of telephone, people added to, and subtracted from, what they heard from their ancestors. Anthropologists perceive the social changes because literacy allows them to compare past and present. Meanwhile, without reading and writing, a preliterate group has no easy way to know that what "we" say now is markedly different from what "they" said then. After all, if the elders are dead, who can challenge the new version of the old myth?

Both the anthropologist and the members of the tribe are outside society; the difference, of course, is the degree of self and social consciousness that literacy offers the anthropologist—and us.

Simmel instructs us to think of our extrasocial nature as a matter of perspective. You could, for example, take a plant and "consider it from the standpoint of its biological development or its practical uses or its aesthetic significance." In the same way you could focus on a person as someone shaped by the society or as an individual who lives in society and who may deviate from many of the society's accepted beliefs, values, and practices. From either perspective this is the essential point: "The within and the without between individual and society are not two unrelated definitions but define together the fully homogeneous position of man as a social animal."[32]

So far, we know that two things make society possible: social categories and our extrasocial nature. Simmel's final insight in "How Is Society Possible" revolves around the inheritance received by all human beings; as each of us utters our first cry, a society already exists and "in spite of all discrepancies between it and ideal standards, social life exists as if all of its elements found themselves interrelated with one another in such a manner that each of them, because of its very individuality, depends on all others and all others depend on it."[33]

Simmel never expects perfect harmony. That is always impossible because of our extrasocial natures. But he does argue that any society demands that "individuality finds its place in the structure of generality, and, furthermore, that in spite of the unpredictable character of individ-

uality, *this structure is laid out,* as it were, for individuality and its functions" (emphasis added).[34]

Think, for instance, of age norms. At birth you encounter a society that
tells you when to marry, when to have children, when to finish your education, and when to retire. If you stop work at fifty, you retired "early";
if you finish your degrees at forty, you are a "late bloomer." In each instance you are blooming late or retiring early in relation to the age norms
that, at birth, laid out the presumed course of your life. You can decide to
reject or refine those norms—to be a deviant—but it is always the preexisting structure that defines the normal and the strange, the correct and
the peculiar.

The beauty of this insight is that it allows us to understand not only
what makes society possible but also what makes it impossible. To the
extent that a structure is not laid out or, even worse, that society lays out
two, three, or four different paths, we are mountain climbers without a
compass, and society is increasingly impossible because it lacks a preexisting consensus about the course to follow. For instance, our age norms
derive from a period in which people's life expectancy was much shorter
than it is today. Traditionally, life is a bell curve, and someone who is sixty
is going down hill. But, suppose like Presidents Reagan and George H.
Bush, I see life as a line that ends when I die. Then, instead of retiring at
65, I can run for a second presidential term at 74 (Reagan) or 69 (George
H. Bush).

We live in a society of lines and curves; there is no one rule of the game.
Although that provides great room for change, it also makes society increasingly impossible because no matter what I do, many others do it
differently—or criticize me for the choice I made. Today individuality has
a much harder time finding itself in the structure of generality because
such a structure is very fragile or, in the extreme, it no longer exists.

Simmel bears no responsibility for our societal predicament. He "only"
explains how society is possible. But in offering insights that are as valid
today as they were a century ago, he shows the great promise of a sociology that focuses on the pure forms of sociation. He never lost that focus,
especially in his sociological masterpiece, *The Philosophy of Money.*

THE PHILOSOPHY OF MONEY

The Philosophy of Money has a goal: Simmel seeks—quite successfully,
by the way—to devastate the labor theory of value. He wants to build a
new floor under historical materialism because Marx missed a crucial
point. Like the hidden cement that supports a pillar, below *any* economic
base is a lively interaction of people adding and subtracting value through
an animated process of exchange. Focus on prices, profits, and the proletariat, and you completely overlook what occurs at the thriving roots of

social life. Down below, people are the *active agents* creating and re-creating the abstract values they attach to whatever objects they exchange. Thus, whether it is feudalism or capitalism, any economic system is ac-tually "based on the mutuality of exchange"; understand this process of exchange (e.g., bartering, swapping, haggling), and you will see how value is created not simply in one economic system but in all societies, all the time.[35]

Value is never inherent in the object itself (e.g., a Chinese porcelain, a house, labor). Like light and shade on a plant, value comes from the out-side—from the minds of people. Value is created when men, women, and children establish a personal and societal scale that extends from the high-est values through indifference to negative values. Objects, like sponges, absorb our value judgments, and we then confront them—for example, a Picasso print—as something that has autonomous value. In reality we added the value and can subtract it at any time.

Today human life is presumably our highest value; meanwhile, we watch the ceaseless rise and fall of other values when we see an object—say, vintage clothing—that was worthless yesterday become quite valu-able today. Or think of toys at Christmas. One object becomes the toy of the season, and with children egging them on, parents stampede to the store to the get the most valuable toy for their anything-but-indifferent child.

Once people add value to objects, exchange is possible *"because exchange presupposes an objective measurement of subjective* values" (emphasis added).[36] Before you come to market, you need to have a scale of personal and societal values in your head and so does the other person. Otherwise how could you *jointly* agree on the value of any object of exchange? Of course, my scale may differ from yours—for example, I really want a BMW and you want a timeshare in Aspen—so Simmel makes room for the variations that occur in the process of exchange. Whether it is labor for money or one car for another, any exchange always involves "a recip-rocal balancing, through which each economic object expresses its value in another object." Simmel uses the words *sacrifice* and *gain* to explain this balancing process; I will part with a lot of money (the sacrifice) to get the watch, house, or painting (the gain) that is the object of my desire.[37]

Remember that Simmel is arguing with Marx about two different points—first is the deepest roots of economic reality; second is the labor theory of value. Thus he examines the notion that usefulness or utility determines economic value. Simmel says this is hogwash. "Utility as such is never able to bring about economic processes unless it leads to demand, and it does not always do so." I can know that a chain saw is extremely useful, but if nobody wants one, the saw has no economic value. Con-versely, "we desire, and therefore value economically, all kinds of things that cannot be called useful or serviceable without arbitrarily straining

ordinary linguistic usage." Twenty years ago Americans paid good money
for pet rocks; many people also gave the rocks names. But even their
greatest advocates would have a hard time arguing that the value of the
rocks derived from their utility.[38]

Simmel tunnels his way to the deepest roots of the economy when he
stresses that "the object in demand becomes a value of practical importance to the economy only when the demand for it is compared with the
demand for other things; *only this comparison establishes a measure of demand.*
Only if there is a second object which I am willing to give away for the
first, or vice versa, does each of them have a measurable economic value"
(emphasis added).[39]

The devastating insight for Marx's theory is that the root of any comparison is not labor but the variable amount of value I (and the larger
society) am willing to attach to the object. Think, for example, of television's *Antiques Road Show*. A person brings in a toy from the 1920s. The
appraiser reports that it is worth $6,000, and as you get off the floor in
shock, he explains why. The toy is in its original box; *in comparison* to other
examples of this Mickey Mouse, you never see the original box. Equally
important, it looks like no one ever played with the toy; maybe the child
hated it or was being punished for life? Who cares? This toy is so valuable
because, *in comparison* to other existing examples, it is "factory fresh."

Simmel summarizes his argument in this fashion. "Practical economic
value is never just value in general"; instead it is a definite sum of value
that results from the measurement of two intensities of demand (e.g., the
toy with and without its original box). Thus, although it may seem that
an object has an absolute value as a result of demand, the truth is that *it
is demand that endows the object with value.*[40] There are no absolutes in Simmel's economic world because value is always relative to fluctuating decisions about sacrifice and gain, based on comparisons that can literally
change with the weather. For example, watch the value of orange juice
before and after the announcement of a frost that just destroyed a large
portion of next year's crop.

Mutual exchange therefore functions like Nietzsche's announcement
about the death of God; it is the "economic-historical realization of the
relativity of all things." Equally important, because people create value
through a process of "lively interaction"—involving a changing mix of
variables—it is wrong to argue "that the essential feature of value is the
socially necessary labor time objectified in it." How, asks Simmel, did
labor power itself become a value? It became a value through the process
of exchange, and that exchange "is affected by other circumstances which
do not involve labor power, such as the need to satisfy wants, whims,
frauds, monopoly, etc." For example, Puerto Rico has experienced an underground labor economy for almost thirty years. Hundreds of thousands
of people work under the table, and for less than minimum wage, because

they do not wish to show the income that can remove their right to receive food stamps. In San Juan and Ponce, the value of labor is often determined by the joint need to avoid the authorities and an exchange that involves one person agreeing to fix another's bathroom—it doesn't matter how much labor time it takes—in exchange for that person agreeing to repair the first person's car.[41]

In an ideal world "exchange is the first and in its simplicity really wonderful means for combining justice with changes in ownership."[42] If each person pays what he or she thinks is fair, then both get a good deal. Unfortunately, in the real world people are positioned very differently when an exchange actually takes place. Illegal immigrants will accept far less than the going wage because their employer has what they need more than anything else: a way to survive in the United States. And adjunct professors work for far less than their full-time counterparts because they need the extra money or because they are willing to make an exchange that gives them prestige (the gain) in place of a fair wage (the sacrifice). Remember, too, the comparisons that are implicit in these exchanges; that is, however bad the pay in the United States, it is far more than the pay in Guatemala, El Salvador, or Mexico.

For Simmel four points are crucial. First, people—and only people— determine economic value in the lively process of attaching worth to the goods and services they exchange. Second, by definition economic value is relative rather than absolute. Third, labor power only acquires value in the process of exchange. And, finally, the value of labor is perpetually influenced by factors that have nothing to do with labor power.

Money finally makes an appearance in *The Philosophy of Money* when Simmel turns not to the nature of exchange but to money's role in the process. Money is a marvelous invention—the means to anything and anywhere—because, with greenbacks in hand, I can easily express the value relationship between the most diverse goods and services; it costs $50 to get someone to paint designs on my nails, $250 to get a plumber to install a new sink, and $30,000 a year to attend America's most prestigious universities.

Money functions like a magician because it is "interchangeability personified"; its dual role is obvious if we remember that "money is measured by the goods against which it is exchanged and also by money itself." I use coins or pieces of paper as a measured means to buy whatever I wish; I also use money to make money—accepting, astonishingly enough, the profits in money form. Think of an interest-bearing savings account. Think, too, of a currency trader using computers to avidly move from dollars to marks to yen in the course of a trading day. The trader has exchanged nothing you can put on the table, yet the pixels on the screen abstractly represent one of money's most incredible characteristics: "Money is one of those normative ideas that obey the norms that they themselves represent."[43] Money serves as an independent source of economic value (e.g., the interest on the bank account) as it simultaneously symbolizes the economic value of anything on earth.

Money is especially important as societies move away from the barter system. Exchange in kind is easy if the values of goods (two pigs for one horse) are "definitely and permanently fixed." But you need money when values are both lively and extensive. Money "offers an exact and flexible equivalent for every change of value"; from both a philosophical and an economic perspective, money perfectly symbolizes the relativity of all values. It possesses an "absolute lack of individuality," and that is its conceptual beauty as a means of exchange. "If money were a specific object it could never balance every single object or be the bridge between disparate objects."[44] Embodied in pieces of paper that in the United States spotlight our presidents, money "is nothing but the relation between economic values," come to life when I happily hold a hundred Jacksons (a $20 bill) or, much better, a hundred Franklins (the $100 bill).

In analyzing money Simmel often explains both its positive and negative consequences. For example, as the common denominator of value, money symbolizes "the general misery of human life"; people suffer because of their constant shortage of money. However, money also underlines *"one of the great accomplishments of the mind"* (emphasis added), that is, our ability to project mere relations into objects. Think, says Simmel, of a wedding ring. It is nothing more than a piece of metal twisted into a particular shape, yet it is also a serious symbol of a moral, legal, and spiritual commitment between two people. In a similar fashion people use money to project value into anything they can buy or sell. Money is "the pure form of exchangeability," and it is a great conceptual accomplishment because it is impossible to conceive of a modern economy without money's ability to cross the gap between different goods, different services, and as with the Euro, different cultures. Money is the bridge that extends around the world; and if money talks, it is a universal language—the language of the lively creation and exchange of economic value.[45]

Simmel now moves to a new topic, "Money in the Sequences of Purposes." Like a series of exclamation points, he even lets his own values show, especially in a section titled "Money as the Most Extreme Example of a Means Becoming an End."[46]

Money means nothing; money means everything. Writing in 1900, Simmel emphatically underlines what he believes is an unprecedented fact of human history: never before has an object that "owes its value exclusively to its quality as a means, to its convertibility into more definite values, so thoroughly and unreservedly developed into a psychological value absolute, into a completely engrossing final purpose governing our practical consciousness."[47]

Simmel tells us that people will do anything for money; and he also explains why. The "ultimate craving for money" occurs because, "as the range of objects made available to money grows continuously," we need money—and only money—to do or buy almost everything on earth. The terrible contradiction is that "as money becomes more and more lacking in quality," it simultaneously becomes ever more powerful in relation to our ability to buy goods and services. *"Its growing importance depends on its being cleansed of everything that is not merely a means, because its clash with the specifics of objects is thereby eliminated"* (emphasis added). Money is the global passport to everything, and its "inner polarity" rests on its being the "absolute means" and "psychologically, the absolute purpose for most people."[48]

Money is soulless and also the ultimate end sought by the soul. Simmel hated this reality because "money symbolizes the established fact that the values for which we strive and which we experience are ultimately revealed to be means and temporary entities." Given the noble achievements of the human mind, it was pathetic to think of a fleeting means as an ultimate end; adding insult to injury, what an "irony of history" that after the death of God, the only replacement people can provide is to embrace the ultimate means as the ultimate end of life. Simmel even argues that with God in his grave, money possesses a great similarity to the notion of God. "The essence of the notion of god is that all diversities and contradictions in the world achieve a unity in him. . . . There arises the peace, the security, the all-embracing wealth of feeling that reverberate with the notion of God that we hold."[49]

In the modern world money is God resurrected and horribly transformed into a transitory nothingness. In fact, "in so far as money becomes the absolutely commensurate expression and equivalent of all values, it rises to abstract heights way above the whole diversity of objects."[50] Like the God who used to be in the heavens, money stands watch as we feverishly pursue the means that has no end. When, after all, can you ever have everything that money can buy?

Money is also responsible for two of modernity's most common psychological conditions: cynicism and the blasé attitude. Cynics have a field day in any modern society because they see two things: if they have money, "the finest, most ideal and personal goods" are available to the most horrible people; and those same goods are denied "to the most worthy" if they lack sufficient amounts of dollars, pesos, or francs. Stock exchanges are "the nurseries of cynicism" because the quick turnover—on December 21, 2001, the Nasdaq exchanged 2.1 billion shares of stock, and the figure for the New York Stock Exchange was 1.6 billion shares—underlines that money can make anyone the owner of anything, anywhere. Your personal worth as a human being is irrelevant when societies openly advertise a "market place for values"; the cynic thrives because he or she perfectly perceives that pessimism is a legitimate response to the realities of a world dominated by money.[51]

If cynicism represents one side of the coin, the blasé attitude is its reverse-side partner. Why not be unmoved when you realize that the "same mount of money can procure all the possibilities that life has to offer?" What is the big deal? And how can I get some excitement in a life that is characterized by the blasé disposition? In 1900 Simmel wrote that out of the blasé attitude, there "emerges the craving today for excitement, for extreme impressions, for the greatest speed in its change." When money buys anything, the only thing that gets our attention is something new, strange, peculiar, or unique. "We have here one of those interesting cases in which the disease determines its own form of the cure. A money culture signifies such an enslavement of life in its means, that release from its weariness is also evidently sought in a mere means which conceals its final significance—in the fact of 'stimulation' as such."[52]

Simmel's pessimism is transparent; although he is writing a book about value, he can see precious little in a world dominated by money. He speculates that "as long as money serves in our consciousness as the only and closest goal of our endeavors it still possesses a quality." Unfortunately, "we would be hard-pressed to formulate what kind of quality it is." People do lust after money, and they joyously celebrate when they make it; it clearly touches the soul and ignites the passions. Yet it is still nothing but an *indifferent* means. How can something that is uncaring, unresponsive, and unmoved have any quality, much less one that is the be all and end all of modern existence?[53]

Simmel answers his own question in this manner: "*The quantity of money is its quality. . . .* With reference to money we do not ask what and how, but how much" (emphasis added).[54] Money's power is its use as a means to anything, so the more you have the more you can buy—and the more influence, prestige, or celebrity you have in the larger society. Think, for example, of the yearly parade presented by *Forbes Magazine*. To national fanfare it lists the 400 richest Americans, and people's position on the national ladder of loot is solely determined by the quantity of money they presently have. In 2001 Bill Gates was worth $54 billion dollars; he was number one. Lawrence Ellison was number four with $21 billion, but he was the year's "biggest loser" because in 2000, he was worth $58 billion. Forbes says almost nothing about how the money was made. Was the person unscrupulous? Does he or she treat others like dirt? Do they perform good deeds on a daily basis? Who cares? Because money's "*quality consists almost exclusively in its quantity,*"[55] Forbes rightfully focuses on the only issue that really matters, the bottom line—how much do you have?

Making world champions out of the rich has consequences that dramatically affect the poor, who get to feel angry, deprived, and envious. Because you can get more and more things with money, because money is the "central and absolute value" of modern life, objects achieve value "only to the extent that they cost money and the quality of value with which we perceive them appears only as a function of the money price."[56] Think of an upscale mall with its Coach leather goods and its Gucci watches. A knockoff may be of better quality than the outrageously expensive product, but the knockoff is useless not simply as a means of conspicuous consumption but as an affirmation of our own commitment to money as the central and absolute value of human life. By agreeing to value objects only to the extent that they are expensive, we consciously or unconsciously embrace the role of money in determining what is, or should be, important to myself, to my family, and to others.

In the 1960s hippies created a counterculture that sought to disregard the power and consequences of money. They wanted to judge people by their worth as human beings. Although this is arguably a laudable goal, Simmel's profound insights lead to this suggestion: it is impossible. To the extent that money allows people to buy anything and everything, it is a prerequisite of modern life. You cannot escape the significance of money because you need it to go to university, to buy a car, or to pay your credit card bills. Money is the indifferent means that allows *anyone* to buy or do *anything*; thus, however crass to the sophisticated, valuing objects by what they cost is simply a reflection of the deepest currents moving modern life. In Simmel's words, "As the range of objects made available to money grows continuously, . . . money becomes more and more lacking in quality yet thereby at the same time becomes more powerful in relation to the quality of things."[57]

Money means nothing; money means everything. "It lacks any content that might be appropriated beyond the mere form of possession"; yet money "obeys us without reservation" as we use it to buy almost anything on earth.[58] As Simmel sees it, those are the facts of modern life. King money rules with little opposition, but however paradoxically, money also offers a wonderful gift to all his subjects. The gift is freedom.

Given Simmel's pessimism about money, it comes as a great and welcome surprise that midway through the book, he includes a chapter titled "Individual Freedom." Simmel now successfully shows "that exchange against money is so far *the most perfect form of solution*" of one of human history's greatest problems. With exchange in kind it often happens that only one person has a specific interest in acquiring or getting rid of a particular object. Like the homeless in many U.S. cities, I can display a sign "Will work for food," but people may have no need for my services, or just as bad, I work and they provide food that I abhor or am allergic to. Because one partner to the exchange has all the power, the weaker partner is clearly behind the eight ball. The "great cultural problem" is "to raise the objectively given amount of value [e.g., the food] to a greater amount of *subjectively* experienced value merely through the change in its owners."[59]

As interchangeability personified, money performs this service in an admirable fashion. Remember that with no money in exchange for his or her work, the homeless person may be forced to accept not only unwanted food but also the additional degradation of eating the food in the basement, the barn, or whatever other location the employer chooses. In addition, the person may need to listen to a long lecture on "how did this happen to you" and "I know a social service agency that can help." Money is liberating because it allows people to use it in any fashion they choose. And, if they choose to eat five cholesterol-laden burgers and an extra large portion of French fries and onion rings, that too increases their degree of freedom. Money allows them the right and the ability to spend the fruits of their labor in any fashion *they* see fit.

Ever the historian, Simmel discusses peasant payments in kind beginning in the twelfth century. Lords often took advantage of their peasants by arbitrarily altering the amounts of produce required to meet local obligations; but once the payment had been "quantitatively and numerically fixed," the lord lost some of his power to take advantage of the peasants.[60] Similarly, once the state allowed citizens to pay their way out of military service, citizens certainly received much greater freedom over their bodies and their chance to live. During the U.S. Civil War, money payments allowed many upper- and middle-class Americans to avoid military service by using money to provide substitutes. General Hooker soon complained that his new recruits included men in a state of delirium tremors; the money turned over in lieu of service was used to purchase the time of any available person with a drinking problem. Incidentally, many of these fellows beat the system by accepting money in one location, quickly deserting, and then accepting money in another location.[61]

Simmel never denies that money brings its own problems. However, the intellectual beauty of his work is that by focusing on forms, he examines an issue from a wide variety of essential perspectives. In this instance his focus is freedom, and his real target is Karl Marx and the socialists.

While it is easy to see the proletariat as a slave, "the slave could not change his master even if he had been willing to risk much worse living conditions." Thinking like Marx, Simmel argues that making labor a commodity that can be bought and sold on the market "eliminates the pressure of the irrevocable dependency upon a particular master." Wage workers must, of course, still subordinate themselves to their employers, but Simmel quickly notes that "there is no necessary connection between liberty and increased well-being which is automatically presupposed by wishes, theories and agitations." After all, *"the freedom of the worker is matched by the freedom of the employer which did not exist in a society of bonded labor"* (emphasis added). Marx justifiably complained that the bourgeois left their workers with none of the fall-back benefits (e.g., land for crops) available under a system like feudalism. Simmel's retort is clear: "The emancipation of the laborer has to be paid for, as it were, by the emancipation of the employer, that is, by the loss of welfare that the bonded laborer enjoyed."[62]

Simmel always underlines "the complete heartlessness of money." He even argues that its heartlessness explains the power of the socialist ideal. Workers understandably want to abolish a system that treats them like a soulless means; so, when socialism promises complete equality, married to an inspiring sense of community, it offers a palliative that is hard to resist.[63] Simmel sees socialism's appeal, but wary of ever achieving complete equality, he suggests some of the additional freedoms of wage labor. Using a contemporary phrase, we might say, "It is just a job"; it is just a way I put bread on the table. Wage labor allows a person to separate his or her personality—his or her soul—from the necessity to work for a living. I go to the factory, I get my paycheck, and when I get home, I use the money earned to do what I want to do, when I want to do it.

Or perhaps you do not want responsibilities or a bright future in the front office. With wage labor you have the potential to earn what you need, and in sharp contrast to slavery or feudalism, you have substantial amounts of "free time," all of which you can use as you see fit.

Simmel refuses any easy solutions. He forces us to see money from a diversity of positive and negative perspectives, including what he calls the "new forms of association brought about by money." Joint stock companies were fascinating because "shareholders were united solely in their interest in the dividends, to such an extent that they did not even care what the company produced."[64] From the perspective of freedom, money allowed a person to "join a group without having to give up any personal freedom and reserve." Today, with mutual funds of every type and description, we have carried the freedom-bearing role of money to unprecedented levels. The only thing mutual about these funds is that you invested money for a certain period of time; today you can even make the investment on a computer screen and never even talk to or meet with another human being. Pixels talk to pixels and that is exactly Simmel's point. "Only money [helped by modern technology] can bring about associations which in no way prejudice the individual member; only money can create . . . a type of organization that unites individuals' non-personal elements in a project. *Money has provided us with the sole possibility for uniting people while excluding everything personal and specific*" (emphasis added).[65]

Simmel's splendid achievement is that he analyzed money from almost every imaginable angle. He tried to forget nothing, yet in the book's final chapter—"The Style of Life"—he offers a summary that is, at times, as angry as Karl Marx and as pessimistic as Max Weber.

Money measures all objects with "merciless objectivity." It is bloodless and bloodthirsty, but in a modern society, it functions alongside other factors that also level the playing field in a totally objective and indifferent manner. The division of labor, for example, creates a world in which "the person can no longer find himself expressed in his work." That was a commonplace insight, extended by Simmel in the following manner. Once labor is a commodity, work is something that the laborer "not only no longer *is*, but also no longer *has*" (emphasis in original). When a cobbler made shoes with his own tools, his labor belonged to him and so too did the shoes. But, once I work via a capitalist division of labor, the product belongs to someone else. "This is most forcefully illustrated where the worker is compelled to *buy* his own product if he wishes to have it."[66] In the contemporary Caribbean, workers take this process a step further by sewing fabric made in the United States, shipping the finished clothing back to the United States, and then buying the same clothing once it is shipped back to Jamaica or the Dominican Republic for the consumption stage of the global division of labor.[67]

Today the worker buys a multinational product, yet the relation to the consumer is fundamentally the same as a century ago. Where a custom product signified a mutual and personally meaningful relationship between producer and consumer, mass production deliberately eliminates—in 1903 and 2003—the personal element. The sweater is made for anyone, and that completes the circle of objectivity and impersonality begun by wage labor under a division of labor. The producer is deliberately separated from the total product; when the producer later buys that product from its corporate owner, it is something made not for him or her but for any anonymous consumer offering the correct payment in money.

In these final pages Simmel argues that along with money and the division of labor, technology, law, and (what he calls) intellectuality also contribute to the objectivity and impersonality that so forcefully characterize modern life. Law is a great leveler because it theoretically treats everyone in the same fashion; law is even "potentially communistic" because it "removes for everyone, those of higher, lower and equal position alike," the status demarcations that traditionally applied. We are all equal under the law, and to the extent this actually occurs, law functions like money. It is a means that manifests "complete indifference to individual qualities."[68]

Intellectuality refers to the accelerating accumulation of knowledge; it too has a link to money because the objectification of knowledge "separates the results of intelligence from its process." Affirming science and rationality, modern societies produce incredible amounts of information that are available to anyone with the wherewithal to read and write. Intellectuality is as democratic as the law or money, yet the wisdom amassed seems like a series of "concentrated abstractions." Science is a means that produces information linked to no particular end. The awful paradox is that anyone can pick the fruits that have ripened on the tree of knowledge, yet that same knowledge often adds more confusion than clarity to the ultimate ends of human life.[69]

Simmel argues that "there has never been an age" in which the means of human life (i.e., money, law, science, and the division of labor) are so disastrously separated from the ends of human life. "Spirituality and contemplation, stunned by the clamorous splendor of the scientific-technological age, have to suffer for it. . . . They feel as if the whole meaning of our existence were so remote that we are unable to locate it and are constantly in danger of moving away from rather than closer to it." We are lost, and "the lack of something definite at the center of the soul impels us to search for momentary satisfaction in ever-new stimulations, sensations and external activities." Like rats, we continuously run on a treadmill that leads nowhere, except to more confusion as a result of the ever-increasing accumulation of knowledge.[70]

This is, to say the least, a pessimistic assessment of modern life. Simmel concludes by arguing that money best symbolizes the "senselessness and the consequences" of our dislocation from ultimate ends. Money is the means that stands above all others and, as such, it is *the gatekeeper of the most intimate sphere*" (emphasis added).[71] Money allows modern humanity to "secure an island of subjectivity, a secret, closed off sphere of privacy— not in the social but in the deeper metaphysical sense—for his personal existence." This compensates for the loss of religion and the ultimate meanings that were God's gift to humankind. With money, we can select the things we need to make life bearable but never expect money to bridge the gap between the means and ends of human life. We are alone in a world where the means deliberately foster objectivity, impersonality, and a devastating indifference to the ultimate ends of human life.[72]

SOCIOLOGY OF WOMEN

Temperocentrism. Sociologists use the word to describe a form of prejudice or bias. In this case people see the world through a lens that focuses on their era or generation as the center of social and historical significance. In its most extreme form, temperocentrism suggests that contemporary insights, beliefs, and values (e.g., about women) are so unique that instead of building on or repeating history, we make it fresh from the bottle. Not much happened before our generation picked up the ball and ran with it.

In the United States feminists often seek a point of origin for the contemporary women's movement in *The Feminine Mystique,* a book published by Betty Friedan in 1963. It was certainly a significant catalyst for social change, but a look back in time could easily point to Simone de Beauvior's *The Second Sex* (published in France in 1948) as the actual origin of the contemporary women's movement.[73] She asked all the important questions. So did Georg Simmel in two essays that are almost a century old. As with all his sociology, Simmel sought to understand the pure forms of sociation, the essences that lay over the exceedingly diverse and tumultuous course of human history.

Simmel grew up in a Germany that often made women's rights a major social issue. August Bebel, a founder of the Social Democratic Worker's Party in 1869, published *Women and Socialism* a decade later. He and his powerful party advocated women's political and economic emancipation; and if we recall that Simmel married a woman with her own writing career and her own fine mind, his interest in the status of women makes perfect sense. What is confusing is his "solution" to the problem. In his essays "Female Culture" and "The Relative and Absolute in the Problem of the Sexes," he argues that self-realization for women depends on understanding a natural fact: "The home remains the supreme cultural achievement of women."[74]

To reach this conclusion Simmel starts from—even for many contemporary citizens—a radical perspective. He argues that as a cultural fact, "the male sex is not merely superior in relation to the female but acquires the status of the *generally human.*" Like a coffin, using the word *man* to denote all human beings buries women under the male category, and "this fact is grounded in the power position of men." Simmel also argues that the "historical relationship" between the sexes is easily understood if we think of masters and slaves. "It is one of the privileges of the master that he does not always need to think of the fact that he is master." That is taken for granted at such a deep level of consciousness that men simply assume they are the center of the universe. Women, on the other hand, never lose the feeling of their subordination to men; in fact, the notion of being second class "forms the subterranean ground of her life that never entirely disappears. All the contents of her life transpire on its basis."[75]

Simmel never focuses on issues like the vote. His is a cultural critique, and as such, it cuts to the deepest roots of male dominance. Like priests, kings, or slave masters, men created an ideology that justified their dominance; in the vast majority of human societies, might makes right in such a powerful fashion that women have no chance for self-esteem, unless it is esteem in the eyes of men. After all, because men set the "absolute standards" for both sexes, any woman behaving like a man is, by definition, masculine in a negative sense. She is aggressive rather than ambitious, pushy rather than eager for achievement. And if a woman behaves like a man dictates, she performs her roles as mother and wife by behaving like a woman—that is, she is gentle, submissive, and frilly—everything that, thankfully, a man is not.[76]

Simmel even argues that men are so selfish that "in general, the average man's interest in women lies in something that is roughly the same in both the seamstress and the princess."[77] Sex is what moves men, "and the fulfillment of sexual desire tends to free the man from the relationship and bind the woman to it." This is so because "fidelity" is at the core of any women's essential nature. She is permanently loyal to a master who couldn't care less. Men move from one sexual encounter to another—"the man may be brought to madness or suicide as a result of erotic experiences"—and they even have a deep-seated "disposition in favor of infidelity." They jump from bed to bed because the appeal of any woman is often lost as soon as the man satisfies his sexual impulses.[78]

Simmel's critics have understandably had a field day with these last lines. He not only had a long affair with the poet and writer Gertrud Kantorowicz, but he fathered a child that he refused to see, even as he continued the affair. His defenders argue that "public admission of his paternity was simply out of the question. The primary concern was to shield themselves [i.e., he and his wife] from public scorn. Furthermore, Simmel's refusal to see his daughter was a way of reassuring his wife of his dedication to their marriage and shielding her from public humiliation."[79]

Skeptics (myself included) might argue that if you believe that, you also believe in Santa Claus, the Easter Bunny, and eternal harmony on earth. Whatever your own judgment, the daughter eventually emigrated to Palestine, and Simmel went on believing that "love negates the authority of marital fidelity. Male desire finds authentic satisfaction beyond social regulation."[80]

Simmel's own behavior mirrored his harsh judgment of the male's self-centered devotion to "fleeting experiences," rooted in a propensity to infidelity. So, given the problem, what was the solution? If modern societies offered a neutral way to judge behavior, women might have a chance for an independent existence. But, "since the relative value of the male and the female is decided on the basis of a male rather than a neutral value idea," women find it impossible to escape from the "vicious circle" created by men. Women will only get negative answers if they continue to judge themselves by male values and beliefs.[81]

"The core of the entire problem" therefore rested on a simple fact: For women to achieve "new nuances" and new extensions to the limits of male culture, they needed to accomplish something *"that men cannot do"* (emphasis in original).[82] With these words Simmel assumes that male culture will not change in any fundamental sense. He could have called for a revolution that challenged both sexes to create a neutral standard. Instead, he called for women to extend the limits of male culture by focusing on those points and occupations "for which distinctively female abilities have a predisposition." In history, for example, "the special observational, empathetic and constructive facilities of the female psyche" offered women a chance to view anything from the Greek Wars to the French Revolution from a fresh perspective. Empathy was never a male strong point, so women would write histories that men could never repeat or surpass.[83]

Women could edge their way into a male-dominated world, but the center of their existence would nevertheless remain the home because "the home is an objective entity whose distinctiveness can be compared with no other. It has been stamped by the special abilities and interests, and emotionality and intellectuality, of the woman, by the total rhythm of her being."[84] Remember that Simmel sought to find something that men could not do. Otherwise, given male dominance, women would only be judged on male terms, and the judgments would be, quite predictably, negative to women.

Simmel saw the nature of male dominance so precisely that he got caught in a web of his own creation. To those who argued that women contributed to culture in an "indirect" manner when they raised children, he noted that this "profound categorical error" confused the transmission of cultural content with a direct influence on culture itself. Women's role as mothers was to act "like the sunshine that made a plant grow"; they taught children how to behave properly, but the content of that education came from men and the world they dominated. Thus, even in the home, all members of the family internalized "the male mode of being."[85]

From this perspective Simmel believed that women could escape "the brutal historical idealization" of male values only by creating a *parallel* sphere of activity. By centering themselves in the home, judgments about self-esteem and societal worth "would no longer turn on an equivalence *within* the general form of objective culture but rather on an equivalence between two modes of existence that have a completely different rhythm."[86] Women would finally dominate because, in the home, they did something that men could not do.

To contemporary ears the argument sounds both self-serving and contradictory. How could the home be an equivalent to the male's world if it only passed on the content created by men? Simmel never resolved this contradiction, but then again, neither have we. The contemporary women's movement would not exist unless the problems perceived a century ago still existed today. What stands out are Simmel's keen insights into the profound dilemmas that women confront when they are asked to root their sense of self-esteem in the values and beliefs of their male "masters." It remains a vicious circle for countless women because, like Simmel, we are still waiting for a solution that eliminates, at its roots, "the power position of men."[87]

STRANGERS IN THE METROPOLIS

His name is Jamal Beghal. In 1965 he and his family emigrated from Algeria to a "gritty suburb" of Paris. He married a French woman, and despite his perfect French and a healthy dose of intelligence, Jamal always remained confined to the margins of French society. "He was stuck on the bottom, drifting between menial jobs in grimy food stalls in an outdoor market near Paris." Eventually, he found a sense of purpose in Islam, and more specifically, the Al Queda terrorist network of Osama bin Ladin. Jamal wanted to do something for Allah, but thankfully, French authorities arrested him before he helped blow up a plane or destroy the American embassy in Paris.[88]

No accurate explanation of Jamal's behavior is possible without taking into account many variables, everything from his personality to the persisting political conflicts between the United States and the Muslim nations in the Middle East. But, despite being published almost seventy years before Jamal's birth, two of Simmel's most famous essays shed significant light on the everyday predicaments of men like Jamal Beghal. Read "The Stranger" and "The Metropolis and Mental Life," and you quickly grasp the sense of loneliness that so often affects Algerian immigrants in Paris or, just as important, the 10 percent of the American people who were born abroad and now live, as strangers, in the United States.

The stranger is a wanderer; because, by definition, he or she brings new values and beliefs to the host society, the stranger's position in the new group is "determined, essentially, by the fact that he has not belonged to it from the beginning, that he imports qualities into it, which do and cannot stem from the group itself." Thus, for the stranger—for any immigrant on earth—there exists a peculiar and uncomfortable tension between the nearness and remoteness involved in every human relation. The immigrant can be squeezed against us in a bus or may provide the food for our lunch, but "in the relationship to him, distance means that he, who is close by, is far; and strangeness means that he, who also is far, is actually quite near."[89]

Think of an encounter in New York, Chicago, Los Angeles, or Houston with an Indian or Pakistani immigrant dressed in robes or a turban. Without saying a word, they are already strange in a literal sense because their clothing is out of step in the United States. You may do a double take because despite being very close to the person, the clothing suggests a continental divide of cultures that can never be bridged. Meanwhile, for the stranger, such an encounter denies their individuality; "strangers are not really conceived as individuals but as strangers of a particular type: The element of distance is no less general in regard to them than the element of nearness."[90]

One common response of immigrants—all over the world—is to live in cultural or ethnic ghettos. In locations such as San Francisco's Chinatown, new immigrants—the strangers—can try to feel a sense of real nearness with compatriots who speak their language, eat their foods, and practice their religion. But even in the cultural oasis, the sense of being an outsider is a permanent, everyday reality. The tourists who tour the open-air food markets gawk at the peculiar fish for sale, and the sight of a row of dead ducks hanging out in a meat market's window moves many tourists to point and giggle. These Chinese people are strange.

Since 1965 more than 25 million immigrants have come to the United States. They keep coming at a rate of almost a million a year, and they live where most of the rest of us do: in the city, in what Simmel called the metropolis. Consider some startling statistics: almost a third of all Americans live in four states—California (34 million), Texas (21 million), New York (19 million), and Florida (16 million)—and our ten largest metropolitan areas house 32 percent of the American people.[91] We have squeezed ourselves into cities; and according to Simmel, the metropolis nurtures a mental life that dramatically accentuates a person's sense of loneliness, of being close to other people, yet simultaneously alienated from them.

"There is perhaps no psychic phenomenon which has been so unconditionally reserved to the metropolis as has the blasé attitude."[92] A city such as Philadelphia, Dallas, or Los Angeles offers all residents an *"enormous intensification of nervous stimulation"* (emphasis added); you can and do see everything in a modern city, so after a while, you feel—with some legitimacy—that nothing can or will move you. You even learn to walk by people lying prostrate on the sidewalk because "the essence of the blasé attitude consists in the blunting of discrimination." You see the person, but you nevertheless glide on by because, in the city, "all things begin to float with equal specific gravity." The difference between an immigrant dressed in odd clothing and a person having a conversation with himself is perceived as insubstantial.[93]

The blasé attitude is a form of self-preservation, "bought at the price of devaluing the objective world." It is necessary for a measure of sanity, as is the sense of reserve, "with its overtone of hidden aversion," that characterizes many a metropolitan encounter. If people seem unfriendly or in a hurry, Simmel argues that a sense of antipathy to others is necessary for our psychic survival. "From both these typical dangers of the metropolis, indifference and indiscriminate suggestibility, antipathy protects us." You walk the streets with a sense of "preparatory antagonism" because that allows you to avoid being touched and bothered. Thus, "what appears in the metropolitan style of life directly as dissociation is in reality only one of the city's elemental forms of socialization."[94]

For the long-term resident, and for a newcomer like Jamal Beghal in

Paris, the sense of reserve, with its overtone of antipathy, produces a very peculiar situation. The city "grants to the individual a kind and amount of personal freedom which has no analogy whatsoever under other conditions."[95] On the one hand, you can be standing in a crowd of 50,000 people and be totally, incredibly alone. The city thus accentuates the sense of strangeness that is the inheritance of any immigrant. On the other hand, you can live in a city of 7 million, and the blasé attitude gives terrorists a leg up in the search for anonymity. Indeed, because city people so often keep one another at arm's distance, the terrorist has a decided advantage in successfully maintaining his or her underground existence. Ironically, the police, aware of their position, then hire as double agents the Algerian (or other) immigrants who have some chance of penetrating the cells built by those who live, as strangers, in cities like Paris, Hamburg, London, or Miami.

To repeat: many variables account for the behavior of a man like Jamal Beghal. Nevertheless, Simmel's insights about the stranger and the city allow us to better understand the sense of profound loneliness that so perfectly meshes with the political, religious, and economic conflicts that characterize our time. By concentrating on forms, Simmel created conceptions that are timeless; they can be plugged into any society on earth, and a hundred years later, they still shed bright light on the important realities of the contemporary world.

STRASBOURG AND DEATH

Speaking in Munich in 1918, Max Weber described German academic life as a "mad hazard." He explained that Jewish professors were, by definition, outsiders in the German system, and he then asked his audience of students this question: "Do you in all conscience believe that you can stand seeing mediocrity after mediocrity, year after year, climb beyond you, without becoming embittered and coming to grief. . . . I have found very few men who could endure this situation."[96]

Weber tried to help Simmel. He supported Simmel's efforts to obtain a chair at Heidelberg University in 1908, where the faculty wrote this summary of Simmel's work to date: "One cannot locate him in any of the general currents; he has always gone his own way. . . . If he can be secured for Heidelberg, then the social science and all their branches . . . would find such a comprehensive representation as exists no where else."[97]

Simmel never got the job. The "sociological artist" saw one mediocrity after another climb the academic ladder while he watched from the sidelines, producing what remains an extraordinarily provocative body of work. Finally, in 1914, he received a chair of philosophy at the University of Strasbourg. Simmel, very reluctantly, accepted this position. Even for Germany, Strasbourg existed at the very margins of the academic world;

like Alaska to the U.S. mainland, it was frontier territory, and especially so in 1914. World War I had just begun; when Simmel arrived, his potential students were dying on the Western Front and the university's lecture halls often turned into military hospitals. In 1915 he tried to obtain a vacant chair in Heidelberg. Once again, his ethnicity and reputation for uniqueness preceded him. Simmel was the preeminent marginal man, denied the recognition he deserved because, *by choice,* he fit into no academic box. Especially in sociology, his focus on forms was so original that, to date, few have followed his lead.[98]

In 1918 doctors discovered that Simmel had liver cancer. He died in September 1918, still trying to obtain what his academic colleagues would never provide, a chair at the center of German university life. The great irony is that Simmel, acutely aware of the prejudices harbored by others, still wanted to be a part of a system that, as Weber stressed, celebrated one mediocrity after another. A psychologist might call this masochistic. A sociologist would note that, understanding what makes society possible, Simmel wanted to make it impossible—at least until the university made room, not only for Jewish professors, but for minds that exemplified the originality universities supposedly champion.

NOTES

1. Georg Simmel, *The Philosophy of Money,* ed. David Frisby, 2nd enlarged ed. (London: Routledge, 1990), 238.

2. William Nicholls, *Christian AntiSemitism: A History of Hate* (Northvale, N.J.: Jason Aronson, 1993), 242.

3. Ibid.

4. Werner Keller, *Diaspora: The Post-Biblical History of the Jews* (New York: Harcourt, Brace and World, 1969), 213–14; also see Nicholls, *Christian AntiSemitism,* 243.

5. Nicholls, *Christian AntiSemitism,* 243.

6. Ibid., 286.

7. Ibid., 304.

8. Ibid., 306.

9. Ibid., 329.

10. Walter Laquer, *A History of Zionism* (New York: MJF Books, 1972), 28–29.

11. Ibid., 29.

12. Ibid., 30.

13. See Lewis S. Coser, *Masters of Sociological Thought* (New York: Harcourt, Brace and Jovanovich, 1971), 194.

14. Simmel, *Philosophy of Money,* 461.

15. Ralph M. Leck, *Georg Simmel and Avant-Garde Sociology: The Birth of Modernity, 1880–1920* (New York: Humanity Books, 2000), 33–34. I have relied heavily on this fine book for a number of the details about Simmel's personal life.

16. Ibid., 29.

17. Ibid., 31–32.

18. David Frisby, *Georg Simmel* (London: Ellis Horwood, 1984), 23. See also Peter Lawrence, *Georg Simmel: Sociologist and European* (Sunbury on Thames: Thomas Nelson and Sons, 1976).

19. Frisby, *Georg Simmel*, 26.

20. Ibid., 27.

21. Leck, *Georg Simmel and Avant-Garde Sociology*, 147–50.

22. Ibid., 153.

23. Frisby, *Georg Simmel*, 32–33.

24. See Leck, *Georg Simmel and Avant-Garde Sociology*. The quote appears on the back cover of the book; its specific source is not cited.

25. See, for example, Simmel, *Philosophy of Money*, 366.

26. Georg Simmel, *The Sociology of Georg Simmel*, trans. and ed. Kurt H. Wolff (New York: Free Press, 1964), 21–22.

27. Georg Simmel, *Conflict and the Web of Group Affiliations* (New York: Free Press, 1964), 61.

28. Georg Simmel, "How Is Society Possible?" in *Essays on Sociology, Philosophy, and Aesthetics*, ed. Kurt H. Wolff (New York: Harper Torchbooks, 1965), 342–43.

29. Ibid., 344.

30. Ibid., 345.

31. Ibid., 347–51.

32. Ibid., 350.

33. Ibid., 353.

34. Ibid., 355.

35. Simmel, *Philosophy of Money*, p. 56.

36. Ibid., *Philosophy of Money*, 81; also 79–82.

37. Ibid., 83.

38. Ibid., 91.

39. Ibid., 91.

40. Ibid., 92.

41. Ronald Fernandez, *The Disenchanted Island: Puerto Rico and the United States in the Twentieth Century*, 2nd ed. (Westport, Conn.: Praeger, 1996), esp. 229–30.

42. Simmel, *Philosophy of Money*, 291.

43. Ibid., 122.

44. Ibid., 125.

45. Ibid., 129–30.

46. Ibid., 232; "Money in the Sequence of Purposes" is the book's third chapter (204–80).

47. Ibid., 232.

48. Ibid., 255–256.

49. Ibid., 236.

50. Simmel, *Philosophy of Money*, 235–237.

51. Ibid., 255–56.

52. Ibid., 256–57.

53. Ibid., 259.

54. Ibid.

55. Ibid.

56. Ibid., 279.

57. Ibid., 232.

58. Ibid., 325.

59. Ibid., 293.

60. Ibid., 287.

61. See, for example, Eugene Murdock, *Patriotism Limited, 1862–65: The Civil War and the Bounty System* (Kent, Ohio: Kent State University Press, 1967).

62. Simmel, *Philosophy of Money,* 300.

63. Ibid., 346.

64. Ibid., 343.

65. Ibid., 343–345.

66. Ibid., 456, see, too, p. 431.

67. See, for example, Ronald Fernandez, *Cruising the Caribbean: U.S. Influence and Intervention in the Twentieth Century* (Monroe, Maine: Common Courage, 1994).

68. Simmel, *Philosophy of Money,* 442.

69. Ibid., 442.

70. Ibid., 484.

71. Ibid., 470.

72. Ibid., 469–70.

73. Betty Friedan, *The Feminine Mystique* (New York: Norton, 1963); Simone de Beauvoir, *The Second Sex* (New York: Bantam, 1961).

74. Georg Simmel, "Female Culture," in *Georg Simmel: On Women, Sexuality, and Love* (New Haven, Conn.: Yale University Press, 1984), 97; on Bebel, see Leck, *Georg Simmel and Avant-Garde Sociology,* 133.

75. Georg Simmel, "The Relative and Absolute in the Problem of the Sexes," in *Georg Simmel: On Women, Sexuality, and Love* (New Haven, Conn.: Yale University Press, 1984), 103.

76. Ibid., 105.

77. Ibid., 125.

78. Simmel, "Female Culture," 71.

79. Leck, *Georg Simmel and Avant-Garde Sociology,* 154.

80. Ibid., 154–56.

81. Simmel, "Female Culture," 74.

82. Ibid., 75.

83. Ibid., esp. 80–81.

84. Ibid., 92.

85. Ibid., 95.

86. Ibid., 101.

87. Simmel, "The Relative and the Absolute in the Problem of the Sexes," 103.

88. Steven Erlanger and Chris Hedges, "Terror Cells Slip through Europe's Grasp," *New York Times,* December 28, 2001, 1, B4–5.

89. Georg Simmel, "The Stranger," in *Essays on Sociology, Philosophy and Aesthetics,* ed. Kurt H. Wolff (New York: Harper Torchbooks, 1965), 402.

90. Ibid., 407.

91. See *Migration News* 7, no. 2 (2000): 7 [www.migration.ucdavis.edu]; for an overview of the immigration process, see Ronald Fernandez, *America's Banquet of Cultures: Harnessing Ethnicity, Race, and Immigration in the Twenty-first Century* (Westport, Conn.: Praeger, 2000).

92. Simmel, "The Metropolis and Mental Life," in *Essays on Sociology, Philosophy and Aesthetics,* ed. Kurt H. Wolff (New York: Harper Torchbooks, 1965), 413.

93. Ibid., 414.

94. Ibid., 416.

95. Ibid.

96. Max Weber, "Science as a Vocation," in *From Max Weber,* ed. Hans Gerth and C. Wright Mills (New York: Oxford University Press, 1946), 134.

97. See Frisby, *Georg Simmel,* 31.

98. Leck, *Georg Simmel and Avant-Garde Sociology,* 36; Frisby, *Georg Simmel,* 32–33; Coser, *Masters of Sociological Thought,* 196–97.

CHAPTER 5

George Herbert Mead

"That is the problem of society is it not? How can you present order and structure in society and yet bring about the changes that need to take place, are taking place?"

George Herbert Mead, *The Problem of Society.*[1]

DIRTY WORK

Do you remember *The Jungle*, Upton Sinclair's 1906 novel about the preposterously unsanitary conditions in Chicago's meatpacking industry?[2] Many students read it in high school and, after finishing the book, found it impossible to eat a hot dog or other mystery meats for a considerable period of time. The book exposed an open sore in U.S. life and led to, among other things, the Pure Food and Drug Act. Congress stepped in and theoretically created conditions that produced, if not the best meat, at least a nonlethal breakfast, lunch, or dinner.

The consumer was safe. But what about the worker? As in 2003,[3] in 1906 a multitude of legal and illegal immigrants killed and cut the meat placed on America's best dining-room tables. They worked long and hard, only to be met by reception committees that included the American Protective Association, centered in the Midwest. The roughly half million members of this organization called "Whiskey Bill" Traynor their anti-immigrant leader. Traynor not only blamed Catholics for the economic problems of the 1890s, but he uncovered a plot as nasty as any in American history. Waving a document titled "Instructions to Catholics," Traynor told anyone willing to listen that the document's author was the Vatican's most famous resident. Traynor argued that the pope meant to take over America and was responsible for the legions of new, job-stealing immigrants from countries like Italy and Poland. "True Americanism" therefore demanded that members take a solemn oath to never vote for a Catholic, to boycott Catholic merchants, and to openly discriminate against Catholic labor.[4]

Over time organizations like the American Protective Association produced a movement to Americanize the immigrant.[5] At the beginning of the twentieth century, countless all-American communities vied with one another to find new ways to make the immigrant blend—willingly or unwillingly—into the American mainstream. Rochester, New York created "Americanization factories" as Theodore Roosevelt stressed that "the country is a crucible, a melting pot in which many different race strains are being fused into one. If some of the material remains an unfused lump, it is worthless in itself and it is also a detriment to the rest of the mixture."[6]

George Herbert Mead stepped into the crucible with a courageous speech delivered in Chicago in 1909. Its title—"The Adjustment of Our Industry to Surplus and Unskilled Labor"—sounds like a strong dose of academic anemia, but its content was as confrontational as a socialist leading a strike. Mead argued that instead of complaining about the immigrant, Americans needed to remember one undeniable fact: immigrants came to the United States "to do the dirty work." They contributed untold benefits to the economy, but instead of appreciation, "I was assured that the business men of the city had absolutely no feeling of responsibility to the immigrant, or the sense of debt which Chicago owes to the immigrant."[7]

These are strong words still today. In 1909 men like Whiskey Bill Traynor were literally on the prowl, eager to forcibly suppress any support for immigrants in general and Catholics in particular. Mead nevertheless reminded his audience that "they come here because there is a demand for them. Many industries have sent their agents abroad to induce them to come. Transportation companies spread their advertisements all over Europe to induce men to come, more than ought to be encouraged."[8]

Mead argued that Americans—especially the businessmen in Chicago—had responsibilities. Immigrants who died in our factories and mines "have just as much right in this America as any one." But have we made a serious attempt to adapt our schools to *their* needs? Do we try to make it possible for these immigrants to learn English? And have we made sufficient efforts to provide the best possible industrial education. "We have not," said Mead, so he proposed a variety of ways to achieve a lifelong goal: the real bringing together of all Americans.[9]

Mead's attitude toward immigrants suggests two of the crucial themes that dominated his teaching, his publications, and his significant community efforts—for more than twenty-five years—in the city of Chicago. First, Mead was always interested in social reform, an activity that he described as "the application of intelligence to the control of social conditions." With a passion as strong as Emile Durkheim's, Mead believed that educated men and women could and should use their intelligence to "maintain order and structure in society and yet bring about the changes that needed to take place." As with the immigrant, if Americans faced the truth and accepted their responsibilities, a serious social problem could become a way to unite rather than divide the American people.[10]

On a second and deeper level, Mead believed that any chance to discover and invent a new future rested on an understanding of the nature and development of reflective intelligence. Like no other animal on earth, human beings have the capacity to talk to themselves about themselves and the world in which they live. I could, for example, reflect on history, the immigrant, the businessmen, and other Americans simultaneously. I could even put myself in the other person's shoes and try to empathize with his or her way of seeing the world. Collectively, we could all see the process of our past development and then decide—after this process of conscious reflection—how we could walk into the future on the basis of a reevaluated and now *conquered* past.

Mead thought of reflective intelligence as a gift that potentially allowed people to control and change one of the most implacable opponents on earth: an institutionalized social order.[11] Thus Mead's focus on the origin and development of self was a search for scientific truth and a deliberate means to a better world. His argument is both enormously eloquent and exceedingly precise. Understand the origin and development of self, and you unlocked the door that explains the nature and functioning of reflective intelligence. Understand the self, and you could conceivably create an America that made a place for everyone—even those who did the nation's dirty work.

MAN FROM OBERLIN

By definition chambers of commerce are famous for hype. Because they try to sell their city, no one is surprised when the chamber engages in hyperbole. In the case of Oberlin, Ohio, the chamber's claim—that it is the "most cosmopolitan small town in America"—actually has deep roots in reality. In 1833 two Yankee missionaries decided to build a town and college at the same place and time. Pledging to live lives that epitomized "the plainest living and the highest thinking," they established a college that in 1833 announced this admission policy: "Youths are received as members, irrespective of color." By the time George Mead entered Oberlin (in 1877), the college and the city both had a well-deserved reputation for rising above the common prejudices and accepted wisdom of the American mainstream.[12]

Born in South Hadley, Massachusetts, on February 27, 1863, Mead came to Oberlin when his minister father accepted a position (in 1869) as chair of Sacred Rhetoric and Pastoral Theology. His mother was a graduate of Mount Holyoke Seminary, so Mead lived in a home where both parents exemplified another Oberlin tradition: in a sexist society, Oberlin was the first truly coeducational college in the United States.

Mead first studied at the Oberlin Preparatory School and formally entered the college in 1879. He quickly became the inseparable friend of Henry Castle, a young man from Hawaii. For twelve years the two men corresponded from all parts of the world, providing a written record that offers tangible evidence of Mead's preoccupations, dreams, and even "making an ass of himself."[13]

As early as 1882 Mead and Castle decided that "no dogmatic philosophy was possible." They serendipitously arrived at this conclusion on the way to class one morning, and "it was an experience that was as profound as any religious conversion could be. It is identified with all the indefinite promise of spring."[14]

It is a great line. Mead knew what he was against but not what he was for. After graduation in 1883 he taught school and tried "to work for others in Christianity." Meanwhile, he also doubted that God even existed. A bit dizzy, he felt "utterly at sea," so in 1884 he worked as part of a crew surveying for the railroads in northeastern Minnesota. It was tough work, with a hard-drinking, foul-mouthed engineer of a boss. As Mead told Castle, "a drunken man howling outside of your tent would destroy the concentration of Socrates."

Castle decided Mead's fate. He entered Harvard in 1887, and so did Mead. At the time Harvard housed philosophers like William James and Josiah Royce. Pragmatism ruled the philosophical day. Mead not only studied with the best minds in America here; he received an offer from James to tutor James's son. In the summer of 1888, Mead lived with the Jameses and "made an ass of himself" when he had a romantic affair with Mrs. James's sister. The great philosopher noted that "Mead was a fine manly fellow and fit object for any woman to adore, but James was not enthusiastic about having to engage in unwelcome spectatorship of such adoration at close range."[15]

With James's help Mead sailed for Germany, now eager to get a Ph.D. in philosophy from the University of Berlin. While he avidly tried to position himself in relation to the doctrines then dominant, the pragmatic bent of his thinking was already evident. As he explained to Castle, "The only inspiring work that can be found is in the practical application of morals to life." Mead especially wanted to settle in one city, immerse himself in its politics, and use science and reason to start the process of significant societal change at its metropolitan core.[16]

Mead remained in Berlin until 1891. He married Henry Castle's sister Helen—she too was in Berlin—but despite his desire for the Ph.D., Mead returned to the United States without completing his dissertation. John Dewey had offered Mead a faculty position at the University of Michigan in Ann Arbor, and the Meads settled there in 1891. It was the beginning of a professional and personal friendship that lasted a lifetime. Despite his embarrassment about never completing his thesis, Mead nevertheless focused on his new teaching and research responsibilities. He never got the Ph.D., and this is arguably a lesson for today's universities. Now, a doctorate is as mandatory as a photo ID at the airport; then, just having a great mind was a sufficient basis for teaching at America's best universities.

Dewey and Mead lived almost side by side. Castle explained that the families seemed to have an idyllic existence. Their homes had "splendid outlooks" because their backyards backed up to the woods. "Ann Arbor is one of the loveliest villages I have seen anywhere; all the streets pretty, up hill and down, fine pasture and forest. George and Helen are fortunate to live in such a place."[17]

The Meads agreed. But when President Harper of the University of Chicago poached other schools' faculty, he only pilfered from the nation's best universities. In 1894 John Dewey received a generous offer to head the University of Chicago's new philosophy department; with carte blanche rights to hire additional faculty, he asked Mead to accompany him to a city that had, instead of the bucolic charm of Ann Arbor, a jumble of skyscrapers facing streets full of crowded trolleys, many on their way to and from the slaughterhouses. Mead stayed at Chicago for thirty-eight years, becoming one of the city's greatest boosters and one of the university's best and most beloved teachers.

One positive proof of Mead's classroom influence is this provocative fact: his students posthumously published the books that are now the basis for Mead's reputation and influence. Others put in print what Mead only offered in class. His reluctance to publish has always baffled anyone trying to understand his career. Go, for example, to the Library of Congress catalog, check the name John Dewey, and 178 books appear. Many are duplicates, but if Mead's mentor and best friend published so much, what stopped George Mead?

One explanation is hard for the status conscious to accept: in Dewey's words, Mead "was remarkably free from the usual external signs of busy activity. He was not one to rush about breathless with the conviction that he must somehow convince others of his activity." In plainer English Mead had nothing to prove, except to himself. From the day he set foot in Michigan, his preoccupation was the "problem of individual mind and consciousness in relation to world and society." Dewey wrote that Mead was the most original mind of his generation but, as if Sisyphus climbing the mountain, that he experienced great difficulty mastering verbal, much less written, expression of his new ideas and insights. "There was not ready and waiting for him any language in which to express himself."[18] Mead developed his own terminology and, with no burning need to impress others with his brilliance, Mead worked and reworked and reworked his lectures and the publications that never made it to the printer's table.

Today Mead would be banished to the academic bullpen or even the hinterland bleachers; in present-day universities you do indeed publish or perish, especially without a doctorate. Thankfully, Mead survived, as a person, a father, a husband, a teacher, and a citizen of a democracy. His son recalled that he most often associated his father with this phrase: "It ought to be possible to do so and so."[19] Dewey called him an idealist, but the remarkable thing about Mead's work is that he did—and does—offer the conceptual tools needed to achieve peaceful yet radical change of the individual and of his or her society.

It is a great body of work, all the more interesting because it was the gift of a teacher to his students and, as if passing the torch, a gift from his students to the rest of us.

"SCIENTIFIC METHOD AND THE MORAL SCIENCES"

William James often emphasized the same point: pragmatism was a *method*, a manner of approaching the facts of life rather than a theory about the course of human history or a dogma setting out the right path to the ideal existence. In a perfect metaphor, James describes pragmatism as a corridor in a hotel; it provides a way to enter "innumerable chambers" by requiring a specific "attitude of orientation" toward the world's storehouse of knowledge.[20]

Say you wanted to know if Jesus Christ was one God or, with Father and Holy Ghost, three gods. Was Christianity monotheistic or polytheistic? James (and students like John Dewey and George Mead) approached such questions in this manner: "What difference would it practically make to anyone if this notion rather than that notion were true? If no practical difference whatever can be traced, then the alternatives mean practically the same thing and all dispute is idle."[21]

With this line James instantly ignored many of the battles that traditionally drove philosophers to argue, with great delight, about the divine light at the end of the tunnel or the principles and categories of knowledge. Want to know if you do or do not exist? Like Rhett Butler in *Gone with the Wind*, pragmatists did not give a damn. Instead, James suggested this philosophical rule of thumb: look away from "first things" and zero in on last things, what he called the "fruits, consequences, and facts" of human thought and action. For pragmatists—and this was crucial for George Mead—"truth in our ideas means the same thing that it means in science." That is, all ideas are true "just in so far as they help us to get into satisfactory relation with other parts of our experience."[22]

From this perspective the search for truth is never completed because even "the most violent revolutions in an individual's beliefs leave most of his old order standing." New truth is "a go-between, a smoother over of the endless arguments between what you were taught to believe and the world that actually exists. In Mead's words, "the facts are determined by conflict."[23] As a pragmatist and a scientist, your task is to resolve the conflict because "to be true only means to perform this marriage function," to assimilate new knowledge into the stock of beliefs that we arbitrarily and involuntarily inherited from others.[24]

George Mead explains the everyday consequences of pragmatism in an essay titled "Scientific Method and the Moral Sciences." Complimenting the work of Sigmund Freud, he notes that psychoanalysis forced people to realize that "we not only do our thinking but our perceiving with minds that already have an organized structure which determines in no small degree what the world of our immediate and reflective experience shall be." Freud focused on issues like dreams and their relation to the unconscious world that influenced our thoughts, beliefs, and actions. As a pragmatist Mead seeks more tangible fruits; he wants to talk about the moral— the social—order that allowed people to live and work together. As a perpetual, historical inheritance from others, we learned to believe that the "process of the universe" favors the creation of "the most admirable order in human society."[25] In the extreme we learned that a moral order preexisted our own existence; like Moses coming down from the mount, social order was given from on high and we simply followed its mandates and tenets.

However comforting, the assumption of a preexisting order offered no solace to a scientist. By definition a skeptic, no scientist could ever say yes to a moral order simply because it had been stamped with the imprimatur of received philosophical or religious wisdom. Nothing was inviolable, least of all a social order untested by "a highly developed form of impartial intelligence," that is, the scientific method.[26]

So far the argument is abstract. Mead comes right down to earth when he discusses democracy and cult values. In civics classes we learn that the citizens of a democracy wisely debate and analyze national and international events. Democratic government supposedly means that "an intelligent public sentiment" decides any issues before the people. In reality, an authoritative public sentiment upon anything is so rare "that my guess is that the number of instances of that in the history of the United States of America could be told on the fingers of two hands, perhaps upon the fingers of one hand." Mead never meant to question the legitimacy of democracy. His target was the received wisdom that assumed an intelligent debate; perhaps we would all be better off if we challenged "old truths" with this argument of then-president William Howard Taft: "We are governed by minorities, and the relatively intelligent minorities are swayed by the import of the issue to these minorities."[27]

The facts are determined by conflict. If theory and reality do not connect, create new truths by introducing received wisdom—hello!—to the world that is actually there.

Mead reserved real bile for "cult values" in general and Christianity in particular. As received wisdom he learned (at Oberlin) the "most grandiose" of all community ideals, that Christianity found its historic expression in the ideals of the Sermon on the Mount, in the parable of the Good Samaritan, and in the Golden Rule. Unfortunately, the real facts prove that "the history of Christendom has been a history of war and strife." For a pragmatist "an institution should arise and be kept alive by its own function but in so far as it does not function the ideal of it can be kept alive only by some cult." In Western societies the church is the "outstanding illustration" of a cult institution; "*its most important function has been the preservation in the minds of the community of the faith in a social order which did not exist*" (emphasis added).[28]

Mead is not against religion. He is against contradiction. When the real world bears no relationship to the received wisdom preached by clerics in pulpits, cult values need to stand aside. The scientific truth is that "there are no absolute values." The best we can do is an endlessly incomplete social order; but we will never achieve even a rough version of that until we dispose of the received wisdom that, like fly paper, keeps us stuck in place.

Few mental comforts exist when citizens try to establish a moral order using the scientific method. Science never has, never will, and never should offer "a vision, given in the mount, of a perfected order of society." Science only argues that we try to solve social and moral problems with the same methods we use to solve the problems of natural science. Substitute functional values (i.e., the actual facts, fruits, and consequences of particular beliefs and practices) for cult values, and you can jump in to what Mead calls the "*great secular adventure*" of human life. It is an amazing experience as long as you always temper your enthusiasm for grandiose schemes as all encompassing as the coming of communism or the perfect democracy.

Mead was an idealist who never, as if Don Quixote, attacked windmills. Focus on "bringing about the immediate adjustment" of people to the immediate problems at hand. "It is the only way in which it [self-conscious change] can proceed, for with every adjustment the environment has changed, and the society and its individuals have changed in like degree."[29] People reform a moral order in increments, and their chance of success is substantially improved if they never forget the weight of the past on the present and the future. "The order of the universe that we live in is a moral order. It has become the moral by becoming the self-conscious method of the members of a human society. We are not pilgrims and strangers. We are at home in our own world but it is not ours by inheritance but by conquest. The world that comes to us from the past possesses and controls us. We possess and control the world we discover and invent. And this is the world of the moral order."[30]

That is pure Mead, pure pragmatism. We move ahead by using reflective intelligence to *conquer* inherited beliefs, values, and practices. Any moral order actually belongs to people only when, after self-conscious and self-critical analysis, they decide if they wish to continue being what the past made them. Mead's great contribution in *Mind, Self, and Society* is to give us the conceptual tools needed to possess and control the social order.

Incidentally, Mead never forgot that it is incredibly hard to conquer the past; but he also emphasized that it is not only quite possible, but it is "a splendid adventure if we can rise to it."[31]

MIND

Mead begins *Mind, Self, and Society* by telling us that he is a social behaviorist. It is an awkward term because it associates Mead with the very perspective he wants to criticize. Seeing behavior only through the lens of stimulus and response, traditional behaviorists acted like the queen in *Alice in Wonderland:* "Off with their heads." Behaviorists forgot about imagery, language, and consciousness, and—the cardinal sin for Mead—they also forgot about introspection. Their strange aim was to observe behavior "without bringing in the observation of an inner experience."[32]

Take this example. In the early 1970s, when college campuses still breathed confrontation and change, I used an expletive in a class. It was a slip of the tongue, but let us call it a stimulus. After class a young man approached me and began to shake my hand. I wondered why. He explained that my use of language was a revolutionary gesture! I tried to be very polite because his response was genuine. Using an expletive (my words included "oh, shit!") was somehow an assault on the bastilles of political, economic, and cultural power.

The rest of my students were indifferent to my use of language. Their response was no response. Fernandez talks like the rest of us. Big deal. I want to go get a beer.

For Mead the key to understanding this encounter is the *process* of interpretation between the stimulus offered by the use of language and the memorable response, the shaking of my hand. Mead puts heads center stage by working from the outside to the inside. He sees the stimulus and then always spotlights how and why the person responded in this or that fashion. An eccentric response would be particularly appealing because a social behaviorist emphasized "the parts of the act which to do not come to external observation."[33] How, based on such a meaningless slip of the tongue, did the student assume that I made a revolutionary gesture?

Mead immediately hints at an answer to this question. He stresses that for a social behaviorist, "the whole (society) is prior to the part (the individual), *not* the part to the whole; and the part is explained in terms of the whole, *not* the whole in terms of the part" (emphasis added).[34]

To help understand the response of my student, you must grasp the influence of society in general and the late 1960s and early 1970s in particular. At our university we even had a student who stood on an orange crate near one of the campus's main thoroughfares. He loudly cursed for minutes at a time; his theory was that by overwhelming us with offensive language, he would eliminate our inhibitions—why be so "up tight"?— and free us to act in a more liberating manner.

As a social behaviorist Mead starts with society and works back to the individual. He focuses on the lively process of interpretation because there is always a *delayed reaction* between any stimulus and response. People think and then they respond to the world that is there. It is a process, a potentially deliberate course of action, because human beings have the remarkable capacity to use their brains to shape and reshape their responses to themselves, to others, and to society.

That brings us to mind. Mead is very frustrating here because, like Durkheim in *The Division of Labor in Society*, Mead only defines this crucial term after 100 pages of prose. And even then, he calls mentality a "relationship of the organism to the situation which is mediated by sets of symbols."[35] It is heavy language that finally catches the thrust of Mead's approach. He will argue that mind is synonymous with self-consciousness and that mind only arises because people have the wonderful ability to use symbols to communicate with one another.

Mead's followers label this approach symbolic interaction.[36] When people communicate using symbols such as words, they make an implicit assumption: that the symbols, the words, mean the same thing to me that they mean to you. When a friend of mine recently learned Spanish, he looked in a bilingual dictionary for the verb "to embarrass." The dictionary gave *embarazar*, so my friend said "estoy embarazado." He thought he said he was embarrassed; in reality he told the other person he was pregnant! In Spanish that is the colloquial meaning of the verb *embarazar*.

Communication failed because the symbols used were not what Mead calls *significant* symbols. They did not arouse in the other person the *same* response they aroused in my friend. On the contrary, interpreting the symbol from a different *societal* perspective, one person looked absurd in the eyes of the other. Even in the most liberal Spanish communities, men never get pregnant.

What is characteristic of any human society is the ability to share symbols. Millions of people can actually and reliably assume that the words I use mean the same thing to me that they mean to them. Mead proves his point with a lovely analysis of bears. Say I point to a footprint and teach you that it means bear. You learn the meaning of the symbol, and we now can both use it to forever identify that this—the footprint—leads to that, the bear we now see in the woods. Because the bear is growling—another symbol we learned to share—our interpretation is rapid and our response is clear: we need to somehow get the hell out of the woods.[37]

Symbols offer all human beings great freedom and flexibility because they "constitute objects not constituted before, objects which would not exist except for the context of social relationships wherein symbolization occurs." Remember that Mead is a social behaviorist. Symbols are therefore the "heritage of man," and meaning is never, fundamentally, a state of consciousness that exists *outside* the field of social experiences. On the contrary, the meaning of symbols should be seen only in the context of a particular set of social and historical beliefs, values, and practices.[38]

Take, as an example, Betsy Ross and the American flag. Pictures of Betsy Ross laboriously darning the American flag dot the pages of countless U.S. elementary and high school textbooks. She is a shared and revered symbol to many Americans, but unfortunately, the Betsy Ross legend "has no substantial foundation in history." Using his freedom to create symbols, Betsy Ross's grandson recounted family tradition—some would say misspoke—at an 1870 meeting of the Pennsylvania Historical Society.[39] Historians believed the grandson, and over time the legend became a shared symbol for more than 250 million Americans. New immigrants even learn about Betsy Ross when they study for citizenship. But, and this is Mead's point, the symbols can only be understood within the context of a particular field of social experiences.

Mead never argues that symbols are accurate or true. As the flag example suggests, people can share and revere symbols that are as trustworthy as cult values. For Mead two points are crucial. First, in the process of social communication, people create, re-create, and discard shared symbols. Symbols establish "new objects in nature" and become, like the Betsy Ross story, the "commonsense" knowledge of a society. Second, think of symbolic interaction as a social act with three parts. Using symbols, one person begins an exchange, the other responds to the symbols offered, and the first person responds to the response of the other. "This threefold or triadic relation" is the basis of meaning. Life is a prolonged and orderly "conversation of gestures" because, in general, you respond as I thought you would—and vice versa.

Shared symbols are a necessity for meaningful interaction—and the proving ground for the development of mind. Mead emphasizes that mind arises in the process of communication, not communication through mind.[40] He believes that both the genesis and the existence of mind are possible only because, in symbolic interaction, I take the attitude of the other toward myself or toward my behavior.

The ability to take the attitude of the other is the foundation stone for any understanding of Mead's work. When I respond to your words or react to your nonverbal (symbolic) expressions of joy, amazement, or disgust, I take the attitude of the other. I see myself in your eyes. This is absolutely essential for the development of mind because it is only other people's attitudes that force me to recognize the existence of my own. For example, I may hate what you said, I may call you every name in the book, but in all likelihood, I am only so upset because you offer me attitudes that diametrically disagree with my own. However brutal, an honest empathy with the critical attitudes of others can be an enormously effective way to precisely recognize and clarify my own beliefs, attitudes, and values.

Mead now moves on to the nature of reflective intelligence. It exists because, by using shared symbols to take the attitudes of others and so achieve self-consciousness, I can then use those same symbols to delay my response to a stimulus and reflect on what was said. Thinking for Mead is nothing more than *internalized conversation;* we stop the action, and even with no money in the bank, we talk to ourselves about ourselves, about others, and about the nature of society. Thus, when "we speak of a person thinking a thing out, or having a mind," we are only underlining the capacity to "pick out a stimulus" and then reflect on what others said to us and we said to them.[41]

For a social behaviorist reflective intelligence is crucial because it is the key characteristic that separates us from other animals. "There is no capacity in the lower forms to give attention to some analyzed element in the field of stimulation which would enable them to control the response. But one can say to a person, 'look at this, see this thing, and he can fasten his attention on the specific object. He can direct attention and so isolate the particular response that answers to it. *That is the way we break up our activities and thereby make learning possible*" (emphasis added).[42]

As social scientists we learn in order to take charge of our selves and our world. With his bow and arrow aimed at only one target, Mead writes that he seeks to "get control," not to settle metaphysical or other idle intellectual questions.[43] Understanding facilitates life; thus, toward the very end of the pages on mind, Mead provides another definition of mentality. Rooted in our ability to use symbols as the mediators of any social situation, mentality now "resides in the ability of the organism to indicate that in the environment which answers to his responses, so that he can control those responses in various ways."[44]

Control can imply something negative, the lockstep behavior of a stimulus that produces the precise response of a controller presumably dressed in a white lab coat. In Mead's work control implies freedom and can equal liberation. Mind emerges in the process of social interaction; by taking the attitudes of others, I achieve the gift of self-consciousness and the associated ability to reflect on self and world. "It is by means of reflexiveness—the turning-back of the experience of the individual upon himself—that the whole process is thus brought into the experience of the individuals involved in it."[45]

We get control by using our minds to understand who controls us. The whole—society—precedes the parts, you and me. We can therefore exercise our minds to see what shaped us, and especially when we grasp the significance of self, we are well on the way to consciously creating a new world. It is an eye opening adventure, revolving, like a carousel, around the concept of self.

SELF

There ought to be a law. Even if it is another Mead, Durkheim, or Simmel, no magnificent mind will ever again be allowed to publish a great book until and unless he or she precisely defines their terms at the very beginning of any long discussion. In Mead's case his students put his books together, so we could blame them if we choose to do so. But, whomever we throw the darts at, the problem remains: Mead offers no exact definition of the self. So, for us self is what you think of you. You could be lying to yourself; you could be firmly rooted in reality. Either way self refers to *your* conceptions of who you are as an object in the world of experience.[46]

This is Mead's logic. If only because we use words to describe our selves, the self does not exist at birth. It arises in the process of social development and as a result of symbolic interaction with other people. Our parents are the most obvious and (in many instances) the most influential others we encounter, but whoever first spoke to you about you initiated the process of your ongoing development of self.

As values of American culture, advocates can applaud the self-made man or woman, all the while listening to Frank Sinatra croon "I did it my way." Meanwhile, Mead will answer with this: nonsense. Because we cannot develop a self unless others initiate the process, our lives are always—and forever—inextricably linked to the attitudes, beliefs, and values of other people. Like the famous Siamese twins, others and the developing self coexist from the first breath taken by any human being, anywhere on earth.[47]

In distinguishing between the self and the body, Mead writes that a body can exist and function effectively without the existence of self. What characterizes the self is that "it can be an object to itself and that characteristic distinguishes it from other objects and the body."[48] The eye can see the foot, and the ear can hear the cracking of our knuckles, but neither can see the body as a whole. The body never sees itself as a totality in the same way that the self gets to grasp the completeness of its existence.

As an object in the world of experience, the self can use the symbols inherited in a language to intelligently reflect on its own existence. This reflexive quality of the self is possible because the self is not only an object to itself; it is also, *simultaneously,* the subject of its own reflections.[49] While this may seem impossible, consider the following example.

You wanted to date a particular person. You finally got the nerve to ask her out, and she said yes. You meet at the student center, you approach her to say hello, but instead of pulling the door in your direction, you push it in on her. Once you pick her up off the floor, she still kindly agrees to dinner. During the meal she reacts to your jokes like a mourner at a funeral. Finally, you spill spaghetti sauce on her white blouse, and she instantly develops a migraine. She must go home at once.

Ten minutes later you are in your dorm room, mulling over your humiliating experience. You are alone, the lights are out, and you are thinking, talking to yourself about your self. When you relive, with your stomach turning, knocking her flat on her back, you are the *object* of your own speculations. But, because you are thinking about yourself, you are simultaneously the *subject* of your own speculations. It is as if the self can be split in two. From one perspective you go over the experiences of the idiot who just made a fool of himself; from the other you are the idiot because the mental pictures are a mirror. You are looking at you.

Mead never argues that we necessarily tell the truth to ourselves as we reflect on the past. Few people want to think of themselves as idiots, so as your thought processes continue, you twist and distort your reflections. She never fell because you slammed the door on her; she fell because she was clumsy. And she never laughed at your jokes because she realized that you were out of her league. Anybody as witty as you would never waste his time on someone as lackluster as she.

Mead offers no "open sesame" to the truth. He only provides the conceptual tools needed to get there.

By reemphasizing the reflexive quality of the self (i.e., its ability to be both subject and object), Mead deliberately repeats a crucial point: no one can be an object to him- or herself until they are first the subject of other people's speculations. Others need to make you the subject of their attitudes, and then, by taking the attitudes of the other, you become an object to yourself. In plainer English you cannot talk to you until others talk to you. And if those others are crazy or confused, your chances for a solid sense of self have appreciably diminished.

Mead stresses that "the unity and structure of the complete self reflects the unity and structure of the social process as a whole. . . . The organization and unification of a social group is identical with the organization and unification of any one of the selves arising within the social process in which that group is engaged or which it is carrying on."[50]

Say you are a second-generation Jamaican born and raised in the northeastern part of the United States. One of your selves is the ethnic identity of being a Jamaican. But because you live in the United States, you are also told—normally *not* by your parents—that you must be a black man or a black woman. As an inheritance from society, the two identities are often mutually exclusive and therefore confusing. You may think the problem is yours, while in reality it derives from the larger society, in the process of taking the attitudes of others. At our campus many students resolve the inherited dilemma by embracing the identity Jamaican and refusing to be black. This, in turn, causes problems with and confusion for many African-American students. The consternation is even greater if the Jamaican who refuses to be black is very dark skinned and the African American is not.[51]

Who are these other people? Is there a way to be more specific about the actual influence of others on your self and mine? Mead answered these questions with a wonderful concept, the notion of the generalized others who provide crucial information about self and world.

The *generalized other* refers to the organized community or social group that gives the individual his or her unity (or disunity) of self.[52] Mead uses the example of a baseball team to show how groups provide the rules of the game and the individual's particular part in it. To successfully play ball, you need to simultaneously take the attitudes of at least nine other people. That includes the eight other players on the field and batter in the box. You can be the catcher, but you also need to know—after many hours of practice—what everyone else on the field can and should be doing. You cannot play successfully unless you have first learned, from others, the rules of the game.[53]

In its widest sense the generalized other refers to American or Cuban or English (and so on) society. However, to get a firmer handle on what happened to any one of us, you can break down the larger society into the specific groups, such as religious, ethnic, family, or political, that offered you their versions of self and world. Whatever the groups, you often learn the rules of the game by playing; but instead of entertainment, *play is very serious business.* "The game represents the passage in the life of the child from taking the role of others in play to the organized part that is essential to self-consciousness in the full sense of the term."[54]

Right down to the camouflaged clothing, GI Joe toys offer children a way to practice and learn about war; whom they learn to kill depends on the nation's contemporary enemy. In 2003 Arabs have replaced Russians as the target of choice. Toy vacuums and ironing boards suggest that housekeeping is also a game, but if you would not buy your five-year-old nephew a toy vacuum or iron, he is probably learning about the rules of the game from the perspective of traditional family beliefs, values, and practices. Presumably, ironing is still women's work.

Play is an essential way to help the individual move from one stage of self-development to another. Mead explains that the first stage includes only an "organization of the particular attitudes of other individuals toward himself and toward one another in the specific social acts in which he participates with them." This might include your parents and your brothers and sisters. They symbolize the *particular* individuals you are likely to meet in your earliest encounters with others. But over and through time, "the self is constituted not only by an organization of these particular individual attitudes, but also by an organization of the social attitudes of the generalized other or the social group as a whole to which he belongs."[55]

Once you know how to "play ball," you no longer need to think about the rules and the positioning of others in the family or religious groups of society. You know how to be a good member of an Italian, Puerto Rican, or Indian family because what was outside (in the attitudes of others) is now inside, that is, internalized at a very deep level in your mind. In the second stage of self-development, the rules have become the accepted "of course" assumptions of social life. You get along well with others because you successfully learned the shared and accepted "universe of discourse" in your society and in the specific social groups that hallmark your particular experiences.

A way to prove the existence and power of the generalized other is to speak everyday English. Say you are planning a wedding and you want to do it right; every "t" will be crossed with class and every "i" dotted with style and sophistication. Your invitations will include a scented piece of onionskin paper inside the cover full of raised-letter printing; and the paper will drift out when you pick up the invitation. Someone questions your choices, and you brilliantly answer with this retort: "That's the way it's done. That's what they say you are supposed to do." You may never get to meet or talk with "they." But it is nevertheless a tangible manifestation of the power and significance of the generalized other. Test this in your own life the next time you use the word *they* to resolve a question of dress styles or seating arrangements or any of the other etiquette predicaments of living properly in U.S. society. In my experience we often have no idea who "they" are. Mead, however, offers us a concrete answer, with the notion of the generalized other.

Like parents to a newborn, others are the indispensable initiators of your or my self-image. Mead lays that groundwork and then moves on to "the central position of thinking when considering the nature of the self."[56] The essence of the self is cognitive; its heart is the internalized conversation that I have with myself about myself and the other people with whom I come in contact. Because Mead wants to grasp the actual nature of that conversation, he uses two pronouns—the "I" and the "Me"—to conceptualize the internal dialogue that we have with ourselves. The best way to prove the persisting brilliance of these concepts is to just talk. Speak street English, and our conversations in the twenty-first century prove the points made by Mead more than eighty years ago.

The "me" is the attitudes of others that one assumes as affecting his or her own conduct. Say, for example, that I have received student evaluations at the end of a course I have taught. I have forty of your evaluations in my hands; some of you just answered the multiple-choice questions, others have written an entire page of the most precise comments and suggestions. For the sake of argument, all forty of you agree: you tell *me* that I can't teach worth a lick. My lectures would put a Starbucks addict to sleep, my tests are totally unfair, and even my clothes stink. Overall, I get an F from the class.

As I think about the evaluations, I ask some questions. Is that what the students think of *me?* Do they really think of *me* in such negative terms? And most ominous of all for my sense of self-esteem, are the students right in what they said about *me?*

Each of the three times I used the word "me" indicates my taking or assuming the attitudes of others. Forty of you told me something, and now I have to respond to what you told me.

The "I" is the response of the individual to the assumed attitudes of others. At least four possible responses are possible: agreement, disagreement, uncertainty, or indifference. In the case of the student evaluations, "I" can agree with what you said about me. You are right. I stink as a teacher.

I can also disagree. You people are wrong about me. "I" am just too intelligent for words, and you responded negatively about me because you are unable to grasp the lasting luster of my brilliant lectures.

Uncertainty could go like this: "I" do not know what to think about what you told me in the evaluations. Give me the weekend, and we can all talk in the next class.

Finally, indifference could be expressed in this fashion. "I" don't give a damn what you think about me or about my teaching. I have tenure, and the forty of you should take a long walk around the mall. It is all the same to me.

My point is Mead's. The "I" is always a varied reaction to the attitudes of others. Indeed, "if you ask, where directly in your own experience the 'I' comes in, the answer is that it comes in as a historical figure. It is what you were a second ago that is the 'I' of the 'Me.' "[57] Remember that the "I" and the "Me" are interconnected and inseparable. But when I stop to respond to what others told me about my teaching abilities (or my obligations to God or my traits as a personality), I look back at a point in history that could have occurred a second ago, a week ago, or ten years ago. The beauty of Mead's conceptualization is that it allows me to look back at my own history—the I "scopes out" the Me—and then decide, with a significant degree of self-consciousness, if others were right about me, and, if not, how I want to change my disposition toward myself, toward others, and toward society.

Society is involved because, since the "Me" gives the form to the "I," the structure of any self is always conventional. We are all inextricably parts of the society's establishment. In fact, we think about our homeroom classes in learning to be a son, a daughter, a husband, a wife, a mother, a father; in each and every instance I can only respond to what others, as representatives of the generalized other, told me about self and world. I can disagree with the attitudes of others, but *even when I disagree*, I am still firmly rooted in a conventional portrait of myself.

Take this example. During the 1960s many young Americans revolted against societal conventions. You—the representatives of "straight" society—tell me that crew cuts are in; I respond by becoming a long hair. You tell me to wear deodorant; I tell you no way. Deodorant masks the real me; I want to be fragrantly natural. And when you tell me to respect authority, I tell you that I will continually question authority—cops are "pigs"—in all its political, economic, and educational manifestations.

Would I as a rebel have long hair unless the representatives of conventional society first told me to have short hair? If the answer is no, then Mead's point is proven. The "Me" gives a standard form to the "I"; it always calls for a certain sort of "I" insofar as we meet the obligations that are given in conduct itself, *but the "I" is always something different from what the situation itself calls for.*[58] In the language of Karl Marx, the relationship between the "Me" and the "I" is dialectical; one acts back upon the other in a never-ending process of stimulus, interpretation, and then response to the attitudes of others.

Mead writes that "the possibilities of the 'I' belong to that which is actually going on, taking place, and it is in some sense the most fascinating part of our experience." The fascination exists because the "I" is what adds novelty and freedom to our existence and to our chances for conscious control of self and world. The "I" is the location of our most important values, and it is "the realization in some sense of this self that we are continually seeking."[59]

The "I" is the locus of the freedom and potential control that Mead promised because, despite the conventional nature of any self, the "I" gives human beings substantial room for personal and social change. This occurs on at least three levels. When "I" disagree with the negative student evaluations, I manifest my freedom to challenge, disregard, or deny the expressed attitudes of others. While my response is something different than was called for, a simply defensive or dismissive response suggests no effort at serious self-consciousness, change, or control.

But if I engage in a deliberate and (to the extent possible) objective reflection about the validity of the attitudes of others—about what the students told me—then I have potentially achieved a greater degree of freedom. I tried to honestly assess what others said about me and to change my self based on that objective assessment.

The third level of response offers the greatest opportunities for freedom, control, and change. Mead defines social control "as the expression of the 'me' against the expression of the 'I.' It (the 'me') sets the limits, it gives the determination that enables the 'I,' so to speak, to use the 'me' as the means of carrying out that is the undertaking that all are interested in."[60] So, thinking of the "I" as reflective intelligence at work, I can see how the generalized other tries to control me, and I can also see the predictable responses I am likely to have, given what they told me. In the case of rebels with long versus short hair, I can see that my response was more or less determined by the conventional attitudes of others. Equally important, I can ask this potentially liberating question: Are a million people with long hair rebels? Or is this simply a new form of predictable conformity?

Great freedom lies in the ability to see not only what they told me but also how I responded to what they told me. Although this level of honesty is very hard to achieve, it is the pregnant promise of Mead's concepts and the reason he argues that the "I" is the location of our most important values. Using the human ability to reflect on our experiences, men and women can find wide latitude for self-expression and self-realization. "I" select what is most important to me and then walk into the future on the basis of my conscious choices. This is a privilege denied to other animals and to the members of many societies. Mead is, after all, a quintessential American. He applauds self-realization, yet many societies do not. In *Fire in the Lake*, an analysis of the Americans in Vietnam, Frances Fitzgerald explains that the traditional Vietnamese family deliberately left little room for self-expression. In fact, instead of using the pronoun "I," youngsters were taught to say "your child" or "your younger brother." Parents tried to make it conceptually impossible for their children to think of themselves apart from the group.[61] By contrast, a society that celebrates the "I" sanctions radical isolation from others. From the outset I see myself apart from and in opposition to the groups that potentially strangle my all-American right to self-expression.

Mead's work always had an underlying goal: control in the service of self-expression and conscious social change. Toward the end of his discussion of the self, he writes that "the situation in which one can let himself go, in which the very structure of the 'me' opens the door for the 'I,' is favorable to self-expression."[62] In sharp contrast to Vietnam, many American parents raise their children to think for themselves. They may forever regret the day their children question their authority, but if you teach "me" to think for myself, do not be surprised when "I" do so. In the

United States, the *conventional structure* of the self is often rooted in the need for self-consciousness and self-expression. To take another example from the 1960s, I knew a couple that only purchased leather couches and chairs for their house. Their children were involved in the process of toilet training, and the parents did not want to inhibit the children's free expression of self. So if the kids urinated on the couches, it was much easier to clean leather.

That is a true story. By contrast, George Herbert Mead was never—thank goodness!—that progressive. But in the final section of *Mind, Self, and Society*, he does offer some provocative ideas about social organization and the "obstacles and promises in the development of the ideal society."[63] It is a proposal for using the "I" and the "Me" as tools for the control and change of social conditions.

SOCIETY

Mead begins with a chessboard. He chooses the great game of strategic thinking because "a good chess player has the response of the other person in his system. He can carry four or five moves ahead in his mind."[64] As if in a game of chess, human beings have the unique ability to comprehend an entire process; they can take the attitude of the other, reflect on what they did and may do, and even strategize about a new way to play the game or organize a society. "The problem is in the hands of the community in so far as it reacts intelligently on its problems."[65]

Mead is fiercely adamant about one thing: social institutions need not squash or constrain individuality. He singles out "the church" for particular criticism because it represents an institution that is "oppressive, stereotyped, and ultraconservative." Churches inhibit or deny individuality, yet there is "no necessary or inevitable reason" that social institutions cannot be organized in a manner that allows people "plenty of room" for free expression. Although I doubt Mead would have sanctioned the child-rearing practices of my friends with the leather furniture, he underlines a point that is as valid today as it was eighty years ago. People can create institutions that free rather than oppress all members of society.

Remember that Mead is writing under the very dark shadow of World War I. No one wanted to see another 10 million dead soldiers, so Mead focused on creating institutions that expressed a "universal" character. His ideal was economic society. People traded with one another, "and then the very processes themselves go on integrating, bringing a closer relationship between communities that may be opposed to each other politically."[66] If people could find a medium of *political* communication that promised the same degree of integration as the pursuit of profit and trade, human beings could conceivably create a future "in which the individual maintains himself as a citizen only to the degree that he recognizes the rights of everyone else belonging to the same community."[67]

Mead confronted the same problem as Emile Durkheim. How, given the widespread praise for self-expression, can you integrate the individual into the social whole? How can you celebrate free expression and nevertheless assume that people will still desire political links that tightly integrate them into local, national, and even international communities?

Mead answers these questions by asking his readers to remember democracy and more specifically, the social contract suggested by authors like Jean Jacques Rousseau and events like the French Revolution. Democracy offered a potentially universal medium of communication because it furnished a way for people to realize themselves "by recognizing others as belonging to the same political organization as themselves."[68]

Mead never lost faith in the power inherent in people's ability to take the attitude of the other. If men and women put themselves in the other person's moccasins, they could create "a highly developed and organized human society." That is, they could create a world in which people recognized their "common social interests,—interests in, or for the betterment of society—and yet, on the other hand, are more or less in conflict relative to numerous other interests which they possess only individually, or else share with one another only in small and limited groups."[69]

Creating this ideal required a clear understanding of one fact: reconstructing society and reconstructing the individual are two sides of the same coin. It is a "reciprocal" relationship because self develops in the process of social experience and therefore contains a conventional structure. Change that structure, and in the process of socialization you could create a self that realizes his or her most important values in affirming common social interests. The "I," the locus of freedom and our most precious values, would *mesh* with the "Me," with the attitudes of others that taught children to realize themselves by focusing on the betterment of society.[70]

If this sounds too idealistic, then so is Thomas Friedman in an editorial in *The New York Times* of December 9, 2001. Friedman compliments President Bush on his handling of the war in Afghanistan and then suggests that the president focus attention on the social values that theoretically set us apart from other nations. The war against terrorism was also a war for the beliefs, values, and practices that set us apart from other nations. So, how about a national campaign to make us energy independent in a decade? How about taking the attitude of the other and demanding that "we Americans, who are 5% of the world's population, don't continue hogging 25% of the world's energy?" And in a suggestion keyed to the nation's youth, Friedman asks us to "imagine if the President called on every young person to consider enlisting in some form of service—the

Army, Navy, Marines, Air Force, Coast Guard, Peace Corps, Teach For America, AmeriCorps, the FBI, the CIA."[71]

When it comes to self-realization through the common good, Friedman is an equal opportunity employer, and so was George Herbert Mead. He grasped the extraordinary potential of meshing the "I" and the "Me" in the service of society and self-realization. However, he also understood the problems that his ideal encountered in the real world.

It was easiest to integrate the individual into the group—the "I" into the "Me"—when the person willingly participated in, for example, one organization, team, church, or association. On a sports team I might even hate the other members of the group, but in the interests of our victory, I will work for the team and forget my personal feelings. Or, in Japan, workers sometimes receive half their pay based on the profits earned by the entire corporation. Thus both the machinist on the factory floor and the engineer programming the computers diligently work for the group because its success is their success. The "I" and the "Me" demonstrate as much harmony as the robots manufacturing a great car.

Problems appear when people participate in two or more different groups, "groups whose respective social purposes or interests are antagonistic or conflicting or widely separated."[72] Mead discusses capital and labor as his prime example of groups whose members are either asocial or hostile. Other examples are easy to find. Any university is a hotbed of conflict between different departments competing for resources; different religions also provide examples of lasting enmity. Growing up in Brooklyn, I was told by nuns to stay away from Protestants. Catholicism was the perfect religion, and when Protestants rejected it, God reserved an especially warm place in hell for all the various manifestations of the Protestant persuasion.

The problems sometimes seem insoluble, yet solutions can and do occur. In the name of harmony, the U.S. Constitution specifically endorses both freedom of religion and the separation of church and state. My teachers in Brooklyn certainly tried to stir up the pot of hate, but in the service of our common social interests, the United States has been remarkably free of religious battles. As President Eisenhower once noted, "Our government makes no sense unless it is founded in a deeply felt religious faith—and I don't care what it is." In addition, "I am the most intensely religious man I know. That doesn't mean I adhere to any particular sect. A democracy cannot exist without a religious base. I believe in democracy."[73]

To bridge the gap between the individual and group—and even between capital and labor—Mead underlined that "a difference of functions does not preclude a common experience." We can take the attitude of the other, imaginatively participate in his or her humanity, and decide to change our behavior because we now understand the other's dilemma. For instance, in Thomas Friedman's *New York Times* article, he suggests that all corporate executives immediately announce that they will take a 10 percent cut in pay so that more average Americans are never laid off.

Although executive pay cuts might be a great way to express our common interests, the principal gap in Mead's analysis is how you move from empathy to action. Like Emile Durkheim, George Mead was a decent man. Many of the rest of us are more selfish. In fact, however great a tool for social change reflective intelligence is, it never guarantees that people will work for the common good rather than for themselves or for the groups to which they belong.

As a great gift, Mead gave us the conceptual tools required for control of self and society. But only we, in the process of *acting* on our empathetic understanding of others, can make Mead's ideal our reality: "The implication of democracy is that the individual can be as highly developed within the possibilities of his own inheritance, and still enter into the attitudes of others whom he affects."[74]

In the service of the common good, the "I" and the "Me" can actually mesh as well as George Mead did into the city of Chicago—and its mountain of social problems.

SERVICE TO SOCIETY

Today we might call it, with an air of disdain, applied sociology. A person happily leaves the ivory tower and, once on the street, actually engages real people, with real problems. As a response to such efforts, many contemporary universities deliberately separate *programs* like social work from *departments* like sociology; contamination is prohibited because no serious scholar wants to mix social theory with a service mentality. By all means, let welfare workers help the community, but please, keep them away from the scholars who need to think about the theoretical solutions to society's social problems.

In Mead's time the example of Jane Adams provided a different model for scholars actively engaged in social activism. Traveling in London in the 1880s, Adams witnessed living conditions similar to those described by Engels in his 1845 *The Condition of the Working Class in England*. Adams also saw the response of some English university students; at Oxford and Cambridge activists reacted by establishing "settlement houses," where they taught workers how to read and write, among other things. When Adams returned to Chicago, she eventually established (in 1889) Hull House, the model for the settlement home established by the University of Chicago in 1894. Historical documents fail to explain when Mead first got involved in the university's efforts, but when he climbed down from the ivory tower, he not only got his hands dirty, he offered a model of applied sociology that challenges today's wisdom.[75]

In 1907 Mead spoke at the university's chapel on "Settlement Sunday."

By now, you have grasped his negative feelings about religion in general and the church in particular, and Mead used his morning in the pulpit to denounce it in no uncertain terms. "The pulpit is called upon to inspire us to right conduct, not to find out what is the right. . . . When, then new problems arise, . . . the pulpit is unable to solve them, because it has not the apparatus, and the scientific technique which the solution of such problems demands. . . . The only overt social issues with which the pulpit in recent time has identified itself have been temperance and chastity."[76]

If the university's chaplain or other ministers were in the audience, Mead offers no indication of their reactions to his sermon. Temperance had its place, but not when Professor Mead spoke about the scientific solution of social problems. "The central fact in all settlements has been that these people have lived where they have found their interest. The corner stone of settlement theory has been that the residents have identified themselves with the immediate portion of the community where their work is found by making their home there." Mead celebrated settlement workers as he simultaneously distinguished them from missionaries or scientific observers. The settlement worker is at home in her community; she has a sense of "neighborhood consciousness," which means that she lives near factories or meat packing establishments, "not to save souls from perdition" but to more intelligently comprehend the "misery" of the people who live next door.[77]

Mead argues that settlement houses offer the scientist a great opportunity. He excitedly describes his encounter with an unnamed pathologist who worked at the famous leper colony established by Father Damien at Molokai, in the Pacific Ocean. The priest was a missionary, whereas the pathologist combined good works with a great scientific problem. Unlike Father Damien, who died from leprosy, "the pathologist knows that he can protect himself from infection." He was "a very lucky fellow" because he had a scientific goal—curing leprosy—that also allowed him to work "under the most favorable circumstances, with unlimited resources behind him." Whether the lepers also saw their circumstances as favorable was apparently beside the point. They were the intriguing problem, and "it is just this difference between an obligation to undertake a disagreeable duty and a growing interest in an intellectually interesting problem that is represented by the attitude of the resident in the settlement house."[78]

In my reading of a number of Mead's papers on social reform, it is exceedingly rare for his enthusiasm to ever blind him to people's pain. The lepers were in no way guinea pigs, yet they nevertheless offered the pathologist the scientific opportunity of a lifetime. Mead saw the same possibilities in any settlement house in the nation because "you will find the settlements at the points where the most intensely interesting problems in modern industrial and social life are centered. It is the good fortune of our time that moral consciousness has been able to tap so large a stream of intellectual interest."[79]

Recall Mead's intellectual roots. He was a pragmatist who focused on the incremental advances that produced tangible fruits, facts, and consequences. The beauty of the settlement houses was that they allowed workers to approach social problems with no preconceptions, "to be the exponents of no dogma or fixed rules of conduct, but to find out what the problems of the community are and as part of it to help toward their solution." Hidden in this commentary is a challenge to the academic comfortably nestled behind a mahogany desk and a high-resolution, flat-screen computer monitor. Maybe theory needs a new introduction to reality? Maybe living in the community will teach us about problems or issues we never imagined, much less encountered firsthand?

As a pragmatist Mead lived by this dictum: truths have "a desperate instinct of self-preservation and of desire to extinguish whatever contradicts them."[80] Mead courageously celebrated the settlement houses because they could challenge accepted beliefs, values, and practices. By incremental steps places like Hull House got us closer to the real truths of the real world; all the while, they provided the most intensely interesting issues for social scientists who wanted to use reflective intelligence to take the attitudes of the thousands of others who lived in misery—just blocks away from a magnificent university built with funds provided by John D. Rockefeller, the general of America's captains of industry.

Mead ended his sermon by focusing on morality. Americans lived in "painful doubt" about the meaning of right and wrong. The settlement houses never offered instant cures, either to leprosy or the abysmal conditions of the working class—especially the immigrants—in Chicago. But the houses did allow us to discover "what the evils are." By combining a practical bent with the scientific method, they even allowed us to "form a new moral judgment."[81]

Mead never noted the precise details of that new moral judgment. It was a work in progress, a moral masterpiece that would only be completed by stepping down from the pulpit and living in a settlement house. You had to work with real people, and for more than twenty-five years Mead did just that. His efforts included not only the settlement houses but also intimate involvement in the school system, in the powerful City Club of Chicago, and in a variety of other civic projects.[82]

Mead may have rejected Christianity, but the good works celebrated at Oberlin were a part of his life until the day he died.

NATIONAL-MINDEDNESS AND OSAMA BIN LADIN

The flags were everywhere. Three months after the hideous terrorist attack on New York's World Trade Center, homes and cars were still filled with American flags of every size and description. On most Connecticut streets, the flags appeared in one doorway after another, for homes with porches, a common touch was to drape a huge flag over the railing. Meanwhile, cars, trucks, and every brand of SUV sported flags in the windows or on the bumpers; in addition, a large or small flag often waved in the breeze, attached to the vehicle's radio antenna. Normally, the flags are their own message of patriotic fervor, but especially in New York City, "God Bless America" regularly appears as an addendum when you read the stickers plastered on the windows of restaurants and stores.

At the attack site, vendors selling souvenirs tried to spoil what is a solemn moment for most of the people obviously overwhelmed by the extent of the destruction. My wife and I cried, and so did many of the other people standing near us. It was simultaneously a good and a terrible feeling because, however incongruous, death, destruction, and hate brought a sense of genuine community to Americans who would otherwise have absolutely nothing in common.

George Mead understood our feelings. In an article published shortly before his death in 1931, "National-Mindedness and International-Mindedness," he wrote that "the hostile feeling is peculiarly favorable to social cohesion."[83] He was especially impressed—and appalled—by what he had seen in the United States during World War I. "To join ourselves with others in the common assault upon the common foe we have become more than allies, we have joined a clan, have different souls, and have the exuberant feeling of being at one with this community."[84]

Mead actually used the Ku Klux Klan as another terrible example of creating community through enmity. Hate brought people together with such passion that nations in search of public policy might use war to create "social cohesion." It was unfortunately a wonderful way to make many millions of people march together with all the practiced precision of a military band. However, to a person using reflective intelligence, the Great War proved that "every war if allowed to go the accustomed way of wars will become a world war, and every war pursued uncompromisingly and intelligently must take as its objective the destruction not of hostile forces but of nations in their entirety."[85]

Mead saw and feared the future. In his day aviation theorists arrogantly argued that airplanes gave modern nations a new weapon of unprecedented power. In England, the United States, and Italy, soldiers and civilians said to forget attacks on soldiers. Bomb cities and you would simultaneously terrorize civilians and destroy the enemy's industrial base. On July 22, 1921, General "Billy" Mitchell mock bombed New York City and allegedly sent thousands fleeing, first from Wall Street and then from Times Square. *The New York Times* reported that Mitchell also planned to attack Philadelphia "but deferred the destruction of that city until next week."[86]

In Mead's mind even reflective intelligence might be no match for the clannishness inspired by red-hot hate of an enemy. "Another catastrophe might be necessary before we have cast off the cult of war." To avoid that worldwide slaughter, Mead turned to a famous essay by William James, "The Moral Equivalent of War."[87] James argued that to dispose of war, nations needed to find an equivalent that provided the "manliness to which the military mind so faithfully clings." To date "war has been the only force that can discipline a whole community, and until equivalent discipline is organized, I believe that war must have its way."[88]

What would replace war? "James seems to have thought that we might substitute some other cult for the cult of warfare and reach the same emotional result." For example, conscripting youth to necessary social labor might provide a peaceful and productive sense of social cohesion—*if* cults could be created with such ease. But that was impossible because of inherited cultures. In a world of nations, people still learned to fuse self and society—the "Me" and the "I"—only when they saw the enemy at the gates. This was "profoundly pathetic" because the tragedy lies in the inability to feel unison with the nation except in the union of arms.[89]

This was no way to live. It was a way to die. So Mead made an argument that is as relevant today as it was in 1929: "If we surrender war there is no way of maintaining national unity except in discovering that *unity in the midst of the diversity of individual concerns*. There is a common good in which we are involved, and if society is still to exist *we must discover it with our heads*. We cannot depend upon our diaphragms and the visceral responses which a fight sets in motion" (emphasis added).[90]

As a specific criticism of Congress and the president, Mead argued that it was a "scandal" for the United States to keep arms distance from an organization like the World Court. How could you possibly create a sense of international mindedness if nations never even appeared in the same place to discuss their differences—and their commonalities?

In the twenty-first century we have the same battle between those who want to expand and those who want to limit the role and power of the United Nations. As Senator Jesse Helms of South Carolina told the United Nations General Assembly on January 31, 2001, in its use of military force in Central America, "the United States did not ask for, or receive the approval of the U.N. to legitimate its actions. . . . The United Nations, my friends, has no power to grant or decline legitimacy to such actions. They are inherently legitimate."[91]

In trying to resolve the battle between national- and international-mindedness, Mead offers no panaceas because none exist. Instead, he offers us conceptual tools like the "I" and the "Me" and a crucial insight into the nature of civilization. *"It is not an affair of reasonableness; it is an affair of social organization. The selfhood of a community depends upon such an* organization that common goods do become the ends of the individuals of the community" (emphasis added).[92]

Long before globalization of the economy and weapons of mass destruction, Mead argued that the real challenge was to create not the moral equivalent of war but a sense of self-realization that was rooted in underlining and embracing the inextricable links between a world of wildly diverse nations, economies, religions, ethnicities, and political ideologies.

International-mindedness was never an ideal devised by a utopian. It was the practical necessity of a pragmatist. "The measure of civilization is found in the intelligence and will of the community in making common interests the means and the reason for converting diversities into social organization."[93]

Mead never lost his faith in the power of reflective intelligence. After World War II, the Cold War, and September 11, 2001, we may be markedly more pessimistic than he about the possibility of finding unity amid diversity. But that is still our challenge. Instead of arms, we could reflectively use the conceptual tools that are the lasting legacy of the work of George Herbert Mead.

NOTES

1. George Herbert Mead, "The Problem of Society," in *On Social Psychology*, ed. Anselm Strauss (Chicago: University of Chicago Press, 1956), 21.

2. Upton Sinclair, *The Jungle* (New York: Heritage Press, 1965).

3. See, for example, Deborah Fink, *Cutting into the Meatpacking Line: Workers and Change in the Rural Midwest* (Chapel Hill: University of North Carolina Press, 1998); for a century-long overview of immigration issues, see Ronald Fernandez, *America's Banquet of Cultures: Harnessing Ethnicity, Race, and Immigration in the Twenty-first Century* (Westport, Conn.: Praeger, 2000).

4. John Higham, *Strangers in the Land: Patterns of American Nativism 1860–1925* (New York: Atheneum, 1971), 81–84.

5. Edward Hartman, *The Movement to Americanize the Immigrant* (New York: Columbia University Press, 1948).

6. Fernandez, *America's Banquet of Cultures*, 152.

7. George Herbert Mead, "The Adjustment of Our Industry to Surplus and Unskilled Labor," *Proceedings of the National Conference of Charities and Corrections* 34 (1909): 222–25 [www.paradigm.soci.brocku.ca/%7Elward/pubs/Mead_1923.html].

8. Ibid.

9. Ibid.

10. George Herbert Mead, "The Working Hypothesis in Social Reform," *American Journal of Sociology* 5 (1899): 367–71 [www.paradigm.soci.brocku.ca/%7Elward/pubs/Mead_1923.html].

11. See, for example, George Herbert Mead, "Scientific Method and the Moral Sciences," *International Journal of Ethics* 23 (1923): 229–47 [www.paradigm.soci.brocku.ca/%7Elward/pubs/Mead_1923.html].

12. See Oberlin College, "Media Information" [www.oberlin.edu/newserv/facts.html].

13. Gary A. Cook, *George Herbert Mead: The Making of a Social Pragmatist* (Urbana: University of Illinois Press, 1993), 1. I have relied heavily on this fine book for many of the details about Mead's life and the development of his thinking.

14. Ibid., 3–4.

15. Ibid., 18.

16. Ibid., 22–23.

17. Ibid., 34.

18. John Dewey, "George Herbert Mead," *Journal of Philosophy* 28, no. 12 (June 4, 1931): 309.

19. Ibid., 312.

20. William James, "What Pragmatism Means," in *Pragmatism and Other Writings* (New York: Penguin Books, 2000), 24–40, esp. 25 and 28.

21. Ibid., 25.

22. Ibid., 30.

23. George Herbert Mead, "Scientific Method and the Moral Sciences," *International Journal of Ethics* 23 (1923): 229–47 [www.paradigm.soci.brocku.ca/%7Elward/pubs/Mead_1923.html].

24. James, "What Pragmatism Means," 33.

25. Mead, "Scientific Method and the Moral Sciences."

26. Ibid.

27. Ibid.; also see Mead's "The Nature of Scientific Knowledge," in *On Social Psychology*, ed. Anselm Strauss (Chicago: University of Chicago Press, 1956), 45–61, esp. 53 and 58.

28. Mead, "Scientific Method and the Moral Sciences"; for an analysis that shows how tightly Mead's and Dewey's thoughts were connected, see John Dewey, *A Common Faith* (New Haven, Conn.: Yale University Press, 1934).

29. Mead, "Scientific Method and the Moral Sciences."

30. Ibid.

31. Ibid.

32. George Herbert Mead, *Mind, Self, and Society*, ed. Charles W. Morris (Chicago: University of Chicago Press, 1962), 2–3.

33. Ibid., 7–8.

34. Ibid., 7.

35. Emile Durkheim, *The Division of Labor in Society* (New York: Free Press, 1984); Mead, *Mind, Self, and Society*, 125, 48.

36. One good overview is Jerome G. Manis and Bernard Meltzer, eds., *Symbolic Interaction: A Reader in Social Psychology* (Boston: Allyn and Bacon, 1967).

37. Mead, *Mind, Self, and Society*, 120.

38. Ibid., 78.

39. Daniel Boorstin, *The American: The National Experience* (New York: Random House, 1967), 374.

40. Mead, *Mind, Self, and Society*, 50.

41. Ibid., 121.

42. Ibid., 95.

43. Ibid., 127.

44. Ibid., 132.

45. Ibid., 134.

46. Ibid., 135.

47. Ibid., 135–36.

48. Ibid., 136.

49. Ibid., 136–37.

50. Ibid., 144.

51. See, for example, Ronald Fernandez, "Our Civilized Neighbors: The West Indians of Hartford," *The Hartford Courant*, January 5, 2001.

52. Mead, *Mind, Self, and Society*, 158, 154.

53. Ibid., 154.

54. Ibid., 152.

55. Ibid., 158.

56. Ibid., 164.

57. Ibid., 174.

58. Ibid., 178.

59. Ibid., 204.

60. Ibid., 210.

61. Frances Fitzgerald, *Fire in the Lake* (New York: Vintage Books, 1972), 148.

62. Mead, *Mind, Self, and Society*, 213.

63. Ibid., 317.

64. Ibid., 243.

65. Ibid., 251.

66. Ibid., 282.

67. Ibid., 286.

68. Ibid., 286–87.

69. Ibid., 307.

70. Ibid., 309.

71. Thomas Friedman, "Ask Not What . . . ." *New York Times*, December 9, 2001, section 4:13.

72. Mead, *Mind, Self, and Society*, 322.

73. Peter Berger, *The Noise of Solemn Assemblies* (Garden City, N.J.: Doubleday, 1961), 63.

74. Mead, *Mind, Self, and Society*, 326.

75. Friedrich Engels, *The Condition of the Working Class in England* (New York: Oxford University Press, 1993); Cook, *George Herbert Mead*, 100; also see Jane Adams, *Twenty Years at Hull House* (New York: Signet Classics, 1986).

76. George Herbert Mead, "The Social Settlement: Its Basis and Function," *University of Chicago Record* 12 (1907–8): 108–10 [www.paradigm.soci.brocku.ca/%7Elward/pubs/Mead_1923.html].

77. Ibid.

78. Ibid.

79. Ibid.

80. James, "What Pragmatism Means," 39.

81. Mead, "The Social Settlement."

82. Cook, *George Herbert Mead*, chapter 7.

83. George Herbert Mead, *International Journal of Ethics* 39 (1929): 385–407 [www.paradigm.soci.brocku.ca/%7Elward/pubs/Mead_1923.html].

84. Ibid.

85. Ibid.

86. "City Wiped Out in Big War Game," *New York Times*, July 30, 1921, 14; see also Edward Meade Earle, ed., *Makers of Modern Strategy* (Princeton, N.J.: Princeton University Press, 1941); and Burke Davis, *The Billy Mitchell Affair* (New York: Random House, 1967).

87. The essay is based on a speech that James gave at Stanford University in 1906. It is available at [www.emory.edu/Education/mfp/moral.html].

88. Ibid.

89. Mead, "National-Mindedness and International-Mindedness."

90. Ibid.

91. Federal News Service, "Remarks by Senator Jesse Helms to the United Nations Security Council," January 31, 2001, [www.derechos.org/nizkor/impu/tpi/helms2.html].

92. Mead, "National-Mindedness and International-Mindedness."

93. Ibid.

CHAPTER 6

Thorstein Veblen

"Veblen hurt. He stung. He wound you up like a clock. . . . He set one going and one couldn't stop. One ticked and ticked."[1]

R. L. Duffus

THE ICHNEUMON FLY

The insect's name may be tough to spell, but Thorstein Veblen loved to irritate listeners with lurid accounts of the ichneumon fly. Except for the southwest, these flies exist throughout the United States. As Veblen told the story, "the female would have her fun and get her eggs fertilized." She then used her extremely long ovipositor—an organ specially designed to deposit eggs—as a powerful drill; the fly often digs through several inches of insect-infested tree trunk to the caterpillars within. When she finds a suitable caterpillar home, the fly deftly deposits her eggs in one of the potential butterfly's many segments. "The caterpillar might know that something had happened but it would not know what." On the contrary, it would happily lead its life until "the little ichneumon grubs would start eating the caterpillar, which being alive, had kept them fresh without refrigeration." Ultimately, the caterpillar was eaten alive; "it would realize what had happened but it would be too late."[2]

One student who heard Veblen tell the story noted that Veblen could be compared to the fly. Veblen loved to deposit dangerous thoughts in people's minds and then walk away. What the recipient did with Veblen's gifts was his or her own business. The professor's job was to deposit the eggs, have fun, and move on to another group of caterpillars.[3]

Although Veblen certainly loved to upset the established order, the fly was also a metaphor for Veblen's assessment of U.S. industrialists. He hated people who got something for nothing. Unfortunately, especially in his formative years, a group of business parasites—the robber barons—stalked the land and ate up the people as rapidly as the grubs ate the caterpillar. Nothing symbolizes the "barbarism" that Veblen always emphasized better than the building of the transcontinental railroad.

The early builders never built a thing. They were the land companies who received vast tracts of public land for the promise to construct a rail link from one end of the continent to the other. Over time the companies received more than 158 million acres of public land. The biggest winners in the federal lottery were the Union and Central Pacific Railroad companies. The latter, building from the West, got 9 millions acres of land and more than $24 million in government bonds. The Union Pacific, building westward from the Missouri River, got more than 12 million acres of land and $27 million in government bonds.[4]

The real trick was to make extraordinary profits without risking a nickel of your own capital. Thus railroad representatives blackmailed local chambers of commerce. It was a nationwide series of stickups underwritten by the federal government. Officials politely told the residents of the affected communities to hand over the money they wanted or they would build a railroad that would never come to that town. "And in every instance where the subsidy was not granted, . . . the effect was just as they said, to kill off the little town."[5]

Another tactic was to create enterprises like Credit Mobilier. This was a construction company formed and owned by the owners of the Union Pacific Railroad. One hand signed construction contracts with the other hand to build track at grossly inflated prices. Over time the pillars of the community pocketed an extra $30 million in profits—all this money coming from the coffers of the federal government. When Congress finally got wind of the scandal, one of the Union Pacific's owners—U.S. representative Oakes Ames—bribed his congressional colleagues. He gave them stock in the Credit Mobilier company, and they all fed, like Veblen's grubs, from the folds in the wallets of Congress.[6]

Meanwhile, 10,000 Chinese immigrants actually built the transcontinental railroad. They worked for a dollar a day—half the wages of "white" men—sometimes under harsh conditions. During the winter of 1866, for example, railroad executives decided that even with snow on the way, workers would drill a tunnel through solid granite. Thousands of Chinese immigrants labored underground in snow tunnels throughout the day and the night. Officials did note that many workers died when avalanches buried them in snow. The bodies were recovered when the spring thaw allowed workers to dig out their frozen comrades.[7]

The railroads also added a bit of so-called folk wisdom to American English. The phrase "not a Chinaman's chance in hell" derives from the railroad boom. When executives and engineers faced a huge rock outcrop called Cape Horn, they needed to cut through the wall of granite. No imaginable detour existed. So, from the peaks of the cliffs, engineers lowered Chinese workers in wicker baskets; the Chinese chiseled holes in the granite, stuck pieces of dynamite in the holes, lit the fuse, and more often than not, they blew up along with the wall of granite.[8]

In 1869 the railroad was finally completed. All Chinese workers were barred from the celebration ceremonies as executives gleefully thanked European immigrants for their wonderful work. Meanwhile, all the Chinese who were just fired walked back to San Francisco. They were not permitted to ride on the transcontinental railroad.[9]

In Congress the Credit Mobilier scandal eventually embarrassed the Grant administration; even Vice President Schuyler Colfax had accepted stock. But Ulysses S. Grant lumbered on, and right after his second term ended, he and his wife went on a world tour of what Veblen later called conspicuous consumption. With the *New York Herald* paying his bar tab, and the U.S. Navy providing much of the transportation, President Grant first visited England and Venice; the president told his Italian hosts "that it would be a fine city if they drained it." In Egypt the dreadful droughts created famine, but the president loved being greeted, in one desolate village after another, as "the King of America."

In India the Grants saw the Taj Mahal and the ghastly results of a drought that killed people as it also made travel for the Grant's a bit dusty. In Calcutta Lord Litton, the British viceroy, accused the president of groping English ladies at dinner. The president responded the viceroy treated him with insufficient respect, and he promptly left for China. In Shanghai 100,000 people turned out to cheer the Grants while a local band played their rendition of "John Brown's Body." It was a wonderful reception except for "fierce, unrelenting heat" and the depressing scenery of hunger and desolation. The worst droughts in Chinese history had just killed between 8 and 20 million human beings. Meanwhile, "nervous American consular officials" noted in their dispatches that without their improved weaponry, "mobs of starving people might have caused a severe political disturbance."[10]

When Grant returned to the United States, he received a tremendous welcome in San Francisco. The *New York Herald* stories about his travels had somehow erased the Credit Mobilier and other scandals. Some political pundits said that were it not for his throat cancer, Ulysses S. Grant might have been reelected president of the United States.[11]

That would have brought a smile to the face of Thorstein Veblen. He never doubted that he lived in a time when barbarians ruled the earth. He would have even remembered that in 1882 Congress formally barred Chinese laborers from the United States. The Chinese were the first people in U.S. history to be summarily refused entrance into ports like San Francisco or New York.[12]

NORWAY, U.S.A.

The sign read: "Speak the American language. If you don't know it, learn it. If you don't like it, move out." This admonition appeared in 1917;[13] about to enter the war, so-called 100 percent Americans wanted to erase the pervasive influence of immigrant languages and immigrant experiences. It never worked because the myth of the melting pot confronted the realities of an America in which many millions of people happily spoke only their native language in communities that distinctly resembled life in the old country.

In 1899 Veblen's brother Andrew founded what is now the oldest *Bygdelag* in America. The word *Bygdelag* refers to organizations composed of descendants of emigrants from particular areas of Norway. The Veblens came from the Valdres Valley, an area roughly 100 miles northwest of Oslo.[14] Norwegian was Veblen's first language, and he first spoke it on a frontier farm in Cato, Wisconsin. He was born on July 30, 1857, in a community that relished, sustained, and nourished Norwegian cultural customs.

Veblen, for example, later exasperated many a colleague with his unwillingness to say a word. Yet his preference for silence had deep roots in Norwegian customs in general and his own home in particular. His father, Thomas Anderson Veblen, stressed that rather than engage in idle small talk, you buttoned your lip. Thus, when the father once bumped into his son in town, he not only remained silent, he never even indicated (e.g., with a smile or a nod of the head) that the son existed. A Freudian could write a book about such a gesture, but for Thorstein Veblen the Norwegian lesson made sense: "If a man had nothing to say, there was no use in talking."[15]

In 1864 the Veblens moved from one farm to another, from Wisconsin to the prairie lands around Northfield, Minnesota. While Norwegian was still the language of choice in Veblen's home, he also learned English from other sources. Irish immigrants lived nearby, and given the relative lack of Norwegian books, Veblen—even then a great reader—made do with a wealth of English fiction and nonfiction. He also spoke German, picking the language up from an immigrant community that lived on the south side of the Norwegians from Valdres.[16]

Veblen's parents announced Thorstein's choice of a college in an interesting fashion. While he was working in the fields, one of his father's workmen came by with the family buggy. Veblen's luggage was already packed, so the seventeen-year-old freshman first learned he was entering Carleton College (in Northfield, Minnesota) when the buggy stopped at the school's doors.[17]

Like most colleges of the time, Carleton's faculty contained a number of clergy, in this case "devout New England Congregationalists." The economics textbook, for example, was forty years old, and its reverend author taught that "God has made man a *creature of desires* and established the material universe with qualities and powers for *the gratification of those desires*." God sowed the seeds, we reaped the benefits of his indulgence, and with God's continued blessing, everyone prospered. It was a thoroughly religious perspective that seemingly had little influence on Veblen. He later joked: "Why believe in God? All it causes is worry."[18]

Veblen's preoccupations centered on money. After Carleton he first went to graduate school at Johns Hopkins, but unable to get a scholarship, he eventually settled on Yale and worked as a teacher. Even then he still struggled to survive, so his father obtained a loan and Veblen remained at Yale until he received his Ph.D. in 1884. He was 27 years old, he had studied with some of the best minds in America, and he even had glowing recommendations from, among others, the president of Yale. The only problem was obtaining a job. "No faculty wanted a Norskie," especially one who joked about God. Veblen also lacked the personal polish required for buttering up his betters; the farm showed though, and his decided reticence added another nail to his academic coffin.[19]

Veblen returned to Minnesota—staying for seven years. He married, he walked the fields with his father, and he sometimes looked for a job. He almost got one at St. Olaf College, but yet again, his religious views got in the way. Finally, his brother Andrew called a family conference, and with money again provided by his father, Veblen arrived at Cornell in the winter of 1891. He was a thirty-four-year-old student who instantly made an impression. When he first visited the office of economics professor J. Laurence Laughlin, Veblen arrived in corduroy trousers and a coonskin cap. He announced, "I am Thorstein Veblen." Laughlin took an instant liking for a clearly unique addition to the Cornell student body. With Laughlin's help Veblen stayed in Ithaca for two years, and when his mentor went to the University of Chicago, Veblen tagged along. At thirty-six the Yale Ph.D. finally had a toehold on his first academic appointment.[20]

Before he left for Chicago, Veblen managed to get even with St. Olaf College. When the school doubted the religious credentials of a prospective student, Veblen wrote the youngster a stinging recommendation; he was "too damned orthodox" to merit the approval of Dr. Thorstein Veblen. That was recommendation enough for the folks in St. Olaf. They gave the youngster the position, and Veblen presumably smiled all the way to Chicago.[21]

The University of Chicago was a hotbed of the nation's best barbarians. Founded with money donated by John. D. Rockefeller, it saw industrialists stumble over one another to endow buildings, schools, and observatories. The architecture was as Gothic as the most extravagant English examples.

Meanwhile, William Rainey Harper ran the institution like a dictatorship. He accepted no lip and had no compunctions about using the school's loot to raid the best universities in the nation. Radicals complained that professors who piously preached higher learning often took the low road that led to Chicago. Money talked, the professors listened, and it was a perfect spot for a man trying to understand the beliefs, values, and practices of the leisure class.

Veblen stayed at Chicago for fourteen years. His started so low on the academic ladder—he had a fellowship rather than an appointment—that it took almost a decade to reach just assistant professor status. He paid dearly for being an outsider in a coonskin cap. But over time, even critics accepted the value of his provocative insights and observations. Consider, for example, an essay that appeared in the *American Journal of Sociology* in 1898. Its title is "The Beginning of Ownership."

THE THEORY OF THE LEISURE CLASS

Without mentioning his name, Veblen begins "The Beginning of Ownership" by opening fire on the theories of Karl Marx. While some people believe that the "ground of ownership" is the productive labor of the owner, no isolated individual is a productive agent. He or she can live from "season to season as the non-gregarious animals do," but significant production is impossible without accumulated technical knowledge, used in the context of an industrial community—the so-called division of labor. It is therefore an "absurdity"—not a word you hear in the journals today!—to argue that the rightful basis of property ownership is the productive labor of the owner.[22]

This is bad enough, but sparks almost fly off the page when Veblen explains that the real "counterfeit" is the notion of corporate ownership. "Ownership implies an individual owner. It is only by reflection, and by extending the scope of a concept that is already familiar," that *society* allows a paper entity called the corporation to invest property rights in capitalists whose only productive effort is to profitably buy and sell shares of common and preferred stock.[23]

Veblen is lecturing his contemporaries. "Look less for the pea under the shell, or the shell itself, and look more at the charismatic face of the conjuror and the metaphysical expectations of the observing underlying population."[24]

Our ideas about ownership are "cultural facts"; forget the nonsense about the isolated individual, and focus instead on a course of habituating citizens to accept a particular set of ideas and practices. For example, "on going back a little way into the cultural history of our own past, we come upon a situation which says that the fact of a person's being engaged in industry was prima facie evidence *that he could own nothing*" (emphasis added). Slaves and serfs worked liked dogs, but nobody offered them property rights. And long before it was fashionable, Veblen noted that "even very recently—culturally speaking—there was no suspicion that a woman's work in the patriarchal household, should entitle her to own the products of her work."[25]

Veblen now makes a distinction that is crucial for understanding any of his later work. He states "that the earliest occurrence of ownership seems to fall in the early stages of barbarism, and the emergence of the institution of ownership is apparently a concomitant of the transition from a peaceable to a predatory way of life."[26] No specific date or culture is mentioned. No analysis of early Italian or U.S. capitalism is ever offered. Veblen focuses only on the counterfeit, on the lies about property rights that millions of people have learned to accept. Somewhere in early history—the time of the savages—the concept of private property did not exist. But when the barbarians took over, societies made a transition from hunting to being hunted; *"the pervading characteristic of the barbarian culture, as distinguished from the peaceable phase of life that precedes it, is the element of exploit, coercion, and seizure"* (emphasis added).[27]

Memorize these words: exploitation, coercion, and seizure are the holy trinity that links Veblen's perception of the U.S. industrial scene. American culture, rooted in metaphysical notions about property rights, actually allows a group of barbarians to eagerly and efficiently exploit the rest of us. It is legal, it is revered, and one of its most perverse consequences is the creation of a leisure class. In essence, we not only let the barbarians exploit us; we use them as role models in every phase of our existence. It is the ultimate scam, wonderfully exposed in *The Theory of the Leisure Class*, Veblen's first and most remembered book.

Many reviewers understandably focused on Veblen's style in this book, published in 1899. Not one page suffers from academic anemia. You smile, you laugh, and you get caught up in the sardonic humor of a writer who never pulled punches. Phrases like "conspicuous consumption" and "conspicuous waste" are now so much a part of our everyday vocabulary that we sometimes forget a simple fact: *The Theory of the Leisure Class* is a first-class piece of sociological analysis; its observations are so sharp that the book is arguably more relevant and penetrating today than when it was first written. To try and prove this point, I will often use contemporary examples in what follows. My aim is to highlight the insights of a writer who always kept his eye not on the pea but on the *cultural concepts* conceived by a well-dressed group of barbarian conjurors.

Veblen uses the notion of exploitation and waste in a literal sense. They bothered him to the core of his Norwegian roots because, he explains, "man is an agent." People "are possessed of a taste for effective work and a distaste for futile effort." In all societies, all the time, human beings have a distinct sense "of the merit of serviceability or efficiency and of the demerit of futility, waste or incapacity." Once again Veblen makes no effort to prove his assertions. He simply calls the taste for effective work "the instinct of workmanship" and uses this instinct as a foil for comparing and contrasting one historical period to another.[28]

Under the rule of "peaceable savagery," people received social esteem for the useful activities that furthered the life of the group. One person emulated another in his or her desire to produce things that served an effective purpose in, for example, food production or health care. When societies passed to barbarism—to a predatory way of life—"the conditions of emulation changed." Those who exploit, coerce, and seize the goods of others are revered not for useful activities but for the "trophies" that provide, for all to see, tangible evidence of prowess under the rule of private property and corporate ownership. Booty serves as a public way to flaunt goods that are inefficient, useless, or unnecessary—or all three at the same time.[29]

Take the "Michelangelo of the hard sell." His name is Tony Razzano, and in a *New York Times* article from 2001, he explains that "you are what you drive." Tony sells used trophies, that is, low-mileage Jaguars, Porches, and Rolls Royces. He sells them to people who do not have enough money for a new version of the real thing. He is Michelangelo because he can work with banks to finance any car for anybody—especially guys with terrible credit. Sales like that tickle Tony's fancy because once you buy the car, "he has you for life." You need the trophy, he has the goods, and his deals with the banks allow you to swap cars at will. You have a Porsche one month, a Jag the next, and your neighbors are dutifully impressed by your prowess and your patriotism. As Tony told customers after the September 11 attack on New York's Twin Towers, "Why would you wait for tomorrow to get what you want today, when tomorrow may never come? Do what the president asks of you. Go out there and spend and be a patriot."[30]

For Veblen, Tony and the buyer are stuck together with a cubic yard of cement. The former provides the essential services that allow the latter to wastefully display his (presumed) success. The guy in the Jag made it, and the rest of us drool with envy. That would make Veblen smile, but what really interested him was the link between individual ownership and the creation of a leisure class.

"It is as elements of social structure—conventional facts—that leisure and ownership are matters of interest for the purpose in hand."[31] Veblen argues that "the motive that lies at the root of ownership is emulation." I compare what I have with what you have, and the winner of the "race for reputability" is the person with the most property. But the race is never finished because there are always more things to get, more ways to out–Rolls Royce your neighbor. Thus, on the foundation of private ownership, Americans in search of social honor build the superstructure of a leisure class. And Veblen is careful to emphasize that the leisure class is *not* characterized by a habitual neglect of work. On the contrary, the leisure class sweats bullets because they can only gain widespread esteem by doing two things: showing "the unworthiness of productive work" and their "pecuniary ability" to waste time and money with all the style of the celebrities depicted on television's *Homes of the Rich and Famous*.[32]

Property equals money, and money gives you the time to gain social honor by being a member of the leisure class. But once they left a small town like Northfield, Minnesota, how did members of the leisure class recognize one another? Especially in a society as diverse as Veblen's America, the barbarian class first needed to create nationally recognized symbols of unproductiveness. After all, how you could impress even close friends unless you both first agreed to be impressed by the same thing?

Knowledge of "fancy-bred animals," polo playing and a ready recitation of the leading players, the ability to wax eloquent about the finest caviar, familiarity with the precise details of setting a proper table, the dos and don'ts of the best weddings: once the leisure class agreed on their standards, their second obligation was to noticeably display their prowess in any and all social settings. The inherent anonymity of a modern society made it difficult for people to know one another by name; you paraded your ability to wallow in waste because that allowed all members of society to easily recognize members of the leisure class and, equally important, accord them the honor and repute they so obviously craved and deserved.

Veblen made lasting distinctions between conspicuous leisure, conspicuous consumption, and conspicuous waste. Like a home run in baseball, they all produced social esteem, but if some home runs barely reached the stands, others sailed out of the park.

Conspicuous leisure included the requirement to have a retinue of servants, the more specialized the better. Man servants—"especially lusty, personable fellows"—provided good care to the master and the mistress, but their real reason for being was to exempt obviously able men from productive work. Opening doors, shining shoes and silver, standing at the master's side during dinner: each of these was a deliberate and public affront to the instinct of workmanship. Servants produced nothing; and the more you had, the less they produced and the greater the employer's degree of social repute. It was especially important that the best servants spend long hours teaching other servants the proper standards of deference and demeanor. In this manner you achieved not efficiency but a public display of the amount of unproductive time required to teach servants how to bow, speak, dress, and serve properly.[33]

Conspicuous consumption required flair and imagination. In Veblen's time the leisure class began the now-common practice of hiring hotel rooms or public restaurants for social functions. Delmonico's (a restaurant in New York) offered Silver, Gold, and Diamond dinners. At one gala every lady in the room opened her napkin and found a gold bracelet with the monogram of the host. "At another, cigarettes wrapped in hundred-dollar bills were passed around after the coffee and consumed with an authentic thrill." Since it was important to announce cost, at a $20,000 dinner one host placed magnificent black pearls in the oysters set before each and every guest. Finally, one fellow gave a dinner for his dog; the total cost was $15,000, and everyone smiled when the host presented his lordship with a diamond-studded dog collar.[34]

This last example underlines conspicuous waste. The trick, of course, was to impress without crossing the line into eccentricity or excessive extravagance. What is your opinion, for example, of this unnamed contemporary of Veblen's? He had a dentist bore little holes in his teeth and then filled them with twin rows of diamonds.[35] He was always a dazzling daylight display, but had the fellow gone too far? Could you waste too much?

Today our own needs for conspicuous consumption are arguably easier to satisfy. In a global economy, the degree of anonymity increases exponentially. To be easily recognizable on the world stage, members of the leisure class need shared international symbols of waste and extravagance. So you can walk through O'Hare Airport in Chicago and buy a thousand-dollar Mont Blanc pen. To those who matter the distinctive markings are evident as the diamonds in that fellow's teeth. And if you walk the streets of Geneva, ten or twenty thousand-dollar diamond studded Rolex watches can be purchased at a wide variety of stores. Strap it on and you will receive social honor from Singapore to London, from San Francisco to Sydney.

Veblen caught our world in its infancy. He ridiculed it with passion because "the leisure class lives by the industrial community rather than in it. Its relations to industry are of a pecuniary rather than an industrial kind."[36] Remember this: Thorstein Veblen had no problems with engineers, even rich ones. Engineers produced machines that could be marvels of efficiency as well as plentiful sources of useful goods for all social classes. But the leisure class produced wealth by passing paper. They bought and sold the engineers' inventions like so many head of cattle, and they then had the audacity to conspicuously distance themselves from the goose that laid the golden eggs.

Veblen discusses the "ceremonial inferiority or uncleanness" of mass-produced goods. Bowls, clothing, or rugs produced by a machine were "common"; so the leisure class let engineers produce them, and with the profits earned by exploiting the engineers, the leisure class demanded hand-made goods produced by little Old World craftsman. If furniture or watchmakers signed the piece, that created an even wider gap between common and uncommon goods. The former were so despised by upstanding members of the leisure class that "even the sight of such goods is inseparable from an odious suggestion of the lower levels of life, and one comes away from their [the common goods'] contemplation with a pervading sense of meanness that is extremely distasteful and depressing to a person of sensibility."[37]

Veblen also accepts the notion of class conflict. As if Karl Marx, he writes that "the salient characteristic of the barbarian culture is an unremitting emulation and antagonism between classes and between individuals."[38] But instead of focusing on a battle between workers and owners, Veblen stresses the conflict between useful and useless, efficient and decadent. In a chapter titled "The Conservation of Archaic Traits," he discusses "survivals" from the stage of peaceful savagery. Characteristics underlined include a conscience, the sense of truthfulness and equity, and "the instinct of workmanship in its naïve, non-invidious expression."[39]

As always, Veblen writes in a tongue-in-cheek style. He gets the reader's attention with humor, but the willingness of the leisure class to squander the fruits of industrialization makes Veblen see red. Machines offered a wonderful way to provide useful goods to more and more people. But instead of sharing the wealth produced by the engineers, the leisure class used its property rights to exploit without conscience and then eat a sumptuous meal at Delmonico's.

Biographers cite the role of Veblen's father in the distinction between the useful engineer and the useless captain of industry. Without turning to Freud, this is a just assumption. Veblen respected his father as a man *and* as an efficient producer of more food for more people. In Wisconsin, for example, Thomas Veblen introduced Spanish merino sheep into that part of the state, and despite the objections of his wife, he sent to New York for the very first two-horse power thresher.[40] We can legitimately trace the distinction to Veblen's farm roots, but whatever its origin(s), Veblen always used the distinction as a sociological benchmark. With the captains of industry at the helm, pecuniary interests would continually dominate the engineers and their machines. Martha Stewart, for example, would be as much of a success in 1899 as she is today because the best inventions were those that allowed the leisure class to find new ways to use more time in a more unproductive manner.

Veblen saw little to no chance for social change. On the contrary, the wide gap between rich and poor produced a perversely complementary form of political and economic conservatism. "The abjectly poor and all those persons whose energies are entirely absorbed by the struggle for daily sustenance are conservative because they cannot afford the thought for the day after tomorrow." Meanwhile, the rich embraced conservatism because, in sharp contrast to the poor, members of the leisure class "have small occasion to be discontented with the situation as it stands today."

They therefore embraced the status quo as a matter of style; what is, is what will be.[41]

Reviews of *The Theory of the Leisure Class* turned Veblen "into the god of the radicals." Go to a gathering of New York's intellectual elite, and they all used quotations from his book. Observers applauded "his withering criticism of aristocratic prejudice" as they drew upon Veblen's prose to distance themselves from the despised leisure class. Meanwhile, "no one was more surprised at the book's reception than Veblen." Popularity scared him. Years later, for example, a colleague arranged a presentation using a microphone. Eighty students showed up for Veblen's talk, but when he heard the effect of the microphone, he quickly threw it into a nearby wastebasket. Veblen then continued in a monotone; students in the first row hardly heard a word; the others naturally left, and Veblen remarked that "Johnson [his colleague] thought he would make me popular. But I fooled him."[42]

Even more than popularity, Veblen disliked reviews that only highlighted the book's satirical approach. He admitted that "the book was not altogether free from satire," but he was using humor as a tool. Others only saw the jokes, and Veblen "came to feel that those who gave the book its popularity were foolish and gullible."[43] Veblen wanted to be taken seriously, but the popular success of his first book reached such proportions that many readers now looked for the laughs rather than serious sociological and economic analysis. Popularity haunted Veblen as the search for satire diminished the reception of his next book, *The Theory of Business Enterprise*, published in 1904.

TIME BALLS, WRISTWATCHES, AND BUSINESS PRINCIPLES

One of the few time balls still left riotously celebrates New Year's Day in New York's Times Square. The ball is now a historical oddity, but in Veblen's youth the balls provided one of the few measures of accurate time in the United States. Typically positioned on top of a tall building, the large metal globes normally rose and fell at noon. People peered through office windows, using the ball's movement as the call to lunch; and ships in ports throughout the nation used time balls to regulate their chronometers.[44]

As Veblen matured, Americans witnessed "a reformation in public time"; the demands of what he called "the machine process" produced a much greater emphasis on calculation, precision, accuracy, and punctuality. People got anxious about schedules—am I on time?—so they began to use little clocks strapped to their wrists.

At first only the richest Americans sported the new necessity; but, especially after the Civil War, the Dennison Waltham Watch Company mass produced "William Ellery" models that were within easy reach of middle-class abilities to pay. That left the poor out in the cold, so they formed watch clubs. Each person contributed a certain amount of money; at the end of the week, club members drew straws and the winner suddenly had the wherewithal to buy a symbol of modernity that was simultaneously a symbol of success. In the Horatio Alger (rags-to-riches) stories of the period, readers learned that gold was better than silver, silver better than gold plate, and gold plate better than base metal. The goal of any modern American was to move from base metal to pure gold as quickly as possible.[45]

Wristwatches still retain their ability to serve as a modern necessity and a means of conspicuous consumption. In contemporary Miami the center of the city easily contains more than 100 stores selling every cheap, expensive, and extravagant wristwatch on earth. Ask a shopkeeper who buys the watches, and they will tell you—in Spanish—that they serve a Latin American market. Buyers purchase a gross quantity of the timepieces and then sell them for a neat profit at home. No clubs are needed; the watch-hungry poor person in Venezuela or Peru instantly boards the modern time machine via a cheap pit stop in Miami. You can easily get three watches for ten dollars.

In the first chapter of *The Theory of Business Enterprise*, Veblen stresses that machines and mass production now ruled America's commercial life. He keys on the "concatenation of interlocking processes" and the "unremitting requirement of quantitative precision, accuracy in point of time and sequence. . . . Standard physical measurements are of the essence of the machine's regime." The word *imbecile* or *barbarian* never appears in this opening chapter. Veblen simply surrenders himself and his contemporaries to the mass-production juggernaut called the machine process. "In the scheme of everyday life, . . . one's plans and projects must be conceived and worked out in terms of those standard units which the system imposes."[46]

Time is suddenly much more than money. To use Durkheim's language, the clock's authority becomes a social fact; it is external to us and capable of exerting a coercive effect. For example, do you and I go to bed when we want to or when it is time to retire? And do we eat when we are hungry or when it is time to eat?

While Veblen dispassionately portrays the new world created by the machine process, his book makes an abrupt about face when he turns to the business enterprise. In theory machines could produce good as well as bad consequences; mass production implied a numbing standardization, but it also offered more things to more people. The trade-off might be worthwhile, but not in Veblen's America. He despised the ups and downs of the so-called business cycle, and he never blamed the machine process for depressions or recessions. The problem was who owned and controlled the machines. In 1904 "industry is carried on for the sake of business and not conversely; and the progress and activity of industry are conditioned by the outlook of the market, which means the presumptive chance of business profits."[47]

Remember the instinct of workmanship, the human taste for effective and useful labor. What drove Veblen up the wall was the captain of industry's utter disregard for "the permanent efficiency" of the industrial system. Captains chased profits; they used machines to make money rather than useful products, so "by and large, it was a matter of indifference to him [the captain of industry] whether his traffic affects the system advantageously or disastrously; his gains (or losses) are related to the magnitude of the disturbances that take place rather than their bearing upon the welfare of the community."[48]

Consider a scandal from the period. A new company called General Electric now controlled the wonderful light bulb invented by Thomas Edison. They competed with Westinghouse and had problems when both used the machine process to produce more light bulbs than anyone wanted to buy. So, in 1896 the two companies began to fix prices; they also pressured Corning Glass to not sell its wares to their competitors. By the time the companies were first convicted in federal courts (in October 1911), they had even pressured machine tool manufacturers to never sell their most efficient machines to anyone competing with General Electric and Westinghouse.[49]

The technical name for such an arrangement is a cartel, a group of manufacturers who provide economic stability by controlling prices, competition, and production. For Veblen this was perfectly understandable, albeit reprehensible. From one perspective the businessman was an entrepreneur; "his aim is to contrive a consolidation in which he will be at an advantage and to affect it on the terms most favorable to his own interest." Simultaneously, the businessman was also an "undertaker"; he ruthlessly buried anyone who got in his way—especially if a competitor could produce better products at even cheaper prices.[50]

The captain of industry was simply the biggest and best undertaker in town. He clearly understood the theory of the modern business enterprise; that is, as long as industrial units remained under different business managements, they worked at cross-purposes. But by eliminating rival businesses, the captain actually served his community; with all competitors buried, "the work of pecuniary management previously involved is dispensed with, with the result that there is a saving of work and an avoidance of that systematic mutual hindrance that characterizes the competitive management of industry. . . . The heroic role of the captain of industry is that of a deliverer from an excess of business management. It is a casting out of businessmen by the chief of the businessmen."[51]

On a deeper level Veblen spotlights the essentially perverse relationship between the machine process and the thirst for profits. Increasingly efficient organization of production allowed competing businesses to produce too many goods and services; because overproduction helped caused the ups and downs in the economy, as a way to produce stability and assure profits, modern business principles demanded everything from price fixing to back-room deals, from strong arming vendors (e.g., Corning Glass) to precise limits on each businesses share of the market.

Veblen was one of the first to suggest that cartels, instead of being an aberration, were an *inherent* part of a capitalism that relied on the machine process. Because the twin enemies of competition and overproduction perpetually threatened profits, the captain ruthlessly destroyed the small competitor and reached a satisfying agreement with relative equals. After all, except in the Bible, Goliath could easily crush David, but if a Goliath like General Electric fought a Goliath like Westinghouse, the result was a battle nobody could win.

In private conversations Veblen described modern business principles in terms of a farmer with a mud hole in front of his home. At first the farmer helped anyone who got stuck; then he began to charge people for his assistance. Over time he gave up farming and earned a living pulling people out of the hole. And during the dry season, he waited until dark to fill up the hole with water from a nearby creek. For Veblen the captain of industry's job was to keep the holes in capitalism full of just enough water to provide profits throughout the year. It was a shell game in the service of money rather than efficiency, waste rather than usefulness. But as Veblen explained to his listeners, "capitalism works." The mud hole kept people employed, even when they used credit rather than real money as a means to business success.[52]

In a chapter called "The Use of Loan Credit," Veblen alternates between anger and bemused astonishment. A captain used credit to extend his business; meanwhile, competitors (also using credit) bid up the prices of the goods bought on credit. As long as people kept buying goods and extending credit, the value of the business enterprise increased. Indeed, "the cumulative extension of credit through the enhancement of prices goes on, if otherwise undisturbed, so long as no adverse price phenomenon intrudes itself with sufficient force *to convict this cumulative enhancement of capitalized values of imbecility*" (emphasis added).[53]

Veblen again perceived an enduring feature of modern capitalism. To make money it was not only unnecessary to make something useful; it was also unnecessary to use real money. Credit increased stock value based on a captain's willingness to gamble that he could withdraw profits before someone discovered that the increased value of his stock depended on an imbecile's willingness to indefinitely extend credit. While Veblen despised this aspect of capitalism, it has endured into the twenty-first century. In a recent book on Silicon Valley, Michael Clark discusses the

rise and fall of Netscape. Historically, capitalists never made a public offering of stock until a company made money for four profitable quarters.
In the mid-1990s "Netscape had nothing to show investors but massive
losses." So, with Veblen rolling over in his grave, trust funds and the
average investor (both often using borrowed funds) provided the increasingly fragile bank balances that allowed Netscape to continue to lose
money as its stock value simultaneously increased. Clark called it "the
new new thing"; but Veblen underlined the essence of the system more
than a century ago. Imbeciles provided the credit, somebody made big
money, and with serviceability always taking a back seat to profits, the
system worked.[54]

Veblen doubted the modern business enterprise could endure over time.
Because the speculative bubbles always burst, "the chronic depression,
more or less pronounced, is normal to capitalism under the fully developed regime of the machine industry."[55] And when socialists and trade
unionists both demanded fundamental change, the captains resorted to
even tighter control of the political and the economic process. Indeed,
"representative government means, chiefly, representation of business
interests."[56]

At some point business principles and values would dramatically lose
their sense of legitimacy because of the inherent contradictions between
the imbecilic demands of business and the rational requirements of science
and the machine process. Veblen presents what amounts to a sociology of
knowledge when he argues that the machine process produces a way of
thinking "that gives no insight into questions of good and evil, merit and
demerit." Like a farmer using his scythe on a field of grass, "the metaphysical basis of the machine process is the law of cause and effect." It so
effectively mows down "conventional truths" that it would soon undermine the cornerstone of the modern business system, the notion that people had a natural right to own a business or manage an industrial cartel.[57]

Science was a close ally of the machine process. It too produced a "skeptical, matter-of-fact complexion, materialistic, unmoral, unpatriotic, undevout." To Veblen it was a "blind guess" whether science or the demands
of the machine process would undermine the legitimacy of a business
system that was built on a series of historically relative beliefs, values, and
practices. He only argued that at some point the skepticism—the iconoclastic mentality—of the engineer and the free thinker would move people
to challenge and change the nature of modern society. Thus, "it seems
possible to say this much, that the full dominion of business enterprise is
necessarily a transitory phenomenon."[58]

The trouble with predictions is that the dues man comes knocking. Veblen stuck his neck out, and the captains of industry, using credit, are still
cutting it off. For example, with his gold buildings and Taj Mahal casinos,
Donald Trump epitomizes conspicuous consumption; and, as of late 2001,

Amazon.com—with more than 371 million shares outstanding—keeps losing more than a billion dollars a year (its net profit margin is minus 37.20 percent), yet investors continue to extend credit, and the system still (sort of) works.[59]

Thorstein Veblen was right; he just hoped he was wrong.

EXILE IN MISSOURI

The Theory of Business Enterprise was published in 1904; two years later Veblen left the University of Chicago. So many scandalous sex stories exist about Veblen's departure that it is best to rely on the facts as we know them. Certainly, Veblen was a less-than-faithful husband; his wife often left him, and even when she was around, he generally refused to take her with him to any social function. In his three trips to Europe, Mrs. Veblen never accompanied her husband.[60]

If one remembers that during the 1896 presidential campaign, President Grover Cleveland admitted to fathering a child out of wedlock, Veblen's behavior was nothing extraordinary. One believable source states that Veblen only discovered late in life that he was attractive to women (he was 47 in 1904) and that he then made up for lost time. Equally important, Veblen "was as often pursued as pursuing."[61]

With his less-than-perfect marriage, Veblen undoubtedly ruffled a great many academic feathers, but by his own admission, something else was the real cause of his abrupt departure from the University of Chicago. An unpublished chapter of *The Theory of Business Enterprise* fell into the hands of university president William Rainey Harper. The chapter ridiculed higher learning in general and the president in particular. So, when Veblen went to Europe with a colleague and the colleague's wife and child, Veblen asserted that President Harper leaked a story about his supposedly adulterous behavior in Europe. While the newspapers refused to print the story without evidence, Veblen's reputation was already ruined. "That left nothing but an added degree of ill feeling between the President and me, and such damage as these endeavors were calculated to yield."[62]

Veblen found a position at Stanford, but once again, his personal life and his radical ideas combined to produce a departure within three years. A student who lived with and assisted Veblen during this period describes a man who was a pleasant enigma. He might say nothing during an entire dinner; he might offer one or two pithy phrases. And he did bring guests home for overnight stays. Indeed, when one of the students staying at Veblen's home referred to a guest as the professor's niece, Veblen "fixed him with a cold and tranquil eye. 'She is not my niece,' he said. And that was that."[63]

Like many professors, Veblen let students serve as personal serfs. In California he discovered that one of his resident guests could type, so he told R. L. Duffus about a machine in the school's executive offices. Duffus's job was to take handwritten manuscript—Veblen did write legibly—and somehow discern what went where. The footnotes, for example, often ran on at great length, and Veblen expressed no concern about proper style. "Stick them in wherever they happened, with lines to set them off." A stickler for detail, Duffus always put the notes at the bottom of the page, yet no matter how hard and long he worked, Veblen never asked a question about Duffus's tedious work on the manuscript. He did, however, want to know what kind of typewriter Duffus used. Unsure, the student mentioned a brand name and then got a question about how the machine worked. When Duffus admitted he had no idea how the reverse ribbon functioned, Veblen "smiled tolerantly. If I were using that typewriter, I couldn't help knowing how it worked. I couldn't operate it unless I knew."[64]

Idle curiosity was more than a mantra for Veblen; his mind never stopped asking questions. That thirst for knowledge helps explain his unique approach to teaching. In a sense students got in the way of time better spent on questions about the functioning of typewriter ribbons or the habits of the ichneumon fly. Veblen did show up for classes, but his teaching style pushed the traditions of academic freedom to their widest limits.

Take office hours. Veblen would actually have to talk to students, plus listen to their problems with grades or—God help him!—campus social life. Custom dictated that professors place a card in the door of their offices, indicating when they would be available. One year the card read: "Thorstein Veblen, 10 to 11, Monday, Wednesdays and Fridays." Soon Veblen changed the time to 10 to 10:30. Then students began to add their own touches. Ultimately, the card read "10 to 10:05, Mondays." Veblen saw the card, smiled, and let it stay on his door the entire semester.[65]

Another way to avoid students included a set of prerequisites that might have stopped Einstein. To get into Veblen's "Economic Factors" course, students needed to have already completed "considerable work" in history, political science, sociology, economics, and whatever other sciences Veblen deemed necessary. They also needed high grades and a letter of recommendation from the head of an academic department. Any student who walked through that minefield then encountered a long reading list, with many of the assignments coming from two-volume works, in English and other languages. When a female student told Veblen she wanted the course because she heard he did not like women in his classes, Veblen smiled and asked if she was a member of a sorority. Puzzled, the young woman admitted membership in two groups but still saw no link between sororities and a course in economic factors. This was Veblen's last word: "I don't say that I will fail any member of a sorority or a fraternity but no member of such an organization has yet passed one of my courses."[66]

Relative to the day of the week, his appearance often produced a second glance. One student recalled that "the first time I saw him coming along the Quad, with a slouch hat pulled down over his brow, with coat and trousers hanging; with unkempt hair and moustache creating a general unkempt appearance, I thought he was a tramp." In truth he was just a man who wanted to be someplace else. No matter what the course catalog said, he taught each and every class as a graduate seminar and droned on in such a low monotone that students often slept rather than listened. Veblen woke them up with an occasional exam, yet even the best students rarely received higher than a C. Sometimes he gave no exams at all, posted a C for every student, and when word got around, fewer students than ever took Veblen's courses.[67]

Only universities tolerate this kind of behavior. Like a magnet, institutions of higher learning often attract people who want to be paid well for following their idle curiosity without any impediments and onerous obligations. Veblen chose the right way to put bread on the table, but the lethal combination of personal eccentricity, marital problems, and radical views finally led to an academic dead end. After his departure from Stanford in 1909, even Veblen's books produced no offers. Finally, a former student fashioned a job at the University of Missouri. Veblen stayed there until 1918. By all accounts, he hated living in a country town like Columbia. For example, when the local chamber of commerce offered a prize for a slogan for the town, Veblen made this suggestion: "It was a woodpecker hole of a town in a rotten stump called Missouri."[68]

Initially, Veblen lived in the cellar of a friend's home. The "apartment" lacked a door, so one of the nation's most renowned scholars entered and left through a window. Eventually, Veblen got his house in order, divorcing his first wife and in 1914 marrying a woman who helped provide a measure of stability in a life with one principal purpose: writing books that made people think.

Veblen published *The Instinct of Workmanship* in 1914.[69] Although it is a great summary of his principal views, the book offers few new insights. However, in *Imperial Germany and the Industrial Revolution* (published in 1915), Veblen provided opinions that, in the middle of World War I, satisfied absolutely no one. He criticizes the English gentleman as "the highest flower of wastefulness," and his negative attitudes toward German *Kultur* never pleased what was then the largest immigrant group in America. Remember that in 1915 fully 10 percent of the American people boasted either German birth or German ancestry.[70]

This did not matter to Veblen. In the preface to *Imperial Germany and the Industrial Revolution*, he explains that his aim is neither political nor polemical. He simply wants "to account for Germany's industrial advance and high efficiency by natural causes, without drawing on the logic of manifest destiny, Providential nepotism, natural genius and the like."[71] Veblen's brilliant argument is that a society can adopt the culture of the machine process without enduring endless years of experimentation and delay. The English needed centuries to create the industrial revolution, and they did it in a society dominated by theories of natural right and fox hunting. But once "the working elements of the [machine process] technology" are available to other nations, the process can be learned without also transferring the useless baggage of British cultural beliefs, values, and practices. In a sense a nation like Germany (or Japan) received a ready-made gift that they "with no great difficulty" adapted to their cultural beliefs and practices. In Germany that unfortunately "meant a policy directed toward warlike success."[72] But a nation could also use the machine process in a peaceful manner. The key insight—sustained to this day—is that any explanation of industrial success must include a ready-made machine process that can be transferred to any society on earth. For contemporary examples consider Singapore or Taiwan, two tiny nations that have marvelously (in economic terms) embraced the rigors and demands of the most sophisticated machine and technological processes.

War censorship soon took Veblen's book off the market. It was too hot to handle, so Veblen decided to create even more controversy by publishing, in 1918, *The Higher Learning in America*. In little more than 200 pages, he not only bit the hand that fed him; Veblen swallowed it whole.

HIGHER LEARNING IN AMERICA

While attending Yale Veblen often appeared at religious ceremonies. They were a part of everyday campus life, and he endured the services because he had no choice. One custom in particular caught his attention. When the services ended students remained standing in their pews; Yale's president then walked down the center aisle, and as he passed each pew, the students turned and, with great solemnity, they "bowed very low."[73]

As an adult Thorstein Veblen bowed to nothing—except the ideals of higher education. The first pages of *The Higher Learning in America* sparkle with an idealism that is both inspiring and surprising. Pursuing Veblen the reader learns to expect sarcasm, satire, and ridicule of the established order. In this book it eventually appears in spades, but not until Veblen first explains the beauty of an endlessly probing mind.

Idle curiosity refers to an impulsive trait of all people, all the time. Human beings seek knowledge, and they value it for its own sake. Like Veblen's need to know how the typewriter functioned, the inquisitive mind wanders in any direction, fueled by a need to acquire information "apart from any ulterior use of the knowledge so gained." Of course, people could turn knowledge to practical account, even making money;

Veblen both accepted and expected such efforts. But the essence of idle curiosity was a disinterested search for whatever information the inquisitive mind wanted to acquire. From its origins in "puerile myth and magic to its (provisional) consummation in the 'exact' sciences of the current fashion," human beings always sought and cherished esoteric knowledge. Thorstein Veblen called this knowledge "the higher learning;"[74] It was the "only end in life that indubitably justified itself," and "nothing more irretrievably shameful could overtake modern civilization than the miscarriage of this modern learning, *which is the most valued spiritual asset of civilized man*" (emphasis added).[75]

Remember how Durkheim used the word *sacred*; it was a category wholly distinct from profane, everyday life. For Veblen universities were literally sacred places because they housed the esoteric knowledge already acquired and because they nurtured idle curiosity and the faculty—who existed to disinterestedly provide what might be of no practical use. "A university is a body of mature scholars and scientists"; and "the university man is, properly, a student, not a schoolmaster." Go to a club if you want to party and a park if you want to play football. Because in Veblen's world, "no man whose energies are not habitually bent on increasing and proving up the domain of learning belongs legitimately on the university staff."[76]

Veblen accepted the need for professional and technical schools; doctors and engineers had to receive an education. But their practical bent meant that they had to be thoroughly separated from the graduate schools that housed the faculty who were perpetual students. Never contaminate the pursuit of disinterested knowledge with demands for practicality; never try to quantify the results of the higher learning; and always keep undergraduates in another location, preferably Siberia. Even more than engineers or technicians, undergraduates promised "the rigid routine and accountancy advocated by the schoolmasters." Let undergraduate methods and standards in the graduate school and, like a house of cards, the sacred enterprise of higher education collapsed. Thus, adolescents were neither seen nor heard in the hallowed halls of a serious university.[77]

If Veblen's ideal sounds far-fetched, it was nevertheless a model shared by a variety of other serious scholars. Along with the philosopher John Dewey and the historian Charles Beard, Veblen helped create—in 1919— the New School for Social Research. Based in New York City, the graduate school only existed to provide disinterested knowledge, and it remains one of the nation's premier schools of higher learning.

Scholars needed protection; they sought an ivory tower but received instead the Gothic counting houses (i.e., the University of Chicago) created by robber barons like John. D. Rockefeller. In a chapter titled "The Governing Boards," Veblen describes a generational change. When he went to Yale, clergymen sat on the board of trustees; now laymen made the rules. This was no problem for an avowed nonbeliever like Veblen, but unfortunately, secularization had nothing to do with scholarship. "The substitution is a substitution of businessmen and politicians; which amounts to saying that it is a substitution of businessmen. *So that the discretionary control in matters of university policy now rests finally in the hands of businessmen*" (emphasis added).[78]

Veblen emphasized a change that is now an institutionalized fact in virtually every U.S. university. A business civilization celebrates its most successful entrepreneurs by placing them on the board of trustees of major and minor universities. Business minds, out to make a buck, decide what happens to scholars who, like Veblen, spend their spare time translating Norwegian classics like *The Laxdoela Saga*. Veblen's translation (published in 1925) "reflects the state of affairs touching the Scandinavian and the English speaking people's at the point of their induction into their feudal and ecclesiastical status in early Christian times."[79]

That was Veblen, a man who despised the idea that higher education could possibly become a business proposition. Instead of Plato's dream of philosophers at the helm, captains of erudition, bankrolled by captains of industry, took over the direction of the pursuit of knowledge.[80] Veblen said to think of the modern university as a department store. It advertised, it ruthlessly competed with other institutions—think of President Harper's stealing faculty from other schools—and as if a sale at Penney's, it sponsored the "public pageants" that allowed parents and students to wallow in the glow of university glitter as they simultaneously displayed "their proficiency in expenditure on seemly dress and equipage." The campus became a showcase for conspicuous consumption because, "broadly speaking, no requirement of the academic routine should be allowed to stand in the way of an available occasion for a scholastic pageant."[81]

Pageants brought customers, but never as many as the ever-expanding curriculum designed to appeal to any educational consumer with the wherewithal to pay the high price of higher education. Universities shamelessly offered any degrees that produced customers, while academic departments competed for bodies with all the energy of an army recruiter. Today those departments also need to bring in foundation and government funding—Can you write grants? is a common question to today's faculty—but either way, defining a university's success in terms of the number of preferably live bodies in the room was a trend that Veblen caught and abhorred.

For those readers who play on a sports team or belong to a fraternity or sorority, rest assured that Veblen thought of your activities as "politely blameless dissipations."[82] He understood that universities sponsored sports teams to attract students and gain repute; but the thirst for college spirit crippled the academic environment by attaching far more significance to winning games than seeking knowledge. In 1918 Veblen stressed that universities got endowment bucks by passing out the Chardonnay and brie at pregame tailgate parties; and a savvy university president always invited the richest fans to his private box.

Greek letter fraternities received high praise; they cultivated the "graces of gentility and were also a suitable place of residence for young men of spendthrift habits." Like President George W. Bush with his gentleman's Cs, fraternities helped downplay the pursuit of knowledge as they simultaneously provided sound training for a life of conspicuous waste and leisure. Son followed father, as they both praised "the corps of workmen and assistants who took care of the grounds, buildings and apparatus." The department store needed to shine, especially before parents appeared for the next round of pompous pageants.[83]

How fair is Veblen's critique? The only just answer to that question is that it depends on your point of view. If, like Veblen, you assume that universities exist to foster nothing but idle curiosity, the introduction of business beliefs and standards certainly contaminated the educational process. However, if you think that sports and students organizations—not to mention undergraduates—have a place at the university, then Veblen's critique simply reflects, among other things, his passion for Norwegian classics.

The one certainty is that, whatever your opinion, Veblen got it dead right on the nature of a modern, U.S. campus. Students and their "we pay the bill" parents are treated like discerning consumers; thus, whether at George Washington University in the nation's capital, Rutgers in New Brunswick, or the University of Nebraska in Omaha, every viable university now has a food court offering cuisine that precisely resembles the offerings of an upscale mall. Luxurious dorms often boast outdoor grills, and (at least for our children) proximity to good bars is as important today as it was in 1918. Meanwhile, university presidents do function as glad-handing seekers of endowments, and faculty are sometimes judged not by the quality of their publications but by the quantity of material that allegedly brings the university repute and distinction.[84]

Veblen saw an emerging world; we inherited it.

THE ENGINEERS AND THE PRICE SYSTEM

True to his ideals, Veblen helped found, in 1919, the New School for Social Research. Located in New York's Greenwich Village, the school made no allowance for young people. For all these professors cared, undergraduates could party in Pittsburgh or play football in Los Angeles. Meanwhile, in a section of New York famous for nonconformity, "a group of men versed in the various branches of knowledge relating to mankind had drawn together for counsel, for the correlations of their investigations and the establishment of a center of instruction and discussion where serious-minded and mature students gather to carry on their studies in a spirit of scientific inquiry."[85]

Veblen could have (and may have!) written these lines about "serious-minded and mature students." They reflected his ideal of idle curiosity, linked to a thirst for serious social change. This was a graduate school with a clear cultural agenda. Its goal is "to seek an unbiased understanding of the existing order, its genesis, growth and present working, as well as those of exigent circumstances which are making for its revision."[86]

Veblen's first contribution at the New School reflected the concerns of one of America's most controversial men, Frederick Winslow Taylor. Legions of workers hated Taylor because, with a green light from the captains of finance, his *Principles of Scientific Management* (published in 1911) instantly enveloped every phase of the worker's day. Consider, for example, Taylor's path-breaking analysis of moving pig iron. Calculating that workers at Bethlehem Steel could load 47.5 tons a day (the average at the time was 12.5 tons), he took a "mentally sluggish man" named Schmidt and "all day long, and at regular intervals, Schmidt was told by the man who stood over him with a stopwatch, 'Now pick up a pig and walk. Now sit down and rest. Now walk, now rest' . . . and at half past five in the afternoon Schmidt had his 47.5 tons loaded on the car."[87]

History calls Taylor the father of the time motion study. Precision instruments in hand, he and his engineer colleagues broke down the elements of any task into its constituent parts. They turned workers into commodities at the service of a clipboard and a stopwatch, yet to Thorstein Veblen, engineers also offered the nation's only hope for a different future. In *The Engineers and the Price System* (published in 1921), Veblen argued that "a Soviet of technicians" should displace the captains of industry, and as five-star generals of the machine process, engineers would use the industrial wealth of the nation to equitably distribute what was necessary rather than frivolous, useful rather than wasteful.[88]

"Sabotage" is the title of the book's first chapter. Veblen explains that the word is derived from *sabot*, French for a "wooden shoe." In America owners flaunting their natural rights to property made the machine process walk in large wooden shoes. In the service of profits and stability, the "Guardians of the established order" nefariously engaged in a successful conspiracy to undermine the marvelous potential of the machine process. Indeed, as if dead to the world, idle plants and idle workmen waited for the owners to once again post the good news of "open for business." If the sign never appeared, workers languished because, as Veblen repeated again and again, corporations were capitalized "on their capacity to produce earnings, not on their capacity to produce goods."[89]

This was vintage Veblen, an insight that was already twenty years old. However, this time the new professor at the New School also offered a plan for radical social change. He stressed that "under existing circumstances there need be no fear, and no hope, of an effectual revolutionary overturn in America."[90] Yet, for those who wanted to think about revolution, here was an engineering blueprint for a new world.

First on the agenda was the abolition of any form of absentee ownership. Only those who habitually and beneficially used property could own it. This meant that in the new order, "the experienced and capable business men are to be rated as well-intentioned deaf-mute blind men."[91] They would watch from the sidelines as the intelligent cooperation of thousands of technically trained men engaged in a "complete *castration* of the country's industrial forces." No matter how you look at it, castration is a strong word; yet Veblen offers no suggestion of a violent revolution. Instead, Americans would finally recognize the debilitating consequences of "the two-cleft or bi-cameral" administration of the nation's industrial process. The technicians, who already managed the machine process, represented the community at large. The businessmen represented the absentee owners who held the technicians (and the rest of the nation) hostage to the natural rights of private property. Just castrate the top cleft of the administrative process, and the machines would work for people rather than profit.[92]

Veblen recommended a "conscientious withdrawal of efficiency"; he preached the efficacy of a general strike "to include so much of the country's staff of technicians as will suffice to incapacitate the industrial system at large by their withdrawal, for such time as may be required to enforce their argument."[93]

High if not impossible barriers to the strike included the following factors. The general public thought of technicians "as a somewhat fantastic brotherhood of over-specialized cranks, not to be trusted out of sight except under the restraining hand of safe and sane business men." The technicians themselves were a group of generally satisfied subordinates who had as much sympathy with the workers and their unions as the captains of industry had for the soviet of workers then under the firm hand of Vladimir Lenin, Joseph Stalin, and Leon Trotsky. It was a panorama filled with pessimism, so Veblen ends with the need "for an extensive campaign of inquiry and publicity" that will alert and convince the American people of the need for a revolution led by engineers waving the banners of efficiency for all, absentee ownership for none.[94]

In judging Veblen's plan, remember the principles of scientific management. In postwar America, not everyone thought of engineers as cranks.[95] Science at the service of the machine process promised to dramatically increase both output and efficiency; so, if Veblen grasped at a straw, it was a straw with a modicum of substance. In addition, the revolution in Russia was still in its infancy. Slaughter and totalitarian control were not yet part of the general public's perception of the Soviet Union. Combining a hint of communism with a large dose of Yankee ingenuity made sense to people seeking radical social change.

Meanwhile, Veblen followed his own advice. In *Absentee Ownership: The Case of America* (published in 1923), he offered the results of an inquiry that, like Paul Revere on his horse, would alert Americans to the realities of their condition. The book includes all of Veblen's familiar arguments. In addition Veblen adds elements that will sound very familiar, especially if you listened to Ralph Nader's critique of business and politics in the year 2000 presidential election.

The biggest change is Veblen's focus on political sovereignty. Especially for kings, sovereignty implied a theological metaphysics; God gave the king divine right over everyone. "The Freudians would presumably call it an inferiority complex with benefit of clergy."[96] However, when kings lost their power, "the retention of this princely sovereignty on behalf of the 'sovereign people' marks the nation as a successor of the dynastic state, chartered to do business on the same lines and with the same powers."[97]

Veblen never accuses Warren Harding or Calvin Coolidge of an inferiority complex. However, he does ridicule the notion of democratic sovereignty. If, instead of the divine right of kings, America is a nation under God, the logic of the argument is that "a loyal member of the underlying population, by Grace of God, owes unqualified and unalienable allegiance to his own person in perpetuity."[98] In reality the people's representatives ran the show, and as World War I proved, they did it in the service of imperial ambitions abroad and business rights and interests at home. The nation had become "a licensed predatory concern" that functioned as part of a coalition that included absentee owners and the country town.[99]

The country town! After twenty years of writing, Veblen used his final book to come home to Minnesota and Wisconsin. Think, for example, of the continuing significance of the illustrations of Norman Rockwell when you read this line: "The country town is one of the great American institutions; perhaps the greatest in the sense that it has and continues to have a greater part than any other in shaping public sentiment and giving character to American culture."[100] For Veblen the country town had turned into a cheerleader for big business and absentee ownership. The self-made man of pioneer days—the farmer—had turned into a captive and supporter of the captains of industry and the political state they controlled. Indeed, when the Metropolitan Casualty Insurance Company actually published pamphlets arguing that "Moses was one of the greatest salesmen and real estate developers that ever lived,"[101] the conjunction of business, political, religious, and cultural (i.e., farmers and their country towns) power was both complete and unassailable. As Calvin Coolidge put it in 1925, the business of America was business.

Absentee Ownership put a period on Veblen's work. He published no additional books. Yet his critique of America's business civilization retains great relevance today. For example, can you see the "long-hair look" of the 1960s or the "grunge look" of the 1980s and early 1990s apart from a need to avoid conspicuous consumption?[102] And what about the following critique from the *New York Times* of November 25, 2001? Economist Paul Krugman notes that Congress's economic stimulus package includes "almost nothing for the unemployed but includes $25 billion in *retroactive* corporate tax cuts—that is, pure and simple lump-sum transfers to corporations, most of them highly profitable."[103]

Krugman wants to know how an $800 million lump-sum payment to General Motors will lead to more investment when the company is already sitting on $8 billion in cash. Veblen would answer that Krugman's question misses the point. Big business exists to make money, not to create jobs. Retroactive tax cuts therefore make perfect sense if Congress is an arm of the corporations, using its divine right of taxation to bless businesses that even in a globalized economy, still trace their success to the country towns of rural America. As President George W. Bush noted on August 13, 2001, "Farm families represent the best of America. They represent the values that have made this country unique and different—values of love and family, values of respect for nature."[104]

The president was serious. And so was Thorstein Veblen.

VEBLEN'S WILL

Veblen retired from the New School in 1926. He ultimately moved to California and died there on August 3, 1929. His will includes the following line: "that no tombstone, epitaph, effigy, tablet, inscription, or monument of any name or nature, be set up in my memory or name in any place or at any time; that no obituary, memorial, portrait or biography of me, not any letters written to or by me be printed or published, or in any way reproduced, copied, or circulated."[105]

As if a Nordic explorer, Veblen's ashes were to be "thrown loose" into the sea. He wanted to disappear, but Veblen remains an American original. He was the immigrant farm boy who came to the big city, the student who exchanged his coonskin cap for one of the most powerful pens in the continuing discourse about the nature and meaning of U.S. civilization.

NOTES

1. R. L. Duffus, *The Innocents at Cedro* (New York: Macmillan, 1944), 78.

2. Ibid., 62. See too, the Web site [www.infoplease.com] for a short summary about the ichneumon fly.

3. Duffus, *Innocents at Cedro*, 62.

4. Matthew Josephson, *The Robber Barons* (New York: Harcourt Brace, 1934), 78–79.

5. Ibid., 85.

6. Edward Winslow Martin, *Behind the Scenes in Washington* (New York: Continental, 1873), 248–57.

7. Sucheng Chan, *Asian Americans* (New York: Twayne, 1991), 31.

8. Ibid., 31.

9. Helen Zia, *Asian American Dreams* (New York: Farrar, Straus and Giroux, 2000), 27.

10. Mike Davis, *Late Victorian Holocausts* (London: Verso, 2001), 1–6.

11. Ibid., 6.

12. Chan, *Asian Americans*, 54.

13. Ray H. Abrams, *Preachers Present Arms* (New York: Round Table Press, 1933), 116.

14. See Valdres Samband, *The Oldest Bygdelag in America*, [www.geocities.com/~valdressamband/].

15. Duffus, *Innocents at Cedro*, 59.

16. Russell H. Bartley, "Unexamined Moments in the Life of Thorstein Veblen: Refining the Biographical References," paper read at the Second Conference of the International Thorstein Veblen Association, June 1996, [www.villa.lakes.com/eltechno/TvbarRI.html]. The evidence about language acquisition is based on letters from Veblen's brother Andrew. Professor Bartley rightly corrects the accounts offered by other writers.

17. Joseph Dorfman, *Thorstein Veblen and His America* (New York: Augustus M. Kelley, 1966), 13. This is a reprint of the original edition published in 1934.

18. Ibid., 58; on the economics text, see p. 23.

19. Ibid., 55.

20. Ibid., 79–86.

21. Ibid., 87–88.

22. Thorstein Veblen, "The Beginning of Ownership," *American Journal of Sociology* 4 (1898–99): 1.

23. Ibid., 4.

24. David Riesman, *Thorstein Veblen: A Critical Interpretation* (New York: Continuum, 1960), 89–90.

25. Veblen, "Beginning of Ownership," 5.

26. Ibid., 6.

27. Ibid.

28. Thorstein Veblen, *The Theory of the Leisure Class* (New York: New American Library, 1953), 29.

29. Ibid., 30.

30. "Michelangelo of the Hard Sell," *New York Times*, November 3, 2001, D1–2.

31. Veblen, *Theory of the Leisure Class*, 33.

32. Ibid., 33, 46.

33. Ibid., 56–57.

34. Josephson, *Robber Barons*, 338.

35. Ibid.

36. Veblen, *Theory of the Leisure Class*, 164.

37. Ibid., 115.

38. Ibid., 151.

39. Ibid., 150.

40. Dorfman, *Thorstein Veblen*, 6.

41. Veblen, *Theory of the Leisure Class*, 140.

42. Riesman, *Thorstein Veblen*, 12.

43. Dorfman, *Thorstein Veblen*, 196–97.

44. Michael O'Malley, *Keeping Watch: A History of American Time* (New York: Penguin, 1990), 87.

45. Ibid., 173–74.

46. Thorstein Veblen, *The Theory of Business Enterprise* (New York: Mentor Books, 1958), 10, 13.

47. Ibid., 19.

48. Ibid., 20.

49. George W. Stocking and Myron W. Watkins, *Cartels in Action* (New York: The Twentieth Century Fund, 1946), 304–62, esp. 307.

50. Veblen, *Theory of Business Enterprise*, 24.

51. Ibid., 29.

52. Duffus, *Innocents at Cedro*, 64.

53. Veblen, *Theory of Business Enterprise*, 55.

54. Michael Lewis, *The New New Thing* (New York: Norton, 2000), 85.

55. Veblen, *Theory of Business Enterprise*, 112.

56. Ibid., 136.

57. Ibid., 148.

58. Ibid., 189.

59. See [www.moneycentral.msn.com/investor/research/profile.asp?Symbol+AMZN].

60. Dorfman, *Thorstein Veblen*, 253.

61. Duffus, *Innocents at Cedro*, 93.

62. Bartley, "Unexamined Moments."

63. Duffus, *Innocents at Cedro*, 98.

64. Ibid., 80.

65. Dorfman, *Thorstein Veblen*, 309.

66. Ibid.

67. Ibid., 248.

68. Ibid., 306–7.

69. Thorstein Veblen, *The Instinct of Workmanship* (New York: Norton, 1964).

70. See Riesman, *Thorstein Veblen*, 133.

71. Thorstein Veblen, *Imperial Germany and the Industrial Revolution* (Ann Arbor: University of Michigan Press, 1966), v.

72. Ibid., 191.

73. Dorfman, *Thorstein Veblen*, 42.

74. Thorstein Veblen, *The Higher Learning in America* (New York: Hill and Wang, 1957), 6.

75. Ibid., 8.

76. Ibid., 13.

77. Ibid., 19.

78. Ibid., 46.

79. Dorfman, *Thorstein Veblen*, 493.

80. Veblen, *Higher Learning*, 57.

81. Ibid., 115.

82. Ibid., 87.

83. Ibid., 90.

84. For a recent critique, see Robert Nisbet, *The Degradation of Academic Dogma* (New York: Basic Books, 1971).

85. Dorfman, *Thorstein Veblen*, 449.

86. Ibid.

87. Frederick Winslow Taylor, *The Principles of Scientific Management* (New York: Norton, 1911), 47.

88. Thorstein Veblen, *The Engineers and the Price System* (New York: Harcourt, Brace, 1963), chapter 6.

89. Ibid., 38, 111.

90. Ibid., 132.

91. Ibid., 138.

92. Ibid., 147.

93. Ibid., 149–50.

94. Ibid., 150–51.

95. See, for example, Reinhardt Bendix, *Work and Authority in Industry* (New York: Harper, 1968).

96. Thorstein Veblen, *Absentee Ownership: The Case of America* (Boston: Beacon Press, 1967), 26.

97. Ibid., 26.

98. Ibid., 27.

99. Ibid., 428.

100. Ibid., 142.

101. Frederick Lewis Allen, *Only Yesterday: An Informal History of the 1920's* (New York: Harper and Row, 1964), 149.

102. See Riesman, *Thorstein Veblen*, 176–77.

103. Paul Krugman, "An Alternate Reality," *New York Times*, November 25, 2001, section 4:11.

104. *New York Times*, August 13, 2001, 1.

105. Dorfman, *Thorstein Veblen*, 505.

CHAPTER 7

Erving Goffman

"The world, in truth, is a wedding."
                    Erving Goffman, *The Presentation of Self in Everyday Life*[1]

NOT MY BUSINESS

It was a right-wing conspiracy. In fact, in the fall of 1964, University of California–Berkeley students and faculty even believed they could pinpoint the source of the problem. During the summer William Knowland, the publisher of the *Oakland Tribune*, allegedly told the university's chancellor that he objected to Berkeley students using state property to advocate the candidacy of certain Republican presidential candidates. In particular, he opposed the students who supported Governor William Scranton rather than his candidate, Senator Barry Goldwater.[2]

Until Knowland's roadblock appeared, students used the sidewalk in front of the university's entrance to hold rallies, set up tables, give speeches, and distribute literature for a kaleidoscope of political and cultural groups. University officials allowed the gatherings because the sidewalk was supposedly city rather than school property. Local officials policed the area, and in Goffman's time (he came to Berkeley in 1958), the police suddenly encountered new and presumably strange people. Beatniks and hippies promenaded down Telegraph Avenue, and with weed, speed, and LSD they added new flavors to a university that already contained a Baskin-Robbins assortment of diverse Americans.

Problems started as soon as students returned for the new semester. School officials indicated that because the sidewalk actually belonged to the university, students could no longer hold any political gathering, of any form on Telegraph Avenue. Students protested and even formed a "united front" of nineteen "off-campus" organizations to protest the school's infringement of a basic American right, free speech.

Proud members of the initial student coalition included the University Society of Individualists, Cal Students for Goldwater, Women for Peace, the W.E.B. DuBois Club, and the Interfaith Council. In hindsight, it seems like a harmless and even laudable assertion of a constitutional right. However, university officials refused to back down. Worried about threats to their state funding, administrators enforced the new ban. As confrontations continued, the united front turned into the free speech movement, one of the most unsettling assertions of student rights in U.S. history.[3]

Early demonstrations included as few as 5,000 students. A majority not only supported the protesters, but they belonged to "no campus political organization." Fully half were attending their first protest rally, and if only 15 percent willingly risked arrest at the beginning of the demonstrations, the speakers so ignited the crowd that 56 percent soon said they would risk arrest "if negotiations broke down an similar demonstrations were necessary."[4]

In a university class on deviance, Erving Goffman reluctantly expressed his beliefs about the relationship between the science of sociology and active support of political movements for civil rights and other social changes. When an activist remarked that "this is all very interesting Professor Goffman, but what's the use of it for changing the conditions you describe?" Goffman was visibly shaken. "He stood up, slammed shut the book he had open on the desk, said, 'I'm not in that business,' and stormed out of the room."[5]

Goffman focused on social order, a commodity in very short supply during the fall of 1964. In October one student refused the request of the university police to leave a table displaying materials for CORE, the Congress of Racial Equality. When officers tried to arrest the student, he folded up like an accordion and the police dragged him to a waiting squad car. A junior philosophy student named Mario Savio urged the students to stay, and they did so. This protest lasted for thirty-two hours and included a "pack-in" in Sproul Hall. Simultaneously, a group of counterprotesters appeared. Throwing eggs, fruit, and lit cigarettes at the demonstrators, the fraternity members helped create such havoc that 500 Bay-area police—carrying riot sticks—suddenly appeared on campus. Finally, standing next to a crumpled police car, a Newman Hall priest quieted the crowd—for the moment.[6]

University chancellor Clark Kerr eventually moved against students involved in these October demonstrations. While his actions immediately and predictably produced a call for new sit-ins (on December 4), it was his reported conversation with the university's board of trustees that inflamed the student body. Like the beatniks, many students earnestly tried to distance themselves from organization men wearing gray flannel suits. Meanwhile, Chancellor Kerr indicated that he made no public announcement of his efforts to liberalize the rules because "would you ever imagine the manager of a firm making a statement in opposition to his Board of Directors?"[7]

On December 3, 1964, Mario Savio answered the chancellor. "I ask you to consider: If this is a firm, and if the Board of Regents are the Board of Directors, and if President Kerr in fact is the manager, then I'll tell you something: The faculty are a bunch of employees, and we're the raw material." No one told budding beatniks they worked in a firm. Standing atop a damaged car, Savio ended with these memorable lines. "There is a time when the operation of the machine becomes so odious, makes you so sick at heart, that you can't take part; you can't even passively take part, and you've got to put your bodies upon the gears and upon the wheels, upon the levers, upon all the apparatus, and you've got to make it stop."[8]

The faculty met in emergency session on December 8, 1964. More than a thousand members piled into a huge auditorium, and no less than a hundred of the faculty made round-trip drives from the campus to the jails where students resided and back again to the university. The faculty debate included a resolution requesting the administration to refrain from any "university disciplinary measures against members or organizations of the University community for activities prior to December 8." Students naturally wanted to attend the debate, but by custom, the faculty meetings remained closed to anyone below the rank of assistant professor. Graduate students were out of the question, so along with undergraduates, they lined the corridors of the building and listened on the steps outside to "a tinny amplification" of the faculty's conversation.

While the printed transcript runs to fifteen tightly packed pages, Professor Rynin of the philosophy department caught the essence of the situation when he stated that "we are gathered here because the University is perhaps in the greatest danger in its career. A supreme effort has been made to save the University." He urged his colleagues to support the students. After a long debate, the faculty passed its resolution of support by a vote of 824 to 115.[9]

Although Erving Goffman's name never appears in the printed debate, he did express his views when he attended one of the student rallies. In an open meeting someone asked, "Professor Goffman, where do you stand?" He responded, "When they start shooting students from the steps of Sproul Hall I guess I'll get involved but not until then."[10] His response stunned onlookers. They expected empathy instead of sarcasm, interest instead of abstinence.

Even with the university in total turmoil, Goffman adamantly avoided political controversy. Students wanted him to speak out, but if it was actually a free speech movement, Erving Goffman certainly had the right to remain silent. The marvelous irony is that the focus of his work was social order. In the midst of a society and university exploding with angry demands for social change, Goffman singlehandedly focused on the "microanalysis" of something he called the interaction order.[11] His work lacks any hint of politics and economics; and you will look in vain for any contemporary analysis of the women's movement, the Civil Rights movement, the gay movement, or the peace movement against the war in Vietnam.

The walls of the university came tumbling down. Meanwhile, Erving Goffman not only found significant social order; he created a body of work that is as unique and important as that of our other magnificent minds. In politics Goffman clearly moved to the sidelines; but when it came to the social order of face-to-face interaction, Erving Goffman went lip to lip—in a profoundly original and enlightening manner.

CITY OF SUNSHINE: DAUPHIN, MANITOBA, CANADA

Like the Italians and Poles in the United States, more than 200,000 Ukrainians moved to Canada between 1897 and 1914. Along with Goffman's parents, they settled in communities that, climatically, resembled their homeland. Max and Ann Goffman first moved to Mannville, Alberta, where, on June 22, 1922, Ana gave birth to their son Erving. The family then moved to the tiny hamlet of Dauphin in the remote reaches of the Canadian province of Manitoba.[12]

Goffman grew up in Dauphin; to draw tourists, Dauphin now calls itself the city of sunshine, but with a population (in 2002) of 8,266, "city" seems like an exaggeration. Roughly ninety years ago, Goffman's parents settled down with other Ukrainian immigrants in a tiny town dominated by agricultural pursuits; it lacked a nearby metropolis, and it naturally possessed a cold climate. Zero is the mean temperature in January, and if the sun shines, even in August the mean temperature is a brisk 65 degrees Fahrenheit. However, Dauphin does host the National Ukrainian Festival, and the Smith-Jackson school proudly boasts a Ukrainian/English Bilingual education program. Admittedly, many of the students lack a Ukrainian ancestry, but for those with roots as deep as Goffman, "the school connects them to their past "and gives them a greater understanding about themselves and their ancestors."[13]

At least for publication, Goffman never wrote about his childhood in Dauphin. He did tell friends about his father's tailoring business; and he declared that "being a Jew and a Russian Jew at that, explained a lot about him." If that meant he was a perennial outsider, caught between his ancestry and the prejudices of the larger society, his position mirrored that of Durkheim or Simmel. However, Goffman never clarified this enigmatic statement; he only suggested that "he saw origins more as a way of indexing others rather than accounting for himself." Maybe he just wanted to confuse everyone. For example, when teaching in Scotland, he liked to call himself "a colonial, a hat in hand visitor to the imperial world of English majesty."[14]

For unknown reasons, Goffman's earliest friends called him "Pooky." He went to a technical high school in Winnipeg (200 miles from Dauphin), and after three years, he entered the University of Manitoba. His first interest was chemistry, his second a career in film working at the National Film Board in Ottawa. A friendship with the sociologist Dennis Wrong pushed Goffman toward the University of Toronto, where, in 1945, he received a bachelor's degree in sociology.[15]

Graduate work sent Goffman to the University of Chicago. It then contained some of the leading lights of American sociology, yet Goffman describes a distinctly narrow curriculum. "In those days there weren't many translations. Having access to these simple texts was a significant thing. It's very hard for a European to understand circumstances where there would be a few professors who had access to the language and none of their students. Those were the circumstances I went to school in." Goffman did read Durkheim's *The Elementary Forms of Religious Life*; and he also mentioned Weber's *The Protestant Ethic and the Spirit of Capitalism*. Beyond that, neither he nor the other students used the classical theories to gain a foundation in sociology. "There were very few of my generation who could read in any effective sense German or French."[16]

Goffman later called himself an "urban ethnographer." It is an apt label for his description of Chicago sociology in the late 1940s. Students read pragmatists like George Herbert Mead, and they then used their knowledge in the field, with firsthand observations of how people actually lived and thought. In Goffman's case, he finished his doctoral dissertation by spending two years living in Unst, one of the small Shetland Isles in Scotland. His designated task supposedly included a "detailed case study" of the community; however, once in Unst, he became intrigued by the way locals behaved with tourists. Visitors expected certain behavior from the supposedly quaint Scots, and if the locals behaved according to the scripts written in tourist brochures, in secret they used a "cryptic, or coded, means of communication." The channel separating people's behavior from their actual beliefs fascinated Goffman; he focused on the masks people wore and got himself into hot water at home. When he defended his dissertation in 1953, reviewers expressed some consternation. Instead of a field study, the student offered "what was primarily a general theory of face-to-face interaction." Ironically, the young man with no grounding in the classical sociologists now produced a provocative theory based on the urban ethnography practiced in Chicago. Meanwhile, he did his research in rural Scotland and happily followed the leads discovered there for the rest of his career.[17]

Goffman married in 1953. Angelica Choate also studied at the University of Chicago, and the couple soon had two children. Tragically, Angelica Goffman experienced serious problems in living. Only 35, she committed suicide in 1964. Goffman later criticized psychiatrists and social scientists for forgetting "that mental symptoms are neither something in themselves nor whatever is so labeled; mental symptoms are acts by an individual which openly proclaim to others that he must have assumptions about himself which the relevant bit of social organization can neither allow him nor do much about." Mental symptoms create family "havoc"; psychiatrists "dismally fail" to examine this havoc, and sociologists ignore it when they treat mental illness merely as a labeling process. "It is this havoc that we must explore."[18]

In his own work Goffman explored a notion called "role distance"; think of the difference between a child blissfully enjoying a ride on a merry-go-round and the child's parent who, with facial expressions, indicates: I'm not enjoying this, I am just along for the ride. Role distance refers to the "effectively expressed separateness between the individual and his putative role." The parent is on the merry-go-round but indicates that the real me is somewhere else.[19]

It is hard to find Goffman's real me. He devoted his entire life to sociology, yet in an interview conducted shortly before his death, he expressed enough role distance to create a large lake. "I'm old fashioned, conservative, and unsophisticated in my epistemology. I have no strong belief in what I espouse." Asked how he labeled himself, Goffman seemed amazed by the concerns of his colleagues. He knew other people used labels to divide the discipline, yet (speaking in 1980) "it's only about eight or nine years old; so, considering the length of time I have been in the business, I can't take any of that labeling very seriously." He did admit to attending sociological meetings and even eating with some of the people making labels. "They are all my best friends. . . . I just don't understand why . . . unless it's a self-defensive process, you know."[20]

One of his former students at Berkeley writes that Goffman believed that "you could be a successful sociologist without becoming a dreaded organization man." Outside of class Goffman dressed casually and "did not like to shave. His speech was neither pedantic nor formal and was always larded with contemporary hip expressions." Goffman was so cool he told graduate students they could avoid joining the American Sociological Association. "He said no, you didn't have to belong, and cited some well known sociologists as examples."[21]

Goffman also liked to play the stock market. He later "boasted that even though he was one of the highest paid sociologists in the United States, he still earned a third of his income from investments and a third from royalties." He also liked to gamble. Colleagues report that he regularly lost at poker but paid his debts "with grace and good humor." In Las Vegas he played blackjack with such aplomb that while researching this particular form of face-to-face interaction, he eventually became a "pit boss" at the Station Plaza Casino. He liked being where the action was and continually opened himself to new forms of research experience.[22]

Only Goffman knew if his level of role distance and self-depreciation was real or a mask. Perhaps he wanted to present an image of himself that, like the islanders in Scotland, had nothing to do with what he really believed and felt. What we have is his work. Erving Goffman indisputably marched to his own drummer; indeed, in the midst of incredible social disorder, he bet on the stock market and found in face-to-face interaction a form of social order ignored by virtually all his label-driven colleagues. As he told a sea of professors when he accepted the presidency of the American Sociological Association in 1982, "The man you have selected from a very short list takes to the center of this vast Hilton field on a hobby horse of his own choosing."[23]

"THE INTERACTION ORDER"

One of Goffman's earliest publications focuses on con artists.[24] The piece perfectly reflects his willingness to study anything that caught his fancy. Nothing human was foreign to Goffman's eye. Glance at his footnotes, and you move from books about cowboys to studies of the film star Greta Garbo to an analysis of baseball umpires. Seemingly random, the supposed madness of the method generally produced significant insights; for example, Goffman knew that successful con artists understood the interaction order as well as any sociologist did.

Consider the case of the "bogus epileptic." In Victorian England this meant "a decent-looking character, a neat, threadbare, hollow-eyed man whose favorite opportunity was a congregation coming out of church or chapel." Just before the worshipers dispersed, the bogus epileptic "collapsed on the ground in convulsions, limbs threshing, foam and cries escaping from his lips." Eventually, the fellow recovered, and after explaining his circumstances, our threadbare tramp produced a letter from a sympathetic clergyman. The letter explained that despite his best efforts, the epileptic endured penury because his ailment prevented him from any form of productive employment. Now moved to tears, the weeping congregation members often dipped into their wallets, and the con artist walked off with as much money as the worshipers put in the Sunday morning collection plate.[25]

This con assumes substantial knowledge of what Goffman later called the social order of face-to-face interaction. On a Sunday morning—and right after church service at that—the congregation would be in a giving, Christian mood. The epileptic looked down on his luck rather than shiftless or worthless. The letter from a clergyman was a nice touch, capped off by the foam coming from the epileptic's mouth. That, incidentally, derived from little pieces of soap shavings slipped under his tongue. He foamed on call, and the worshipers opened their hearts and wallets to save a soul who failed through no fault of his own.

Sometimes the bogus epileptic cried with too much pain. A helpful hand called a doctor, and when the epileptic got a clean bill of health, he soon got something else as well: a one-way ticket to jail. All face-to-face interaction assumes risk; people make mistakes. Yet Goffman nevertheless argued that "it appears to me that *as* an order of activity, the interaction one, more than any other perhaps, is in fact orderly, and that this orderliness is predicated on a large base of shared cognitive presuppositions."[26] Those presuppositions guided the con artist; he knew what people thought and how they would behave in particular situations. Thus, if he sustained the assumptions maintained by the congregation, he celebrated social order as he simultaneously cheated it and the congregation.

On the opening page of *Relations in Public*, Goffman suggests that face-to-face-interaction is a "form of government." Quoting Herbert Spencer, he writes "that this kind of government, besides preceding other kinds, and besides having in all places and times approached nearer to universality of influence, has ever had, and continues to have, the largest share in regulating men's lives."[27]

That is Goffman's argument. And it flows, like honey, from the assumptions and goals of his research. He remains skeptical of labels but, when pushed, sees himself as a "traditional structural functionalist." He openly admits that his ideal is "the kinship system of a preliterate society." Granted, he never expected to find that kind of "functional whole" in a modern culture, yet he nevertheless sought to study social order because, "in the last analysis, when you get down to studying something, well, you are interested in showing that there is some sort of organization, or structure to it. Otherwise, you haven't found anything presumably."[28]

In face-to-face interaction—in the hundreds of focused encounters that make up everyday life—Goffman perceives an order that allowed heterogeneous masses of people to successfully interact and, as in a wedding, ceremoniously support social order. "The central theme remains of a traffic of use, and of arrangements which allow a great diversity of projects and intents to be realized through *unthinking recourse* to procedural forms" (emphasis added).[29]

Goffman analyzed those procedural forms for a lifetime because of the astonishing degree of social order they produced *and* because the procedural forms of face-to-face encounters allowed him to "systematically study" aspects of life "worn smooth by constant repetition on the part of the participants." He certainly understood the need and desire to study the "macroscopic entities" favored by Marx, Weber, Simmel, Durkheim, and Veblen. Focus on the economy, religion, and social solidarity if you wished; but you could get a much better handle on face-to-face interaction because "the forms themselves are anchored in subjective feelings and thus allow an appreciable role for empathy." In essence, you could put yourself in the other person's head and, like Weber, try to grasp the subjective meanings women and men attached to their actions, expressions, and reactions.[30]

Explaining his approach, Goffman would definitely receive an F in any graduate course on methods. He indicated that as an "ethnographer of small entities," he worked alone. He seemed proud that "I don't work in terms of large grants employing anybody. I don't think I've ever employed anybody in my life."[31] He read widely and referred to his method as scholarship rather than research. "It is a sort of freewheeling, literary kind of thing." He collected a large number of illustrations, thought about them in a systematic way, and produced, especially in his early work, "papers that I wrote off the top of my head."[32]

One of those papers is "On Face-Work." It is "an analysis of the ritual elements in social interaction" and a perfect bridge into the work of a man who sometimes sounded like Thorstein Veblen. "There's nothing in the world we should trade for what we do have; the bent to sustain in regard to all elements of social life a spirit of unfettered, unsponsored inquiry; and the wisdom not to look elsewhere but ourselves and our discipline for this mandate."[33]

"ON FACE-WORK"

When reading Goffman, it helps to make a distinction between the self-inside and the self-outside. The former is what you think of you; as in the work of George Herbert Mead (see chapter 5), the self-inside is your more-or-less stable evaluation of you as a human being. The self-outside is the self you show to others; it may be the same as the self-inside (e.g., you think you are wonderful, and you let others know it), but Goffman continually spotlights the self we display to others—*and* how we maintain that self in the face of opposition, contradictions, and mistakes.

In "On Face-Work" Goffman talks about "lines." In any social encounter involving face-to-face interaction, a person acts out a line, that is, "a pattern of verbal and nonverbal acts by which he expresses his view of the situation and through this his evaluation of the participants, especially himself."[34] In our con artist example, the line is that of a person down on his luck through no fault of his own. The soap that produces the foaming at the mouth is a nonverbal part of the line taken. *Face* refers to the "positive social value" a person claims for himself when he takes a line during any encounter. Goffman immediately emphasizes that any claim always involves the larger society. The elements of any line "tend to be of a legitimate institutionalized kind" and *by entering a situation in which he is given a face to maintain, a person takes on the responsibility of standing guard over the flow of events as they pass before him* (emphasis added).[35]

Standing guard is something we all do, all the time. You put a face into the line you offer, and you want others to toe the line and endorse the face that you assume they do, will, or must see. For example, have you ever made a mistake when talking to a person with an ego? They have a heart attack because you forgot to use the label Doctor, Attorney, Vice President of Widgets, and so on. That is the face they offer, but in making the mistake, you underline a point that is crucial for Goffman and his focus on social order: "While his social face can be his most personal possession and the center of his security and pleasure, it is only on loan to him from society; it will be withdrawn unless he conducts himself in a way that is worthy of it. Approved attributes and their relation to face make of every man his own jailer; this is a fundamental social constraint even though each man may like his cell."[36]

Goffman loves everyday language. "Jailer" and "cell" are metaphors for the larger society that constrains our actions. No line can work unless others share the same set of assumptions you do. You internalized those assumptions in the process of socialization, and they are the literal and figurative lines you memorized. Once you take a line and claim a face, you are on the line and exposed; you are in the interaction cell you just created. And you will act like a jailer because, "just as the member of any group is expected to have self respect, so also he is expected to sustain a standard of considerateness." Simple decency requires that I sustain your face as you sustain mine. Sadists want to crush others, but Goffman argues that most people learn to guard the face of others as they hope that others guard their face. You are "heartless" if you disregard the feelings of others (i.e., their line and offered face), and you are "shameless" if you willingly expose to the scrutiny of others, the indignities and dishonorable sides of yourself as a human being.[37]

When people guard each other's faces, they impose "an important conservative effect upon encounters." You watch out for me; I watch out for you. And in the process of staying in the social cell, we maintain, nourish, and sustain our learned social lines and the ritual order of everyday life. This ritual order contains a distinct religious feel and character. You offer a face, and then, in interaction, that face is a player in a ritual game in which people are "sacred objects." I can commit heresy, and so can you. Thus, even if you make a mistake about your face, you do not have "the license to forgive the event." You can say you are sorry, but only others can accept the apology, and it is a *"safe prerogative"* for them to do so because they want to save your face or because they want to sustain the encounter. Alternately, you graciously accept their apologies—or overlook their mistakes—because you are a decent person or because the person out of face is your boss, your parent, your wife, your friend, your professor, and so on.

Face-to-face interaction functions like the U.S. Constitution: "One finds a system of checks and balances by which each participant tends to be given the right to handle only those matters which he will have little motivation for mishandling. In short, the rights and obligations of an interactant are designed to prevent him from abusing his role as an object of sacred value."[38]

Go back to Berkeley and the free speech movement. The campus was falling apart, and police with nightsticks often waited outside the university's gates. Yet even in the midst of such havoc, the checks and balances of *face-to-face interaction* can easily stay in place for most members of the university community, not to mention the rest of the society. Even political radicals are unlikely to endorse focused interactions that constantly expose them to heartless or shameless behavior.

From this perspective face-work refers to the "actions taken by a person to make whatever he is doing consistent with his face." A person offering a face of sophistication is unlikely to admit that he or she does not know which knife or fork to use; if they have poise they will subtly drop their napkin, pick it up with an apology for their clumsiness, and then use the fork they saw others employ. That is face-work, and Goffman stresses two things: "The ritual code itself requires a delicate balance and can be easily upset by anyone who upholds it too eagerly or not eagerly enough, in terms of the standards and expectations of the group."[39] The group is paramount because "you cannot go from the individual to the society. Given society, society has got to make use of individuals or constitute individuals in such a fashion that social organization can be sustained."[40]

First is social organization. Second are individuals who fit into that preconceived social organization. For example, Goffman criticizes those who discuss the social construction of reality because "I don't think the individual himself or herself does much of the constructing. He rather comes into a world, already in some sense or the other established."[41] In face-to-face interaction, that established society creates a ritual order that is conservative and accommodating; equally important, the overall sense of order is so pervasive "because the person normally stays away from the places and topics and times where he is not wanted and where he might be disparaged for going."[42]

The free speech activist is not going to chill out in the frat house responsible for the rain of fruit and vegetables. On the contrary, like the rest of us, he *"cooperates to save his face, finding that there is much to be gained in venturing nothing"* (emphasis added).[43]

Face—not justice, equality, or freedom—is the axis of the ritual order.

We continually cooperate to sustain and save all presented faces, and we do it because we lack individuality. "Universal human nature is not a very human thing. By acquiring it the person becomes a kind of construct, built up not from the inner psychic propensities but from the moral rules that are impressed on him from without." In Goffman's world of face-to-face interactions, we are socially determined; we dutifully follow an inherited set of rules establishing the "ritual organization of social encounters," and we follow those moral rules because society taught us to be "usable participants" in its ritually organized system of social activity—of face-to-face interaction.[44]

Goffman is neither sad nor happy—and certainly not judgmental. The ritual order exists, and it provides a remarkable degree of stability. In *The Presentation of Self in Everyday Life*, Goffman begins to delineate the structure and function of performances. Critics will instantly accuse him of being the ultimate cynic; it is an odd label indeed for a sociologist who focused on the power of society to produce the ritual and moral order of everyday life.

THE PRESENTATION OF SELF IN EVERYDAY LIFE

Goffman starts with an assumption in *The Presentation of Self in Everyday Life*. When people engage in face-to-face interaction, they will and do have "many motives" for trying to control the impressions others receive. It could be something as innocent as trying to do well in a job interview or putting on a big smile when you chew the absolutely awful appetizer that a loved one prepared especially for you. Alternately, you could be a corporate executive trying to deceive reporters during an interview about corporate finances or a U.S. president lying to the public because you are unable to reveal secret information about troop movements or the internal affairs of another nation. For Goffman the motives are extraneous to his sociological aims and efforts. In this book, "I shall be concerned only with the participant's dramaturgical problems of presenting the activity before others."[45]

Maybe Goffman should have used another word. *Drama* implies that, with Shakespeare's "all the world's a stage," people are nothing but a bunch of actors trying to entertain or mislead others. However, Goffman is a serious sociologist, trying to understand how people present lines and faces in the course of interaction. Drama is a perfect term as long as we remember that the focus is everyday encounters; *how* do people manage to impress one another and so achieve not only deception, but also the ritual order of everyday life? When Goffman writes that "the world, in truth, is a wedding," he means that many people offering performances happily and genuinely "highlight" society's official values. Proper presentations are crucial because everyday interactions are also ceremonies that act "as an expressive rejuvenation and reaffirmation of the moral values of the community."[46]

Because performances are at the center of any presentation of self, Goffman quickly offers this definition: "A performance is all the activity of a given participant on a given occasion that serves to influence in any way any of the other participants." The elements of any performance are non-verbal as well as verbal, so Goffman begins with "front"—that is, the "expressive equipment of a general kind" that functions "to define the situation for those who observe the performance." As part of front, furniture and decor are the social scenery of any performance and crucial for the ritual order. Imagine going to a doctor's office and seeing that the physician has paintings of nudes on the office walls. The carpets are a garish red, and the chairs are those floppy vinyl seats full of little balls. You sink as fast as a rock in water.[47]

Society teaches that a doctor's office is antiseptic. As expressive equipment of a general kind, it ought to be as bland as fake butter or, before the nurses say a word, you may be out the door. Meanwhile, those nurses need to maintain, as other elements of front, an "appearance" and "manner" that offers all patients the proper impression. A nurse wearing a soup-stained uniform raises immediate flags, and if he or she treats us in an imperious, arrogant, or disrespectful manner, we may rightfully get the wrong impression.

Front instantly provides a set of clues about the impressions offered by others. Picture a visit to a home where the couches—and even the lamps—wear a transparent cover of plastic and you make a squeaky sound when you sit down. Or recall a friend wearing as much eye shadow and lipstick as the staff of a fine department store's makeup section. Without saying a word, the person conveys an immediate impression; front opens the door to face-to-face interaction, and even though it is a background factor, bad front can spoil a presentation as quickly as a dentist with dirty fingernails and terrible teeth.

To effectively manage the impressions received by others, we all offer performances all the time. They can go well or badly, but a structural factor in performances is the dilemma of "expression versus action." Suppose you work like a dog and do a great job, but nobody knows because you spend no time telling others how great you are. Meanwhile, the jerk in the other office does nothing, but he is such a great performer that he successfully takes credit for your work. Goffman calls these "interaction constraints." They are factors "that play upon the individual and transform his or her activities into performances." No one can rest on their laurels because people often judge not the activities you perform but the impressions they receive from your dramatic presentations of self in everyday life.[48]

Examples of structural constraints include what one scholar calls "groupthink."[49] Seven or ten people meet in a government, corporate, or educational office to decide policy. Many people disagree with the policies proposed, but in the interests of consensus or in the interest of not offending the boss who proposed the moronic policy, six or seven people make a terrible judgment. From a decision-making perspective, that proves one thing: seven minds are not necessarily better than one. From a dramaturgical perspective, it shows that work activity often turns into a performance. This is as normal as a shower in the morning, but for Goffman, the crucial point is the structural forces that turn people into fine performers—even when that is neither their aim nor their desire.

Another structural constraint is the necessity to offer an "idealized impression"; a performer accentuates the positive and neglects to mention the negatives. Say you are a campus guide when the university has its open house. You genuinely love the school, and you believe in what you are doing. Yet you neglect to mention the school's abysmal record with advising students, and you deliberately ignore a food service with all the appeal of bread and water. We could argue that you are lying; or we could simply highlight the structural factors that move you, the tour guide, to tell visitors what they need to hear about your great institution.

This is an undeniable fact for Goffman: "Whether honest or dishonest, all human beings must take care to enliven their performances with appropriate expressions, exclude from their performances expressions that might discredit the impression being fostered, and take care lest the audience impute unintended meanings." The proper maintenance of the ritual order demands that we perform admirably whether the face-to-face encounter is a stand-alone performance—or as a member of a team.[50]

A team is "any set of individuals who co-operate in staging a single routine."[51] It could be the staff at a fast food restaurant or the press personnel working in the White House's West Wing. Goffman's point is that face-to-face interaction often occurs in group or team settings. You still present a self to others, but that self belongs to the group, and your role is to convey effectively the impressions desired by management. In the Caribbean the competition for tourists is so intense that the "front" of many hotels maintains the spit-polish shine of a marine's dress shoes; the staffs are often well trained and "delighted" to see you. In fact, the team performances are now so intense that people literally fall all over themselves trying to assist their guests.

If only because of interaction constraints, individuals often struggle to convey the proper impression; teams have far greater problems because they need to get hundreds or even thousands of people to maintain what Goffman calls "dramaturgical loyalty." Like patriots, staff need to wave the team's flag, and even if they know things that can damage the team's presentation, they need to button their lips and keep people outside of what Goffman calls the back "regions" of the team's business.

A region is "any place that is bounded to some degrees by barriers to perception."[52] Think of a receptionist guarding the closed doors that provide access to the executive offices or the swinging doors that lead to the kitchen in a restaurant. The team members theoretically project the right impression as long as they keep us away from what Goffman calls the nether regions possessed by any team. For example, when a waiter or waitress is on the floor, they are *onstage*, behaving with courtesy even when the person at table three is rude and demanding. "Backstage," in the kitchen, they scream about the "creep" pretending to be a customer, yet as they walk through the swinging doors separating the kitchen from the restaurant floor, a scowl becomes a smile. Again onstage, the waiters and waitresses behave like members of the team. They smile their way through the meal because they need their jobs and their tips. Meanwhile, social order (and the team's presentation) prevails because the staff release their venom only in the safe regions backstage.

Goffman sometimes hesitated when asked about the generality of his insights. He deliberately presented a restrained image of self by publicly arguing that his insights only related to a "small section of the middle class in America." In reality, that was "just a verbal device." He actually believed that "no one really knew the boundaries of these things."[53] My own argument is that the boundaries are as wide as the world, especially if we consider the archival recesses of any government on earth. Stamp a piece of paper secret, and in Great Britain it often takes fifty years for the backstage to become onstage, that is, for the government's line to be potentially challenged by scholars examining the documents that show what was actually said and done. Remember, too, that, like the United States, Britain eventually opens many of its archival doors; in other countries the truth stays buried or is instantly shredded by the team loyalists, who guarantee that the official line is the only line.

Goffman's work is also instructive if we spotlight the largest bankruptcy in U.S. business history, the collapse of the Houston-based Enron Corporation. In public Enron presented itself as a cutting-edge leader in the world's energy industry. Thousands of employees believed this line with such passion that they genuinely presented the corporate line on a daily basis, in many thousands of face-to-face interactions. Meanwhile—backstage—executives used a variety of devices (e.g., more than 600 corporate—"paper"—entities in the Cayman Islands alone) to escape everything from federal taxes to close scrutiny of their corporate ledgers. In a colossal and clever scheme, they also created "on-the-side" partnerships that hid corporate losses as they grossly overstated company profits. These transactions contained so many complexities that even after an explanation of the chicanery, some corporate officials never understood the truth. Finally, as bullpen members of the team, auditors at Arthur Andersen and the bankers who lent billions for the partnerships helped management present Enron's public posture of profitability.[54]

Backstage the corporation experienced significant team and personal turmoil. The formal bankruptcy filing occurred on December 2, 2002, yet as early as February 2002, auditors met to discuss the corporate house of cards. While accountants chewed their nails, they never threatened the corporate presentation of self. Enron vice chairman J. Clifford Baxter, who later committed suicide, "complained mightily" throughout the spring, but instead of going public, he simply resigned. In August Enron vice president Sherron Watkins prepared a two-page memo for Chairman Kenneth Lay. She explained that "she was incredibly nervous" that the company "might implode in a wave of accounting scandals." Lay read the memo, initiated an internal examination of corporate finances, and as he told investors and employees to continue buying stock, Sherron Watkins never "blew the whistle."[55]

From Goffman's perspective, Watkins was a potential dramaturgical traitor. If she let the general public know the truth, thousands of employees might still have a pension plan. However, instead of going public, she remained on the job and, shortly before the official bankruptcy, prepared another memo for Kenneth Lay. This one (in late October) laid out a "public-relations plan" to place blame on others and announce to the world that despite the farcical business practices, Enron would prevail because Lay and his team now knew the truth. As the *New York Times* editorialized, Watkins did the right thing backstage, but the corporation's only hope for survival rested on "traitors" who "went public with their concerns as early as possible. That would have given this sordid tale a true whistle-blower."[56]

The trouble is that many loyal members of the team despise whistle blowers with such passion that the act of going public—of becoming a dramaturgical traitor—is a "life-changing event." "Reprisals are almost certain. Almost half of all whistle blowers are fired and, of those, half lose their homes, and of the ones who lose their homes, more than half will lose their families as well."[57]

From the audience, bravery seems easy; newspaper editorialists abound with suggestions that Watkins and her colleagues never did the right thing because they wanted to save themselves, maintain the stock's price, or have a future when Enron eventually imploded. Backstage the situation is fraught with personal and institutional peril. It is easy to find a host of rationalizations for toeing the corporate line; as any of us might have said, "Why should I stick my neck out?"

This sketch of the Enron debacle underlines Goffman's conclusion to *The Presentation of Self in Everyday Life:* "It seems to me that the dramaturgical approach may constitute a fifth perspective, to be added to the technical, political, structural and cultural perspectives."[58] Use high beams to spotlight impression management, and the "end point of analysis" suddenly orders the facts of social life in a thoroughly original manner. For example, a political analysis focuses on leadership, on the way one person directs thousands of others; but a good leader also needs, at times, to keep strategic secrets from other members of the team. And to lead others successfully, "it will be necessary, regardless of the power position, to convey effectively what he wants done, what he is prepared to do to get it done and what he will do if it is not done. *Power of any kind must be clothed in effective means of displaying it, and will have different effects depending upon how it is dramatized*" (emphasis added).[59]

The cultural and dramaturgical perspectives intersect if we turn to the maintenance of moral standards. Any group presentation of self is firmly rooted in the beliefs, values, and practices of the host culture. So when executives at Enron or Citibank called the White House to get backing for additional corporate financing, they focused on the moral effects of a collapse of the seventh-largest corporation in the United States. How would world markets react? Would people sell too many other stocks and thus threaten healthy as well as corrupt corporations? And, the most morally ominous question of all, would millions of Americans begin to wonder if the entire economy could or might implode in a series of accounting scandals?

When the president and the secretary of the treasury assure the nation that all is well—that Enron is nothing but a blip on the nation's financial screen—their required presentation of self performs a meaningful role in maintaining social order. Backstage they may actually think or know that accountants, executives, bankers, and greedy investors failed to protect the economy and the nation. In public they engage in impression management; and that is Goffman's wonderfully original contribution. With a focus on personal and team presentations of self, we gain an additional perspective on human behavior, on the ways in which good actors play a leading and essential role in the maintenance of social order.

"REMEDIAL INTERCHANGES"

Face-to-face interaction rests on a series of responsibilities and obligations. You enter an encounter knowing what you should (or should not) do, and you expect that others will (or will not) behave in a certain manner. Extend your hand to another, and you expect a hand in return. Say "pleased to meet you," and you expect something similar in return. In all cases you never say "good bye" when first meeting someone, and you rarely kiss the clerk at the local supermarket. Goffman argues that these are moral responsibilities and expectations. Unfortunately, when people come into one another's presence, they also "bring to the scene a vast filigree of trip wires"; people make mistakes, "and this ensures that circumstances will constantly produce potentially offensive configurations that were not foreseen or were foreseen but undesired."[60]

Social control is essential and indispensable. However, instead of a criminal justice system, replete with police officers, judges, courts, and prisons, in Goffman's world people provide their own social control by engaging in remedial interchanges. "The function of the remedial work is to change the meaning that otherwise might be given to an act, transforming what could be seen as offensive into what can be seen as acceptable." The offender helps him- or herself (and the moral order) by using three main devices: accounts, apologies, and requests.[61]

You pass by an office at corporate headquarters or, even better, in the university's administration building. Inside, a coworker (or a professor) is energetically making a great speech to an empty room. He is alone in the room, and you watch the apparently mad performance through the window. He spots you and, with a gesture, motions you to enter. You do so but with a good measure of trepidation. What is going on here? Your coworker could do nothing, but aware of his responsibilities and your expectations, he offers an account of his behavior. For example, he is making a speech at a company conference next week and he was practicing. Would you mind listening? Or he is an advocate of old-fashioned Gestalt therapy. His psychiatrist told him to talk to the empty chair (or the empty room) and let out his childhood, adolescent, and adult aggressions. He was engaging in therapy, and you earnestly accept his account but suggest that he put a shade over the office window and lock the door.

Apologies are a second form of remedial interchange. For example, if our lonely speaker really was rehearsing a speech, you might apologize for the interruption and then add the icing of an account. "I saw you talking to the wall. It looked quite strange. Sorry for the interruption."

Requests are a third way to accept your responsibilities and maintain the other's expectations. "A request consists of asking license of a potentially offended person to engage in what could be considered a violation of his rights."[62] We make requests all the time when we, for example, inquire of a friend, "Can I ask you something personal?" The request is "based on the assumption that when a violation is invited by he who normally would be its victim, it ceases to be a violation and becomes instead *a gesture of regard* performed by this person" (emphasis added).[63]

Whether an account, an apology, or a request, any remedial interchange highlights a remarkable attribute of the self: our ability to split ourselves in two. One part of the self jumps out of the interaction and joins hands with the other members of the face-to-face encounter. For George Herbert Mead this indicated people's ability to reflect on their behavior, even in the course of interaction. For Erving Goffman the split functions to sustain and nourish social order. One self apologizes or accounts for the other self, and in the process, the offender's remedial work shows that "whatever happened before, he now has a right relationship—a pious attitude—to the rule in question, *and this is a matter of indicating a relationship, not compensating a loss*" (emphasis in original).[64]

Paradoxically, by righting a wrong, the remedial worker maintains and nourishes the social order. Remember, too, that in accepting his or her responsibilities and satisfying the expectations of self and others, the individual uses scripts written by the society and techniques of impression management that stipulate everything from facile characteristics to proper tonal qualities. Try, for example, to offer an apology in a tone of voice out of tune with socially approved melodies and mannerisms.

Sometimes individuals do remedial work even when they are not engaged in focused interaction. Goffman calls this "body gloss," or gestures in the round.[65] A person at a bus stop with others will "lean over the curb" and, with all the proper facial expressions, watch for the bus; this way others know he truly belongs to and with the group. He is not a loiterer or, even worse, a potential thief. A person waiting in a train station or the airport cautiously approaches a newspaper left on an empty seat. He picks it up but does so in a "diffident manner, so that at a moment's notice he can relinquish his claim and reconstitute the paper into someone else's property." Finally, when a person who left something at a store returns to retrieve it, he or she "breaks into a mock run as they enter the store, and, shaking their heads, they silently broadcast support of the bad opinion that others might have of someone who is so obviously forgetful."[66]

These seemingly random examples of remedial work make a point that fascinates and bemuses Goffman. He understands that when people "come together, many contingencies arise that could reflect discreditably on them." Remedial work is necessary because no one engages only in his or her own business; on the contrary, "we go about constrained to sustain a viable image of ourselves in the eyes of others." But in a world full of hippies, yippies, and others, "it is strange, and more Durkheimian than it should be, that when the individual can get almost everything else off his back, there remains the cross of personal character—the one he bears, albeit lightly, when he is in the presence of others."[67]

STIGMA

Critics charge that the federal government has rules for everything. Although that is an exaggeration, in the late 19th century, the government did indicate the precise size of the brand it put on the faces of U.S. Army deserters. Regulations stipulated a mark of one-and-a-half inches. Placed under the eye with a red-hot iron, the capital D supposedly served two purposes. It acted as a deterrent to other deserters—seeing the stigma on a friend's face, no one would want to look like that—and the prominent D brand helped recruiters avoid making a second mistake. Americans often enlisted for the bonuses offered and then deserted to get another bonus in another part of the country. The D was an indelible mark of permanent disapproval; it stigmatized the person for the rest of his life.[68]

Goffman wrote a book titled *Stigma;* as usual, social order is one of its prominent themes. Before people meet one another in face-to-face interactions, "society establishes the means of categorizing persons and the complement of attributes felt to be ordinary and natural for members of each of these categories." Because we know what to expect, we need not think. In fact, attributes designated by society allow us to anticipate categories (e.g., male/female, well dressed/slob) that Goffman calls social identities. We place the people we meet in these preestablished boxes, and "we lean on these anticipations, . . . transforming them into normative expectations, into righteously presented demands."[69]

Sometimes interaction gives us a mental kick in the rear end. What we expected—the *virtual* social identity—clashes with what we see, the *actual* social identity. Any face-to-face interaction with a man wearing a capital D under his eye will certainly cause us to think. The discrepancy between expectations and reality is Goffman's meat and potatoes. He wants us to see not only the "deeply discrediting" attributes but also their role in maintaining the norms established by society. For example, the dreadful D establishes my normality as it simultaneously confirms the deserter's inability to function effectively in everyday life.[70]

In understanding a stigma, remember that the discrediting mark always reveals a *relationship* between an attribute and a stereotype. Focus not on the scar but on what society says the scar indicates about this type of person. Broadly stated, societies designate three types of relationships between a stigma and the stereotype. First are "abominations of the body"; these include everything from blindness to the loss of limbs. Second are "blemishes of individual character"; they may be harder to spot, but alcoholism, mental illness addiction, and a prison record are stigmas when perceived by others. Finally, "there are the tribal stigma of race, nation and religion, these being stigma that can be transmitted through lineages and equally contaminate all members of the family." In nations like Guatemala or Peru, anyone stigmatized as an "Indian" can expect treatment as harsh as anything reserved for other contemptible members of the society.[71]

Encounters between the stigmatized and the normal often engender anxiety for all concerned. Especially if the attribute is an abomination of the body, the normal person may want to show sympathy for the stigmatized person's plight but worry that any mention of the scar or size (e.g., a dwarf) embarrasses and shames the individual who already has an obvious problem. Meanwhile, the stigmatized person knows that we know, we realize that they know we know, and they realize we know that they know we know. It is such a dizzying string of knowledge that Goffman criticizes the social psychology of George Herbert Mead. By taking the role of the other, we learn how to begin the "infinite regress of mutual consideration," but we never learn how to end it.[72]

Goffman offers some help when he focuses on how the stigmatized hide their deeply discrediting marks of Cain. From this perspective, "the issue is not that of managing tension generated during social encounters but rather that of managing information about his failing." How do people hide who they are? How do the stigmatized manage to avoid the mountain of speculations that arise as soon as they enter the presence of so-called normal people?[73]

To grasp the process of information control, Goffman introduces the notion of personal identity. Despite the innumerable interactions in any person's everyday life, an informed observer still sees "a structure holding the individual to one biography." People can be uniquely differentiated from one another because, over time, "a single continuous record of social facts can be attached, entangled, *like candy floss*, becoming then the sticky substance to which still other biographical facts can be attached."[74]

It is a lovely metaphor. As if the cardboard container holding the candy, traits stick to our perception of the individual; we see him or her as a unique person, and in that uniqueness lies an opportunity for information control. For example, officers sometimes put the D on a deserter's behind instead of below his eye. The mark on his cheek proves a "shady past" regarding his *social* identity. But "the way he handles that information about this past is a question of *personal* identification." As long as we never see his cheek, we only focus on the biographical facts—the personal identities—available for inspection.[75]

Given the great rewards that attach to a normal social identity, "almost all persons who are in a position to pass will do so on some occasion by intent." In an anti-Semitic society, some Jewish people change their names; light-skinned African Americans historically passed for white, and until Native Americans began to make money running gambling casinos, many Americans successfully hid their social identities as Indians. If we only see the personal identity that attaches to the person, he or she is safe. We never penetrate the wall that surrounds their shady past or tribal mark of shame and inferiority.

Another technique of information control is covering. This is so widespread "that many of those who rarely try to pass, routinely try to cover."[76] For example, to the extent that old age is now a stigma, many Americans seek plastic surgery to remove wrinkles from their foreheads. The doctor shaves the hair over the front of your skull; the doctor then cuts you from one side to the other and pulls up the skin over the forehead, snips off the excess baggage, and sews together the two sides of the cut skin. Once the hair grows back, the scar is covered, and only your doctor (and banker) knows the truth.

Another example of covering comes from the hard of hearing. To hide their stigma they learn that at a dinner party, it is best to sit next to someone with a loud voice; they use chokes, coughs, and hiccups to mask a sentence they failed to hear, and they often ask questions even though they already know the answers.[77]

The gap between personal and social identity allows the individual to successfully cover or pass. The stigma never mars a face-to-face encounter, but on the level of ego identity, the person still needs to deal with how he or she feels about stigma and its management. Ambivalence is "inevitable" because, in trying to satisfy those without a problematic attribute, the stigmatized accentuate their deviation. Do I associate with my own kind or with "them"? And if I associate only with them, am I betraying myself and all others like me?

One response to questions like these is to become a militant. The individual not only associates with his own kind, but he takes their case to the larger society. The goals can be as distinct as full assimilation or complete separation, but whatever choice is made, the society exerts a powerful form of social control. After all, "his disdain for a society that rejects him can only be understood in terms of that society's conception of pride, dignity and independence. In short, unless there is some alien culture on which to fall back, the more he separates himself structurally from the normals, the more like them he may become culturally."[78]

Goffman chronicles this vicious circle with both insight and compassion. He believes it is a worthwhile and meaningful object of analysis. However, in the conclusion to *Stigma*, he also makes a rare value judgment. He criticizes sociologists who "have so quickly become comfortable in using the term deviant." His colleagues seem to believe that those to whom the term *deviant* is applied "have enough in common so that significant things can be said about them as a whole." Goffman not only doubts that assertion, but he even argues "that there are categories of persons who are created by students of society and then studied by them." The deviance is in the eye of the beholder rather than in the group so labeled.[79]

Goffman worried about the specializations so prevalent in sociology. Thus he classified a variety of stigmatized persons under the same umbrella, but to achieve that aim, he extracted something "from the traditional fields of social problems, race and ethnic relations, social disorganization, criminology, social pathology and deviance." These commonalities (e.g., the difference between virtual and actual social identity) suggested that once we know what the fields share, we would also see where they differ. Ultimately, sociologists might elect to retain the "old substantive areas." Goffman had serious doubts, "but at least it would be clear that each is merely an area (e.g., deviance) to which one should apply several perspectives and that the development of any one of these analytic perspectives is not likely to come from those who restrict their interest exclusively to one substantive area."[80]

Goffman never restricted his focus; on the contrary, his willingness to break down arbitrary barriers helps account for the persisting relevance of his insights and his pointed (if rare) criticisms of a science he loved—sociology.

FRAME ANALYSIS

Published in 1974, *Frame Analysis* offers yet another perspective on face-to-face interaction. Goffman uses new concepts to tread over old turf, and the result is a book that remains as provocative as it is worthwhile.[81]

"Primary frames" box in all forms of face-to-face interaction. Like the wide array of do-it-yourself models available at an art store, primary frames provide the elemental structures required for orderly interactions. They are the *definitions of the situation* provided by the society, and they are primary because they neither depend on nor hark back to any prior or original definitions. Enter a library, and you know the frame that structures interaction. Sit in the bleachers in New York's Yankee Stadium, and you expect everything from foul language to obscene gestures to drunkenness. Primary frames are the basic building blocks required for interaction because, once learned, they render "otherwise meaningless aspects of the scene" into meaningful behavior.[82]

With his foundation stone now in place, Goffman explains how we move from primary frames to other definitions of the same situation. "Keys" refer to "a set of conventions by which a given activity, *already meaningful in terms of some primary framework,* is transformed into something patterned on this activity but seen by the participants to be something quite else" (emphasis added).[83] Say there are two children, and one says to the other, "Let's play house." The request is a key that transforms a buried (in your mind) set of primary frames into make-believe. After all, the children could not play unless they already knew how to wash dishes, set the table, and prepare dinner. Even the toys they employ are meaningless unless they already know the frames that provide the rules of the family game. From this perspective, the key announces the make-believe that allows children to rehearse the frames required for an orderly adult life.

Another key is the set of conventions that surround "contests" like fox hunting, horse racing, or boxing. The primary frame provides a backdrop, but no fight in a street or bar has, as on television from Las Vegas, an announcer dressed in a tuxedo, a bizarrely clothed entourage leading the combatants, and a scantily dressed young woman walking around the ring between rounds holding up the number of the next round.

Keys offer one way to move from primary frames into another form of face-to-face interaction. Keys are ubiquitous, and so too are the fabrications that turn a primary frame into a deliberate form of deception. Once again, Goffman argues that deception is crucial for social order—and the preservation of face. But to separate good from bad intentions, he distinguishes between *benign* and *exploitive* fabrications.[84]

A benign fabrication "claims to be engineered in the interest of the person contained by it, or if not quite in his interest and for his benefit, then at least not done against his interest."[85] It is an ambiguous definition for an ambiguous world. For example, if I pretend to like the way you are dressed (actually, I think your outfit is ghastly), most of us would call that a benign fabrication. Why hurt another person's feelings? Why be truthful when it is obvious that the other person has spent both time and money making this fashion statement? Protecting another is generally acceptable, but what about "experimental hoaxing," fabrications in the interest of science?

In the 1960s Stanley Milgram staged a series of controversial experiments centering on the issue of obedience to authority. He wanted to see if people—for four dollars an hour—would give another person a series of painfully escalating electric shocks. However, instead of telling participants the truth, Milgram lied. Based on primary frames, he told his subjects that this was a study focused on memory and the role of punishment in increasing a person's ability to remember. After the experiments ended, people learned the truth. Some left the experiments thinking of themselves as potential death-camp guards. Some might say the end justifies the means; others might say that nothing justifies the pain these people unwittingly endured. Whatever your decision, the ambiguity stressed by Goffman makes sense.[86]

Exploitive fabrications refer to interactions in which "one party contains others in a construction that is clearly inimical to their private interests," here defining "private interests" as the community might.[87] An easy example is the sale that turns out to be a trick. Using the primary frame of a real sale, a store catches our attention with spectacular prices on certain items, but when we enter the store, the sale items are already gone. Store owners hope that we buy another item rather than express our outrage or, even worse, report the store owners to the local Better Business Bureau.

Ambiguity intrudes itself if we turn to other business practices. For a fee (about $25,000), a U.S. corporation can now incorporate itself in Bermuda. There is no need for an office, staff, or even a fax machine. The payoff is no federal taxes. Register in Bermuda, and like Ingersoll Rand or Stanley Tools, you can avoid "at least $40 million dollars annually in American corporate income taxes." So, when these corporations prominently display huge American flags at their stateside corporate headquarters, are they engaging in an exploitive fabrication or simply doing what is best for their shareholders?[88]

Another example is clearly exploitive, but the person exploited thanked his exploiter. For two years (1972–74) President Richard Nixon lied to the nation about his involvement in the Watergate break-in and in a series of "dirty tricks" perpetrated by members of his campaign staff. Many Americans expressed outrage at the lies, but not presidential speechwriter Raymond Price. He explained that "the President had done me a favor by deceiving me. It meant that I'd be able to write for him honestly."[89]

Politics does make strange bedfellows. Equally important, we can use the Watergate scandal (or President Clinton's long list of fabrications) to underline what Goffman calls "structural issues in fabrications." The security chief of President Nixon's reelection committee headed the Watergate break-in. That was quite embarrassing in its own right, but like the underwater iceberg hit by the Titanic, the real problem was structural. If reporters discovered the truth about Watergate, one lie could easily lead to another: everything from the campaign's Mexican money laundering to its undermining of Democratic presidential campaigns might suddenly appear on the front page of the nation's newspapers. Thus, the president and his closest aides lied and stonewalled in the interests of structural issues in fabrications—in the interest of not opening the can of worms that led to the Oval Office.

A conversation in that Oval Office underlines what Goffman refers to as the "transformational depth" of any particular fabrication.[90] Whatever their motives, when people lie they place a *layer* of deception over the primary frame. Transformational depth raises the issue of how many layers a person adds before stumbling over their own mountain of lies.

On March 21, 1974, John Dean, legal counsel to the president, met with Richard Nixon. Dean indicated that because of the Watergate scandal, the administration faced a "cancer on the Presidency." The primary frame is a conversation between two people. The president added a layer by never telling Dean that he knew about Watergate from its inception. Dean added a second layer by never telling the president that for weeks, he had been speaking to federal prosecutors about the lies emanating from the White House. The president added a third layer by not telling Dean that he had a tape recorder secretly turned on. Dean added a fourth layer when, although suspecting the bug, he said nothing about it or his suspicions. Conceivably, this conversation also contained a fifth level of deception: the president suspected Dean's suspicions but said nothing about them.[91]

Ideally, people can add as many layers of deception as they please. In reality, even players as practiced as President Nixon and John Dean will eventually stumble over the layers of deception that, like quicksand, bury them in their own words.

In the conclusion to *Frame Analysis*, Goffman reiterates his central point: "People have the capacity and inclination to use concrete actual activity—activity that is meaningful in its own right—as a model upon which to work transformations for fun, deception, experiment, rehearsal, dream, fantasy, ritual, demonstrations, analysis and charity." Ordinary activity is anything but ordinary, especially when, following Goffman, we use primary frames to see the extraordinarily complex—and utterly fascinating—realities of everyday life.[92]

ASYLUMS AND THE "INSANITY OF PLACE"

Asylums are "total institutions," places "where a large number of like situated individuals, cut off from the wider society for an appreciable period of time, together lead an enclosed, formally administered round of life." Prisons and military bases are other examples of total institutions. In each instance all "aspects of life" occur in the same location and under an all-encompassing authority. Each facet of any member's day occurs in the presence "of a large batch of others," all treated in the same way and all required to do the same things together. Life in any total institution is tightly scheduled by a group of officials obeying precise rules and regulations. Finally, "the various enforced activities are brought together into a single rational plan purportedly designed to fulfill the official aims of the institution."[93]

Goffman's book *Asylums* spotlights the moral career of the mental patient. How did inmates manage to survive? With walls and barbed wire, society cut them off from their loved ones as it simultaneously mortified them through a process of "regimentation and surveillance." Asylums horrified Goffman so much that he made a rare and pointed political judgment: "An asylum is not merely a bad deal, it is a grotesque one."[94]

In trying to comprehend why society treated the insane in such a monstrous fashion, Goffman ultimately wrote an essay called "The Insanity of Place." Insanity is, for him, an *unprecedented encounter with disorder;* he finds everything from confusion to havoc and suggests that people become inmates because the grammar of conduct breaks down. Society offers no frames—primary or otherwise—that fit the behaviors of those defined as insane.

Start with the difference between biological and social norms. The former offer a model with these characteristics: we get sick, we take medicines or endure surgeries designed to produce "restorative counteractions," and we get better or the biological system is destroyed.[95]

Social norms are different. Instead of a physical relationship, our relationship to social norms is political. We legitimate them or we do not; and if we violate the norms, society uses institutions like asylums to exert various forms of social control. It uses the biological model as a frame of reference even though the control model implied by biological norms breaks down. "For when an offense occurs (e.g., I refuse to bathe for three months or I wash so frequently that I rub my hands raw) it is by no means the case that sanctions are applied, and when negative sanctions *are* applied, or when unanticipated penalizing consequences occur (e.g., people refuse to interact with the offender) it is by no means generally true that diminution of the deviation results."[96] Instead of getting better, or dying, people who violate social norms may increase their deviations to such a degree that they threaten to drive the rest of us crazy.

The offenders—and the rest of us—have a serious social problem. Instead of easily entering some form of corrective, medicinal, or surgical cycle, they need to engage in face-work, in remedial exchanges. Provide an apology or an account of your deviations, and your family, friends, or coworkers normally welcome the chance to restore social order. A request for help is also an indication that you support the same norms as the rest of us. After all, why ask for assistance if you do not want to get back on society's track?

But what happens if the offender, instead of making efforts to restore order, becomes more disorderly than ever?[97] Perhaps the person says that she has an atom bomb in her stomach. Or the individual decides he is Jesus, dresses in long white, flowing robes, and preaches the Sermon on the Mount at family dinners.[98]

By refusing to engage in remedial work, the offender creates "organizational havoc"; he or she openly embraces face-to-face disorder as a way of everyday life. It is havoc that the asylums—"the philosophy of containment"—ignore because "mental symptoms "are neither something in themselves nor whatever is so labeled; mental symptoms are acts by an individual which openly proclaim to others that he must have assumptions about himself which the relevant bit of social organization can neither allow him *nor do much about*" (emphasis added).[99]

Focus on those last words. You can walk by the "weirdo" on the street or sympathetically read case histories provided by others. But if the offender is your spouse, your parent, or your child, disengagement is almost impossible. Your relative refuses to sustain the grammar of conduct that allows for everyday social order. *"His behavior strikes at the syntax of conduct, deranging the usual agreement between posture and place, between expression and position"* (emphasis added).[100]

Asylums provide a prison for those who refuse to engage in remedial work and benign or exploitive fabrications. We exile the insane to "grotesque" warehouses; meanwhile, their behavior is a terrible reminder of the fragility of social order. Especially for family members, "the social significance of the confusion he creates may be as profound and basic as social existence can get."[101]

In a terrible way "the insanity of place" highlights the entire thrust of Goffman's work. He focused on social order but also taught us about the havoc that ensues when people refuse to endorse the primary frames that, like steel girders, maintain everyday order in any society on earth.

Erving Goffman died of cancer in 1982. He liked to belittle the significance of his work—"it was an exploratory, tentative undertaking"[102]—but
in reality, his books and essays offer a perspective that is as fresh and
original as anything sociology has to offer.

Goffman was different. And however ironically, he was quite proud of
never fitting into the orderly molds provided by sociology and its specialized subdivisions.

NOTES

1. Erving Goffman, *The Presentation of Self in Everyday Life* (Garden City, N.J.:
Doubleday Anchor, 1959), 36.

2. See *The Berkeley Free Speech Controversy, Preliminary Report*, December 13,
1964, [www.fsm-a.org/stacks/GradStudentReport.html]. A group of graduate political science students prepared this report.

3. Ibid., 4–5.

4. Ibid., 7.

5. Gary Marx, "Role Models and Role Distance: A Remembrance of Erving
Goffman," *Theory and Society* 13 (1984): 649–62, [www.sobek.colorado.edu/~Marxg/
ascervg.html].

6. See "Berkeley Activism," [www.uga.berkeley.edu/resource/webfiles/r10_
3.html].

7. "Mario Savio's Speech before the Free Speech Movement Sit-In," [www.fsm-
a.org/stacks/mario/mario_speech.html].

8. Ibid.

9. "Resolution of the Academic Senate of the University of California, Berkeley," December 8, 1964, [www.fsm-a.org/stacks/ACSenate.html].

10. Marx, "Role Models and Role Distance," 5.

11. Erving Goffman, "The Interaction Order," *American Sociological Review* 48
(1983): 1–17.

12. *Contemporary Authors Cumulative Index* (Detroit: Gale Research, 1993), 326.

13. For the school's program, see [www.home.merlin.mb.ca/~school1486/]; for
the city of Dauphin, see [www.town.Dauphin.mb.ca/ourcity/OurCity.html].

14. Tom Burns, *Erving Goffman* (London: Routledge, 1992), 9.

15. *Dictionary of Contemporary Authors*, 325.

16. Jeff C. Verhoeven, "An Interview with Erving Goffman," *Research on Language and Social Interaction* 26, no. 3 (1993): 325–26.

17. Burns, *Erving Goffman*, 11; also see *Dictionary of Contemporary Authors*, 326.

18. Erving Goffman, "The Insanity of Place," in *Relations in Public: Microstudies
of the Public Order* (New York: Basic Books, 1971), 356–57.

19. Erving Goffman, *Encounters: Two Studies in the Sociology of Interaction* (Indianapolis: Bobbs Merrill, 1961), 108.

20. Verhoeven, "Interview with Erving Goffman," 327, 320, 335.

21. Marx, "Role Models and Role Distance," 4.

22. *Dictionary of Contemporary Authors*, 326.

23. Goffman, "Interaction Order," 1.

24. Erving Goffman, "On Cooling the Mark Out: Some Aspects of Adaptation to Failure," *Psychiatry* 155 (November 1952): 451–63.

25. Kellow Chesney, *The Victorian Underworld* (London: Penguin, 1970), 233.

26. Goffman, "Interaction Order," 5.

27. Erving Goffman, *Relations in Public: Microstudies of the Public Order* (New York: Basic Books, 1971); the quote from Spencer appears right after the dedication page.

28. Verhoeven, "Interview with Erving Goffman," 318, 334.

29. Goffman, "Interaction Order," 6.

30. Ibid., 9.

31. Verhoeven, "Interview with Erving Goffman," 323.

32. Ibid., 321.

33. Goffman, "Interaction Order," 17.

34. Erving Goffman, "On Face-Work," in *Interaction Ritual* (Garden City, N.J.: Anchor, 1967), 5.

35. Ibid., 9.

36. Ibid., 10.

37. Ibid., 10–11.

38. Ibid., 32–33.

39. Ibid., 40.

40. Verhoeven, "Interview with Erving Goffman," 323.

41. Ibid., 324.

42. Goffman, "On Face-Work," 43.

43. Ibid., 43.

44. Ibid., 45.

45. Goffman, *Presentation of Self*, 15.

46. Ibid., 35.

47. Ibid., 15.

48. Ibid., 65.

49. See Irving Janis, *Groupthink* (Boston: Houghton Mifflin, 1983).

50. Goffman, *Presentation of Self*, 66.

51. Ibid., 79.

52. Ibid., 106.

53. Verhoeven, "Interview with Erving Goffman," 325.

54. Kurt Eichenwald and Diana B. Henriques, "Web of Perils Did Enron In as Warnings Went Unheeded," *New York Times*, February 10, 2002, 1, 28–29.

55. See, for example, Caroline E. Mayer and Amy Joyce, "Blowing the Whistle," *Washington Post*, February 10, 2002, H01.

56. Editorial, *New York Times*, February 15, 2002, A 20.

57. Mayer and Joyce, "Blowing the Whistle."

58. Goffman, *Presentation of Self*, 240.

59. Ibid., 241.

60. Erving Goffman, "Remedial Interchanges," in *Relations in Public: Microstudies of the Public Order* (New York: Basic Books, 1971), 99, 106.

61. Ibid., 109.

62. Ibid., 114.

63. Ibid.

64. Ibid., 118.

65. Ibid., 125.

66. Ibid., 131, 133, 135–36.

67. Ibid., 183, 185, 187.

68. Jack D. Foner, *The United States Soldier between Two Wars: Army Life and Reforms, 1865–1898* (New York: Humanities Press, 1970), 42, 82.

69. Erving Goffman, *Stigma: Notes on the Management of Spoiled Identity* (Englewood Cliffs, N.J.: Prentice-Hall, 1963), 3.

70. Ibid., 3–4.

71. Ibid., 4–5.

72. Ibid., 18.

73. Ibid., 42.

74. Ibid., 57.

75. Ibid., 57, 64.

76. Ibid., 102.

77. Ibid., 104.

78. Ibid., 114.

79. Ibid., 140.

80. Ibid., 147.

81. Erving Goffman, *Frame Analysis* (New York: Harper, 1974), 21.

82. Ibid., p. 21.

83. Ibid.; these are the theme of chapter 4, 83–123.

84. Ibid., 87.

85. Ibid., 87.

86. Stanley Milgram, *Obedience to Authority* (New York: Harper and Row, 1974).

87. Goffman, *Frame Analysis*, 103.

88. David Cay Johnston, "U.S. Corporations Are Using Bermuda to Slash Tax Bills," *New York Times*, February 18, 2002, A1, A12.

89. See Ronald Fernandez, *The I, the Me, and You: An Introduction to Social Psychology* (New York: Praeger, 1977), 245; the quote was drawn from Theodore White, *Breach of Faith: The Fall of Richard Nixon* (New York: Atheneum, 1975).

90. Goffman, *Frame Analysis*, 182–88.

91. Fernandez, *The I, the Me, and You*, 248; see especially John Dean, *Blind Ambition* (New York: Simon and Schuster, 1976).

92. Goffman, *Frame Analysis*, 560.

93. Erving Goffman, *Asylums: Essays on the Social Situation of Mental Patients and Other Inmates* (Garden City, N.J.: Doubleday, 1961), 3, 6.

94. See Goffman, "Insanity of Place," 336.

95. Ibid., 346.

96. Ibid., 348.

97. Ibid., 350–51.

98. For the atom bomb example see R. D. Laing and A. Esterton, *Sanity, Madness, and the Family* (Baltimore: Penguin, 1970); also see Milton Rokeach, *The Three Christs of Ypsilanti* (New York: Knopf, 1964).

99. Goffman, "Insanity of Place," 356.

100. Ibid., 367.

101. Ibid., 389.

102. Verhoeven, "Interview with Erving Goffman," 328.

CHAPTER 8

Peter L. Berger

"The genius of sociology is negative, and paradoxically, it is as negation that sociology can make its best contribution to any positive
cause. . . . Sociology must return to the big questions."[1]

Peter L. Berger, *Sociology Reinterpreted*

JESUS THE OUTDOOR MAN

Bruce Barton helped found one of the most successful advertising agencies
in America. He argued that the first words ever uttered—Let there be
light!—divinely constituted advertising's charter, so, in 1925, Barton published a book about Jesus, *The Man Nobody Knows*. For two straight years
(1925–26), Barton's work was the best-selling nonfiction book in the
United States. Readers ate up the good news of the gospel as they also
embraced Barton's principal insight: Jesus Christ was the founder of modern business, an executive of such genius that he "picked up twelve men
[i.e., the apostles] from the bottom ranks of business and forged them into
an organization that conquered the world."[2]

Peter Berger rightly calls Barton's book a "notorious bestseller."[3] If, like
Berger, you think of Jesus as God, Barton's interpretation skipped heresy
and immediately boarded an express train to blasphemy. In a chapter
titled "The Outdoor Man," Barton explains that "it will seem almost ir-
reverent to suggest that Jesus was physically strong." But he was: "Think
of what his years of hard toil must have done to his arms and back and
legs." Jesus was a "women's man," a guy who rippled with muscles as
powerful as the words of his father in the sky.[4]

Barton's business interpretation of Jesus had deep roots in America's past. For example, between 1877 and 1925, Protestant minister Russell Conwell delivered the same lecture more than 6,000 times—120 speeches a year about the "Acres of Diamonds" that, like rocks, were waiting to be collected in any American's backyard. Conwell preached, "I say you ought to get rich and it is your duty to get rich." And to those who criticized a Protestant minister devoting his time "to going up and down the country" telling young people to make money, Conwell offered this religious retort: "I say you should have money. If you can honestly attain riches, it is your Christian and godly duty to do so. It is a mistake of these pious people to think you must be poor to become pious."[5]

Bruce Barton owed a debt to his predecessors. But to date no one has ever surpassed his unique mix of simultaneous praise for Jesus, business, money, and the American way of life. In the chapter on the outdoors, Jesus could be hawking camping gear for the then-popular Sears catalog. Jesus loved being outside so much that he "spent all his days in the open air." After preaching, he always turned his back on the hot walls of the city and slipped away into the healthful freshness of the Mount of Olives." He liked mountain breezes so much that "the vigorous activities of his days gave his nerves the strength of steel."[6]

Barton's claims are so bad they are good. You read the words, smile because they are unbelievable, and then Barton takes yet another astonishingly blasphemous leap of faith. In his discussion of the parable of the wedding at Cana, in which Mary approaches Jesus and complains that "the wine is gone," Barton writes, "Well, what of it?" With a hundred people at the wedding why did Jesus have to do something? And, while he did eventually turn the water into wine, it was not to please his mother. Jesus Christ liked a good time. He wanted "to keep a happy party from breaking up too soon," and equally important, he sought "to save a hostess from embarrassment." What would the gossips of Cana say if the bride's family failed to fill every cup to the brim—again and again and again?[7]

Chapter 6 of Barton's book is titled "The Founder of Modern Business." Remember when Mary and Joseph scoured Jerusalem to locate the missing Jesus? His mother "pictured a hundred calamities," so when they found him in the temple gabbing with a bunch of elders, Mary asked, "Son, why hast thou thus dealt with us? Behold thy father and I have sought thee sorrowing." Barton writes that Jesus responded with deference but also with a sense of astonishment: "How is it that ye sought me? Wist ye not that I must be about my father's *business?*"[8]

The emphasis is in the original. Barton meant to leave readers with no doubt about Jesus' real mission on earth. Forget about redemption in heaven, and also forget about sin, hell, and contrition. Jesus came to wheel and deal; instead of the Sermon on the Mount, consider his clear "business philosophy." For example, "whoever will be great must render great service." Jesus Christ understood that work and religious work were synonymous. He therefore asked that we all pick up those waiting acres of diamonds, and in the process of making a buck we would finally grasp the real reason for the divine visit of *The Man Nobody Knows*.

Peter Berger published his first book almost forty years after the success of Barton's blasphemy. Yet so little had changed that Berger's *The Noise of Solemn Assemblies* is a thorough and lucid critique of American religion in general and Protestantism in particular. If the business of America is business, the role of American religion is to put its imprimatur on the secular, "OK world" of U.S. life. Berger argues that while the churches may add "a heavier dosage of religious vocabulary," in truth they only celebrate a "cultural religion" that justifies and sanctifies everything from big business to democracy, from two cars in every garage to a prime roast beef in every convection oven.[9]

Written for the National Student Christian Federation, Berger's book offers readers specific suggestions about how to approach God. To those who study the Bible, it is clear "that the God of the prophetic message stands sovereignly above all nations and empires. He cannot be evoked as a safe political ally." Where Barton puts Jesus behind a cash register, Berger stresses that Jesus "broke the Sabbath. He associated with those outside the norms of the culture of that day. And in human terms his life was a total failure." Jesus cast divine light on eschatology, on the final events in the history of humankind. He came from and led us to *another world;* thus, by definition, to follow the real message of Christ in the United States is to be led, "of necessity, to a measure of alienation from the culture."[10]

Can a sociologist offer advice about God? Can a scientist tell us how to safely enter the next world? Berger's answer is unequivocal. Absolutely not. As a sociologist, my responsibility is to "ruthlessly"[11] examine the world that is there. Once the scientific examination is complete, I can then make value judgments, not as a sociologist but as a Christian, a citizen, a parent.

Berger talks about "de-ideologizing"; it is a rare use of a clumsy word, yet it catches a theme that perfectly characterizes forty years of his work. "De-ideologizing means the process of radically honest thinking and communicating by which systematic illusions are breached." Berger has spent a lifetime asking his readers to fundamentally rethink the deepest assumptions of their social, political, religious, and economic worlds. For example, as early as 1960, Berger courageously took issue with conventional attitudes about homosexuality, the death penalty, and the role of African Americans in U.S. life.[12] He uses sociology as a bulldozer; it is a science that levels illusions. Then, once its work is done, the rest of us can make judgments as human beings. In Berger's case he is still searching for *The Far Glory*[13] of the next world. But even when he finds it, we will always have a body of work that ceaselessly uses sociology in its classic and most significant sense: to ask the big questions first posed by Marx, Weber, Durkheim, and Simmel.

THE PRECARIOUS VISION

Peter Berger has a great sense of humor. He openly admits to being an inveterate joke teller, and he is a person with such a passion for humor that he even wrote a monograph titled *Redeeming Laughter*. It seems appropriate, therefore, to begin this short sketch of his life with three jokes from this, his most recent book.

About religion: "What happens if you cross a Unitarian with a Jehovah's Witness? A person who goes from house to house and doesn't know why."

A sick joke: "A child: May I play with grandmother? The mother: No, I'm not going to unscrew the coffin a third time."

On Freudian psychoanalysis: "Two Jewish ladies are talking. 'My son is in psychoanalysis,' says the first, 'It seems that he has an Oedipus complex.' To which the other lady replies, 'Ach. Oedipus, Shmoedipus. Main thing, he loves his mother.' "[14]

Freud practiced in Vienna. Peter Ludwig Berger was born there on March 17, 1929. He grew up in a world at war and escaped it by first traveling to England. He studied for a short time at the University of London, and in 1946, he came to New York City, a stranger who was also "very poor."[15]

Religion, and more specifically Lutheran Protestantism, has always been at the center of Berger's life. One of his first jobs in the United States—he was an office boy in the headquarters of the Methodist Church—moved him to quickly question what he calls "the Protestant smile." He vividly recalls "walking down long corridors and looking through open doors into the offices: Almost every office was occupied by a formidable looking woman. . . . Almost every one of these women was smiling." Berger wanted to know why. He "didn't quite trust" the Protestant smile or the "omnipresence" of the American flag in the churches he attended and visited. Based on his education in Austria, "the Christian faith could never be identified with any culture, not even a culture that one finds morally acceptable or even admirable."[16]

While Berger tried to decipher the meaning of the smile—"it was one of my early preoccupations"—he also went to school. He graduated from Wagner College in 1949 and did his graduate work at the New School for Social Research in Greenwich Village. Recall the school's origin in 1919. Scholars like Thorstein Veblen and Alvin Johnson settled there because it was a new school that gave free rein to idle curiosity and deliberate challenges to the established order. Classes tended to include a large number of middle-aged adults, and the notion of advising students seemed somewhat outrageous. At the New School students came because they wanted knowledge. No one filled up your cup with wisdom. You did that yourself, or you got very thirsty.

Berger arrived when the sociology faculty included a number of German expatriates—Alfred Schutz, Karl Mayer, and Albert Salomon. These scholars gave the school a distinctly German perspective. While statistics had their place, it was not in the classroom. Even in the late 1960s, the U.S. focus on methods and coefficients never penetrated the New School's hard walls. Rooted in disciplines like history and philosophy, the sociologist relied on imagination and (this is a Berger mandate) prose that sought to be elegant as well as informed. Meanwhile, Max Weber, not Karl Marx, dominated theoretical discussions. Berger, for example, is fond of quoting what he calls "one of the most chilling statements I know in the history of Western thought." When a friend asked Weber how he could continue writing books that came to such pessimistic conclusions, Weber responded in this fashion, "I want to see how much I can take."[17]

Berger stresses that Weber heavily influenced his own conservative perspective. For the humanism that also dominates Berger's thought, there is of course religion but also the influence of teachers like Salomon and Mayer. These men not only spoke a number of languages and displayed an array of knowledge that stretched from classical to modern thought. More important, they were extremely decent human beings, who created an intellectual atmosphere of genuine warmth and concern. Mayer's wife always accompanied him to every class, and their relationship left a distinct, positive impression on many students. Salomon inherited a frail body, but when you listened to him talk about friendship in the essays of the sixteenth-century French philosopher Michel de Montaigne, Salomon was as impressive a human being as he was a sociologist.[18]

Berger "lucked out." He managed to find in Greenwich Village a group of teachers who were anything but strangers to his cultural roots. He got his Ph.D. in sociology from the New School in 1954 and, with the draft in effect—became a U.S. citizen in 1951. Berger then spent two years in the U.S. Army. The following year he served as research director of the Evangelical Academy in Bad Boll, Germany.[19] All the while Berger struggled to position himself in relation to God and the vocational direction of his life. Thus Berger spent another "very happy" year at the Lutheran Theological Seminary in Philadelphia. He studied to be a minister, but "while all biographical decisions are murky, this one was essentially simple: I felt that I could not be a Lutheran minister unless I could fully assent to the definition of faith as stated in the Lutheran confessions, and I drew back from this role because I doubted whether I could give such unqualified assent. In other words I doubted that I, for one, could preach that."[20]

"That" refers to a liberal Lutheran position. Berger then doubted whether he could do it justice. He is ruthlessly honest not only in his sociology but also about his lifelong search to establish a relationship with God. Where conventional Christianity maintains that there is a contradiction between belief and unbelief, Berger explains that "God has not exactly made it easy for us to believe in him." There is nothing sinful about unbelief; on the contrary, "a just God will not hold it against us if we do not manage the exercise."[21]

Berger, however, maintains his own faith with such passion that "theology, at least for me, seems to be a disease that lies dormant for years and then breaks out at more or less regular intervals." In a discipline where the classical sociologists treated the notion of God as a superstition to be overcome, Berger indicates in 1992 that "the morning *will* come. The burden of God's silence will be lifted and He will return once more in the dawn, with flaming fire at his right hand, in the fullness of his glory."[22]

With great care, Berger tries to keep his sociology separate from his writings about God and redemption in the next world. Read his work about the sociology of knowledge, and you would struggle indeed to find the man of faith on the pages you examine. He is vigorously objective as a social scientist, but the moral imperative that is at the center of his deep religious commitment nevertheless informs his work in a fascinating manner. For example, consider this comment, made after he first visited Mexico at the invitation of the radical priest Ivan Illich: "I can say with confidence that the human misery of Third World poverty and oppression has shocked me as deeply as it can anyone coming from the comfortable West and I have been and continue to be fully convinced of the urgency of seeking alleviation for it."[23]

In sharp contrast to many of his sociological contemporaries (e.g., Goffman), Berger lets us know that he has been moved, that he bleeds and cries, that it is perfectly acceptable for a scholar to manifest "an impulse of outraged humanity." His faith in God drives his work as much as his belief in the positive effects of a sociology whose genius is negative. With Berger we enter new territory because, along with sociological theory, we encounter a proud political conservative's sharp questioning of the established order and a serious Christian's quest for a measure of morality on a planet where "all of history is one endless massacre stretching back to the dawn of mankind."[24]

Berger is an original, a man with a great sense of humor and faith, in a world full of massacres, many committed in the name of God.

INVITATION TO SOCIOLOGY

Berger starts *Invitation to Sociology* by defining a social situation. It is any encounter in which "people orient their actions towards one another."

This includes everything from criminal behavior to the classroom, from marriage to the sales techniques used by the home shopping networks. What interests the sociologist is "the web of meanings, expectations and conduct resulting from such mutual orientation." How do the men and women on the shopping networks dress and behave; and if their folksy techniques move merchandise, what is the set of shared meanings that allows them to so successfully connect with their listeners?[25]

Any social interaction can interest a sociologist, but because the discipline is first and foremost a *form of consciousness*, Berger explains the "special sort of abstractions" that, like a fish lure, attract a sociological mind. Borrowing a phrase from Lutheran sacramental theology, he argues that the sociologist hones in on what is present "in, with and under" any social activity. "To ask sociological questions presupposes that one in interested in looking some distance beyond the commonly accepted or officially defined goals of human actions." While the sociologist may not be a total skeptic, he or she generally manifests a healthy suspicion about official interpretations of the way the world works. The "art of mistrust" is at the root of sociology as a form of consciousness.[26]

Think of it as empathy in the service of upsetting society's apple cart. Sociologists put themselves in everybody else's shoes because that is the best way to get in, with, and under any social situation. The sociologist sees things from all perspectives, but in the process, "the sociologist will be driven time and again, by the very logic of his discipline, to debunk the social systems he is studying."[27] Whatever their own personal beliefs, all sociologists are by definition subversives; in always going the extra mile to try and understand the world they encounter, sociologists ask deeply disturbing questions about any society they examine. For example, if Americans self-centeredly complain about the rate of divorce and "mixed" families, the sociologist looks at history. People often married two or three times in the nineteenth century because their first spouse died, mixed families are a historical constant, and if parents supposedly did a better job in the good old days, how can we explain a story like Cinderella? Perhaps evil stepmothers (and stepfathers) existed long before the twentieth century? And finally, if we consider a play like Shakespeare's *King Lear*, it is even arguable that serious conflicts between parents and children are normal, rather than abnormal. Maybe Americans in pursuit of family happiness are searching for a learned illusion rather than an achievable reality?[28]

The questions are a consequence of the form of consciousness. And they are subversive because, in addition to the specific issues about family life, the questions suggest that all societies are plastic; they imply that throughout human history, people have and do mold values, beliefs, and norms into a variety of forms, none of which is immutable. Thus, *"not only is the world not what it appears to be, but it could be different from what it is"* (emphasis in original).[29]

Even in an Armani suit or a Dior gown, sociologists lack respectability because the discipline's genius is negative rather than positive; it is by definition a jolt of caffeine rather than a measured quantity of valium. As such, its subversive quality "has always been sensed, almost instinctively, by dictatorial regimes of every ideological coloration." Sociology forces you to see the relativity of all social forms; that is its beauty as well as its potential for being a liberating force in modern life. Berger stresses that there are definite restrictions on the amount of freedom that sociology promises. We inherit a society, and that inheritance sets limits on the amount of change that can occur. But sociology nevertheless opens up new areas of choices as well as forcing us to see the unintended as well as the intended consequences of our actions. For example, progress comes with a price; some people lose their sense of meaning and if the sense of normlessness is sufficiently great, we should not be surprised by the appearance of religious and political movements that offer people simple answers to the most complex social problems.[30]

As sociologists, we only set out the possible choices and the likely consequences of this or that course of action. Then, as citizens, as parents, as politicians, we all make the "moral and existential choices" for or against this or that policy. "But, whichever choice is finally made, the individual who makes it will at least have a clearer idea of what he is up against. *And that is no small contribution"* (emphasis added).[31]

Berger also argues that the negative genius of sociology is in short supply in the United States. His books rarely display a sense of sarcasm or self-importance, yet he did write this line in *Invitation to Sociology:* "The sensible person reads the sociological journals mainly for the book reviews and the obituaries and goes to sociological meetings only if he is looking for a job or has other intrigues to carry on."[32]

Berger is critical of the fixation on statistical techniques that lead to "little empirical studies of narrowly confined topics." Numbers are supposedly proof that sociology is a hard science; the narrow topics—for example, the class system of some hamlet or the dating habits in a university—are especially conducive to results that can be quantified with coefficients as reliable as the sun in August. Unfortunately, small topics are for small minds. "All parochial approaches in sociology entail a loss of intellectual substance." If you want to know "why more teenagers pick their noses in rural Minnesota rather than in rural Iowa," go for it. But do not assume that such questions express the genius of sociology. The sociological perspective should always be comprehensive and comparative, and if American sociology is to have any long-lasting significance, *"sociology must return to the big questions."*[33]

What are those questions? For Berger they revolve around the nature of the modern world. How, following Durkheim, can we achieve a sense of social solidarity in a world that puts the individual ahead of the group, self-realization ahead of self-sacrifice? How has capitalism changed? And in comparison to socialism or any other alternative system, what are capitalism's benefits and deficiencies? Does anybody have the right to bet a generation's future on what globalization may bring? And as countries as diverse as the Philippines, the Dominican Republic, and Turkey are actively *exporting millions of people* as a means to economic growth, what does that tell us about the supposed trickle-down theory of Third World development?[34]

Finally, and most important, how do we get sociologists to focus on the act of interpretation that was at the center of Max Weber's sociology? For Berger the act of interpretation is far more than an "arid methodological consideration." He argues that "human phenomena don't speak for themselves; they must be interpreted." And the act of interpreting has a "moral, even a humane dimension." We agree to see the world as it is, not as it ought to be. We agree to "respect other people and their intentions, hopes and ways of life." And we agree to interpret the consequences of modernity by always using "cross-cultural, global comparisons, in historical depth as well as in contemporary terms." The sociologist is always a cosmopolitan rather than a provincial because the greater the range and depth of comparison, the greater the chance for interpretations which are simultaneously original and liberating, provocative and humanistic.[35]

Berger asks us to think about a puppet show. "We see the puppets dancing on their miniature stage, moving up and down as the strings pull them around, following the prescribed course of their various little parts." Similarly, we can see ourselves dancing on the stage of society. But unlike the puppets, we can use the process of interpretation to stop the show and see how we learned to think and act as we do. We can see who is pulling the strings, and "in this act lies the first step towards freedom. And in this same act we can find the conclusive justification of sociology as a humanistic discipline."[36]

SOCIOLOGY OF KNOWLEDGE

Woody Allen once wrote a short story, "The Metterling Lists," ridiculing academics. Laboring over an intellectual history, a noted scholar is so focused on details that he needs to know what socks Metterling wore when he wrote his masterpiece. Were they blue, black, or argyle? It matters because the socks are, for obsessive academics, the noxious passport required to penetrate the true meaning of the master's thought.[37]

Peter Berger never wrote about socks. But in 1966 he and Thomas Luckmann published *The Social Construction of Reality*. It remains one of the most influential theoretical treatises written in the last forty years because the authors quite successfully redefined the sociology of knowledge. They argue that instead of focusing on intellectual history—on an endlessly deep understanding of the history of ideas—sociology needs to focus on everyday life. Spotlight what passes for commonsense knowledge rather than ideas, and you will suddenly discover the "fabric of meanings" essential to human beings in France, India, Egypt, or Chile.[38]

Like the key to a set of handcuffs, the effort is liberating because anyone who understands how social reality is constructed also understands how to reconstruct it. Society can be very different indeed, especially when sociologists use a set of conceptual tools that explain the footings that hold up any society on earth.

"Commonsense knowledge is the knowledge that I share with others in the normal, self-evident routines of everyday life."[39] It is what I take for granted; it is what I expect will happen when I enter any particular social situation. For example, because many states now allow drivers to make a right turn at a red light, I now take it for granted that many of my opponents on the road will no longer stop at the light. They will roll through, so, given my commonsense knowledge of driving habits, I maintain a healthy degree of caution whenever I approach a light.

In everyday life—when you go to work, when you enter an elevator, when you eat in a restaurant—commonsense knowledge is most evident when we use the "continuum of typifications" that allow otherwise anonymous individuals to successfully interact. Customer and clerk, teacher and student, husband and wife: each pair of labels underlines that "most of the time, my encounters with others are typical in a double sense—I apprehend the other *as* a type and I interact with him in a situation that is itself typical."[40]

What guides these typecast encounters is the common stock of knowledge that we all internalize as children. "Recipe knowledge" is the shorthand used by the authors, and it perfectly catches the taken-for-granted ingredients (including tone of voice and facial expressions) that, as a recipe, guide encounters. For example, if a young man calls a young woman for a date, she knows what to say, and how to say it, if she wants to accept the invitation. In addition, she also has, stored in her stock of internalized knowledge, a list of recipes that politely explain her inability to accept the offer. "I just broke up with someone and I need time to get my bearings before I date again." Or "my parents are angry with me and I am grounded for the next two months (two years, the next century)."

The recipes work as long as they are taken for granted by both partners to the exchange. But if recipes change, interactions can fail. In an elevator today, who gets out first? It is often up for grabs. My own recipe is to let aged women out first; however, if the other passengers are middle aged and below, my recipe is every person for him- and herself. Sir Walter Raleigh can be polite; I am out the door and on my way.

Recipe knowledge guides everyday life; recipe knowledge often changes. The seeming paradox is resolved in one of the book's most original sections. In trying to explain how societies (and people) are simultaneously fixed and fluid, Berger and Luckmann freely draw on the work of, among others, Marx, Durkheim, Simmel, Schutz, and Weber. They soon create, while standing on the shoulders of giants,[41] a new and very convincing map of how and why people think and act as they do.

At the center of their map are "the three dialectical moments in social reality." Each of these moments endlessly acts back on the other; in everyday life they are as interconnected as a baby to its umbilical cord. And any "analysis of the social world that leaves out any one of these three moments will be distortive": (1) society is a human product, (2) society is an objective reality, and (3) man is a social product.[42]

Society is a human product. Among other things, this affirms the commitment to a humanistic sociology because it is rooted in the notion that people—and only people—construct social reality. Men and women create everything from beliefs to values, from social institutions to the recipes for getting in and out of an elevator. But, and this is a *huge* but, when any of us is born, we inherit—before we construct a thing!—a social world that was made by others for us. Our inheritance is shared, learned, and also arbitrary. Admittedly, I once had a student who proudly told the class that he had chosen his society and his parents in a past life; but unless you or I can also make such a claim, we all inherit, arbitrarily, a world of already-constructed recipe knowledge and social typifications.

Society is an objective reality. Before we appear on the scene, society exists *out there*—as an objective, tangible reality—in the minds of others, in the books we read, in the myths and legends that we learn as children and repeat as adults. For Berger and Luckmann, "all human activity is subject to habituation." If only because people need a degree of predictability to successfully interact, the possibility of "institutionalization is incipient in every social situation continuing in time." That human possibility becomes an objective reality "whenever there is a reciprocal typification of habitualized actions by types of actors." In fact "any such typification is an institution."[43]

From this perspective the Pentagon and the rules for interacting with a clerk are both examples of institutions. The former is of course inordinately more complex and enveloping than the latter, but both fundamentally involve the typifications and recipe knowledge that allow any society to function, to "tend to hang together." This last phrase is especially important because it represents a frontal assault on anyone arguing that social institutions, by definition, "hang together, functionally, let alone as a logically consistent system"[44] Berger and Luckmann ask us to consider a straight male, a bisexual female, and a lesbian. All are guided by recipe knowledge, "and there is, after all, no reason why two processes of erotic habitualization, one heterosexual and one Lesbian, cannot take place side by side without functionally integrating with each other." They may; they may not. Nothing can be assumed; the proof is in everyday life. But even when institutions are integrated, "their integration is not a functional imperative for the social processes that produce them." On the contrary, it occurs in a "derivative" fashion.[45]

This is a crucial point, with significant implications for the analysis of any social institution. Whether in the Pentagon or at the mall, "individuals perform discrete institutionalized actions within the context of their biography." An individual uses recipes to interact, but instead of being specific to the individual, those recipes are socially shared and articulated. Thus any degree of institutional integration, functional or otherwise, occurs "by way of this detour of socially shared universes of meaning." Integration starts and ends with people. If men and women do not use the same recipes and typifications, any society's institutions will, instead of hanging together, collapse like a bunch of steamed broccoli.

Man is a social product. Societies achieve a variable measure of integration and solidarity by making what is "out there"—in the minds of others—"in here," that is, in your mind or mine as the stock of recipe knowledge required to successfully negotiate everyday life. In essence, the objective reality of society becomes the subjective reality of personal existence when you and I internalize and take for granted the recipes created and provided by others. It is only with "the transmission of the social world to a new generation that the fundamental social dialectic appears in its totality." When a baby is born, and its parents begin the process of socialization, the child's cry renews the social world and begins again the endless dialectic of society shaping people as people simultaneously shape society.[46]

The rub, of course, is that instead of beginning life at step one of the dialectic—society is a human product—we begin at steps two and three. A society exists before we do, and it shapes us before we can shape it. All human beings respond to society based on the recipes others provide about living fruitfully in that society. Like a gambling casino, the odds favor the house to such a degree that Berger and Luckmann talk about socializations that are so successful, people forget who authored—and authors—the social world. *"Man is capable of producing a reality that denies him"* (emphasis added).[47]

Reification is the term the authors use to conceptualize this astonishing lapse of memory. "It implies that man is capable of forgetting his own authorship of the human world, and further, that the dialectic between man, the producer, and his product is lost to consciousness. The reified world is, by definition, a dehumanized world."[48] It is as impersonal as the most overpowering bureaucracy because a reified world erases step one of the dialectic; it forgets that society is a human product, that people and only people construct social reality.

Take the concept of race. Microbiologists can now prove that only fifty of our roughly fifty thousand gene pairs have anything to do with the color of our skin. In other words, .001 percent of our genes absurdly determine the basis for racial classifications like *Negroid* or *Caucasian*. Scientists continually argue there is only one race—the human race—but not only do Americans continue to define each other via a racial divide, they even argue that they are *colorblind* as they simultaneously use the colors black and white as the basis for self-identification. Meanwhile, immigrants from India, who are often darker than many African Americans, do not get a color. We call Indians "others" because they do not fit in to our reified racial categories.[49]

The conceptual importance of the three-part dialectic is that it allows us to see that for the apprehension of reification as a modality of conscious, I need to have achieved a "relative *de*reification" of consciousness. To see how society determines my way of thinking, I need to be able to step back from the process and (with Durkheim, Weber, Marx, Simmel, and Mead) reflect on what I see. This is a "comparatively late development" in any individual biography but especially prominent in modern societies because, for example, the plurality of worldviews makes it much harder for people to assume that their recipe knowledge is the best or the only recipe in town. A Borders Books of recipes exist, so in modern societies, it is much easier to step back from our inheritance and momentarily underline only part one of the dialectic: society is a human product. There is room for conscious social change.[50]

In summarizing the implications of their focus on the social construction of reality, Berger and Luckmann stress that sociology needs to take its rightful place as a science that deals with man *as* man. It is a humanistic discipline that must engage in a continuous dialogue with history and philosophy "or lose its proper object of inquiry." For example, the three-part dialectic suggests crucial philosophical questions about the limits of human freedom. If we are first social products, to what extent can people liberate themselves from the world they inherit? And if people need society in order to be social beings, to what extent should they try to liberate themselves from society? Are hermits running away from society or to a sense of freedom that can only be found alone, away from the social world that created the hermit in the first place?

Questions like these suggest the need for a dialogue that always includes history and philosophy. Any society is part of a human world, "made by men, inhabited by men, and, in turn, making men in an ongoing historical process. It is not the least fruit of a humanistic sociology that it reawakens our wonder at this astonishing process."[51]

SARIN GAS AND *THE HOMELESS MIND*

Peter Berger stresses the need for a conversation with history. This of course means a close reading of what happened in the societies that preceded us. As in the earlier discussion of "the charge of the light brigade" (chapter 3), there is no substitute for an intimate knowledge of what people actually said and did at a particular point in human history.

The facts are important, yet Berger's special stress is to put human beings into an overall or *overarching* historical context. Words like *modernity* refer to specific *historical* processes, with observable consequences. In *The Heretical Imperative* Berger talks about "the vertigo of relativity induced by modernization."[52] People receive, as their social inheritance, such a bewildering banquet of possibilities (e.g., about sexual orientation, about religion, about careers, about family) that they regularly become as dizzy as Jimmy Stewart when he reached the tower in Alfred Hitchcock's frightening film *Vertigo*.

Dizziness, especially about important beliefs and values, is often so terrifying that as a consequence of modernity, we cannot be surprised by the existence of cult groups, even one capable of the apocalyptic violence practiced by the Aum in Japan. Led by Shōkō Asahara, Aum members, on March 20, 1995, filled Tokyo's subways with sarin gas, a deadly concoction designed to save the world by destroying it.[53]

In explaining the Aum's existence, Robert Jay Lifton contends that a specific historical factor is of particular importance. Many Japanese refuse to accept their nation's responsibility for, among other things, the massive slaughter of civilians during the bombing of Nanking (in 1937) and the enslaving of 3 million mostly Chinese and Korean citizens for wartime labor projects. Instead, the Japanese stock of knowledge now includes a sense of "victim consciousness" (for Hiroshima and Nagasaki) linked to a desire for a national greatness. These societal beliefs arguably predispose people to accept "a movement with apocalyptic claims to resolving all conflict and restoring collective glory, claims of a purification that would wash away all evil."[54]

Following Berger, the specific history needs to be placed in the context of modernization. Interviews with Aum members indicated the profound sense of "psychohistorical dislocation" that they experienced as a result of the rapid modernization of Japanese society. Exposed to extremes including simultaneous social, political, and cultural transformations, many contemporary Japanese adolescents and adults inherit "social and institutional arrangements" that never anchor them in any meaningful way. In relation to commonsense knowledge, "what are impaired are the symbol systems that have to do with family, religion, social and political authority, sexuality, birth and death, and overall ordering of the life cycle." Feeling the vertigo of relativity, many Japanese are open to cults or movements that offer to provide answers that will eliminate dizziness, even as they eliminate human societies. People save themselves by destroying themselves—and the rest of us.[55]

This grotesque result symbolizes a profound problem produced by modernization: people feel alone in the universe. They experience a terrible sense of "homelessness" because "faith is no longer socially given but must be achieved individually." For example, instead of a religious commitment, a person has a religious *preference*. Like brands of food in the supermarket, I have a penchant that can be changed if and when a better deal appears. As our inheritance from modernity, the social stock of knowledge offers possibilities rather than certainties, options rather than answers.[56]

The homeless mind includes a sense of identity (of who I am) that is peculiarly open, differentiated, reflective, and individuated.[57] A person is *open* in the sense of being unfinished as he or she enters adult life; we endlessly search for a self-realization that can be achieved in church or, if it is your preference, via a set of expensive tapes purchased from the latest guru on the home shopping network.

Identity is *differentiated* because we experience a plurality of possibilities, each of which relativizes the other. Back in that supermarket, all the brands seem the same; I do not know which is best, so "the individual seeks to find his 'foothold' in reality in himself rather than outside himself." In the extreme I become the most interesting thing in my own life because, in modern societies, "subjectivity acquires previously unconceived depths."[58]

Identity is *peculiarly reflective*. The welter of ever-changing options forces the individual to think. Feeling tense is normal because, instead of sheep peacefully grazing on an English countryside, the citizens of modern societies are sheep being buzzed by an airplane. We are restless and frenetic, and we reflect because we need the answers that will, we hope, restore a sense of serenity and harmony.

Finally, modern identity is peculiarly *individuated*. Freedom, autonomy, and individual rights "come to be taken for granted as moral imperatives of fundamental importance, and foremost among these individual rights is the right to plan and fashion one's life as freely as possible."[59]

Because the homeless mind is a consequence of modernization, Berger and his coauthors carefully define their object of inquiry. They discuss *"modernization as the institutional concomitants of technologically induced economic growth."* And in an especially important qualification, they write that *"there is no such thing as a 'modern society' plain and simple; there are only societies more or less advanced in a continuum of modernization"* (emphasis in original).[60] For example, if our focus is being wired for the twenty-first century, Finland is arguably the lead society. Helsinki's citizens are justifiably famous for using cellular telephones in an endlessly "advanced" manner. Cross the Baltic in a (Norwegian-built) hydrofoil, and you find Estonia, a society that joyously celebrates its modernization; but given the nation's wonderfully bucolic countryside, Estonia still has a long way to go.

Institutional concomitants is, admittedly, a mouthful, but it precisely catches one focus of *The Homeless Mind.* Using the redefined sociology of knowledge as a benchmark, Berger wants to understand the "everyday consciousness" of people subjected to technologically induced economic growth. *How* do people think? "What is their cognitive style? What organization of knowledge is intrinsic to technological production?"[61] For example, two (of many other) prerequisites are a "pervasive quality of *implicit abstraction*" and *"anonymous social relations."* Think of the worker on a Korean, Japanese, Mexican, or North American automobile assembly line that is full of people and robots. The line's logic demands that you abstract yourself and your task from the whole process; by definition you are a cog in a well-oiled process of scientific management, and the robots graphically illustrate the level of anonymity that so often characterizes low- and high-technology production.[62]

The Homeless Mind also analyzes the everyday consciousness induced by one of modernity's other omnipresent companions: bureaucracies. Whether, for example, political, educational, or business, bureaucracy's cognitive style produces a need for characteristics like *orderliness, predictability, and moralized anonymity.* Job-holding professionals are put into pigeon-holed categories (this is the associate vice president for academic affairs) where their responsibilities are defined by job descriptions written in deliberately lifeless language, endlessly scrutinized by lawyers who also bloodlessly dot every *i* and cross every *t.* Meanwhile, by definition, the occupant of any bureaucratic position must be morally blind. Whether you are young or old, a man or a woman, Latino or Asian, everyone is to be treated in the same morally anonymous fashion. To show favoritism is to inject an element of subjectivity into the mind-set of a person who must, as a bureaucratic mandate, treat everybody in the same neutral fashion.[63]

As a less than neatly wrapped package, modernization includes a sense of homelessness linked by a process of "mutual contamination"[64] to the cognitive styles nurtured by bureaucracy and technologically induced economic change. One consequence, especially in more traditional societies, is a continual collision of cognitive styles, of different forms of everyday consciousness. Distinct ways of thinking clash, and the result is often a pronounced sense of disillusionment—for the modernizers and for their traditional opponents. For example, many Caribbean and Latin American nations have a relaxed sense of time; natives joke that Caribbean time means *mañana,* whether I live in English-speaking Jamaica or the Spanish-speaking Dominican Republic. Meanwhile, the executives of global corporations ask consultants this question: How do I get somebody to answer my e-mails? These people have no sense of schedules, dead-lines, or "tasking." If the parties cannot work it out, one serious conse-quence is that the corporations move their facilities to nations with a more modern cognitive style.[65]

Get modern or get left behind. This suggests one of *The Homeless Mind's* most intriguing conclusions: "Modernization, counter-modernization and demodernization must be seen as *concurrent processes.*"[66] If the most basic function of social institutions is "to protect the individual from having to make too many choices," modernization implies a leveling process that forces choices across the board. In religion, politics, education, gender roles, and answering e-mails, a citizen needs to make choices on a bewil-dering variety of levels, all the time, everyday. So, if the Aum in Japan are a grotesque reaction to the sense of homelessness, a more restrained response is "resurgent religion," what Berger calls the desecularization of the world. He is especially impressed with the astonishing growth of evangelical movements throughout Latin America and with the rapidly increasing significance of commitments to Islam in nations that extend from North Africa to Southeast Asia. Recall that one in five inhabitants of the earth is a Muslim and that Indonesia has by far the largest number of Muslim believers.[67]

In Afghanistan Osama bin Laden and the Taliban represented (and rep-resent) a desire for counter-modernization. They slaughtered civilians to help produce a return to eighth-century realities. But whether it is a brutal rejection of modernity or a peaceful resurrection of religious beliefs, the crucial insight is that, however "absurd politically or aesthetically" (think of the Taliban destroying the magnificent Buddhist statues at Bamian), these movements have a distinctive, everyday logic.[68] You cannot have modernity without the processes that concurrently resist and reject it.

Toward the end of *The Homeless Mind*, Berger notes "that anyone who claims to know the outcome of these efforts is foolhardy indeed." Soci-ology's genius is negative, so it can only offer significant help in under-standing the concurrent results of modernization. But because society is a human product, people can use the negative insights to produce positive results. There is no inherent reason that we cannot experience "genuinely new" alternatives to the violent clashes that now characterize so many modern and modernizing societies.[69]

POLITICAL ETHICS AND SOCIAL CHANGE

Peter Berger says that he can be provoked. If someone presses the proper buttons, "I can deliver myself of a conservative credo literally drip-ping with such medievalism as to get me excluded from faculty parties from here to eternity."[70] We hope that that will not happen, but Berger's conservative perspective is anything but typical. He is a self-identified liberal in religious matters and borders on extremist if we turn to questions of morality (e.g., death penalty, Vietnam War, homosexuality) and aesthetics. Yet "I see no contradiction between my 'radicalism' in some of these areas and my conservative predispositions in the socio-political sphere."[71]

Consider this very useful distinction between two types of conservatives. The first is "adversely disposed toward change because they consider the institutional arrangements of the status quo as being intrinsically good, natural or even sacred." These conservatives have such a faith in the righteousness of the established order that they perceive threats to its legitimacy as "evil, perverse, or even blasphemous." Because Berger is a sociologist, he is by vocational choice a zealous debunker of all established orders. An intrinsic faith in the status quo is impossible if you contend that "history posits the problem of relativity as *a fact*, the sociology of knowledge *as a necessity of our condition*."[72]

Berger has "a prejudice against change" not because of any beliefs in the sanctity of the status quo but because he "has profound suspicions about the benefits of whatever is proposed as an alternative to the status quo. Pessimists and skeptics by inclination, these are the conservatives by lack of faith."[73] With a good degree of legitimacy—think of terrorist groups in Colombia, Spain, Sri Lanka, and the Middle East—Berger argues that "all of history is one endless massacre stretching back to the dawn of mankind. Wherever we are in history, we stand on a mountain of corpses, and, however terrible the thought, we are the beneficiaries of all this carnage."[74]

Given that pessimistic assessment, a person needs to" think daringly but act prudently."[75] Berger is a conservative humanist who, to his great credit, profoundly challenged his own beliefs after he visited Mexico in 1969. Invited to teach in Cuernavaca, Berger explains that "I can say with confidence that the human misery of Third World poverty and oppression has shocked me as deeply as it can anyone coming from the comfortable West and I have been and continue to be fully convinced of the urgency of seeking alleviation for it."[76] In Berger's case he wrote a splendid book— *The Pyramids of Sacrifice*—that simultaneously challenges the capitalist myths of growth and the socialist myths of revolution. Berger is on no one's side, except perhaps the people who live and die in the Third World garbage dumps that offer, as development's promise, a humanly intolerable "calculus of pain."

Consider Mexico City. Close to 20 million people produce more than 8,000 tons of refuse a day. In the poorest areas the city lacks any means of collecting the trash, so locals simply burn their garbage as a way to kill rats and control flies. As a result, in the city's open-air garbage dumps, fires rage with such force that nearby neighborhoods are sometimes evacuated. The city could purchase more trucks and even build better plants, but at the time Berger first visited, garbage produced big profits for the powerful underworld organization that then controlled the resale of anything valuable—that is, the metals, timber, plastics, and bottles discarded by the minority of Mexicans who make money from the developmental transformation of the Third World.[77]

Crews of garbage collectors first roam the affluent neighborhoods, scavenging through the trash and removing anything of easy value. The remaining garbage is then transported to the city's dumps, where a second-level crew of collectors takes over. Using *pepenadores* (in Mexican Spanish, *pepenar* is the verb "to pick up"), the overseers direct a labor force that slavishly earns its subsistence by combing through the trash heaps that they call home. Thousands of people construct shacks of corrugated iron or cardboard. They share their dump space with vermin, while the crew bosses are so successful that in the late 1970s, some became federal deputies of the ruling PRI, or Institutional Revolutionary Party. All the while the fires rage with such force that to talk of breathable air is to believe that the PRI was actually a force for change, rather than a filthy supporter of the status quo.[78]

This situation hints at what moved Peter Berger to a sense of urgency. Morally outraged and intellectually provoked, he used sociology to challenge existing assumptions and point the way toward a development process that never forgets this fact: "The most pressing human costs are in terms of physical deprivation and suffering. The most pressing moral imperative in policy making is a calculus of pain."[79]

Incidentally, Berger never neglects the difference between science and social policy. He strives for objectivity in his critical analysis; but "since value-free policy is an absurdity," moral judgments are a necessity once we move from the world that is, to the world that will, can, or should be.[80]

When Berger published *Pyramids of Sacrifice* in 1976, socialism and capitalism both vied with one another in a cold war that was also a fight about developmental schemes. Today capitalism has few viable competitors, and given the realities of globalization, Berger's critique of the myth of growth is more relevant today than it was twenty-five years ago. He punched holes in capitalism's bubble long before it won the war for the bank accounts and strategic plans of societies as distinct as Korea and Mexico, Taiwan and Panama, Thailand and Brazil.

The myth of growth has a heart: it is the cargo cult, the belief that capitalism will transport to the Third World "all the wondrous gifts of modernity in plentiful supply for all." Unfortunately, the cargo ship never arrives, or if it does, it docks near one of the garbage dump cities that exist in any developing nation on earth.[81]

What happened? One answer is that development takes time. Give the capitalist model more of a chance to work its magic, and the "trickle down" or spread effect of growth will occur. It happened in Europe and

North America when they transformed their economies, so have some
patience, and the same spread of wealth, accompanied by consumer
goods, will bear plentiful fruit throughout the Third World. Berger is skeptical for at least two reasons. In countries like Brazil the environment is
being forever destroyed in an unprecedented fashion, and equally important, "it is obviously difficult to disprove an argument which depends for
verification on an empirically inaccessible future." The proponents of
growth can always plead for more time; meanwhile, the gap between rich
and poor grows within a developing nation *and* between already developed and developing nations.[82]

To explain the lack of spread—and the disastrous growth of shack cities
in Ankara, Turkey, or Caracas, Venezuela—an analyst needs to assess the
difference between being first and last in the development line. The myth
of growth assumes that what occurred in Europe will also occur in the
Third World, but this is a terrible error because, instead of being the first
case in history, developing nations enter the process when "a fully developed and enormously powerful international capitalist system already
exists." It is like asking a heavyweight to box with a flyweight, especially
when the flyweight is painfully dependent on the already-existing capitalist system for everything from technology to direct investment.

Consider, as a contemporary example, the Northern Marianas, a group
of fourteen islands that lie just North of Guam in the Pacific. These tiny
islands—as U.S. territories—now (in 2001) export about a billion dollars
a year in garments that are stamped "Made in America." Meanwhile, the
workers receive far less than minimum wage, and even more interesting,
fully 84 percent of the garment industry's workforce is foreign, mostly
Chinese brought in on a temporary basis to exploit the manufacturing and
tax loopholes created by Congress. The serious profits flow out of the
Marianas, and whatever trickle-down benefits occur are not only quite
limited, but Congress can instantly eliminate them because of the Marianas' place in the development line, that is, very close to dead last.[83]

As a general conclusion, "the Marxist diagnosis that capitalism is bad
for the Third World makes a lot of sense." Dependency creates enormous
problems because, as the World Bank notes in a report titled "Entering
the Twenty-first Century," investors sent (in 1996) "only one-quarter of
their money to the developing world." And, at that, only five countries—
Argentina, Brazil, China, Mexico, and Poland—got 50 percent of the
money investors finally agreed to send to developing nations. Berger
stresses that breaking free of dependency on the developed world is such
a great impediment to success that the problems cited by socialist critics
(e.g., mounting debts, deteriorating terms of trade) "are not inventions of
Marxist ideologists, but empirical facts readily available to any objective
observer."[84]

My deliberate use of contemporary data underlines the persisting relevance of Berger's insights. He caught the significant problems, but equally important, he also raised issues that the economic experts often miss or utterly disregard. *"There are no experts on the desirable goals of human life"* (emphasis added). So, to the extent possible, all people "ought to participate in the fundamental choices to be made, choices that hinge not on technical expertise but on moral judgments."[85]

Capitalism has been "singularly unsuccessful" in dealing with questions of community and social solidarity. This follows if we recall Simmel's insight (see chapter 4) that money—a means—is the ultimate value of many developed societies. Thus, when development strategies erase or significantly weaken the hold of traditional community or religious groups, they replace it with nothing. "In sociological terms the main cost of capitalist freedom has been anomie." A sense of normlessness accompanies the widening gap between the rich and the poor; so, looking out from the garbage dumps or from the profit statements of global giants, people can rightfully feel that socialism—or some other ultimate solution—is a better development choice than capitalism.[86]

Here are some questions the experts need to ask the people. If productivity is a viable goal—the Chinese now have more than 1.5 billion men's shirts stockpiled in warehouses; the figure for "extra" bicycles is 20 million[87]—for how long a period of time and at what "noneconomic" costs? Is general affluence—a rising gross domestic product—more important than sharing the wealth with ever greater percentages of the people? Do the profits from development trickle down or, instead, rocket on up to the developed world and to a developing society's small upper class? "And, most importantly, what values are given moral priority: Individual freedom or collective security? Pluralism or community? Enterprise or harmony?"[88]

In resolving these issues Berger demands that policy makers consider the "calculus of pain" and the "calculus of meaning" that must accompany, like conjoined twins, any process of strategizing about Third World development.

In discussing a capitalist nation like Brazil and a socialist nation like China, *"the models assume the sacrifice of at least one generation for the achievement of their respective goals."* But because Berger presupposes *"that policy should seek to avoid the infliction of pain,"* any justification of the grief endured by the population must be justified in moral rather than economic terms. In northeast Brazil about one-third of the children died before they reached the age of three. The dead economic data discuss unemployment and income distribution; meanwhile, these numbers are "realities that kill human beings."[89] This is a literal "massacre of the innocent" that revolves around the difference between affluence and hunger. "The present critique of the Brazilian model is not that it is insufficiently egalitarian but that it condones the starvation of children as an acceptable price for economic growth."[90]

Turning to China, Berger asks an awful question: "Assuming that the Chinese have more to eat today than they had before (the revolution in) 1949, is this fact *in any way* due to the fact that millions of their number were killed by the regime. Nowhere in the apologetic literature is the question posed in this way. The reason, no doubt, is because the answer is all too clear."[91]

Similarly, the same questions can be put to Fidel Castro in Cuba. After I traveled from one end of the island to the other in June 2001, certain pictures stand out in my mind. The oxen plow the fields as the few available tractors move people in the carts built to carry sugar cane. In Havana people spend as much as five hours a day using grotesquely crowded public transportation to travel to and from work. The U.S. embargo certainly plays a role in the people's daily fate, but the Cuban government's failed economic strategies must accept primary responsibility for a result that Berger also found in China. This regime has succeeded in making one of the liveliest people in the world walk Havana's, Camaquey's, and Santiago's streets with little laughter and less noise. Cubans see daily life as *la lucha* (the struggle), and their gargantuan doses of pain are as questionable as the penalties paid by the Chinese or Brazilian people.[92]

The use of contemporary examples again suggests the continuing relevance of the questions posed by Berger. People's pain must be part of any strategic calculus and so too the meanings that people gain and lose when a nation experiences modernization. As noted in *The Homeless Mind*, becoming modern means "a transformation of the meanings by which men live, a revolution of the structure of consciousness."[93] As much as two plus two equals four, the onset of modernization equals "a severe trauma, a collapse of the old certainties, and, for better or worse, the beginning of a journey into new worlds of meaning."[94] When the experts inevitably encounter resistance, if they call that resistance ignorance or superstition, they are not only ethnocentric, they are to some extent inhuman—inhuman in the sense that the experts refuse to calculate the lost meanings and moorings that occur as an integral part of modernization.

Empathy is an essential trait for any developmental expert. Forget a calculus of meaning and you risk ignoring that in principle, "all worlds of consciousness are equal." People's beliefs must be considered, and for more than moral reasons; "policies that ignore the indigenous definitions of a situation are prone to fail." Speak a different language of meaning— work from totally foreign recipes for knowledge—and the experts will talk by the peasants who ultimately raise a desperate flag of surrender from the garbage heaps they call home.[95]

Besides empathy, humility is another essential tool for humane development. Experts tend to neglect the "postulate of ignorance"; they forget that "most political decisions must be made on the basis of inadequate knowledge." Development implies a strategy, not a certainty; mathematical formulas and so-called laws generally collapse when they meet the unintended consequences of social action. Life is anything but an exact science, and anyone who understands this fact will move "*very gingerly toward policy options that exact high human costs.*"[96]

Ultimately, Berger offers this cast-iron shield to protect the people from the experts. Begin with nay-saying. Use loud speakers to say "NO to children living in garbage, no to exploitation and hunger, no to terror and totalitarianism, no to anomie and the mindless destruction of human beings."[97]

Because the genius of sociology is negative, it is sometimes easier to know what is wrong rather than what is right. Rooted in his Christian conception of humankind, Berger argues that people from many different ideological camps can coalescence around a series of "nos." And "from these concrete instances of saying no, one may then move ahead to the painstaking task of finding alternatives which will not only be morally acceptable, but which will work."[98]

Given the manic logic of global capitalism—it is "one world, ready or not"[99]—Berger's questioning of all brands of development seems more relevant today than when he first published *Pyramids of Sacrifice* in 1976.

RUMORS OF ANGELS

Religion is one of Peter Berger's central sociological preoccupations. To date he has written six books—and scores of articles—focusing on religion from a wide variety of different perspectives. However, by his own reading, *The Sacred Canopy* is unique. Intended as a theoretical contribution, the book actually reads "like a treatise on atheism, at least in parts." At one point Berger actually counsels readers that "every inquiry into religious matters that limits itself to the empirically available must necessarily be based on a *methodological* atheism."[100]

Berger is of course correct. If social reality is a human construction, then religion is no different than political, family, or economic institutions. Each is a human product; religion, in particular, "is the human enterprise by which a sacred cosmos is established."[101] Once constructed—by men and women—this cosmos "both transcends and includes man." In fact, whether called heaven or some other world(s) inhabited by the gods, this cosmos confronts man as "an immensely powerful reality other than himself." One of religion's perennial wonders is that the gods not only talk to us; they locate us in an "ultimately meaningful universe."[102]

We talk (pray) to the gods. And they respond. The divine dialogue is a human constant, "but since every religious world is based on a plausibility structure that is itself the product of human activity, every religious world is inherently precarious in its reality."[103] For example, in the modern world, in a world dominated by science, rationality, and empirical verification, you can talk to God and it is called prayer. But if God talks to you it is called schizophrenia.[104]

Berger, for example, talks about the "corrosive effects" of pluralism. Instead of a religious consensus that makes surrender to God both plausible and meaningful, the citizens of any modern society confront a situation in which they choose their maker based on a extensive potpourri of possible religious preferences. "In premodern situations there is a world of religious certainty, occasionally ruptured by heretical deviations." In the modern world we inherit—partially because of the science of sociology—religious uncertainty, "occasionally staved off by more or less precarious constructions of religious affirmations."[105]

One way to conceive of our predicament is to follow Berger and label it "the heretical imperative." For the citizen of any modern society, heresy is a necessity because "modernity creates a new situation in which picking and choosing becomes an imperative."[106] Refuse to choose and one dizzying alternative is to embrace the nausea of the existentialists, symbolized by Sisyphus endlessly rolling his rock up the hill, only to have it tumble down at the peak. Why are we here? Who knows? Life is an endless, rocky road to nowhere.[107]

Berger offers alternatives based on the difference between knowing and believing. Traditionally, Christians make a distinction "between faith and lack of faith, belief and unbelief." Commit the ultimate heresy—God does not exist—and the lack of belief in God is defined as sin. But because "God has not exactly made it easy for us to believe in him," defining unbelief as sin seems quite unfair. As a substitute Berger proposes a distinction "between belief and knowledge. If we know something, there is no reason to believe; conversely if we say that we believe something, we are implying that we don't know." In a world where everything is taken for granted, people think they know what is true and false; they do not need to believe because they know. But given that religion is a human construction, we *know* that all religious realities are made and remade by people. Belief implies faith instead of knowledge; and part of Berger's tremendous contribution is that he simultaneously shows us the power of sociology as a science and the predicament of modern man in general—and Peter Berger in particular—in the face of the social construction of religious and other realities.[108]

Some people engage in "cognitive bargaining." It is a dialogue that says, for example, "All right, there is no way of holding on to the miracles of Jesus. But we won't give up on the resurrection. Or, we'll stipulate that Jesus didn't say a number of things he is reported to have said in the New Testament. But we will insist that he instituted the Lord's supper!" Berger's response, in a truly memorable line, is that "one needs a very long spoon indeed if one is to dine with the devil of doubt; without it, one is liable to end up as dessert."[109]

Rejecting all the other forms of cognitive bargaining (e.g., Jesus walked on water and that is that), Berger talks about the "signals of transcendence" that can often be discerned in the most commonplace situations.[110] To affirm these signals is a matter of faith, of belief; Berger never contends that he knows that these signals are valid. Instead, using lawyer language, he talks about "hearsay evidence concerning transcendence."[111]

Take humor, one of life's best signals of transcendence. Any joke or funny occurrence hovers, like a cloud, over normal, everyday reality because it posits, for a while at least, a reality where the "assumptions and rules of ordinary life are suspended." We stop for a joke, and this is "transcendence in a lower key" because it normally involves no religious beliefs or insinuations. For example, even many jokes about priests and rabbis revolve around secular activities, in many instances, their alleged sexual encounters.

But some laughter is "redeeming" in a religious sense because it "makes life easier to bear, at least briefly." A memorable joke or an especially funny movie or book—such as Mel Brooks's *Blazing Saddles* or Philip Roth's *Portnoy's Complaint*—does in fact provide a measure of enduring solace and support, especially when everyday life is disastrous or, more typically, just plain difficult.[112]

Seeing humor as transcendence in a higher key requires a leap of faith, perfectly symbolized by the game of peek-a-boo. "God's dealings with mankind can be seen as a cosmic game of hide and seek. We catch a glimpse of him and then he promptly disappears. His absence is a central feature of our existence, and the ultimate source of all our anxieties. Religious faith is the hope that He will eventually reappear, providing that ultimate relief, which, precisely, is redemption."[113]

Berger has great faith in Jesus Christ. He believes—he does not know— that Jesus is God, and his faith sustains him as he (and we) walk toward our inevitable grave in the ground. Or, for those who prefer cremation, our inevitable waft of ashes floating, however fleeting, over a cliff or a city we loved.

Berger's faith is a genuine religious affirmation in the face of his own scientific work. God exists even though religious and all other social realities are human—and only human—constructions. Skeptics might call his signals of transcendence nothing more than faith in illusions, but, like Berger, skeptics do not *know* they are right. They choose not to believe, and Berger chooses to affirm faith in a future that transcends all people, all the time.

The last words definitely belong to Peter Berger. As he notes in the final lines of *The Far Glory*, "The morning *will* come. The burden of God's silence will be lifted and He will return once more in the dawn, 'with flaming fire at his right hand,' in the fullness of his glory."[114]

THE CAPITALIST REVOLUTION

Recall Berger's request: sociology must return to the big questions. God is certainly at the top of any such list, but in the modern world, the nature and logic of capitalism also poses questions of global significance. *The Capitalist Revolution*[115] offers fifty propositions about prosperity, equality, and liberty. Each is interesting, but the block of propositions concerning East Asian economic development are especially provocative in their own right—and because they say a great deal about Berger's approach to sociology. From his first books in 1961 until his most recent publications, he stresses the need for "relentless intellectual honesty." If theory and reality conflict, theory makes way for the facts; intellectual maps are guides that must be ignored if they refuse to let reality challenge the assumptions of any theory.[116]

In *Pyramids of Sacrifice* Berger stressed that the central proposition of Latin American critiques of "developmentalism" was true: "Underdevelopment can only be understood if one understands the basic facts of dependency."[117] But ten years later, "the development of the capitalist societies of East Asia is the most important empirical falsification of dependency theory. . . . One cannot go on doing dependency theory while ignoring this region of the world, but its development cannot be explained from within the theory."[118]

Take, for example, Hong Kong and Puerto Rico. Critics would argue that because each (at least in 1985) was a colony—a state of dependence by definition—neither should be able to successfully develop "in a condition of dependency upon the international capitalist system." Yet within that system, Hong Kong has managed a significant degree of self-sustaining economic growth while Puerto Rico remains mired in its failed 1950s strategies.[119] Defenders of dependency theory call Hong Kong (or Singapore or South Korea) an example of "dependent development," but Berger argues that despite this admirable bit of "verbal legerdemain," the truth is obvious: "The East Asian evidence falsifies the proposition that successful development cannot occur in a condition of dependency upon the international capitalist system."[120]

Bad news for dependency theorists is accompanied by equally bad news for those who argue that "state interventionism is bad for economic development." Champion, as do many U.S. Republicans and Democrats, a laissez-faire (a government hands-off) approach to growth, and you are confronted with another series of discomforting East Asian facts. Because the Four Dragons (Singapore, Hong Kong, South Korea, and Taiwan) are characterized by "interlocking directorates" between government and business, "the East Asian evidence falsifies the idea that a high degree of state intervention in the economy is incompatible with successful economic development."[121]

Berger now argues that "the inclusion of a Third World country within the international capitalist system tends to favor its development." This is a cautious proposition indeed, but if that is all theory can say at a particular point in time, then theory works from the realities that exist, rather than the millennial hopes that persist. Relentless intellectual honesty offers its advocates no other choice.[122]

In 1985 Berger established at Boston University the Institute for the Study of Economic Culture. Its specific purpose is to do research "on the relations between socio-economic change and culture," that is, the beliefs, values, and lifestyles of different human groups. Over the years the institute has sponsored a variety of projects, but *Many Globalizations: Cultural Diversity in the Contemporary World* (2002) yet again underlies Berger's focus on the big questions. He and his colleagues successfully tackle the myths surrounding globalization with facts, intelligence, and a number of provocative insights. True to his word, Berger still believes that the "genius of sociology is negative." Debunk the conventional wisdom and you subversively open the door to the world that is actually there.[123]

NOTES

1. Peter L. Berger and Hansfried Kellner, *Sociology Reinterpreted: An Essay on Method and Vocation* (London: Penguin, 1981), 13, 16.

2. See Frederick Lewis Allen, *Only Yesterday* (New York: Harper and Row, 1931), 149.

3. Peter L. Berger, *The Heretical Imperative: Contemporary Possibilities of Religious Affirmation* (London: Collins, 1979), 116.

4. Bruce Barton, *The Man Nobody Knows* (Indianapolis: Bobbs Merrill, 1924), 35.

5. Russell Conwell, *Acres of Diamonds* (Kansas City, Mo.: Hallmark, 1968), 3, 24, 26.

6. Barton, *The Man Nobody Knows*, 43.

7. Ibid., 49–50.

8. Ibid., 105.

9. Peter L. Berger, *The Noise of Solemn Assemblies* (Garden City, N.J.: Doubleday, 1961), 41, 63, 93.

10. Ibid., 132–34, esp. 133.

11. Ibid., 137.

12. Peter L. Berger, *The Precarious Vision* (Garden City, N.J.: Doubleday, 1961), 193–94.

13. Peter L. Berger, *The Far Glory: The Quest for Faith in an Age of Credulity* (New York: Free Press, 1992).

14. Peter L. Berger, *Redeeming Laughter: The Comic Dimension of Human Experience* (New York: Walter De Gruyter, 1998), 57, 59, 61.

15. *Current Biography* (New York: H.W. Wilson, 1983), 28.

16. Peter L. Berger, "Confessions of an Ecclesiastical Expatriate," *The Christian Century*, October 24, 1990, 964–69.

17. Berger, *Facing Up to Modernity* (New York: Basic Books, 1977), xiv.

18. These comments are based on my own experiences at the New School.

19. *Current Biography*, 29.

20. Peter L. Berger, "From Secularity to World Religions," *The Christian Century*, January 16, 1980, 44.

21. Peter L. Berger, "Protestantism and the Quest for Certainty," *The Christian Century*, August 26–September 2, 1998, 782–96.

22. Berger, *Far Glory*, ix, 218.

23. Berger, "From Secularity to World Religions," 41.

24. Peter L. Berger and Richard John Neuhaus, *Movement and Revolution* (Garden City, N.J.: Doubleday, 1970), 57.

25. Peter L. Berger, *Invitation to Sociology: A Humanistic Perspective* (Garden City, N.J.: Doubleday, 1963), 29.

26. Ibid., 30–31.

27. Ibid., 38.

28. See, for example, Philippe Aries, *Centuries of Childhood* (London: Penguin, 1962).

29. Berger and Kellner, *Sociology Reinterpreted*, 13–14.

30. Ibid., 109, 79.

31. Ibid., 79.

32. Berger, *Invitation to Sociology*, 10–11.

33. Berger and Kellner, *Sociology Reinterpreted*, 16.

34. See for example, Peter Stalker, *Workers without Frontiers* (Geneva: International Labor Office, 2000).

35. Ibid., 17–23.

36. Berger, *Invitation to Sociology*, 176.

37. Woody Allen, *Getting Even* (New York: Random House, 1978).

38. Peter L. Berger and Thomas Luckmann, *The Social Construction of Reality* (Garden City, N.J.: Doubleday, 1966), 14.

39. Ibid., 23; the authors express their debt to, especially, the work of Alfred Schutz. See, for example, Alfred Schutz, *The Phenomenology of the Social World* (Chicago: Northwestern University Press, 1967); and Alfred Schutz, *Reflections on the Problem of Relevance* (New Haven, Conn.: Yale University Press, 1970).

40. Berger and Luckmann, *Social Construction of Reality*, 30.

41. See Robert Merton, *On the Shoulders of Giants* (New York: Harcourt, Brace, 1985).

42. Berger and Luckmann, *Social Construction of Reality*, 58.

43. Ibid., 51.

44. Ibid., 59.

45. Ibid., 61.

46. Ibid., 58; for the comment about renewal, see Berger's dedication in *Far Glory*.

47. Berger and Luckmann, *Social Construction of Reality*, 82–83.

48. Ibid., 82.

49. See, for example, Jared Diamond, *Guns, Germs, and Steel* (New York: Norton, 1998); also see Scott Malcomson, *One Drop of Blood: The American Misadventure of*

Race (New York: Farrar, Straus and Giroux, 2000); on the genes see Ronald Fernandez, *America's Banquet of Cultures: Harnessing Ethnicity, Race, and Immigration in the Twenty-first Century* (Westport, Conn.: Praeger, 2000), chapter 5.

50. Berger and Luckmann, *Social Construction of Reality*, 83, 85.

51. Ibid., 173.

52. Berger, *Heretical Imperative*, 10.

53. Robert Jay Lifton, *Destroying the World to Save It* (New York: Henry Holt, 1999).

54. Ibid., 246–49.

55. Ibid., 236–37.

56. Peter Berger, Brigette Berger, and Hansfried Kellner, *The Homeless Mind* (New York: Random House, 1973), 81.

57. Ibid., 77–79.

58. Ibid., 78.

59. Ibid., 79.

60. Ibid., 9.

61. Ibid., 23–24.

62. Ibid., 28–32.

63. Ibid., chapter 2, esp. 49–52.

64. Ibid., 165.

65. This example is based on consulting work done in the Caribbean and Latin America.

66. Berger, Berger, and Kellner, *The Homeless Mind*, 189.

67. Ibid., 187; also see Peter L. Berger, ed., *The Desecularization of the World: Resurgent Religion and World Politics* (Grand Rapids, Mich.: William Eerdmans, 1999); see also Don Belt, ed., *The World of Islam* (Washington, D.C.: National Geographic, 2001).

68. Berger, Berger, and Kellner, *The Homeless Mind*, 200.

69. Ibid., 230.

70. Berger, *Facing Up to Modernity*; see the essay titled "Intellectual Conservatism: Two Paradoxes," 115.

71. Berger and Newhaus, *Movement and Revolution*, 21.

72. Peter L. Berger, *A Rumor of Angels* (Garden City, N.J.: Doubleday, 1969), 48.

73. Berger and Newhaus, *Movement and Revolution*, 21.

74. Ibid., 57.

75. Berger, *Facing Up to Modernity*, xvii.

76. Berger, "From Secularity to World Religions," 41.

77. Alan Riding, *Distant Neighbors: A Portrait of the Mexicans* (New York: Random House, 1984), 376. I used this fine book because it most closely approximated the conditions Berger saw when he first visited Mexico. For a more contemporary view, see Kathryn Kopinak, *Desert Capitalism: Maquiladoras in North America's Western Industrial Corridor* (Tucson: University of Arizona, 1996).

78. Riding, *Distant Neighbors*, 376.

79. Peter L. Berger, *Pyramids of Sacrifice: Political Ethics and Social Change* (Garden City, N.J.: 1976), xiii.

80. Ibid., 136.

81. Ibid., 45.

82. Ibid., 48.

83. U.S. General Accounting Office, *Northern Marianna Islands: Garment and Tourist Industries Play a Dominant Role in the Commonwealth's Economy,* GAO/RCED/ GGD-00-79 (Washington, D.C.: General Accounting Office, February 2000), esp. 11, 19–20.

84. Berger, *Pyramids of Sacrifice,* 57–58; on the World Bank, see World Bank, *Entering the Twenty-first Century: World Development Report, 1999–2000,* [www.worldbank.org], 2001.

85. Berger, *Pyramids of Sacrifice,* 59.

86. Ibid., 65.

87. *Migration News* 4, no. 9 (1997): 20; this wonderful publication is housed at the University of California at Davis and is available at [www.migration. ucdavis.edu].

88. Berger, *Pyramids of Sacrifice,* 66.

89. Ibid., 157–59.

90. Ibid., 159.

91. Ibid., 177.

92. I visited Cuba in March 2000 and in June 2001. My research allowed us to move from one end of the island to the other.

93. Berger, Berger, and Kellner, *The Homeless Mind,* 102.

94. Berger, *Pyramids of Sacrifice,* 192.

95. Ibid., 201.

96. Ibid., xiii.

97. Ibid., 252.

98. Ibid.

99. William Greider, *One World, Ready or Not: The Manic Logic of Global Capitalism* (New York: Simon and Schuster, 1997); for a more optimistic assessment, see Thomas Friedman, *The Lexus and the Olive Tree: Understanding Globalization* (New York: Farrar, Straus and Giroux, 1999); also see George Soros, *The Crisis of Global Capitalism* (New York: Public Affairs, 1998).

100. Peter Berger, *The Sacred Canopy* (Garden City, N.J.: Doubleday, 1967), 100; for Berger's assessment of the book, see the introduction to *Rumors of Angels,* ix–x.

101. Berger, *Sacred Canopy,* 26.

102. Ibid., 26.

103. Ibid., 50.

104. Thomas Szasz, *The Second Sin* (Garden City, N.J.: Doubleday, 1973), 42.

105. Berger, *Heretical Imperative,* 28; also see Berger, *Far Glory,* 41.

106. Berger, *Heretical Imperative,* 28.

107. See, for example, Albert Camus, *The Myth of Sisyphus* (New York: Knopf, 1955).

108. Berger, "Protestantism and the Quest for Certainty," 2.

109. Berger, *Far Glory,* 42.

110. Berger, *A Rumor of Angels,* 65.

111. Berger, *Far Glory,* 139.

112. Berger, *Redeeming Laughter,* 205.

113. Ibid., 211.

114. Berger, *Far Glory,* 218.

115. Peter Berger, *The Capitalist Revolution: Fifty Propositions about Prosperity, Equality, and Liberty* (New York: Basic Books, 1986).

116. Berger, *Precarious Vision*, 151.

117. Berger, *Pyramids of Sacrifice*, 58.

118. Berger, *Capitalist Revolution*, 128.

119. On Puerto Rico, see, for example, Ronald Fernandez, *The Disenchanted Island*, 2nd ed. (Westport, Conn.: Praeger, 1996); also see James Dietz, *Economic History of Puerto Rico* (Princeton, N.J.: Princeton University Press, 1986).

120. Berger, *Capitalist Revolution*, 156.

121. Ibid., 158.

122. Ibid., 129.

123. Peter L. Berger and Samuel P. Huntington, eds., *Many Globalizations: Cultural Diversity in the Contemporary World* (New York: Oxford University Press, 2002); also Berger and Kellner, *Sociology Reinterpreted*, 13.

Conclusion

"Thus, if we are competent in our pursuit (which must be presupposed here) we can force the individual, or at least we can help him, to give himself an *account of the ultimate meaning of his own conduct.*"
Max Weber, *Science as a Vocation*[1]

SOCIOLOGY, THE COMPARATIVE METHOD, AND INCONVENIENT QUESTIONS

In the introduction I argued that sociology is the most liberating discipline in the modern world. Now I aim to summarize my argument by beginning with a problem. All over the industrialized world, women refuse to have children. The reasons vary, but one certainty is that Italy and Spain compete with one another for the lowest fertility rates on earth. In each nation the rates (as of 2000) hover at 1.2 children for each woman, and that means—quite obviously—that the Spanish and Italians are not replacing themselves.

Many of us still sleep at night; the news is not that earth shattering until, along with the United Nations, we consider the implications of fewer and fewer children in most European societies and in nations like Japan and Korea.[2]

One consequence of such low birth rates is an increase in the percentage of senior and very senior citizens, of people 65 or older. In Spain and Italy the present numbers are 17 and 18 percent of the population over the age of 65. If nothing is done about producing more children, the United Nations (UN) estimates that in 2050, Spain will have 37 percent of its people over the age of 65; the estimate for Italy is 35 percent. As a home point of reference, the figure for the United States (where the fertility rate is a bit higher) is 21.7 percent of the people over the age of 65 in 2050.[3]

With such substantial increases in the number of aged citizens, one obvious question is this: Who will pay for the retirement benefits? Many European nations offer state-endowed retirement plans that are far more generous than those in the United States. How will the Spanish, Italians, French, or Germans fund those programs if there are fewer and fewer young people to make the tax contributions that keep senior citizens happy, healthy, and still out of the work force?

Read the pages of *El Pais* in Spain, and you can witness a debate that is also worldwide. One alternative is to bring in large numbers of immigrants. Morocco now sends thousands of legal and illegal workers to Spain, and their birth rate is above replacement levels. However, many Spanish prefer the relative homogeneity of their society, and they adamantly refuse to accept the newcomers, who are so very different than they. In Belgium and Italy conservative political movements actively try to prevent more immigrants from ever arriving.

Another option is to extend the age of retirement. Forget immigrants, and let aged citizens work for much longer periods of time. UN estimates suggest that without migration and more children, the present rate of benefits can only be paid if Americans and French workers retire at 74. The figure for Germany, Italy, and Japan is 77, and the figure for South Korea is an astonishing 82 years of age. In South Korea people could retire on their way to the graveyard.[4]

Yet another option is to reduce benefits to older citizens. However, in many nations the aged are extremely well organized; for example, in the United States AARP (the American Association of Retired Persons) can muster more political muscle than the finest exercise salon. Cutting benefits is not a likely option if older citizens think that state support is an entitlement rather than a privilege, a right rather an erasable line of any nation's budget.

The ultimate option is for Spanish or Italian women to have as many children as their grandmothers and great-grandmothers. With modern medicine we can keep the children alive, and the population balance would quickly shift in a manner that substantially increased the proportion of young people. However, to the extent that women want the same rights and privileges as men, it is hard to imagine women having five or six children—especially if men still refuse to do their fair share of the massive amount of work required to rear children.

The options, possibilities, and problems are as endless and unsettling as the science of sociology.[5] Using the comparative method, the UN study alerts us to one of sociology's most powerful and intimidating insights. All social arrangements are relative. Nothing is permanent, and paradoxically, many societies in the midst of social change share a host of similar problems and possibilities. One beauty of sociology is that, using the comparative method, we can learn from one other and then use our particular culture as the basis for a unique adaptation to any social problem or issue.

Sociology also specializes, following Weber, in inconvenient questions. The UN data suggest that societies throughout the world may want to radically rethink the notion of retirement. Say you plan to retire at sixty and life expectancy in your nation is eighty. That equals *25 percent* of your life in retirement; how many of us want to watch repeat episodes of *Friends* or *I Love Lucy* for that many years? Should societies be thinking of ways to allow older citizens to work more productively? Should we replace the notion of life as a bell curve—if I am sixty I am going downhill—with the notion of life as a line? It ends when we die, and we no longer enter life with the inherited expectation of disengaging from it at fifty-five or sixty-five.

Sociology forces us to think especially about what Berger calls the big questions. Capitalism and God, money and the nature of reflective intelligence, higher learning and the lower classes. Examine the work of the eight minds analyzed here, and you receive meaningful and often profound insights about society's greatest problems. For example, Durkheim posed the issue of a sense of social solidarity among people who increasingly had less and less in common. In his wonderful essay about the Dreyfus case, he pointed to the "individual in general" as an axis that could unite France and, potentially, the world. To date we have failed to embrace his idea, but it is arguably as relevant as ever. Durkheim suggested that we could actually achieve social solidarity if we learned to express sympathy for all that is human, if we learned "a broader pity for all sufferings, for all miseries, a more ardent need to combat them and mitigate them, a greater thirst for justice."[6]

Just words? Perhaps. But they are words that shape the mind, and Durkheim's words provided part of the foundation for a human rights movement that now speaks a universal language; it is an idiom that celebrates the inherent rights and dignity of any human being, anywhere on earth.

The rub, of course, is real life. If sociology is as liberating as I suggest, how do we deal with Goffman's (or Durkheim's) argument that inherited beliefs and practices are external to the individual and capable of exerting a coercive effect on the development of any human being? Instead of being free, people are socially determined.

Equally important, if sociology can help produce justice, what about the assertions of Berger and Weber? In a world that recently witnessed everything from the genocide in Rwanda to the savage attack on New York's World Trade Center, the "ethical irrationality" posited by Weber seems quite obvious. It is even possible to agree with Peter Berger's harsh conclusion: "All of history is one endless massacre stretching back to the dawn of mankind. Wherever we are in history, we stand on a mountain of corpses—and, however terrible the thought, we are the beneficiaries of all this carnage."[7]

Remember Weber's sociological injunction. The discipline offers insights that are inconvenient not only for others *but also for our own beliefs and practices.* Thus, how can I argue that sociology is liberating in the face of social determinism and a sea of corpses from one end of the world to the other?

Here is my answer. People are free and socially determined at the same time. The paradox is real, but the possibilities for change are nevertheless endless. Recall Mead's arguments about reflective intelligence. We can mentally step out of our own skins and, using the concepts provided by sociology, achieve a solid measure of internal freedom, that is, a substantial degree of insight into the forces that shaped us and our world.

At its best sociology turns us into eager tourists using the Empire State Building for a first glimpse of New York; sociology lets us view self and society as if they were strangers. And in that startling encounter, we can achieve insights that move us to deliberately and freely *reconstruct* our inherited beliefs, values, and practices.

That is the promise and power of sociology.[8] But returning to the unavoidable sea of corpses, keep two things in mind. We have the power to achieve internal freedom, but actually doing so is an effort of our wills—not sociology's conceptual insights. In 1929 Mead wondered why it took evil to provide an amazing sense of social solidarity during World War I. We can, in theory, reconstruct a world that roots unity in positive rather than negative attributes and beliefs. But the choice is ours. To loudly echo Weber, for a sociologist the world is disenchanted, and that means that only men and women are responsible for what becomes of them and their children.

None of us deserves the world we inherited. But we may deserve the ones we are willing to tolerate. Sociology offers great hope; however, only people can do the exceedingly hard work required to turn hope into a world of value judgments as dignified and decent as the ones envisioned by our group of magnificent minds.

To quote Goethe in *Faust:*

And to this thought I hold with firm persistence,
the last result of wisdom stamps it true,
he only earns his freedom and existence,
who daily conquers them anew.[9]

NOTES

1. Max Weber, "Science as a Vocation," in *From Max Weber: Essays in Sociology,* ed. Hans Gerth and C. Wright Mills (New York: Oxford University Press, 1946), 152.

2. Population Division, Department of Economic and Social Affairs, United Nations Secretariat, *Replacement Migration: Is It a Solution to Declining and Ageing Populations?* (New York: Population Division, Department of Economic and Social Affairs, United Nations Secretariat, March 21, 2000).

3. Ibid., 6.

4. Ibid., 22.

5. See, especially, Peter Berger and Hansfried Kellner, *Sociology Reinterpreted: An Essay on Method and Vocation* (London: Penguin, 1981).

6. Emile Durkheim, "Individualism and the Intellectuals," in *On Morality and Society*, ed. Robert N. Bellah (Chicago: University of Chicago Press, 1973), 48–49.

7. Peter L. Berger and Richard John Neuhaus, *Movement and Revolution* (Garden City, N.J.: Doubleday, 1970), 56–57.

8. Ronald Fernandez, *The Promise of Sociology* (New York: Praeger, 1975), 24–25.

9. Johann Wolfgang von Goethe, *Faust: A Tragedy* (New York: Modern Library, 1950), part 2, 241.

Bibliography

In the interests of space, this bibliography includes only selected works, followed by selected biographical material, of each of the eight sociologists discussed.

KARL MARX

Marx, Karl. *Capital*. 3 vols. London: Penguin Classics, 1991.
———. *The Economic and Philosophic Manuscripts of 1844*, ed. Dirk J. Struik. New York: International Publishers, 1964.
———. *The Eighteenth Brumaire of Louis Bonaparte*. New York: International Publishers, 1963.
Engels, Friedrich. *The Condition of the Working Class in England*. New York: Oxford University Press, 1993.
Manuel, Frank E. *A Requiem for Karl Marx*. Cambridge, Mass.: Harvard University Press, 1995.
McLellan, David. *Karl Marx: His Life and Thought*. New York: Harper and Row, 1973.
Padover, Saul K. *Karl Marx: An Intimate Biography*. New York: McGraw Hill, 1978.

EMILE DURKHEIM

Durkheim, Emile. *The Division of Labor in Society*. New York: Free Press, 1984.
———. *The Elementary Forms of Religious Life*. New York: Free Press, 1965.
———. *Professional Ethics and Civic Morals*. London: Routledge, 1992.
———. *The Rules of the Sociological Method*. New York: Free Press, 1964.
Giddens, Anthony. *Capitalism and Modern Social Theory: An Analysis of the Writings*

of Marx, Durkheim, and Max Weber. Cambridge, England: Cambridge University Press, 1971.

Lukes, Steven. *Emile Durkheim: His Life and Work, a Historical and Critical Study.* London, Penguin, 1973.

Nisbet, Robert. *Emile Durkheim.* Englewood Cliffs, N.J.: Prentice Hall, 1965.

MAX WEBER

Weber, Max. *From Max Weber: Essays in Sociology,* ed. Hans Gerth and C. Wright Mills. New York: Oxford University Press, 1946.

———. *The Protestant Ethic and the Spirit of Capitalism.* New York: Charles Scribner's, 1958.

———. *The Sociology of Religion.* Boston: Beacon Press, 1964.

———. *The Theory of Social and Economic Organization.* New York: Free Press, 1964.

Honisheim, Paul. *On Max Weber.* New York: Free Press, 1968.

Mitzman, Arthur. *The Iron Cage: An Historical Interpretation of Max Weber.* New York: Grosset and Dunlap, 1969.

Weber, Marianne. *Max Weber: A Biography,* ed. Harry Zohn. New Brunswick, N.J.: Transaction Books, 1988.

GEORG SIMMEL

Simmel, Georg. *Conflict and the Web of Group Affiliations.* New York: Free Press, 1964.

———. *Essays on Sociology, Philosophy, and Aesthetics,* ed. Kurt H. Wolff. New York: Harper Torchbooks, 1965.

———. *The Philosophy of Money,* ed. David Frisby. 2nd enlarged ed. London: Routledge, Kegan Paul, 1990.

———. *The Sociology of Georg Simmel,* ed. Kurt H. Wolff. New York: Free Press, 1964.

Coser, Lewis S. *Masters of Sociological Thought.* New York: Harcourt, Brace and Jovanovich, 1971.

Frisby, David. *Georg Simmel.* London: Ellis Horwood, 1984.

Leck, Ralph. *Georg Simmel and Avant-Garde Sociology: The Birth of Modernity, 1880–1920.* New York: Humanity Books, 2000.

GEORGE HERBERT MEAD

Mead, George Herbert. *Mind, Self, and Society,* ed. Charles W. Morris. Chicago: University of Chicago Press, 1962.

———. *Movements of Thought in the Nineteenth Century,* ed. Merritt H. Moore. Chicago: University of Chicago Press, 1936.

———. *On Social Psychology,* ed. Anselm Strauss. Chicago: University of Chicago Press, 1956.

———. *The Philosophy of the Act*, ed. Charles W. Morris. Chicago: University of Chicago Press, 1938.

Cook, Gary A. *George Herbert Mead: The Making of a Social Pragmatist.* Urbana: University of Illinois Press, 1993.

Dewey, John. "George Herbert Mead." *Journal of Philosophy* 28, no. 12 (June 4, 1931): 309–14.

Manis, Jerome G., and Bernard Meltzer. *Symbolic Interaction: A Reader in Social Psychology.* Boston: Allyn and Bacon, 1967.

THORSTEIN VEBLEN

Veblen, Thorstein. *The Higher Learning in America.* New York: Hill and Wang, 1957.

———. *The Instinct of Workmanship.* New York: Norton, 1964.

———. *The Theory of Business Enterprise.* New York: Mentor Books, 1958.

———. *The Theory of the Leisure Class.* New York: New American Library, 1953.

Dorfman, Joseph. *Thorstein Veblen and His America.* New York: Augustus M. Kelley, 1966.

Duffus, R. L. *The Innocents at Cedro.* New York: Macmillan, 1944.

Riesman, David. *Thorstein Veblen: A Critical Interpretation.* New York: Continuum, 1960.

ERVING GOFFMAN

Goffman, Erving. *Frame Analysis.* New York: Harper, 1974.

———. *The Presentation of Self in Everyday Life.* Garden City, N.J.: Doubleday, 1959.

———. *Relations in Public: Microstudies of the Public Order.* New York: Basic Books, 1971.

———. *Stigma: Notes on the Management of Spoiled Identity.* Englewood Cliffs, N.J.: Prentice Hall, 1963.

Burns, Tom. *Erving Goffman.* London: Routledge, 1992.

Drew, Paul, and Anthony Wootton, eds. *Erving Goffman: Exploring the Interaction Order.* Boston: Northeastern University Press, 1988.

Verhoeven, Jeff C. "An Interview with Erving Goffman." *Research on Language and Social Interaction* 26, no. 3 (1993): 317–48.

PETER L. BERGER

Berger, Peter. *The Capitalist Revolution: Fifty Propositions about Prosperity, Equality, and Liberty.* New York: Basic Books, 1986.

———. "From Secularity to World Religions." *The Christian Century,* January 16, 1980, 41–45.

———. *The Heretical Imperative: Contemporary Possibilities of Religious Affirmation.* London: Collins, 1980.

———. *Pyramids of Sacrifice: Political Ethics and Social Change.* Garden City, N.J.: Doubleday, 1976.

————. "Reflections of an Ecclesiastical Expatriate." *The Christian Century*, October 24, 1990, 964–69.

Berger, Peter, and Thomas Luckmann. *The Social Construction of Reality*. Garden City, N.J.: Doubleday, 1966.

"Epistemological Modesty: An Interview with Peter Berger." *The Christian Century*, October 29, 1997, 972–78.

Index

and Simmel, 136; and Weber's
"Politics as a Vocation," 101
World War II, 246
Wristwatches, 184–85
Written record, 117

Wrong, Dennis, 207

Yale University, 177

Zionism, 111
Zola, Emile, 53

About the Author

DR. RONALD FERNANDEZ is Professor of Sociology at Central Connecticut State University. A widely recognized author on sociological issues, including multiculturalism and Hispanic-American concerns, his latest book is *America's Banquet of Cultures: Harnessing Ethnicity, Race, and Immigration in the Twenty-First Century* (Praeger, 2001).